Lincoln's Lost Legacy

UNIVERSITY PRESS OF FLORIDA

Florida A&M University, Tallahassee
Florida Atlantic University, Boca Raton
Florida Gulf Coast University, Ft. Myers
Florida International University, Miami
Florida State University, Tallahassee
New College of Florida, Sarasota
University of Central Florida, Orlando
University of Florida, Gainesville
University of North Florida, Jacksonville
University of South Florida, Tampa
University of West Florida, Pensacola

Lincoln's Lost Legacy

The Republican Party and the African American Vote, 1928–1952

SIMON TOPPING

University Press of Florida
Gainesville · Tallahassee · Tampa · Boca Raton
Pensacola · Orlando · Miami · Jacksonville · Ft. Myers · Sarasota

13 12 11 10 09 08 6 5 4 3 2 1

Library of Congress Cataloging-in-Publication Data
Topping, Simon.
Lincoln's Lost Legacy: the Republican Party and the African American vote, 1928–1952/Simon Topping.
p. cm.
ISBN 978-0-8130-3228-3 (alk. paper)
1. African Americans—Politics and government—20th century.
2. Republican Party (U.S.: 1854–)—History—20th century.
3. Voting—United States—History—20th century. 4. Party affiliation—United States—History—20th century. 5. National Association for the Advancement of Colored People—History—20th century.
6. Presidents—United States—Election—History—20th century.
7. Lincoln, Abraham, 1809–1865—Influence. I. Title.
E185.6.T67 2008
323.1196'073—dc22 2007050372

The University Press of Florida is the scholarly publishing agency for the State University System of Florida, comprising Florida A&M University, Florida Atlantic University, Florida Gulf Coast University, Florida International University, Florida State University, New College of Florida, University of Central Florida, University of Florida, University of North Florida, University of South Florida, and University of West Florida.

University Press of Florida
15 Northwest 15th Street
Gainesville, FL 32611–2079
http://www.upf.com

To my parents, George and Ena Topping

Contents

Preface

"There's a book in that," was Robert Cook's immediate reaction when I mentioned examining the relationship between the Republican Party and African Americans in the 1930s and 1940s as part of my master's degree. The origins of this idea were fairly humble. I was reading Harvard Sitkoff's "Harry Truman and the Election of 1948: The Coming of Age of Civil Rights in American Politics," in the *Journal of Southern History* (37 [1971]), which mentioned, barely in passing, that the Republican Party had proposed stronger planks on civil rights than had the Democrats in both 1940 and 1944. This seemed curious: the "conservative" Republican Party offering African Americans more than the "liberal" Democratic Party? Of course, I knew about Abraham Lincoln, the Civil War, Emancipation and the Thirteenth, Fourteenth, and Fifteenth Amendments, but it seemed that African Americans had voted Democratic for an eternity. Intrigued, I decided to find out when and why African Americans had abandoned the party of Abraham Lincoln and embraced the party of Jefferson Davis. Perhaps even more remarkable than the startling nature of this realignment was the realization that no historian had deemed the Republican reaction to it as worthy of serious study.

This study fills a number of significant gaps in the historiography of the Republican Party and the early civil rights movement and provides an indication of the increasing importance of the African American vote. It explains why the Republican Party lost the African American vote, examines its failed efforts to regain it, and looks at how African American voters adjusted to the changing American political landscape of the 1930s and 1940s. I offer insight into the tactics and philosophy of the Republican Party over a period of nearly a quarter century and note that, however well-intentioned, the party failed to grasp the realities of life for African Americans.

I have been fortunate enough to win a number of research grants to help me carry out my work. I would like to thank Hans Krannebaum and the Roosevelt Study Center, in Middleburg, the Netherlands, for a grant, in the summer of 1998, to look at the papers of Franklin Roosevelt, Eleanor Roosevelt, and Harry Truman, as well as the *Congressional Record*. Particular thanks go to Arjen Westerhoff.

The Faculty of Arts Research Executive (FARE) at the University of Hull generously funded two research trips to the United States. In 1998, I traveled to the University of Indiana, Bloomington, to look at the papers of Wendell Willkie, and then in 2000 I went to the University of Rochester, New York, to look at the papers of Thomas Dewey.

The staff at the Lilly Library at the University of Indiana was extremely helpful throughout my stay in Bloomington, but Helen Walsh and her son Alan merit a special mention.

My research was funded in part by an Alfred M. Landon Historical Research Grant funded by the Kansas State Historical Society, Inc. I would like to thank David Haury and all the staff at the KSHS for their cooperation during my time with them.

I was also greatly assisted by the Herbert Hoover Presidential Library in West Branch, Iowa, and its award of the Herbert Hoover Grant in 2000. Everywhere I went in America I was impressed by the knowledge and dedication of librarians and archivists, but never more so than at the Hoover Library. Special tribute has to be paid to Pat Wildenburg (and family) for both his considerable knowledge and his equally considerable hospitality and friendship.

In Rochester, I am indebted to Mary Huth and the archival staff at the Rush Rhees Library; I am also very grateful to Mary Menard for her generous hospitality during my stay. Thanks are also due to Tony Badger and the Mellon Fund for their assistance on my frequent visits to Cambridge University to look at the NAACP Papers.

Thanks to Henrice Altink, Kris Allerfeldt, and Harry Bennett for proofreading and suggestions; to Emily Gilbert and Sean Kelly for various instances of hospitality; and to Dave Masterson and the staff of the Hooper Building, University of Lincoln.

I am deeply indebted to both Professor John Ashworth and Dr. John White, especially for JA's skill as a historian and "Jay Dubya's" extensive knowledge of the civil rights movement and eye for detail.

I am extremely grateful to all the staff of the Department of American Studies at the University of Hull for their help and support during my six years with them; I would like to pay particular tribute to Dr. Jenel Virden and Dr. John Osborne. Thanks are also due to my fellow graduate teaching assistants at the University of Hull. Thanks also to my colleagues in the Department of Humanities at the University of Plymouth, particularly

Harry Bennett, our irrepressible head of school. Thanks are also due to Eli Bortz, Heather Romans, and Meredith Morris-Babb at the University Press of Florida for their patience as my manuscript inched toward completion.

A very special mention must go to Dr. William Riches, my undergraduate mentor at the University of Ulster, for his infectious enthusiasm for American history and his encouragement and unswerving belief in me. Without Bill's guidance and encouragement over the last fifteen years, my career path would have been very different and undoubtedly much less rewarding.

Love and thanks to my family for their unfaltering support. My brothers, Phil and Andrew, have been utterly indispensable, but this book is dedicated to my parents, George and Ena, who recognized the value of a good education, ensuring that their sons became the first generation of our family to go to university. This book is a testament to their love and foresight.

INTRODUCTION

The Mantle of Lincoln

A highly symbolic part of Abraham Lincoln's legacy to the Republican Party was the loyalty of African Americans. For over a half century after his death, Lincoln's role as the "Great Emancipator" was invoked at election time, and this rallying cry was usually enough to remind African American voters where their allegiance ought to lie; the alternative was, after all, the party of the Klan, the Confederacy, Redemption, and Jim Crow. Yet, in four short years in the 1930s, this inheritance was lost and never regained. African Americans abandoned the Great Emancipator in favor of an aristocratic New Yorker, who now led the erstwhile party of the Old South, in perhaps the most dramatic, and least expected, political realignment in American history.

Six years into his presidency, George W. Bush made his belated debut at the National Association for the Advancement of Colored People's (NAACP) annual convention in 2006. It was a potentially uncomfortable encounter given the hostility of America's premier civil rights organization to both the president and his party; the NAACP was, moreover, a staunch supporter of the Democratic Party, which had commanded the support of some 90 percent of African American voters in both 2000 and 2004. President Bush told his audience, arguably with neither conviction nor sincerity, that "I consider it a tragedy that the party of Abraham Lincoln let go of its historic ties with the African American community," but he offered no suggestion as to how these "historic ties" could be renewed.[1] He was not alone among modern Republicans in recognizing the historic bond with Lincoln and also the chasm that existed between his party and African Americans. At the 2000 Republican convention, retired African American general and future secretary of state Colin Powell declared that "the party of Lincoln has not always carried the mantle of Lincoln." Neither had it taken the initiative in "reaching out to minority communities," the African American community in particular.[2]

Powell's words echoed across a century of disappointment and disillusionment among African American Republicans. In 1952, for example, Rev.

Archibald Carey, foreshadowing Martin Luther King's plea to America at the Lincoln Memorial more than ten years later, urged the Republican Party to "let freedom ring."[3] In 1944, Robert R. Church, one of the few African American Republicans able to operate in the South, urged the party to be "courageous enough to rededicate itself to the principles upon which it was founded."[4] Powell's speech demonstrated that the words of Church, Carey, and countless others had gone unheeded. The "party of Lincoln" had clearly not found the courage that Church invoked. It had failed to reconnect to those founding principles or its hitherto staunchest allies.

This is hardly surprising. After the Civil War, the Republican Party quickly lost interest in the newly enfranchised former slaves, yet African Americans remained spiritually Republicans; the diminishing numbers of those who could vote in the dark aftermath of the Civil War invariably marked their cross for the party of the architect of Emancipation. They had little choice; Frederick Douglass famously declared the Republican Party to be "the deck, all else is the sea," but more pertinently, and less famously, he revealed the true and asymmetrical nature of the relationship when he asserted, "I knew that however bad the Republican party was, the Democratic party was much worse." African Americans were Republicans by default.

By the 1930s this had changed, and African Americans *did* have a choice. The memory of Lincoln had faded; the mythical debt seemingly settled. Those African Americans who had moved to the North as a result of the Great Migration, the Depression, and then World War II exercised their democratic rights free from the hindrances that made them only nominal citizens in the South. The Democratic Party, at least in the North, made tentative steps to win their votes, while the Republican Party, certainly during the Hoover years, seemed to be doing its utmost to foster African American disaffection. Most important of all, these votes were an increasingly important currency in American politics; their concentration in key northern states made them potentially the deciding factor in any close presidential election, resulting in the "balance of power" argument becoming a recurring theme in campaigns. The 1930s would fundamentally change African Americans politically, and the black vote would, in turn, fundamentally change American politics.

The decade saw a wholesale switch of African American allegiance from the Republican to the Democratic Party. The roots of this shift are to be found earlier, but it is apparent that, beginning with the midterm elections of 1934, a majority of African Americans voted Democratic. This book will examine, from the Republican perspective, both the context and the process of African American political realignment from the late 1920s to the early 1950s. It will illustrate not only that the process of African American defection from the Republican Party is evident as early as 1928, but that African American alienation from the "Grand Old Party" (GOP) was affected and dictated by a number of interrelated racial, political, and economic concerns. Moreover, the loss of the African American vote by the Republicans must be viewed in the context of the overall political situation in 1930s and 1940s America, when the GOP's problems were exacerbated by the Depression and then compounded by persistent electoral failure. Viewed in this respect, Republican neglect of African Americans, or specifically the Republican leadership's neglect of African Americans, makes much more sense.

It could be argued that the Republican Party did its utmost to regain the African American vote between 1928 and 1952, and that it offered genuine alternatives to the New Deal and the Fair Deal. Furthermore, it could be argued that the party remembered its history and acted upon it, and, as such, the leadership deserves much more credit than it receives. This would make an interesting and controversial thesis; it would also be utterly unsustainable. Certainly the GOP did more than it has previously been given credit for, but its approach to civil rights was stuttering, inconsistent, and half-hearted. The Republican Party was not hostile to the aspirations of African Americans, but it was unquestionably ambivalent. What emerges is a political strategy that was, at best, ill-defined and contradictory, and at worst, insincere and deeply cynical; while not characterized by overt bigotry, it still reflected the latent racism of contemporary American society.

When considering the Republicans' attitude, a number of important factors must be considered. It can be concluded, for example, that the transfer of the African American vote during the New Deal was part of an ongoing process, in that it is glaringly apparent that the black vote in the 1930s and early 1940s was for Franklin Roosevelt and *not* the Democrats. Many African Americans were still not entirely happy, and perhaps were even embarrassed, with the prospect of being Democrats, yet they nonetheless recognized the benefits of the New Deal and enlisted in the "Roosevelt Coalition." Indeed, African American realignment continued under Truman, but the longevity of this alliance was by no means assured in the 1930s (when a majority of African Americans remained registered Republicans) and the 1940s. The reasons for the initial switch were largely, but not exclusively, related to the economic benefits of the New Deal, but a number of other issues—for example, lynching, fair employment opportunities, and the poll tax—and the influence of Eleanor Roosevelt and the "Black Cabinet" were also important.

This study establishes why the Republican Party lost the African American vote, what it did to try to win it back, the impact that internal party difficulties throughout the period had on these efforts, and why they ultimately failed. The party was unmistakably and hopelessly split throughout the period, and, amid the "bigger" crises that engulfed both party and country, African Americans, never a major priority, were further neglected. The situation faced by the party in the 1930s was unprecedented; there was a genuine fear that it was on the verge of extinction. Under these circumstances, it is perhaps not very surprising that African Americans were overlooked by the GOP; the period 1932 to 1952 was, after all, the Republicans' longest spell in opposition and represents the party's nadir.

In 1932, around 70 percent of African Americans voted for Herbert Hoover. By 1936, the same percentage backed Franklin Roosevelt, and an even greater proportion would vote for Harry Truman in 1948 and Adlai Stevenson in 1952. Of all the groups that pledged allegiance to Franklin Roosevelt during the 1930s, none was more unexpected, nor less sought, than the African American voter; indeed, no group has remained as loyal to the Democrats as African Americans. Conversely, prior to 1934, no group was more stubbornly faithful to the Republicans. It is implicit in the historiography that the Republicans merely wrote off this constituency and made only token efforts to regain these votes in the years after 1934. This does not, however, tell the whole story.

Many historians have dealt with aspects of the Republican Party's attitude toward civil rights and African Americans, but the period of this study has been largely passed over. Between Richard Sherman's *The Republican Party and Black America from McKinley to Hoover, 1896–1933* and Robert Burk's *The Eisenhower Administration and Black Civil Rights*, no historian has made a serious effort to examine this relationship.[5] There is, then, a gaping hole in the historiography. Scholars examining this period all refer to the GOP's relationship with African Americans, but none deem it especially important. The centrality of the New Deal in the switch of the African American vote and the effects of its programs on African Americans have, however, been examined in some detail by Harvard Sitkoff and Nancy J. Weiss among others, but the response of the GOP to the transfer of the African American vote throughout the 1930s and, perhaps more importantly, the 1940s and early 1950s has been barely touched.[6] While it would be folly to dismiss its importance, it is apparent that the New Deal, although the most important factor in African American realignment, was not, as Sitkoff and Weiss imply, either the start or the end of this recasting of loyalties; at best, it represented only a partial culmination of the process.

The pervading difficulty with the existing historiography is that it only investigates what happened once African American allegiance had transferred to the Democrats, not the process itself. There is an underlying assumption that the loss of the African American vote by the Republicans and their subsequent efforts to regain it can be explained relatively simply. This is not the case. The relationship between the Republican Party and African Americans was extremely complicated and constantly evolving and, as such, merits serious attention. For example, there is a presupposition that the GOP did little or nothing to win back the African American vote, which must be, if not completely refuted, then at least properly explained.

This lack of even a cursory examination is all the more unusual given that in the 1940s the African American vote became large enough to determine the outcome of a presidential election, and demonstrably did so in 1948. The historiography on the period 1928 to 1952 is, therefore, self-evidently incomplete. There is undeniable scope for a serious examination of the relationship between the Republican Party and African Americans during these years. Yet it would be misguided to overemphasize the importance of this relationship; it was obviously peripheral when viewed in the context of the upheaval caused by the Depression, World War II, and the early Cold War. Nevertheless, it is still something that needs to be addressed if there is to be a broader understanding of not only the political realignment that took place in American politics in the 1930s, but also the more general historiography of the civil rights movement and the Republican Party.

The loss of the African American vote by the Republicans, and their attempts to regain it, will be analyzed on a number of levels. The relationship between the GOP and African Americans on a national level throughout the period is examined, starting with the events of the "Republican Ascendancy" from 1920 to 1932. The presidential elections from 1932 to 1952 perhaps provide the best gauge of public opinion, and a detailed analysis of Republican electoral strategy in these contests is offered. An understanding of the role of the NAACP and the growth of African American political power throughout the period is also essential. Officially nonpartisan, and undergoing a reevaluation of its role, it is clear by the late 1930s that the NAACP's fate was becoming inextricably linked with that of the Democratic Party, which had, in turn, begun to recognize the strategic value of African American votes. This tacit alliance was fraught with difficulty, and, in some respects, African Americans, in the form of the NAACP (although it is worth stressing that the two were definitely not synonymous) were as frustrated by the incumbent Democratic administration as they had been with the previous Republican one. Regardless of this, the NAACP became increasingly alienated from the Republican Party. Finally, these issues must be considered within the overall context of the contemporary political situation. This was a period when the certainties with which Americans had lived were threatened, not only by the Depression but also by the radical and unprecedented nature of the New Deal. In looking at these various themes collectively, an overall picture will emerge of how problematic the relationship between African Americans and the Republican Party actually was. The transition of African Americans from Republicans to Democrats was undeniably a more complex process than has been previously recognized.

The experience of Republican rule from 1920 to 1932 laid the foundations for future African American discontent with the GOP. It can be convincingly demonstrated that the roots of the African American defection from the party of Lincoln are to be found during the presidency of Hoover. The crucial point is that while the record of Republicans in the White House in the 1920s was undoubtedly poor from an African American perspective, Hoover's apparently willful insensitivity made the transfer of African American allegiance to the Democrats a much less arduous and controversial experience than it could have been.

The Republican Party was facing the biggest crisis in its history during the 1930s and was unsure of how to cope with the new and uncomfortable political realities confronting it. Moreover, African Americans were only one of a number of constituencies estranged from the GOP during the 1930s, and the party was slow to recognize the overall realignment that was taking place (continually underestimating, for instance, the importance of the Democratic urban vote). It is easy with hindsight to view the Republican Party in the 1930s merely as a haven for the most reactionary and extremist elements of American politics, yet it has to be remembered that there were those who were genuinely fearful about where the New Deal was leading and Roosevelt's cavalier attitude toward the Constitution.

This is an unapologetically broad study that deals with major themes on a national rather than a state or local level. Critics could argue that this is essentially a "top-down" history, an approach often dismissed as hopelessly old-fashioned, viewing history solely through the eyes of generals, presidents, and monarchs. Yet given the scope of the topic and the time frame involved, a largely top-down approach is considerably more of a virtue than a vice. Moreover, this in no way suggests that African Americans were mere spectators while their history was being made around them and for them. There is no doubt that the period of this study saw the nascent civil rights movement begin to emerge from the shadow of Redemption and Jim Crow, and the importance of these years to the eventual high tide of civil rights protest in the 1950s and 1960s has finally been recognized. Historians such as Patricia Sullivan and Robert J. Norrell have demonstrated that African Americans were, often tentatively in the South, lighting the fires of freedom.[7] Yet the concerns of this study are largely national, or perhaps even northern, in character: after all, in the South during these years the Republican Party existed virtually in name only, while precious few African Americans could exercise their political rights. Regarding state or local studies, New York is the only state given special attention, as its governor, Thomas Dewey, was the pivotal figure in Republican politics throughout the 1940s. Other state or local studies are, unfortunately, beyond the scope of this work.

In order to focus on the Republicans and civil rights over a twenty-four-year period, there are inevitable, if unavoidable, gaps in this study. There is, for example, no prolonged discussion of the Roosevelt administration and its decidedly mixed record on race. Eleanor Roosevelt's role and that of the Black Cabinet and the Supreme Court are passed over, as is the impact of the Great Migration.[8] Where the latter is concerned, the consequences—that is to say, the concentration of African American voters in key northern states—are much more important than the processes that caused African Americans to abandon the South. Similarly, some of the momentous developments of the Truman years (*To Secure These Rights*, for instance) are dealt with briefly, not to minimize their importance, but simply because they have been dealt with in considerable detail elsewhere. There seems little to be gained by synthesizing the numerous works relating to Truman or the Roosevelts in a book on a topic upon which little or nothing has been written.

For the purposes of this piece, it is considerably more beneficial to have an idea of the broader political situation than to provide an examination of the minutiae of American political life in the period of the emerging civil rights movement. As a result, this study will give a more complete understanding of the political realignment of African Americans and add to, particularly, the historiography of the Republican Party, the civil rights movement, and presidential elections between 1928 and 1952. Its primary concerns are, however, twofold: Why did the Republican Party lose the African American vote, and how did it attempt to regain it? In answering these questions, it will be demonstrated how and why Lincoln's legacy was lost.

1

The Lily-White House

If the roots of the African American realignment are to be found during the New Deal, then the seeds can be found during the presidencies of Warren Harding, Calvin Coolidge, and Herbert Hoover from 1920 to 1932. The process was accelerated by the Great Depression and New Deal, but this realignment neither began nor was completed by the presidency of Franklin Roosevelt. By the 1920s, African American alienation from the party of Lincoln was acute but had no viable outward expression: quite simply, African American voters had nowhere else to go. African Americans had rarely sat comfortably within the GOP's electoral alliance, and, in reality, the relationship had always been an uneven one. Whatever liberal or moral impulse had motivated the founders of the party and the post–Civil War radicals had disappeared with the party's embrace of business by the 1880s. Yet the Republicans had much to gain by courting African American voters; indeed, they could do this without betraying their roots. Nonetheless, from the 1890s to the 1930s, as Sherman notes, "GOP politicians appealed to the myth of Lincoln and to their party's egalitarian ideals, even when their practices belied their words."[1]

The alternative was no better; the Democrats—the party of the South, slavery, and Redemption—neither sought nor wanted African American votes. In the early 1920s, the African American vote was both negligible and northern; ignored by the Democrats, it was taken for granted by the Republicans. It is in this neglect, especially once Hoover assumed the presidency, that the source of the black desertion of the GOP is to be found. More than any other Republican, Hoover fractured the historic alliance between the party of Lincoln and the descendants of the slaves he had freed. The Hoover years starkly illustrate the extent to which the Republican Party had departed from its historic, if momentary, role as the protector of African Americans.

The presidencies of Warren Harding (1920–23) and Calvin Coolidge (1923–28) were unremarkable for African Americans, but they did create a pattern that Hoover would continue. Any hope African Americans may have had that the Republican Party would provide an antidote to the racial retrenchment of the Wilson years was misplaced. Neither president, for example, even lukewarmly endorsed antilynching legislation. Under Harding, the Dyer antilynching bill negotiated the House of Representatives in January 1922 but died in the Senate in December after a southern Democratic filibuster.[2] In Harding's defense, he cannot be held entirely responsible for the failure to secure even the most limited of civil rights legislation. His Interracial Commission died in a congressional committee, the antilynching bill was scuppered by a Democratic filibuster, and discrimination in national life was too ingrained to be removed easily.[3]

Harding's successor, Calvin Coolidge, believed in minimal federal involvement to improve the lot of the less fortunate members of society; the business of America was, after all, business. Coolidge's reputation was not helped when he showed no interest in antilynching legislation or, crucially, by the perception that he was ambivalent toward the Klan. The Klan, claiming 4–5 million members, had a considerable influence in American politics in the 1920s and was particularly strong in the Republican Party in Colorado, Indiana, and Ohio.[4] At the Republican convention in 1924, a plank to condemn the Klan was blocked, as was an attempt to repudiate the organization publicly. The Republicans were further damaged when the Democrats narrowly failed to pass a plank condemning the Klan (by the smallest margin in convention history), and their presidential candidate, John W. Davis, condemned the organization in a speech. Davis asked Coolidge to do the same to eliminate the Klan as an election issue; the Progressive candidate, Robert M. Follette, did likewise, but Coolidge remained silent. This stance made him the most attractive candidate to members of the Klan, provoking condemnation from the *New York Times*: "Either Mr. Coolidge holds his peace for mistaken reasons of politics or policy or he tolerates the Klan. . . . He has shown himself by his silence deficient in judgment and courage."[5]

Coolidge's inaction undoubtedly contributed to the desertion of the party by African Americans in the 1930s.[6] For example, in 1925, despite widespread public opposition, he again demonstrated his ambivalence to the Klan when it was allowed to parade in Washington, D.C., without protest from the White House.[7] African Americans were clearly low on the GOP's list of priorities, and the small number of votes they cast were not needed to maintain the party in power in the 1920s. As well as helping to facilitate Garveyism, this inaction began the process of African American disengagement from the GOP. The lack of concern by the Republican Party reflected a more general apathy among white Americans about the plight of African Americans and, as such, was as much a by-product of the age as an active process of deliberate alienation.

"Tradition and Inertia"

The experience of African Americans under Republican rule in the 1920s led many to believe that their future lay outside the GOP. The Wilson years had been bad, seeing, for example, increasing segregation within the federal government, but the administrations of Harding and Coolidge were extremely frustrating for African Americans. Nothing, however, could have prepared even the most estranged for the Hoover presidency. By the time Hoover left office in March 1933, he had offended almost every segment of African American opinion; many prominent African American Republicans who were personally very loyal to Hoover in 1928 refused to support him or have anything to do with his campaign in 1932. Suspicions about Hoover arose even before he had been nominated; foremost among them was the fear that he wanted a lily-white party in the South. This concern proved to be well founded, and the attempted reform of the southern wing of the GOP would continue throughout Hoover's presidency. By 1928, many African Americans were coming to the conclusion that northern Democrats were as liberal as their Republican counterparts, while southern white Republicans and Democrats were equally racist. Kelly Miller, an eminent African American educator, articulated this concern to Hoover when he argued that only "tradition and inertia" tied African Americans to the GOP.[8]

By 1931, Hoover had tried to appoint an avowed segregationist to the Supreme Court, offended the mothers of dead African American soldiers, failed to prevent the effective disbandment of the country's most famous black regiments, and, of course, launched his fundamentally flawed southern strategy, all of which happened against the background of the worst depression in American history. In the election of 1932, not only had Hoover alienated many African Americans, but the southern policy on which he had staked so much lay in ruins; the gains made in the region in 1928 were erased as the Democrats swept into power.

Hoover's cause in the South in 1928 was aided by the Democrats' controversial decision to nominate Governor Alfred Smith of New York, a liberal, "wet" Catholic, as their presidential candidate. The candidacy of Smith was not about to precipitate a wholesale desertion of the GOP by African Americans, but it at least brought the issue of bigotry to the fore as his

Catholicism made him a target for many southern Protestants. There were those in the South, declares George Mayer, who "disliked [Smith] for what he was, and [he] could not have won their support even if he had advocated the re-enslavement of Negroes."[9] The candidacy of Smith, therefore, finally gave the Republicans an opportunity to crack the so-called "Solid South." The destination of the African American vote gave further hints of an impending realignment in American politics. *Collier's* commented: "the Republicans and the Democrats are both worried, and no small part of that worry is caused by the uncertainty regarding the colored brother's vote."[10] The importance of the black vote was overstated, but it encouraged a feeling that if Smith could hold onto the South, then he would only need New York, Illinois, Pennsylvania, and Indiana to achieve an overall victory, essentially a prediction of the future potential importance of the black vote.

The African American vote may have been deemed more important than ever, but some things remained resolutely unchanged. Both party conventions, for example, were segregated, and this was especially galling to African American Republicans.[11] African American leaders were so disillusioned by the actions of the Republican Party that they now began to desert the GOP to such an extent that the party had trouble finding people to serve on its Colored Advisory Committee. Five men, including prominent Memphis Republican Robert R. Church, publicly declined to join, citing GOP policy. Ironically, the Democrats had no trouble finding African Americans to serve on their colored voters division. The African American press, which could usually be counted on to support the GOP, was initially neutral or backed Smith. The *Chicago Defender*, however, was openly hostile to the Republicans: "our readers are entitled to know that the Ku Klux Klan is taking an active part in the campaign and that it is NOT aiding the Democratic candidate."[12] The Democrats were, nonetheless, reluctant to alienate their racist southern constituency by exploiting any potential rift between the Republicans and African Americans.[13] The Republican Party was also aided by the fact that, outside of New York, many African Americans were skeptical about their chances of betterment under Smith. The Democrats, regardless of whatever liberal veneer Smith provided, were still the party of the South, the Wilson years were fresh in the collective memory, and many African Americans were also wary of Smith's Catholicism. A frustrated NAACP issued a manifesto condemning the racism of both parties.[14]

Walter White was a key figure in the NAACP. A light-skinned, blue-eyed, technically "colored" Atlantan, White had risen to prominence in the early 1920s through his investigations of lynching in the South, which had yielded one best-selling book and identified him as the rising star of the association.[15] His endorsement, therefore, would be invaluable to any presidential candidate wanting the black vote. This was recognized by Smith's publicity director, who asked him to head the Democrats' "Negro" division.[16] White's usefulness to the Democratic Party was also appreciated by the NAACP's Moorfield Storey and Arthur Spingarn and the latter's law partner Charles Studin, who felt that an endorsement could be advantageous to the association. After much thought, White eventually refused, partly because he disagreed with the concept of segregated campaign bureaus.[17] Approached again prior to Smith's nomination and conveniently on leave from the association, White was tempted. He asked Smith for a forthright statement on the plight of African Americans, clearly wishing to test his sincerity on the race issue. This statement, written by James Weldon Johnson, was never issued, reflecting Smith's fear of further offending the South. White, nevertheless, campaigned for Smith in a private capacity, despite the Democratic candidate's reticence.[18] The fact that such a prominent member of the NAACP, constitutionally nonpartisan, could even consider working for the Democrats reflected the association's increasing hostility toward the Republicans.[19]

There was also a feeling that the two parties were equally unsympathetic to African American aspirations. W.E.B. Du Bois felt that the candidates offered little choice: "in our humble opinion, it does not matter a tinker's damn which of these gentlemen succeed. With minor exceptions, they stand for exactly the same thing: oligarchy in the South, color caste in national office holding and recognition of the rule of organized wealth."[20] He did, however, urge African Americans to choose their congressmen very carefully.[21] A characteristic expression of dissatisfaction with the GOP came from Neval Thomas, the president of the NAACP's District of Columbia branch and a member of the Republican Party: "I refuse to allow a crowd of oppressors who are opposed to everything Republican masquerade in its sacred name. This aggregation now parading in its name stands for everything that Republicanism condemned and destroyed. They are in solemn compact with the Bourbon South in their wicked schemes against the Negro."[22] African American alienation from the party of Lincoln was becoming increasingly vocal, but the alternative remained frustratingly unappealing. Hoover won the election easily and commanded huge support among African Americans, yet there were already signs that the unshakable grasp that the GOP had on the African American vote was beginning to weaken. Republican analysis noted that in traditionally solid northern cities anywhere between

10 percent (Chicago) and 30 percent (Cleveland) of African Americans had opted for Smith, hinting at the change that would occur in 1934.[23]

"This Knowledge Could Be Judiciously Used in the South"

The Republicans' "southern strategy" was the first of the many controversies that would exacerbate African American disaffection with the party and particularly with Hoover. It was a long-held GOP desire to win the Solid South, with both Harding and Coolidge trying and failing. In 1928, the candidacy of Smith and the apparent willingness of Hoover to embrace lily-whitism offered the GOP its best chance ever to win southern white votes. Kansas senator Henry J. Allen wrote to Hoover arguing that the African American vote was lost, and that the Republicans should exploit the racial situation to their advantage: "it seems rather certain for the moment that we are going to lose the colored vote in the North. If this knowledge could be judiciously used in the South, it would be helpful to us."[24]

While the circumstantial evidence implicating Hoover in the formulation and execution of the GOP's southern strategy is quite convincing, an element of doubt remains. Even if the intention of his southern strategy was not to disenfranchise African Americans, that was certainly the result. Alfred Kirchhofer, the Republican publicity manager in 1928, however, challenged the contention that Hoover closely controlled the southern campaign in 1928. Kirchhofer explained that "there was little by way of direction, except that Mr. Hoover specified three areas [prohibition, Smith's religion, and Mrs. Smith] in which nothing should be said without prior approval."[25] This can be interpreted in perhaps two ways: if official Republican Party literature dealt with any of these issues, then Hoover can be held directly responsible for it. Alternatively, the fact that most of the less savory propaganda disseminated during the campaign can be attributed to anonymous or unofficial sources does help to distance Hoover from it, although it does not necessarily exonerate him.[26] Kirchhofer places the blame for the bigotry of the southern campaign at least in part with Mabel Willebrandt, an assistant attorney general and friend of the Hoovers.[27] He also states that whatever efforts Hoover made to disclaim bigotry had little effect on those preaching it.

Regardless of Hoover's duplicity, Republican tactics were successful. The party managed to carry West Virginia, Kentucky, Tennessee, Virginia, North Carolina, Florida, and Texas, a hitherto unthinkable achievement.

Not only did the Republicans have their best showing in the South since Reconstruction, but they also managed to carry all the northern states with large African American populations.[28] The success of the 1928 campaign meant that the Republicans were more willing than ever to repudiate or at least reconsider their historic commitment to African Americans. African Americans, for their part, viewed the southern strategy with a mixture of suspicion and anger.[29] The seeds of discontent with the Republican Party in general and Hoover in particular were, therefore, sown prior to his taking office, and started a process that would reach at least a partial culmination with the African American desertion of the GOP by 1936.

The support given to Smith by some African Americans merely confirmed the lack of options that they actually had in 1920s America. As Lichtmann notes, African Americans were confronted with "a Republican party whose friendship . . . was a tarnished memory and . . . by a Democratic party wedded to southern racism."[30] In 1928, the Democratic Party offered little and promised nothing, and African Americans passively supported the Republicans. Yet a vote for Smith could have helped to assert African American political independence by forcing both parties to stop taking them for granted, a strategy that may even have lessened the influence of the South on the Democratic Party. Nonetheless, it is clear that the failure of African American leaders to prise voters away from the Republicans in 1928 reflected the rather limited influence they, and African Americans generally, actually had in national politics at the time. This would, of course, change over the next eight years; in the meantime, however, the prospect of a Hoover administration can only have left African Americans extremely pessimistic about the chances for immediate progress. Hoover seemed determined to purge the Republican Party in the South of African Americans, while paying little attention to those in the North.

As if to emphasize the short-termism of the Republican strategy in 1928, and predicting the electoral problems the party would face in the 1930s, a majority of urban voters backed the Democrats for the first time. This would be much more important politically than Hoover's short-lived success in the South but was largely ignored by the press and contemporary commentators. Furthermore, the Democrats began to make inroads in the Midwest. These trends are associated with Roosevelt and the New Deal, but it is clear that the wider realignment of American politics preceded both the Depression and the New Deal. The Republicans did not recognize that politics was changing, particularly in the cities, and this would, of course, help condemn the GOP to minority status throughout the 1930s and 1940s.

"The Best Use of Tea since the Night It Was Thrown into Boston Harbor"

Having secured the presidential nomination, Hoover pressed ahead with reform of the Republican Party in the South, where it was divided between "black and tan" and "lily-white" factions. Black and tans were interracial and were a throwback to the days of Reconstruction; the lily-whites felt that the only way to reestablish the GOP in the South was to exclude African Americans. Indeed, lily-white Republicans shared only a name with the national party, and most lily-white and black and tan factions were nothing more than skeleton organizations.[31] It was no secret that Hoover owed his nomination at least in part to these factions, causing him considerable discomfort. He now sought to put into practice his philosophy of having honest men looking after the interests of the party.

The *New York Times* agreed there was a need for reform, but warned that the course of action pursued by Hoover "clearly foreshadows a Republican party in the South almost as purely a white man's party as the Democratic party there." It predicted that "a heavy political price may yet be paid" if Hoover excluded African Americans from the party.[32] African Americans were deeply concerned about Hoover's plans. The *World* cited numerous editorials from African American newspapers, noting that "Negroes are engaging in a real insurrection against the Republican Party." Moreover, African Americans were "stirring up trouble" in northern "balance of power" states such as Indiana and Illinois, while some Republicans were questioning the worth of the southern strategy.[33] Robert Church warned Hoover that his southern strategy would "leave the Republican party a wreck upon the shores of the political ocean."[34]

Hoover and his supporters insisted that they were only interested in reforming the party in the South and not in purging African Americans, but this was a highly dubious claim. There were, for example, no attempts made to end corruption or remove incompetent politicians elsewhere in the country. Furthermore, as the only people prosecuted or removed in the South were African American, the sole conclusion that can be drawn is that the Republican policy was essentially racist and designed to create a lily-white party in the region. Ultimately, there was a realization that this strategy would cost African American votes in the North, and for this reason the proposed purge of African American Republicans in the South was delayed until after the election.

That there was a need for reform is beyond doubt. The Republicans had to disassociate themselves from Reconstruction and the perception, inaccurate though widely accepted, that it was a time of black rule and corruption in government, if they wanted to reestablish a two-party system in the region. Yet, it is apparent from the evidence that most southern white Republicans were only interested in purging the party of African American corruption. The real motivation of Republican reformers stemmed more from the importance of the southern states at the national convention rather than from any realistic belief that the GOP could have a viable party organization in the South in the foreseeable future. That reform targeted African Americans is abundantly clear from the efforts to convict Mississippi black and tan leader Perry Howard, among others, of corruption and the complete lack of similar action against lily-whites. The charismatic and longevous Howard, who would attend Republican national conventions as a committeeman from the state until 1960, was twice charged with corruption in the distribution of federal patronage. He was first acquitted in December 1928 and then again in May 1929, both times by all-white Mississippi juries. It was clear that the juries in each case, as well as the white power structure in the state, regarded Howard's acquittal as essential to prevent lily-white Republicans threatening the Democratic Party's grip on the state, as he was almost certainly guilty of the charges against him, notably the selling of patronage positions to, ironically, Democrats.[35]

Regardless of Howard's fate and the motivation of reformers, the Republican Party in the South, whatever its composition, was inherently weak. It could be argued, therefore, that the most Hoover's southern policy could hope to achieve was the replacement of one group of essentially paper organizations with another. Consequently, Hoover's southern policy was flawed not only because it alienated African Americans in the North but also because it was based on a misunderstanding of the nature of the "Hoovercrat" bolt from the Democrats in 1928, which represented opposition to the Smith candidacy rather than anything more than a temporary shift toward Republicanism.[36] Whichever way Hoover's southern strategy is viewed, therefore, it was fatally flawed both in both concept and execution.[37] Ultimately, as Milton Viorst argues, "subsequent events showed that 1928 was a particularly poor time for the Republicans to abandon proven old friends on behalf of dubious new ones."[38]

The election of 1928 saw the first African American returned to Congress for nearly a quarter century when Oscar De Priest replaced the late Martin

B. Madden in a predominantly African American ward of Chicago. Controversy swirled around De Priest because it was traditional for the First Lady to invite the wives of newly elected congressmen to the White House. An invitation to De Priest's wife, Jesse, would therefore be offensive to southerners and hinder Hoover's southern ambitions. After careful preparation by Lou Hoover, the visit by Mrs. De Priest went ahead on 12 June 1929. Mrs. Hoover ensured that the rest of her guests on that day would not be offended by the presence of Mrs. De Priest and would, on the contrary, make her very welcome. Southerners duly raised a storm of protest. Despite meticulous planning, the De Priest tea was a disaster for Republican hopes in the South. It gave southern Democrats a basis from which to attack Hoover's southern policy and undermine Republican gains in their region. De Priest also saw the political importance of the tea and was keen to capitalize on the publicity generated by the ensuing controversy; indeed, it can be argued that he cannily used his wife's invitation to the White House to undermine the Republican Party's southern policy as well as boosting the political cause of African Americans.[39] It seems that Republicans were not prepared for De Priest's exploitation of the invitation; moreover, De Priest believed that the furor over the invitation would actually rally African Americans to the Republican standard.

If De Priest's goal was to undermine Hoover's southern strategy, then he was at least partially successful. By the end of 1929, for example, Henry Anderson, a senior Republican from Virginia who had worked on the southern campaign, believed that the "unfortunate De Priest incident" was being used against Republicans in the state.[40] De Priest did, however, reflect uneasiness among many within the party about the direction that the GOP was taking. Given subsequent events, De Priest's efforts to keep African Americans inside the Republican Party and his courting of the NAACP may have been a better way forward for the party. Robert McCormick of the *Chicago Tribune* was pleased, and argued that if this incident served to drive southern fanatics out of the party, then it was "the best use of tea since the night it was thrown into Boston harbor."[41] The rumpus over the De Priest tea meant that Hoover was keen to avoid any further controversy involving African Americans.

"A Great Judge or a Conspicuous Southerner?"

The nomination of North Carolinian John J. Parker to the Supreme Court in 1930 demonstrated not only how insensitive Hoover had become to the aspirations of African Americans, but also the growing confidence of the NAACP and the increasing importance of the black vote. The defeat of the Parker nomination has been traditionally attributed to the opposition of labor, with the NAACP assigned a mere supporting role. More recent scholarship challenges this interpretation, arguing that, on the contrary, it was the NAACP that took the lead and was ultimately responsible for the most embarrassing setback Hoover suffered in relation to appointments.[42] What is absolutely certain is that the defeat of the Parker nomination represented the NAACP's greatest political victory to date and made public African American disaffection from the GOP. It could be argued that the damage caused by the Parker nomination both eroded remaining African American enthusiasm for Hoover and helped to ease the transfer of African American allegiance from the Republicans to the Democrats.

The NAACP's opposition to the Parker nomination followed the well-worn path of lobbying, but it also spawned a variety of new tactics, notably the targeting of specific elected representatives who had supported the nomination. At this time, litigation was perhaps the most significant and effective tactic used by the NAACP, hence any changes to the Supreme Court were extremely important. The Parker case can, therefore, be seen as the first major engagement in the African American rebellion against the Republican Party. Parker was the Republican candidate in the gubernatorial election in North Carolina in 1920 and did relatively well, polling around 230,000 votes, some 63,000 more than any previous Republican. His nomination to the Supreme Court in 1930 was, therefore, vitally important to Republican plans to reform the party in the South. Hoover was indebted to North Carolina for his victory in 1928, and had considered appointing Parker as attorney general in early 1929 because Parker was a member of the southern elite that Hoover wanted to attract to the party. It should perhaps be added that Parker was both well qualified and generally highly rated by many within the judiciary.[43]

Many people, in both the Democratic Party and the NAACP, felt that Parker's nomination was another phase in Hoover's southern strategy, as he would replace a fellow southerner on the Court. The *New Republic* wondered whether Hoover was choosing a "great judge or a conspicuous southerner."[44] Walter White, who had just succeeded James Weldon Johnson as the NAACP's executive secretary, checked Parker's background and discovered comments he had made about African Americans in the 1920 North Carolina gubernatorial election. Among other things, Parker had declared that in the South, "we recognize the fact that he [the African American] has not yet reached the stage in his development when he can share the burdens and responsibilities of government.[45] The NAACP decided to telegraph Parker to see if he still held these beliefs; he did not reply, and on 28 March 1930 the organization's campaign to thwart his nomination began. Parker's comments and Hoover's decision to nominate him to the Supreme Court outraged African Americans. The *Chicago Defender* was scathing: "If ever there was evidence for a president's disregard for opinion and welfare of a great number of his constituents, it is being shown in this particular case."[46]

Organized labor also opposed Parker because he had ruled favorably in a case involving "Yellow Dog" contracts.[47] White appeared before the Senate Judiciary Committee on 25 April 1930 at the same time as William Green of the American Federation of Labor (AFL), although White felt that Green was keen to avoid any suggestion that labor was working in conjunction with the NAACP.[48] White argued that Parker lacked the impartiality necessary for a Supreme Court justice, but it was the argument of the AFL on the issue of labor contracts that finally persuaded three members of the subcommittee to vote against Parker.[49] White, questioned by the committee, admitted: "frankly, we had never heard of him until he was nominated."[50]

Many Republicans were nervous. Robert R. Moton, the head of the Tuskegee Institute, warned Hoover: "I know of nothing that would so effectively turn the tide of Negro support against the president and the party . . . as to deliberately place on the Supreme Court a man who has openly declared his contempt for them."[51] Hoover stubbornly refused to take advice, believing that Parker was being victimized. Even Senate Majority Leader James E. Watson and Vice President Charles Curtis, neither noted for his sympathy toward African Americans, urged Hoover to either withdraw the nomination or get a retraction from Parker on his racial views, but Hoover refused.[52]

Hoover sought the support of Senator Arthur Vandenberg of Michigan, where both African American and labor votes were important. The NAACP, however, had kept Vandenberg well briefed, and, as a result, he refused to support the nomination, stating:

> The authority of the Supreme Court depends upon the measure of public confidence it enjoys. Therefore if 18,000,000 [*sic*] colored citizens of the United States have a basis for feeling that Judge Parker is prejudiced against their political rights, it is impossible to ask them

> that they still give him their confidence in respect to these constitutional questions.[53]

Writing to a constituent, Vandenberg described himself as a "literal constitutionalist" and talked of "our responsibility in a democracy where majorities must be scrupulous in respecting the rights of minorities. The Fourteenth and Fifteenth amendments to the Constitution are the heart of the Constitution as far as the colored citizen is concerned."[54] Vandenberg was heavily criticized in his home state for his stance, and his cause was not helped by his refusal to explain publicly his decision.

The NAACP had African Americans bombard their congressmen with telegrams and letters condemning the nomination of Parker, and many were surprised by their militancy. NAACP members, for instance, sent hundreds of telegrams to the two senators in Illinois as well as to Vandenberg's colleague in Michigan, and all four, who were Republicans, voted against the nomination. The Senate Judiciary Committee rejected Parker on 21 April 1930, while on 7 May 1930 the nomination was rejected in the Senate by 41 votes to 39.[55] The debate in the Senate had been more about labor than race, but Senator Robert Wagner of New York linked the two: "I see a deep and fundamental consistency between Judge Parker's views on labor relations and his reported attitude toward the colored people of the United States. He is obviously incapable of viewing with sympathy the aspirations of those who are aiming for a higher and better place in the world."[56] The Associated Negro Press (ANP) was quick to give the NAACP credit for the victory.[57] Hoover concurred, further widening the gulf between himself and African Americans. From the middle of April until the end of the campaign, the race issue increasingly dominated Parker's correspondence, perhaps confirming the central role of the NAACP in his defeat. The consequences of the defeat of the Parker nomination were very clear, representing the NAACP's greatest victory to date while hampering the Republican Party's plans for the South.

The defeat of Parker became the NAACP's "rallying cry throughout the 1930s," according to Kenneth W. Goings.[58] The campaign had far-reaching repercussions; it was a "black insurgency movement" against the GOP and led some African Americans to consider the Democrats a viable alternative to Hoover's lily-white Republicans.[59] A combination of factors contributed to the defeat of the nomination, and not everyone opposed it for the same reasons. For example, there was a fear among southern Democrats that

Parker's nomination would help to reestablish the GOP in the region. This is particularly pertinent as it shows that there were those Democrats who feared that the Republicans could successfully create a lily-white two-party system in the region. It is, therefore, not surprising that many southerners voted against the nomination.[60]

Southern Democrats were clearly in a quandary: if they defeated Parker and ended the Republican Party's southern reform, they would also be affronting southern race relations by seemingly siding with the NAACP. Alternatively, if Parker was nominated, it would strengthen the Republican Party in the South and the Democrats could lose their monopoly on the lily-white vote. The outcome of the nomination depended on southern Democrats, and with half of them voting against it, they demonstrated that the Republicans could not reward southerners with office. Liberal northern and border state Republican senators voted against Parker not only on the basis of issues of labor and race but also because they opposed a lily-white party in the South. Ultimately, 29 Republicans voted for the nomination and 17 against, while 10 Democrats were for and 23 against. To each party, the nomination of Parker seemed to epitomize Hoover's southern policy, and factions within each party had good cause to oppose it. In any event, Walter White was correct when he declared that "Negroes have delivered an effective blow against the Republican party's lily-white policy."[61]

Hoover later admitted that the Parker defeat had damaged the prestige of his presidency, and he put the blame for this defeat squarely at the door of African Americans in general and the NAACP in particular: "I don't know what the country is coming to if things are to be run by demagogues and Negro politicians."[62] Hoover refused to deny that he had made these remarks, and this seemed to confirm to African Americans that he wanted them out of the Republican Party.[63] Despite the importance of the Parker fight, it should be remembered that the campaign lasted only six weeks. The effect that it had upon the NAACP, however, was profound in that it had been the first time that the organization had prevented a major candidate from achieving office. A decision was taken by the NAACP board in July to campaign against Parker's supporters in the Senate; Du Bois duly printed the names of pro-Parker senators in the *Crisis* and urged his readers to "paste this [list] in your hat and keep it there until November 1934."[64]

The campaign against those senators who had supported Parker concentrated on those with large African American constituencies such as Republicans Allen of Kansas and Roscoe C. McCulloch of Ohio. Kelly Miller urged White to be cautious, arguing that African Americans were too weak to play what he called the "vindictive game in politics."[65] There was no doubt, however, that the tactic did have some success. Allen was duly defeated, and his vanquisher, George McGill, stated that he would not have succeeded without the efforts of the NAACP to help him win the African American vote.[66] Where McCulloch was concerned, White claimed that the NAACP was "taking no position with regard to the Republican Party," but the association was increasingly seen to be helping McCulloch's opponent.[67] Although McCulloch was defeated and the African American vote shifted to the Democrats, there were other factors involved, notably the Depression, McCulloch's "dryness," and the opposition of labor. When White went to Indiana to oppose James Watson shortly after two lynchings in the state, he linked the activities of the Klan to the Republican Party.[68]

Attacks on pro-Parker Republicans not only emphasized how vital the ballot was but also made it more acceptable for African Americans to vote for the Democrats. Watson, for instance, was duly defeated in 1932, albeit as part of the Democratic landslide, and it should also be noted that some of Indiana's NAACP branches actively supported the senator. By 1934, the campaign against Parker and his supporters was over. In December of that year, the *Crisis* boldly announced that "all the senators who voted for Parker who could be reached by the colored voter have been defeated," but at least noted that African American voters had not acted alone in this endeavor.[69] The Parker episode cemented the NAACP's position as the nation's preeminent African American organization and increased white and African American awareness of the potential importance of the African American vote; African Americans were, therefore, politicized before the advent of the New Deal. They were, as Goings argues, "becoming active players, not just potential voters waiting to be seduced into the New Deal coalition," something particularly evident in those states with large African American populations.[70]

Hoover's relationship with the NAACP had never been good, and the Parker nomination ensured that there would be no reconciliation. Hoover disliked "politicians," and into this category he placed the NAACP, refusing to see the association as a nonpartisan pressure group and even suggesting that it was funded by the Democrats. "This serious blind spot," argues Donald J. Lisio, "cut him off from a basically non-partisan organization that generally used non-political legal methods of which Hoover would have approved."[71] Hoover was not helped in this matter by the fact that his secretaries often prevented the NAACP from contacting him.[72] The NAACP became increasingly vitriolic in its attacks on the administration, but in doing so effectively ended what little chance there was of advancement under Hoover.

"The Party Label Means Nothing"

Concurrent with the Parker episode was a controversy surrounding the Gold Star Mothers. In short, the mothers of American soldiers killed in the Great War were given the opportunity to visit the graves of their sons in Europe, but the mothers of white soldiers would travel on navy ships while those of African American soldiers would have to go on commercial liners. Hoover, with typical disregard for the feelings of African Americans, not only refused to become involved but also refused to deny that he had ordered segregated transport; in doing so, he sustained a controversy that would cloud the rest of his administration. Only 58 of the 450 African Americans who had asked to go on the trip actually did so; other trips followed, but not many African Americans went. *The Nation* commented: "surely there was no time in the history of our country when segregation was less necessary and more cruel."[73] As Sherman notes, "Hoover turned a well meaning gesture into a painful insult."[74]

In the 1930 midterm elections, Du Bois urged the abandonment of loyalty to party labels: "we can afford to vote for northern liberal Democrats in spite of the South . . . the Republicans are supporting the rotten boroughs of the South just as steadfastly as the Democrats. The party label, then, means nothing. The individual candidate is everything."[75] Moton suggested the creation of a "Black Cabinet" to Hoover; this recommendation, however, became lost amid the election campaign (but would be famously taken up by Franklin Roosevelt).[76] The Republicans did little to hold the African American vote in 1930; Hoover ignored African American leaders and refused to make any direct appeal to African American voters. One consequence was that the Democrats managed to win 25 percent of the African American vote in Harlem.[77] The *Pittsburgh Courier* was scathing: "it looked like the President tried to do everything in his power to humiliate faithful Negro Republicans."[78] Fourteen of the twenty-four Republicans elected to Congress from the South in 1928 were defeated in 1930, while the African American press rejoiced in the downfall of a number of other Republicans.[79]

When the Republicans assessed their performance in 1930, they managed to display some optimism. Yet what is perhaps most significant about the "Republican Party General Political Survey" of April 1931 is that it seemed to recognize the futility of attempting to break the Solid South. The report contended that the Democrats were not popular in the country at large, but it also made the rather obvious observation that they were very deeply entrenched in the South.[80] The report maintained, however, that while "the country prefers a Republican in the Presidential office," people were not satisfied with the current situation.[81] If this was not food for thought enough for Hoover, the report's assessment of the African American vote would have made depressing reading. It noted that "one of the most notable features of the 1930 congressional elections in the states north of the Potomac and the Ohio was the support given to Democratic nominees by the black vote."[82] This turn of events saw seven thousand African Americans register as Democrats in Baltimore, while two judges and one assemblyman were elected in New York on the Democratic ticket.[83]

After the 1930 elections, there was at least a partial realization by Hoover of the gravity of the situation relating to African Americans. This was coupled with an acknowledgment that many southern white Republicans were interested in patronage rather than reform. Had Hoover attempted to consolidate the African American vote in the North, it would have made little difference to the Republican Party in the South, but it might have checked the desertion of the GOP by northern African Americans. In May 1931, White asked Hoover to supply a message of greeting to the NAACP's annual convention, providing the president with the possibility of repairing relations not only with the NAACP itself but also with the wider African American community. Hoover's dislike of the NAACP led him to offer only a curt message, to which White responded with a vigorous attack on the president.[84] White portrayed Hoover as antiblack and outlined numerous grievances that the community held against him. Hoover failed to respond to his unpopularity among African Americans, and the problem was exacerbated by the controversy surrounding the Tenth Cavalry.

The Tenth Cavalry was the country's most famous African American regiment and had represented the link between African American military service and citizenship since the Civil War. It was, therefore, of huge symbolic importance to African Americans. In August 1931, however, as part of military reforms, General Douglas MacArthur decided to reduce the size of the regiment. There was an immediate outcry, and Hoover was warned that this could cost him African American votes in northern and border states if he did not act to save the regiment. Hoover did nothing, and the regiment suffered the ignominy of being effectively disarmed and essentially reduced to noncombat status.[85]

In April 1932, *Opportunity*, the journal of the National Urban League, reported that over half of African Americans intended to vote for the Democrats. By May, the proportion had grown.[86] African American discontent with Hoover and the Republicans was becoming increasingly vocal, most notably in September, when erstwhile Republican and owner/editor of the *Pittsburgh Courier*, Robert L. Vann, announced his break from the party. Vann, who had been continually passed over for patronage positions, made a speech entitled "The Patriot and the Partisan" in which he famously predicted the end of African American support for the Republican Party. "I see millions of Negroes," he declared, "turning their pictures of Abraham Lincoln to the wall. This year I see Negroes voting a Democratic ticket."[87]

Ironically, given subsequent history, the Democrats' choice of presidential candidate in 1932 actually helped the Republicans. Franklin Roosevelt, the governor of New York, was cultivating support among southern states to the point where it sometimes appeared that the Klan had helped him. Many African Americans viewed Roosevelt—who had spent considerable time in Georgia receiving treatment for polio and did little for African Americans while governor of the Empire State—with deep suspicion.[88] The nomination of Roosevelt, together with the selection of John Nance Garner, a Texan, as his running mate and the lack of any mention of African Americans in the Democratic platform, meant that there was little alternative to Hoover.[89] African American Republicans emphasized the possibility that southerners would dominate a Roosevelt administration or that his vice-presidential nominee, John Nance Garner, could become president.[90]

Opportunity, nevertheless, leaned toward Roosevelt: "there appears to be convincing evidence that it [the black vote] has partially broken away from its traditional moorings."[91] The *Crisis* commented on the lack of merit of either candidate: "Mr. Roosevelt's record on the Negro problem is clear. He hasn't any, [while] Mr. Hoover's record on the Negro problem is not clear and in that respect it resembles his record on everything else."[92] Predictions that the Democrats would make gains among African Americans in Harlem, Pittsburgh, Indianapolis, St. Louis, Detroit, Manhattan, and Kansas City proved to be accurate. This perhaps illustrated a more general shift to the Democrats in urban areas, but it should be noted that the Republicans actually increased their support in the African American communities of Chicago, Cleveland, Knoxville, Cincinnati, Philadelphia, and Baltimore.[93] Roosevelt did not inspire much confidence among African Americans, and, as a result, most continued to vote Republican.[94]

Arthur Krock of the *New York Times* argued in *Opportunity* that African Americans had not become politically independent, although they were moving toward independence, but had turned against the Republicans, largely because of the Depression. He continued: "to my mind, it was a splendid revolt. The Negro, in brief, voted as a citizen on Hoover and Roosevelt, forgetting Lincoln and Jefferson Davis." He felt that any switch of the African American vote to the Democrats would be temporary: "he will vote Republican again when that party shows the least reason to merit it."[95] But were they voting for Roosevelt or against Hoover? If the latter were true, then it would be merely a temporary protest vote. In the South, the Republicans achieved their lowest vote since the Civil War, dropping from 1.5 million in 1928 to less than a half million in 1932, exposing the folly of the southern strategy; the Republicans had thus succeeded in beginning to alienate African Americans without cracking the Solid South.

Throughout the so-called "Republican Ascendancy," from 1920 to 1932, the GOP's record was bad on appointments, antilynching, and the Klan because it had little to gain by addressing black concerns genuinely. Furthermore, Republicans would continue to take African Americans for granted so long as their loyalty to the GOP was considered guaranteed. Ignoring their history and political necessity, the GOP did little to cultivate northern black voters, suggesting a loss of idealism within the party combined with what Sherman terms "a lack of political good sense as too many Republicans clung to an outmoded concept of America."[96] The Republicans refused to adapt to America's increasingly urban, multiethnic society, whereas the Democrats embraced it.

Hoover's record was even worse than that of his immediate predecessors, and a number of factors combined to make his presidency the catalyst for the desertion of the GOP by African Americans. The 1920s saw a rise in the expectations of African Americans, which, combined with their growing numbers in the North, meant that their votes became more important with every election. Often exaggerated by African American leaders, particularly Walter White, this new dynamic in American politics was at least recognized by liberal northern Democrats. As a consequence, by the late 1920s this wing of the party was courting the African American vote actively. This coincided with Hoover's southern policy, which symbolized the GOP's apparent abandonment of African Americans.

The historic relationship between the Republican Party and African Americans was, therefore, being reassessed by both. By the onset of the 1930s, African American allegiance to the GOP was, as Sherman observes, "an anachronism" based on "legend and habit" rather than on constructive polices.[97] Moreover, African Americans were hit hardest and helped least when the Great Depression struck. The apparent indifference of Hoover to the economic plight of African Americans further imperiled the relationship between descendants of the emancipated and the party of their emancipator. Hoover had no consistent approach to the plight of African Americans and little understanding of their problems. A prime example of this is Hoover's antagonistic attitude toward the NAACP. In viewing it as a "political" organization that was possibly a tool of the Democrats, he demonstrated a complete absence of any understanding of the organization's purpose, and, by robbing himself of a very important potential ally, he actually created his most effective opposition among African Americans.[98]

There can be no doubt that in the 1920s most African Americans still saw the Republican Party as their spiritual home, but in 1928 there were discordant voices within the community urging a change; by 1930, the Democrats began to breach Republican citadels in the North. In 1932, the Democratic ticket offered little comfort to most African Americans and 70 percent supported Hoover. By 1934, however, the New Deal had begun to appreciably improve the lives of African Americans, and for the first time a majority of them voted for the Democratic Party.

The shift away from the Republican Party by some African Americans in 1928, eight years before the major shift to the Democrats would occur, confirms that it was not the New Deal alone that caused African Americans to change their allegiance. Rather, it was a combination of factors, many of which preceded both the Depression and the New Deal, and this suggests that events during the New Deal continued a process that had already begun, a process that was mirrored in other voting groups and illustrated the serious weaknesses within the Republican electoral coalition. These weaknesses would be magnified by the events of the 1930s, and one consequence of this, among many, was that the Republican Party would lose, and never regain, the votes of African Americans.

2

Abraham Lincoln Is Not a Candidate

The 1930s represented the lowest point in the history of the Republican Party. The GOP saw itself as the natural party of government, having occupied the White House for fifty-six of the seventy-two years since the start of the Civil War, but it was now dealing, for the first time, with the prospect of a prolonged period in opposition. "The election of 1932 was more than the defeat of a political party," contends E. E. Schattschneider, "it was something very much like the overthrow of the ruling class."[1] The Republicans, George Mayer asserts, did not know how to deal with defeat: "the unfamiliar frustrations of minority status embittered GOP leaders, clouded their judgment, and goaded them into political errors. Each blunder led to mutual recriminations and a deterioration of morale, which in turn provoked a fresh disaster at the polls."[2] The party, a diminishing force in Congress and blamed for the Depression, was losing its traditional core constituencies. Fundamentally weak in large parts of the country, it was deeply split over how to extract itself from the morass in which the scale and manner of the 1932 defeat had left it. The GOP's long exile from government was a deeply unhappy one; leaderless, split, and groping for issues, the party staggered from one electoral catastrophe to the next. Consequently, the party's neglect of African Americans can be best understood against the background of its divisions and serious difficulties during the early years of the New Deal.

The internal problems of the GOP illustrate that the party had priorities other than the maintenance of the votes of African Americans and even other traditional constituencies. Moreover, the Republicans' misinterpretation of the new political realities with which they were confronted goes some way to explaining their attitude toward African Americans. It is essential, therefore, to consider the loss of the black vote in the context of the problems faced by the GOP throughout the decade. Implicit in much of the historiography is the assumption that not only was the switch of the African American vote virtually inevitable, but that it can be explained relatively simply. There is certainly worth in this argument as the benefits brought by the New Deal—or perhaps the contrast between little or no positive action by successive Republican administrations compared to the help given to African Americans by Roosevelt—go a long way to explain the shift, but they by no means tell the full story.

The party was divided between progressives, or liberals, and conservatives, with the former based primarily in the West and the latter in the East. As the midterm elections of 1934 approached, the party had to decide how it was going to contend with the remarkable popularity of the New Deal. A serious problem was that the figure of Herbert Hoover still loomed large over the party, and he and his supporters wanted to oppose the New Deal in its entirety. Hoover's supporters had seized control of the Republican National Committee, which they then used to assail the New Deal, implicitly criticizing those Republicans in Congress who had backed it and threatening their prospects for reelection as a result.[3] The election of 1934 is noteworthy since, traditionally, the party that wins the presidency loses ground in midterm elections. Despite a few predictions of GOP gains, the election of 1934 reversed this trend. This year is also extremely significant as it marked the point at which a majority of African Americans voted Democratic for the first time. The Democrats strengthened their position by gaining 19 seats in the House (increasing from 313 to 332) and 10 in the Senate (up to 69). The New Deal had won, announced Arthur Krock, "the most overwhelming victory in the history of American politics."[4] The Republican Party was now in full retreat across the nation.[5]

Many within the GOP felt that the Democrats had poured relief into strategic areas: "it was more like an auction than an election," moaned one.[6] Clinging to this rationale, Old Guard conservative Republicans did not view the defeat as representing a sea change in voting patterns, whereas liberal westerners saw it as a repudiation of conservative leadership. The Republicans were faced with a dilemma: did they continue to oppose the New Deal and go down the road of conservatism, or did they embrace aspects of it and become more liberal? William Borah, a senator from Idaho since 1906 and a nonconformist fixture in the party's progressive wing, was in no doubt: "unless the Republican party is delivered from its reactionary leadership, and reorganized in accord with its one-time liberal principles, it will die like the Whig party of sheer political cowardice."[7] One problem was that the only alternative the Republicans were offering to the New Deal was the Constitution, and, as Borah rightly pointed out, "you can't eat the Constitution."[8]

Borah, for all his faults, at least recognized the seriousness of the Republican predicament.[9] He repeated his call for liberalism in December 1934, arguing that the party had reached its "lowest ebb," and that this was at least partly due to an unwillingness to "meet the great problems confronting us upon a broad and humanitarian basis."[10] He maintained, however, that he did not want a third party or the abandonment of the Republican name. The Republicans, he argued, risked losing disenchanted voters permanently if they did not start to represent the views of ordinary Americans.[11] Charles McNary, the Republican floor leader in the Senate, backed Borah's call, arguing that the party "should quit its abstractions and alarms and get down to the level of human sympathy and human understandings." There was, he believed, little to be gained by complaining about "regimentation and bureaucracy" when people did not know where next month's rent was coming from.[12]

By the beginning of 1935, the Republican Party, according to Clyde Weed, "reflected a coalition of groups that had come to feel extraordinarily threatened by the policy changes induced by the realignment then underway, and this severely limited the party's ability to undertake electoral readjustments."[13] Midwestern elements now felt that they should set the agenda. Easterners had largely controlled the GOP since its inception, but it was becoming clear, even to them, that they were an electoral liability.[14] It was obvious that if the party was to have any chance of victory in 1936, it had to dissociate itself from eastern business interests and look to the West for a candidate.[15] With this in mind, western Republicans met in Topeka, Kansas, in January 1935, and, despite the election being nearly two years away, Alfred Landon, the governor of Kansas, was being suggested as a potential presidential candidate.[16] The westerners urged the GOP to advocate both liberal policies and candidates, and agreed to meet again to discuss a declaration of principles. This effort to revive the fortunes of the party was met with approval in both the West and the East, particularly in New York.[17]

William Allen White, the noted Republican editor from Kansas, welcomed the move to liberalize the GOP. Articulating, but clearly exaggerating, the concern that many Republicans had about the New Deal, he expressed fear that, unless something was done, "America may drift into fascism." He stated that there was currently a challenge to "our ancient democratic liberties" that could only be countered by offering the common man more in terms of economic security; he also urged Republicans to turn away from business and return to the "humanity of Lincoln." "We can save America," he concluded, "but America cannot be saved by merely denouncing the faults of Roosevelt."[18]

A "Grass Roots" Republican convention began on 10 June in the highly symbolic setting of Springfield, Illinois, the home of Abraham Lincoln. The convention would only discuss principles; candidates and talk of candidates were forbidden.[19] The main theme of the convention was expressed in the phrase "save the Constitution," and there was even talk of changing the name of the party to the Constitutional Party.[20] Interestingly, some of those advocating the name change did so to appeal to conservative white voters in the South, suggesting that the folly of Hoover's southern policy had not been entirely recognized. There was a private acceptance by easterners that the next Republican presidential candidate must come from the West and must not be a conservative.[21]

Another GOP faction, the "Republican Crusaders," announced a platform in Cleveland, Ohio, on 10 July 1935. The Crusaders were from six states, Kentucky, Michigan, Ohio, Pennsylvania, Tennessee, and West Virginia, and apparently had the blessing of party chairman Henry Fletcher, a New Yorker unpopular with many westerners. They declared their allegiance to the principles of the Republican Party and the Constitution and claimed that Roosevelt was trying to replace the Constitution with a dictatorship. Among other things, they condemned lynching as the "oppression of the colored race" and demanded a federal law that would "conform to the Constitution."[22] A number of regional Republican conventions had, therefore, taken place in an attempt to dictate the future course of the party, but it seemed that the eastern wing of the party would yield to the West over the choice of presidential candidate and the composition of the platform; moreover, it was glaringly obvious that Hoover's renomination, however much he wanted it, would be political suicide for the party.[23]

The prospects for African Americans did not look bright regardless of which faction gained control. African Americans were faced with a Republican Party that, on the one hand, had a liberal western faction whose liberalism did not extend to supporting antilynching legislation and, on the other, a conservative eastern wing that decried the liberalism of the western wing and the New Deal. The most vocal westerner was Borah, and his opposition to antilynching legislation was well known; in fact, aside from

Arthur Capper of Kansas (an NAACP member), it was difficult to identify any Republican senator prepared to be publicly and vocally associated with the push for antilynching legislation occurring on Capitol Hill throughout the period. The prospects of the Republican Party embracing a civil rights agenda, therefore, were poor. This is unsurprising: Republicans in the Far West had few African American constituents and therefore had little to gain by advocating civil rights. Nevertheless, those in the Midwest (particularly Illinois and Ohio) and in New York and Pennsylvania should have realized that an appeal to African American voters, even on the basis of self-interest, made sense politically. That they did not makes them more culpable than Borah for the party's failure to regain the African American vote.

It seemed that the West had won the argument when Landon, the front-runner for most of the previous year, was nominated on the first ballot in June 1936.[24] Eastern conservatives were by no means vanquished, and the foolhardy campaign they and others waged against the New Deal contrasted with the more liberal philosophy that westerners had hoped to promote. The election of 1936 represented the Republicans' nadir and still did not resolve the vexed question of whether the party was going to adopt liberal or conservative principles. Bloodied, the GOP sought an alliance with southern Democrats, an alliance that would dominate American politics for more than ten years.

"Abraham Lincoln Is Not a Candidate in the Current Campaign"

The Democratic victory in 1936 is vitally important to any assessment of the Republican loss of the African American vote. Indeed, in terms of the growth of African American political power, the election of 1936 was, in many ways, a watershed in the history of racial politics in the United States. This election is usually remembered as one of the greatest landslides in American history, with a thankful electorate endorsing the program of Franklin Roosevelt. While this is undoubtedly true, there is a danger that, with the benefit of hindsight, this landslide can be seen as entirely predictable. The reality is that in 1936 many pundits (and not just those from the infamous *Literary Digest* poll) were predicting a close election, one in which each party had to campaign for special-interest votes.[25] African Americans were, arguably for the first time, paid special attention due to their increasing numbers in the North, and this makes the election of 1936 a pivotal moment in the emergence of African American political power. The election of 1936 confirmed that African Americans were no longer wedded to the Republican Party; memories of Lincoln had faded amid the despondency of the Depression and grew even dimmer when the New Deal offered renewed hope. The switch of the African American vote was by no means sudden; it was, nevertheless, remarkable, and the scale of it more remarkable still, but more important was the long-term impact of the realignment on American politics.

The 1930s were a very bad time for the Republicans to alienate further any of their core constituencies, however apparently insignificant. The lack of concern shown by Republicans for African Americans had never been an electoral handicap as there had never been enough African Americans voting to make any difference, whereas any perceived or overt sympathy could have been electorally damaging. Since the Civil War, the Republicans believed that they could maintain the African American vote with a minimum of effort, and this was certainly true until 1934. The situation was now very different. The *Crisis* argued that the Republicans could no longer rely on "Lincoln, flag-waving and mammy stories . . . to charm votes into ballot boxes," while the *Baltimore Afro-American* pointedly reminded the GOP and African Americans that "Abraham Lincoln is not a candidate in the current campaign."[26] The national press, too, recognized the importance of the African American vote, but even the *New York Times* was reluctant to predict which party would eventually win it.[27] The fact that the destination of the black vote was a matter of serious debate would have been unthinkable barely a few years before.

The African American vote was reckoned to hold the balance of power in at least ten states. The Democrats were alive to this possibility and were able to capitalize on it, whereas the Republicans were reluctant to substantially modify appeals that had been used for generations. By mid-decade, an appeal to African Americans in the North based on the tradition and history of the Republican Party was much less effective in the face of a Democratic appeal on the basis of relief and employment opportunities. The onset of the Depression and the benefits provided by the New Deal meant that African Americans no longer voted on the basis of traditional loyalty or mere habit; they now, for the first time, would vote as poor people rather than as people with a perceived political debt to repay. The Republicans, no longer assured of this vote, actually had to campaign for it.

To the NAACP, and many African Americans, the main issues of the 1936 election were relief and antilynching legislation, and the party that offered these would be best placed to win the African American vote. The Republicans were hurt in this regard when William Borah, the implacable foe of antilynching legislation, emerged as a potential presidential candidate; he soon replaced Parker as the NAACP's bogeyman and would be successfully halted during the primary elections. Eventual Republican candidate Landon was quite progressive on racial matters but lost ground with African Americans due to the suspicion that he would give control of relief distribution to the states.[28]

The loss of the African American vote by the Republican Party could not have come at a worse time. By 1936, African Americans could compare four years of the Democrats with twelve years of the Republicans, and the gains made in these four years put into perspective the inaction of the previous twelve. Moreover, the increasing number of northern African American voters, negligible in the 1920s, coincided with a new political awareness among African American leaders, particularly within the NAACP. This meant that African Americans had to be courted by politicians in the same way as any other group. The Republicans only partially grasped this, and failed to regain the African American vote not only because of their prior neglect but also because their appeal was fundamentally flawed. The GOP advocated orthodox but conservative economic policies built around the concept of a decentralized federal government and a balanced budget, but this was unlikely to win the votes of many African Americans at the height of the Depression.

It was apparent that the 1936 presidential election would be unlike any other for African Americans. Walter White, for example, realized that the election could be close and urged African Americans to ignore party labels in favor of individual candidates.[29] White also recognized, and often exaggerated, the potential of the African American vote, and in subsequent elections he would repeatedly remind African Americans, the press, and politicians about the "pivotal nature" of the African American vote. And he was not alone in this analysis; Arthur Krock predicted that four groups would decide the outcome of the election: new voters, African Americans, labor, and agriculture, but new voters and African Americans had not been adequately canvassed to determine the destination of their ballots.[30] White also declared that African Americans would vote for "men and measures" rather than political parties and would sell their votes to the "highest bidder." In 1936, White sought to put the African American vote on the political map, and there was no doubt that he had a point about its importance. He claimed, for example, that it could be pivotal in up to seventeen states with a combined electoral vote of 281 (out of a total of 535) in 1936. He felt that the African American response to both the Parker nomination and Borah's attitude to antilynching legislation were a good indication that the black community was largely united on the main issues affecting it.[31]

Analysts frequently mentioned Illinois, Michigan, New York, New Jersey, Missouri, Indiana, Ohio, and Pennsylvania as states where the African American vote could prove important. Of these, New York, Michigan, Ohio, Pennsylvania, and Illinois were usually Republican strongholds, but had all gone Democratic in 1932, taking with them 157 electoral votes. These states, together with Indiana, Missouri, Kentucky, and Tennessee (already thought to be safely Democratic), had enough African American voters to swing the election either way. In all, the states where the African American vote was considered important accounted for over 200 electoral votes, compared to the South's 140.

The logic of the NAACP was quite simple: the African American vote in the North could negate or exceed that of the white South, and both the Republicans and Democrats needed to appreciate this. It was theoretically possible, therefore, to win the election without the South. Furthermore, predicting that African Americans would vote for one party offered the potential of wringing concessions from the other, assuming, of course, that African Americans would vote as a bloc. Both parties therefore, should have been extremely wary of offending African American voters in potentially pivotal northern states by appealing to relatively unimportant lily-white sentiment in the South. Rhetoric alone, therefore, would no longer convince African Americans of the merits of a particular party.[32] White maintained that African Americans' main problem with Roosevelt was his perceived dependence on southerners, and warned that the administration had to decide whether it was going to listen to a handful of southern white voters or the "thoughtful people of both races in the seventeen states with more than twice as many electoral votes."[33] White was confident that southern Democrats would not bolt from the party on the race issue as they would lose their influence on congressional committees.

"It Is Hard to Convince a Man That It Is Unconstitutional to Save His Life"

The NAACP was determined to thwart William Borah's presidential ambitions in 1936. When it became evident that Borah would be seeking the Republican nomination, Walter White wrote to him on the subject of lynching, the Idahoan having deemed federal antilynching legislation unconstitutional. Citing Borah's role in the defeat of both the Dyer bill of 1922 and the 1935 Costigan-Wagner bill, White stated that Borah had "the somewhat dubious honor of having been the executioner of two distinctly hopeful opportunities to pass federal legislation."[34] White reminded Borah that fourteen people had been lynched recently: "do you feel proud of your handiwork, Senator Borah? And does it disturb your conscience to the slightest extent that there is the possibility that had the Costigan-Wagner bill passed that [these] lynching[s] might not have occurred?"[35] White noted that African Americans might hold the balance of power in the forthcoming presidential election. "There are many Americans," White continued, "who no longer believe in the sincerity of members of the Senate who forget states' rights when such issues as prohibition are being discussed, but wrap themselves in the mantle of 'constitutionality' when the lives of human beings are being taken by lawless mobs."[36] The NAACP, and White in particular, saw the chance for a new political crusade akin to that against the Parker nomination.

Early in 1936, the association warned the Republicans of the possible consequences of a Borah candidacy.[37] Borah, in an interview with the Associated Negro Press, tried to mend fences with African American voters: "I regret so much that Negroes over the country feel as they do toward me. Why, there is not a member in the United States' Senate that thinks more of the Negro than myself."[38] He reiterated that he was not opposed to an antilynching bill in principle and understood the need to stop the crime, but he maintained that those bills brought before the Senate were unconstitutional. When consulted by the bill's sponsors, he restated this view, explaining, "I couldn't see the sense of going through the motion of doing something that would not benefit the Negro race."[39] He stated that many in the Senate agreed with his stance, but those with large African American constituencies "got scared and left me holding the bag."[40] Borah believed that his major error was to state his views publicly when other politicians refused to.

Hamilton Fish, a congressman from New York and Borah's eastern campaign manager, was becoming frustrated by attacks on the senator, writing to White demanding that the NAACP publicize the views of other potential Republican candidates and President Roosevelt on the constitutionality of the Costigan-Wagner antilynching bill. Fish then challenged White to make their views public.[41] The association demurred, however, preferring to trawl Borah's past to damn the senator with his own words; it certainly had plenty to choose from. "I will say very frankly," Borah had told the Senate in 1914, "I am one of those who believe that it was a mistake to bestow upon the colored people at this particular time [after the Civil War] the right to vote."[42]

The association's concerted campaign against Borah aided his defeat in the Ohio primary. The *Chicago Tribune*, a staunch Republican (and vehemently anti-Roosevelt) newspaper that was not insensitive to the party's historic links with African Americans, reported that Borah was blaming his defeat in the Ohio primary on the antilynching question and the fact that he was honest in his opposition while others were insincere in their support.[43] Borah then lost in Illinois, where there were 226,000 potential African American voters, by 80,000 votes, and this effectively ended his bid for the Republican nomination. White claimed another triumph, declaring: "the Negro vote is coming of age and is no longer the chattel of any one party."[44] A precedent had been set, he believed, whereby African Americans could no longer be taken for granted. White wrote a gloating letter to the senator attributing his defeat to an "entire record [which] has been one of almost invariably consistent hostility to the Negro's ambitions, and when your attitude was not characterized by hostility it was at best one of indifference and apathy."[45] White finished his attack by quoting political commentator Jay Franklin: "it is hard to convince a man that it is unconstitutional to save his life."[46]

More so than the Parker nomination, the demise of Borah's ambitions cannot be attributed solely, or even predominantly, to the efforts of the NAACP. Borah had always been a maverick, divisive influence within the GOP, and had an inconsistent voting record and little support outside his native Northwest. He had turned down Coolidge's offer of the vice-presidential nomination in 1924, implying that he himself should head the ticket; he then failed to campaign for Hoover's reelection. This latter point and his advocacy of a liberal party in the wake of the 1932 and 1934 elections had alienated him from conservative Republicans, and in all likelihood had cost him the, admittedly slim, chance he had of being the GOP's standard bearer. This not only helps to explain his failure to win the party's presidential nomination in 1936 but also supports charges made by the NAACP that his opposition to antilynching legislation on constitutional grounds was incompatible with the stance he took on other issues. Moreover, by the time of his defeat in the Illinois primary, his support had largely dissipated.

That Borah was never a serious candidate for the nomination is not the fundamental issue. What remained important throughout the episode was that African Americans were very vocally refusing to be taken for granted, and with their potentially crucial votes, they could not be. The Republicans clearly suffered in this regard; Borah was, after all, one of their own. The *Norfolk Journal and Guide* declared that "Borah stultifies whatever reason the Negro might have had for holding out any hope that the GOP might be his salvation. The party . . . comes forward with a prospective leader for 1936 who openly and unashamedly opposes a measure that would safeguard his human rights."[47] It warned that African Americans would desert the Republican Party completely if Borah were nominated. The fact that Borah could even be considered by the Republicans as a potential presidential candidate proved to many African Americans that the party simply could not be trusted.[48]

"In the House of His Friends"

The Republican convention in Cleveland did little to reassure African Americans. There was a continued preoccupation, although much less overt than in 1928, with establishing the party in the South; the Credentials Committee seated lily-white delegations from Florida, Louisiana, and, initially, South Carolina (as well as a black and tan delegation from Mississippi led by "the elusively surviving" Perry Howard).[49] No evidence of wrongdoing was found against these states, but there was a fear that the party's southern policy could cost it 1–4 million votes in the North.[50] Several African American delegates threatened a floor fight against the lily-white southern delegations, and, as a result, "Tieless Joe" Tolbert's black and tan delegation from South Carolina was seated, overturning the previous decision to seat the lily-white delegation from the state.[51] Walter White warned that the seating of the lily-whites would hamper Republican efforts to win over African American voters.[52]

The GOP did, however, set a precedent by having an African American minister, Bishop James W. Brown, give the opening prayer at the night session of 12 June 1936.[53] After the Democratic convention, the *Crisis* remarked acidly, "if the Republicans said little of the Negro in their platform, the Democrats went one better by saying nothing."[54] The *Crisis* did not pretend to be surprised by the Democrats' stance on lynching, but "only the Lord knows what curious quirk of reasoning kept the Republicans from mentioning the crime."[55] The association recognized that lynching, in the context of the economic plight of African Americans, was probably not a major issue in the campaign, but it maintained that the problems of African Americans, which also included suffrage and education, were all linked. There was, however, a glimmer of hope for African Americans as the two candidates seemed "much better than their platforms."[56]

The *Crisis* argued that the Republicans had learned nothing from their preoccupation with the South in 1928 and their defeat in 1932. It expressed concern that the GOP was too dependent on old-style, conservative African American "Dixie delegates," who did not "speak for the three million Negroes in the North who have the vote."[57] It stressed that as the South would remain Democratic, it made more sense for the Republicans to listen to those African Americans who could vote, citing Parker and Borah as evidence that northern African Americans "mean business."[58] The *Crisis* identified two main concerns of African Americans: equal employment opportunities and pay and removing all restrictions on the right to vote: "with these two pledges carried out the Negro himself will take care of such matters as education, lynching, segregation and discrimination."[59]

If the Republicans were serious about attracting African American votes, then they had got off to an inauspicious start. To their credit, they did at least supplement their usual rhetoric with a "Negro" plank, albeit under the heading "Furthermore" at the end of their platform. In this, the Agricultural Adjustment Administration (AAA) was attacked for pushing African American sharecroppers toward poverty; Roosevelt's silence on racial issues was condemned, as were the lack of antilynching legislation and the inaction of the Justice Department on interstate lynchings. The Republicans, obviously hoping that African Americans had forgotten their inactivity from 1920 to 1932, stressed that Roosevelt's inaction was particularly difficult to justify as the Democrats had majorities in both houses of Congress. The platform summed up: "we condemn the present New Deal policies which would regiment and ultimately eliminate the colored citizen from the country's productive life, and make him solely a ward of the federal government."[60] Landon approved the platform in "word and spirit" and prepared to campaign on the basis of it.[61] Indeed, in August the party announced "plans for the most intensive campaign among the Negro race ever waged by the Republican party."[62]

Landon was one of the few Republicans to win office in 1932 when he became governor of Kansas. Admittedly, his victory had come in a three-cornered contest, but his record as state chairman from 1928 and as governor had, as noted, been good enough for him to be viewed as a potential presidential candidate as early as January 1935. Landon realized that the African American constituency was one of the many that had to be brought back to the GOP fold, and, as a result, he became the first modern Republican presidential candidate to campaign actively for the black vote. This did not go unnoticed among African Americans. In the *New York Times*, the NAACP's Henry Lee Moon contended that "the present Republican campaign for the Negro vote differs from that of previous years. It is no longer a gesture to hold these votes. It is now a strenuous effort to woo these voters back from the Democrats."[63]

Landon had a decent record on race and progressive issues. He had bolted from the party on two occasions, siding with Theodore Roosevelt's Progressives in 1912, and then joining William Allen White's campaign against the Klan in 1924. When he was Kansas state chairman in 1928, he appointed William M. Bradshaw as assistant chairman, the highest position held by an African American in the Kansas Republican apparatus, and he complemented this with the appointments of three more African Americans at the party's state headquarters. In 1929, Bradshaw was promoted to special assistant to the state attorney general, and then charged with courting the black vote in Landon's 1932 gubernatorial campaign. Landon wanted, Donald McCoy argues, to help "Negroes feel that they were part of the party."[64] In keeping with this, Republicans advocated equality (without actually defining it), and this was in all likelihood to counter rival candidate John W. Brinkley, another advocate of "equality." In 1934, Landon had been one of nine governors who petitioned Roosevelt, urging him to support an antilynching bill.[65] The Republican candidate did, therefore, offer something more than words to African American voters in 1936.

Landon's comments and record did not necessarily mean that the Republican Party was about to start taking the concerns of African Americans seriously. The NAACP had submitted a document to the Republican convention demanding: antilynching legislation; an end to relief, welfare, and employment discrimination; the enforcement of the Fourteenth and Fifteenth Amendments; an end to photographs on civil service applications; and an end to discrimination in educational funding.[66] Landon would make only a partial commitment to the NAACP's program by going on record opposing lily-white Republicans, condemning lynching, and urging an end to discrimination in civil service recruiting.

The election of 1936 was to be a referendum on the New Deal and its perceived benefits. The Republicans, fearful of losing the African American vote permanently, had to come up with an alternative to the New Deal that was consistent with both their conservative attitude toward the role of the federal government and their traditional alliance with African Americans. On the one hand, the GOP appealed to history. For instance, Landon told African Americans:

> When the Negro maintains his allegiance to the principles of the Republican party, he is in the house of his friends. The Thirteenth and Fourteenth Amendments are Republican Amendments. They made the word citizen a real word in the lives of the colored people and brought them under the protecting shelter of the Constitution and the Bill of Rights.[67]

At the same time, however, there was a conscious effort to offer an alternative to the New Deal, specifically the negative effect of relief. Landon argued that "the attempt of the New Deal to use relief rolls as modern reservation[s] on which the great colored race is to be confined forever as a ward of the federal government . . . is not only disastrous to a great people but of alarming consequence to our entire economic and social life."[68] The Republican National Committee (RNC) proclaimed Landon's words as a "new Emancipation Proclamation," and there were pockets of enthusiasm for him in the African American press. "Your Party," gushed the *Chicago Defender*, "never had a better candidate than Landon," contrasting his vocal stance on racial issues with the silence of Roosevelt.[69] Overall, however, the African American press was unsympathetic. The *Afro-American* saw Landon as an advocate of states' rights and told its readers that it would be "plain suicide" to support him.[70] African Americans had long memories, and many simply did not trust the Republicans.

Francis E. Rivers, a New Yorker and eastern campaign manager of the RNC's Negro Voters Division, followed Landon's line of attack:

> Negroes should not fall for the confusing tactics of the president, who exploited the personality and liberal viewpoint of his wife. Nor should they be led astray by the sham social progress promised by the myriad New Deal agencies. The real colors of the president's party were to be seen in his refusal to appoint any Negroes to permanent Civil Service and his choosing to segregate them in emergency colored divisions.[71]

Rivers condemned many New Deal agencies. For instance, the AAA used African American labor because it was cheaper; the Federal Emergency

Relief Agency (FERA) discriminated in its payments; the Works Progress Administration (WPA) put most African Americans in unskilled jobs; and social security legislation excluded many more. These were all extremely valid criticisms of the New Deal, but, as Nancy Weiss argues, too many African Americans had benefited from New Deal programs for this approach to be effective: "it was a sophisticated argument but there was no way it could appeal successfully to the majority of black Americans in the 1930s."[72]

Robert Church met Landon on 5 October 1936 and issued a statement on the candidate's behalf: "in common with all law-abiding citizens of this country, I am unalterably opposed to lawlessness in all its forms and, of course, this includes lynching, which is a blot on our American civilization. We must devise some legal means which will be effective in ending this great menace to our institutions."[73] Landon also demanded equality in relief distribution and federal employment based solely on merit. White was not convinced, describing the term "some legal means" regarding antilynching legislation as "puzzling." By not directly advocating either state or federal laws to combat lynching, White suspected that Landon was being deliberately vague. It is possible that Landon was advocating state action on lynching as Kansas had an antilynching law (passed before his governorship) and he had referred to it on occasion during the campaign.[74] The NAACP did, however, praise Landon's belief that more jobs needed to be created for African Americans as "a significant statement which goes to the root of the Negro's economic plight," but it asked for more specifics on how this would be achieved.[75] The *Crisis* expressed hope that the focus on providing jobs was part of a maturation of Republican policy: "the fact that the GOP promises to do it [provide jobs] shows that the party is at last beginning to come out of the Abraham Lincoln clouds to solid earth."[76] The association agreed that relief was not the answer, but it professed deep concern about the governor's "recently acquired enthusiasm for the doctrine of states' rights."[77]

Four million African Americans were on relief, and one of the reasons they had begun to turn to the Democratic Party was that it had provided federal relief that, while not free from discrimination, did at least benefit them.[78] African Americans wanted relief to continue to be administered by the federal government and not by the states. If the states, and especially southern states, were given control of relief budgets, then there was the very real prospect of discrimination. Moreover, there was a justifiable concern that a reelected Republican Party, advocating the decentralization of federal power, would transfer relief into the hands of the states. Unfortunately,

Landon confirmed African American fears by advocating state control of relief, drawing immediate and predictable condemnation from White.[79] Roosevelt had only been partially successful in keeping discrimination out of relief, but, as the *Crisis* noted, "even with their failures, they [relief agencies] have made great gains for the race in areas which heretofore have set their faces steadfastly against decent relief for Negroes."[80]

The Democrats had other advantages over the Republicans. Eleanor Roosevelt was very important in their quest to win black votes, and there can be no doubt that her sympathy for African Americans and her friendships with Mary McLeod Bethune and White were utterly sincere.[81] Eleanor Roosevelt did her husband no harm and actually allowed him to be vicariously portrayed as an advocate of African American rights through her good deeds. Harold Ickes, the secretary of the interior and a former Republican, served a similar function for Roosevelt when he addressed the NAACP convention in 1936, declaring that "political calculus took precedence over moral outrage" where lynching was concerned.[82] The "Black Cabinet," a number of unofficial African American advisers on racial matters, was also of great value to the Roosevelt administration. In reality, the Black Cabinet's importance was more symbolic than substantive, but, as Weiss asserts, "it shows once again the skill of Franklin D. Roosevelt in turning limited departures from past racial practices to his own advantage."[83] It also demonstrated that the African American vote could be rallied to Roosevelt's cause without him uttering a single word on civil rights.

In September, Landon was faced with accusations of racism and anti-Semitism, accusations he vehemently refuted: "if ever in this country there is an attempt to persecute any minority on grounds of race, religion or class, I will take my stand by the side of the minority."[84] It would be harsh to question Landon's sincerity on racial matters, but ultimately he was fighting a losing battle. Most African American churchmen, usually Republican stalwarts, were backing Roosevelt, as was most of the black press.[85] Perhaps most embarrassing of all, however, were the reports that Republican meetings in Topeka were segregated and Landon's African American employees' claim that they were underpaid, his cook declaring that she would be voting for Roosevelt.[86]

The Republicans' task became even more difficult when Joel Spingarn, the NAACP president, decided to campaign for the Democrats. Spingarn's stance was a departure for the traditionally nonpartisan NAACP, and although he campaigned nominally as a private citizen, the implication was clear: his usefulness to the Democrats, as he was well aware, stemmed from his association with the NAACP, while other NAACP officials had been prevented from campaigning for the Republicans.[87] Roosevelt, Spingarn argued, had done more for African Americans than "any Republican since Lincoln." He was careful, however, to emphasize that he was not representing the NAACP, which would remain nonpartisan: "I am not speaking for the Association but for myself when I say that in this election we must not think of the Democratic party but of Franklin Roosevelt."[88] Spingarn made speeches in eight cities where the African American vote was important, and, in a number of instances, posters and literature emphasized his link to the NAACP.

The Republicans also sought to woo African American voters by recruiting Jesse Owens. He had just returned from the notorious Berlin Olympics with four gold medals and had rejected overtures from the Democrats in order to campaign for the Republicans. His attitude, however, demonstrated a lack of real enthusiasm among many African Americans for either party: "I do not want to knock the present administration; President Roosevelt has done something, but not enough, to benefit the people of the colored race. But I believe that the election of Governor Landon will be good for the people of America and the colored race. Governor Landon does not promise very much, but what promises he does make I think he will keep." This was hardly a ringing endorsement of Landon's candidacy.[89] When Owens later visited Indianapolis for the Republicans, four of the nine cars in his motorcade sported FDR stickers.[90] Owens was, in fact, handsomely paid for his services to the GOP in 1936, and would refer to his participation in the Republican campaign as the "poorest race I ever ran." He worked for the Democrats in 1940.[91]

"Roosevelt, *in Spite* of the Democratic Party"

Despite some predictions, Roosevelt won a crushing victory, and the African American vote was not a vital factor in his triumph. Roosevelt won 27,751,597 popular votes to Landon's 16,679,583, and 523 Electoral College votes to Landon's 8. The New Deal had received an overwhelming endorsement from the electorate, including northern African Americans, 76 percent of whom voted for Roosevelt; and in every northern city except Chicago, at least 60 percent voted Democratic (in Chicago, the figure was 49 percent). The Democratic vote among northern African Americans had increased by between 60 percent (New York) and 250 percent (Cleveland).[92]

Republican appeals to history and attacks on the New Deal had little impact in the face of the palpable benefits African Americans had seen since 1932; African Americans had demonstrated both support for the New Deal and rejection of the GOP. Four years of the New Deal and a liberal Democratic administration had shown how some government intervention could appreciably improve the lives of African Americans, but even limited intervention remained an anathema to most Republicans. African Americans, it must be emphasized, had not been targeted for special treatment by the New Deal; it took the Great Depression and the millions of whites it put onto the relief rolls to bring African Americans into the protective embrace of the federal government. African Americans were clearly accidental beneficiaries of the New Deal, but they were beneficiaries nonetheless. They had been among the most stubborn Republicans until 1934 and, historically and presently, had good reason to remain so when confronted by a Democratic Party apparently controlled by reactionary southern whites. The *Crisis* asserted that African Americans had "voted for Roosevelt, *in spite* of the Democratic party" and "had a feeling that Mr. Roosevelt represented a kind of philosophy in government which will mean much to their race."[93] It believed that antilynching legislation, reform of the civil service, and an end to discrimination would be the price Roosevelt would have to pay for continued African American support.

It would be unfair to attach too much blame to Landon for the GOP's failure to regain the African American vote. He paid the price for the sins of previous Republican administrations, despite being altogether more progressive on race relations than his counterparts in the 1920s; indeed, he had a better reputation than Roosevelt on the issue. He had made strides to liberalize the GOP in his own state as governor, but in 1936 he was tainted with states' rights, from which he made little effort to distance himself, and African Americans were worried that he would subvert the gains that they had made under the New Deal.

In 1936, economics lay at the heart of the Republicans' dilemma: African Americans were wedded to the New Deal primarily by economics rather than any real racial liberalism within the administration, but the GOP was not prepared to take the action deemed necessary to alleviate the plight of African Americans. It was unfortunate for the Republicans that African Americans became the unintended beneficiaries of the New Deal at a time when their votes in key northern states were becoming potentially crucial in presidential elections, a fact as apparent to many Republicans as it was to African Americans. The Republicans tried to redeem themselves in the eyes of African Americans in 1936, but their efforts failed for a number of reasons. Paramount among these was the success of the New Deal in providing relief to African Americans. Republicans argued, not without some justification, that relief was being given in marginal wards (although not specifically African American areas) that affected voting patterns: "you can't run against Santa Claus," Landon would later say of his defeat.[94]

After the Republican rout in the presidential election, White wrote to Chester C. Bolton, a sympathetic Republican congressman from Ohio who had been swept away in the Democratic deluge. White outlined why he thought the GOP had lost the African American vote. One reason, he argued, was

> the almost incredible stupidity of much of the publicity put out by the Republican party so far as Negroes were concerned, and a general ineptitude, especially on the part of some of the older Negro politicians who have long since lost caste with thoughtful Negroes. Some of these politicians seemed to be able to only fool white people.

White contended that the Republican cause would have been helped had the party endorsed an antilynching bill. He stressed, however, that he believed that the African American vote would now be fluid.[95]

The traditional Republican–African American alliance had, in many respects, run its course. The Civil War, slavery, and Emancipation all seemed a long time ago to many younger African Americans. They were drawn to urban liberal Democrats in the North, who were often keen to distance themselves from the party's southern wing. Furthermore, 1936 was the first time that the African American vote had anything beyond symbolic relevance in a presidential contest, and this in turn generated a greater political awareness among African Americans, especially new voters. African Americans, therefore, looked at the policies of the two main parties rather than their history, and Roosevelt offered a better deal. Republican efforts, although more determined than ever before, remained inadequate. African Americans had been let down just too often and were now prepared to break from the past. The election of 1936 was, therefore, something of a turning point in American political history. The Republicans, admittedly, had more pressing problems with their party split and their electoral coalition disintegrating, but while other constituencies would eventually come back to the fold, never again would the African American vote be "in their top pocket."

"Parties Unknown"

The persistence of lynching in the 1930s represented the most visible reinforcement of African Americans' second-class citizenship. Thus the campaign for antilynching legislation simultaneously demonstrated both the continued precariousness of life in the United States for African Americans and the growing, although perhaps misplaced, confidence of the NAACP. To the NAACP, antilynching legislation was a test of political sincerity on racial issues, and this quest became a panacea for the association and the particular obsession of Walter White. The campaigns of the 1920s and 1930s also reflected the shifting loyalties of African Americans: in the 1920s, antilynching drives, although infrequent, were the almost exclusive preserve of Republicans; by the 1930s, the GOP was conspicuous by its apathy.[96] Antilynching should have provided the Republicans with an opportunity to revive their flagging fortunes among African Americans; instead, it illustrated just how far the party had departed from its roots. The party was not hostile toward antilynching legislation, but it was certainly ambivalent.

Almost every session of Congress between 1934 and 1940 saw an attempt to pass an antilynching bill. Each endeavor followed a familiar ritual: at the start of a congressional session, the bill would pass through the House of Representatives without too much trouble; it would then be dropped by the Senate after a southern filibuster to make way for more "important" legislation, reflecting a lack of commitment from supporters, the absence of encouragement from the White House, and the resolution of southern Democratic opponents. The bills were all variations on the original Costigan-Wagner bill of January 1934, but it would not be until 1940 that a Republican sponsored antilynching legislation publicly, and even this was tainted by its cynical motivation. Clearly most politicians, Republican or Democrat, were not prepared to make anything more than a token stand on antilynching, and, in reality, these bills gave politicians the chance to pay lip service to African American needs without actually having to do anything substantive. There were, of course, exceptions; Republican Arthur Capper and Democrat Robert Wagner, for example, had sincere and consistent records on racial matters. Moreover, while few northern politicians actively opposed antilynching legislation, most lacked any real commitment to it.

By the early 1930s, the NAACP felt that the time was right for another attempt to secure antilynching legislation. The Parker episode had shown that the organization could have some influence on national politics, but in the process it had alienated Hoover, thus making any action on lynching during the remainder of his presidency unlikely. After the election of Roosevelt in 1932, White, the architect of the campaign, decided to try again. Because lynching was extremely difficult to justify and an antilynching bill potentially only an oblique challenge to the southern caste system, attempts to eradicate the crime could attract support from some whites as well as Republicans and Democrats. The election of the liberal Roosevelt together with the increasing importance of the African American vote meant that any bill's chances of success were better than ever. Conversely, any optimism was tempered by the continued strength of the Democrats' southern wing and recognition of how low African Americans were on the Republican Party's list of priorities.[97] Although the association nonetheless hoped to garner cross-party support, the reality was that it was Democrat, not Republican, backing that was vital. The Democrats would dominate political life in America throughout the 1930s, and in the North the party had finally begun to acknowledge the potential of the African American vote. It should, therefore, come as no real surprise that it was the Democrats who championed antilynching legislation.[98]

Not only did the Republicans seem ambivalent toward antilynching legislation, but the most vocal opponent of the bills from outside the South was, again, William Borah. Borah argued, as he had during the 1920s, that a federal antilynching law would be an unwarranted intrusion into the affairs of the states and would, therefore, be unconstitutional.[99] Borah's stance was particularly damaging as he was a potential Republican presidential candidate in 1936 and a Republican with a high public profile. The NAACP was, as noted, determined to stop him. For the most part, other Republicans, whatever their feelings on the need for, or the constitutionality of, the measure, remained largely silent, either due to indifference or as a reflection of the party's weakness in Congress. What is certain is that it was in Republican interests to see conflict among the Democrats by allowing them to fight among themselves (a tactic used again in 1937 when Roosevelt attempted to reform the Supreme Court).[100] Whatever the political benefits of silence, this tactic resulted in the Republicans appearing indifferent about lynching.

The NAACP also realized that the antilynching battle had the potential to embarrass the Democrats. Northern Democrats knew that supporting antilynching legislation was one way to court black voters, but they also knew that it could potentially split the party; in other words, strengthening the party in the North with black voters could be offset by enhancing Republican chances of breaking the Democrats' hold on the southern white vote.

This would be especially likely if there was a suspicion that northern Democrats were becoming too liberal on the race question. Roosevelt, therefore, faced the daunting prospect of having to reconcile the two divergent wings of his party, knowing that to take the side of one would be to alienate the other. Like Harding in the 1920s, he was not prepared to sacrifice his entire legislative program on the altar of an antilynching bill; moreover, Roosevelt, unlike Harding, had the added problem of placating a southern bloc that was irredeemably hostile to the legislation. Despite entreaties from the NAACP, Roosevelt would not commit himself to antilynching legislation publicly.[101] The president's silence appeased the South; the public support of antilynching bills by his wife, Eleanor, and various members of the Black Cabinet appeased African Americans and northern liberal Democrats.

"The Ablest Men in the Senate"

The renewed effort to pass antilynching legislation began in early January 1934 when the Costigan-Wagner bill was presented to the Senate for the first time. Sponsored by Democrats Edward Costigan of Colorado and Robert Wagner of New York, this bill, framed by the NAACP the previous November, was a response to twenty-eight known lynchings in 1933.[102] White, appealing to Democratic self-interest, told Eleanor Roosevelt of "the great strategic value of an overwhelmingly Democratic Congress passing such legislation." This would provide "a valuable weapon," he continued, in the forthcoming midterm elections, especially in balance of power states.[103] Roosevelt refused to become involved publicly in the debate, although at least he did meet White at the White House on 6 May.[104] The lynching of Claude Neal, an African American from Florida, in October 1934 reinvigorated the NAACP's campaign as Neal had been taken from custody and his lynching advertised.[105] Democrat gains in November 1934 meant that the Costigan-Wagner bill could theoretically be passed in both Houses without any southern votes and would be successful if Roosevelt made it a priority piece of legislation.[106] When Costigan announced his intention to resubmit the antilynching bill to the Senate in April 1935, Arthur Krock commented that it "hangs over . . . the President's program like a poised avalanche, with destruction its promise."[107]

The *Crisis* provided a list of the bill's supporters, but some were much more enthusiastic than others. A number of the twenty-five remaining Republican senators came out in support of the bill, including: Norris (Nebraska), Capper (Kansas), Vandenberg (Michigan), McNary (Oregon), Cutting (New Mexico), Johnson (California), Couzens (Michigan), La Follette (Wisconsin), Barbour (New Jersey), Hastings (Delaware), and Nye (North Dakota). Of these, only Capper, Barbour, Vandenberg, McNary, and Nye had any long-term future in Republican politics. Couzens failed to be renominated; Hastings and Barbour were defeated in 1936 (although Barbour would be reelected in 1938); Johnson was elderly; and Cutting would die later in the year. Norris and La Follette, increasingly exasperated by the conservative course of the party, would become an Independent and a Progressive respectively in 1937 (undoubtedly extending their careers in the process).[108] Not all of those listed in the *Crisis* actually supported the measure; many simply said that they would consider it carefully.

The Republicans had at least finally begun to show some interest. "Senator McNary has," White told Eleanor Roosevelt, "pledged his unqualified support and both he and Senator Hastings have stated that we can safely count on all the Republicans voting for the bill."[109] This, of course, could have been a veiled threat to the president. The implication was that the Republicans, with one eye on the presidential election of 1936, were taking the bill seriously in an attempt to regain the African American vote.[110] The Costigan-Wagner bill did eventually reach the Senate, but by early May it was dropped to enable the passage of more pressing matters.[111] Borah had not intended to become embroiled in the debate but was goaded by comments from Costigan. Borah maintained that, as with the earlier Dyer measure, the Costigan-Wagner bill was unconstitutional.[112] Borah insisted that to pass the antilynching bill and have it sustained by the Supreme Court meant that state sovereignty would be "utterly annihilated."[113] He also claimed that the Costigan-Wagner bill would not stop lynching, and that this could be done only by education and influencing public opinion.[114]

The *Crisis* declared that "many so-called friends of the Negro and haters of lynching *from the North and West* did not support the bill with their votes and did nothing to break the filibuster."[115] Many of these senators, including Republicans Norris and Couzens, abandoned the bill in order to pursue more "important" legislation and were, in the eyes of the *Crisis*, more culpable than senators from Tennessee and Kentucky who wavered before voting for an adjournment. Particular ire was, as always, reserved for Borah.[116]

In January 1937, in the aftermath of Roosevelt landslide, Wagner and Joseph A. Gavagan reintroduced the antilynching bill in both houses of Congress.[117] The *New York World Telegram* reported that the Republicans would back antilynching legislation either to recapture the African American vote or to thwart the New Deal.[118] Moreover, White argued that Roosevelt had nothing to lose by supporting the bill as he would not be seeking reelection.[119] With the backing of the eighty-nine Republican congressmen who had survived the Democratic onslaught, the Gavagan bill passed the House on 15 April by 277 votes to 119, and it went to the Senate as the slightly different Gavagan-Wagner–Van Nuys bill.[120] White privately commented on "how grand a job several of the Republicans did."[121] The difficulty, as always, was not in securing enough votes for a bill to pass in the Senate—the NAACP was confident that this could be achieved—but in overcoming the inevitable filibuster so that a vote could take place at all. There was the added danger that Roosevelt's decision to increase the size of the Supreme Court, a controversy that had divided the Democrats, would delay the bill.[122]

Southern Democrats successfully, although less vociferously, filibustered and the Gavagan-Wagner–Van Nuys bill was not passed. Senate Minority Leader NcNary facilitated the filibuster by preventing Vice President Garner and Majority Leader Barkley from sidestepping the bill. The Democrats hoped to dispense with the bill as painlessly as possible, but McNary sought to exploit Democrat divisions, giving credence to the view that the Republicans were using antilynching to discomfort the Democrats.[123] It also suggests that many Democrats wanted to heal the divisions the bill had caused by quietly dropping it.

In early 1938, seventy-four senators from both parties pledged their support for the Gavagan-Wagner–Van Nuys bill if it reached the Senate floor, but an extended southern filibuster dampened their enthusiasm.[124] Borah was once more at the forefront of the opposition, announcing to the Senate that the South was doing very well in combating lynching.[125] McNary told the NAACP that he was in favor of the bill but did not want the Senate to give up its right to unlimited debate; the Republicans, could not, therefore, vote for cloture, a Senate mechanism to curtail debate. McNary's commitment was called into question, however, when the NAACP learned that he had actually voted in favor of cloture in nine out of the eleven occasions it had arisen since 1917 and had signed cloture petitions five times.[126] It was becoming apparent that even those senators who were nominally supporting the bill had no real desire to see it become law.

The Gavagan-Wagner–Van Nuys bill was laid aside on 21 February after a six-week filibuster. Efforts by the two senators to force cloture twice failed, and on the second occasion no Republicans voted in favor.[127] The bill was eventually shelved to make way for Roosevelt's $250 million emergency relief bill. Wagner expressed regret that Republican members of the Senate had refused to vote for cloture, but McNary countered by stating that while the GOP was in favor of the bill (the only Republicans against were Hale of Maine and, inevitably, Borah), it was up to the Democrats, with their large majority, to invoke cloture, and they had demonstrated little genuine enthusiasm for this. Barkley reminded the Republicans that while they may have given the bill their tacit approval, no GOP senator had actually spoken out in support of it.[128] White was livid. "I want to tell you," he wrote Lewis Strauss, "something of the inside story and particularly of the awfully stupid politics McNary and some of the other Republicans, as well as some of the Democrats, are playing."[129] Arthur Vandenberg was one senator who opposed cloture on general principle. Not unsympathetic to the aspirations of African Americans, he later took the time to write to the NAACP explaining that he only ever envisaged voting for cloture on questions of national defense.[130] The supporters of the bill had little choice other than to give it up; they would have lost hard-won sympathy had they persevered. White offered the meager consolation that both the emergency relief and antilynching bills "were aimed at the alleviation of human suffering."[131]

The antilynching crusade further strained relations between the NAACP and the Republicans. When White criticized McNary publicly over the failure of cloture, the Senate minority leader vowed not to support any future measure backed by White. John D. Hamilton, the Republican Party chairman, pointed out to White that there were only sixteen Republican senators against seventy-six Democrats, and that any criticism should be directed at the White House. Hamilton had a point; the Republicans, even if they had wanted to, were really in no position to dictate legislation. The breakdown of relations between White and senior Republicans did not necessarily mean that the black vote would remain securely and overwhelmingly in the Democratic column; indeed, many Democrats were concerned about the effect of yet another defeat for an antilynching law, but by 1938 there was little chance of cooperation between the GOP and the NAACP. The problem of lynching was serious enough for Roosevelt to meet an African American delegation at the White House. As usual, nothing tangible resulted from the meeting, but it reaffirmed White's belief that the African American vote was becoming too important to be taken for granted.

The NAACP hoped to reintroduce an antilynching bill after the midterm elections of 1938. These elections saw Democratic reverses, plus a failed purge of conservatives, and this meant that party liberals were in no position to fight strenuously for another antilynching bill. As usual, plenty of congressmen were willing to back the bill, but it would be 1940 before another serious attempt was made. Antilynching legislation could have provided the Republicans with the ideal opportunity to drive home this rare political advantage and also accentuate Democratic divisions. The GOP decided, however, that an alliance with southern or conservative rather than northern or liberal Democrats was much more useful. The ideological battle within the GOP had reached a stalemate by this point, but the party at least felt confident enough to challenge effectively the New Deal, and to do this they needed the assistance of southern Democrats. The Republicans felt that if they were to be electable in 1940, then they had to offer a conservative rather than a liberal alternative to the New Deal, and this would not be achieved by joining forces with northern Democrats to champion antilynching legislation. Once again, congressional Republicans' halfhearted commitment to antilynching legislation in particular, and African Americans generally, had been exposed; once again African American interests were supplanted by a broader political agenda.

"Trying to Buy Back the Colored Vote"

In 1940, there was yet another drive to pass an antilynching bill. Despite its eventual failure, this attempt is notable because it was sponsored actively by a Republican. Hamilton Fish, a congressman from New York, was the first Republican since the 1920s to be associated so publicly with an antilynching bill. Fish had served as an officer in an African American regiment in World War I; nonetheless, his support appeared curious given his involvement in Borah's abortive campaign for the presidency in 1936. Fish's approach to antilynching bills was inconsistent, and his defense of Borah in 1936 was in marked contrast to his own record. In 1935, he had introduced a bill identical to Costigan-Wagner and had been a passionate supporter of the 1922 Dyer bill. White recognized Fish's "long record of sincere service to the Negro" but was uneasy about his support for Borah in 1936. He was worried that Fish's introduction of an antilynching bill in 1935 had been merely "a political gesture" to secure black votes.[132] There was clearly some kind of reconciliation between White and Fish by 1940, together with a divergence between Fish and Borah prior to the latter's death in January 1940.[133] Defending his 1940 bill, Fish declared, "I am absolutely convinced and I have been for 20 years of the constitutionality of this type of legislation, the need for it and the right of the Negro to have it."[134] Perhaps the inconsistencies of Fish should have been a cause for concern to the NAACP, but the association was grateful for allies wherever it could find them.

The Gavagan-Fish bill passed the House in early 1940 by 252 to 131, with 140 Republicans and 109 Democrats supporting the bill, and 123 Democrats and 8 Republicans against. The Republicans were keen to take credit for this, refuting accusations that they were, in the words of Democrat Arthur Mitchell—the nation's only African American congressman—"trying to buy back the Colored vote."[135] A Republican National Committee press release challenged Mitchell's assertion and demanded to know whether the motivation of the Democrats and the NAACP ("an organization most favorable to the New Deal") was equally questionable.[136] Vandenberg was again the most senior Republican to support the bill, but once more he opposed cloture, explaining that he was against "deliver[ing] the complete control of the United States to any transient majority that comes along."[137] Fish demanded to know where Roosevelt stood on the bill, arguing that the president seemed more interested in foreign rather than domestic policy. He insisted that "one word from the White House and that bill would come flying through the Senate and be enacted into law."[138] Given the lack of leadership from the GOP in previous attempts to pass antilynching legislation, his association with Borah, and the proximity of the election, Fish's efforts to appeal to African American voters appear quite cynical.

One could even speculate on a much more sinister reason for Fish's support for an antilynching bill. He was from the isolationist wing of the Republican Party and was heavily involved in the "America First Committee" and various pro-Nazi groups prior to the United States' entry into World War II. He was also regarded as an anti-Semite and a fascist, with an internal White House memorandum commenting that "Fish belongs to that small group of Congressmen and Senators who are trying to inject racial and religious issues into Congressional debates in order to foster their political aims."[139] At a time when America was rearming, many suspected that Roosevelt was determined to drag the country into the war. It could be argued, therefore, that an antilynching bill and the filibuster it would attract could delay the defense program. This could be a grave injustice to Fish, but serious questions remain about his true motivation.

By October 1940, the political climate was dominated by the war in Europe. Against this backdrop, McNary and Barkley polled their colleagues and found little enthusiasm for a renewed effort on antilynching. Barkley stated that "in the midst of our international situation, [and] our defense program . . . it is impractical at this time to make a futile effort to obtain a vote on the bill."[140] In dropping the bill, Barkley protested that the NAACP had made "insistent and sometimes peremptory demands that, regardless of anything else, the anti-lynching bill should be brought forward."[141] Despite this, he still claimed to hope that the bill could be considered at a later date. Vandenberg questioned the sincerity of those who fought for antilynching bills in the Senate by noting that they never tried to break the filibuster "with round-the-clock sessions with a quorum intact."[142] The implication was that those who supported antilynching measures did so because they were more concerned about African American votes than African American lives.

Both parties had good reason to avoid controversy. After the debilitating internal struggles and electoral setbacks of 1938, the Democrats did not want to risk fragile party unity in an election year. The Republicans, for their part, seemed more concerned about maintaining their alliance with conservative and southern Democrats against any liberal legislative program. It is also possible that the passing of an antilynching bill was slipping down the NAACP's list of priorities. When the Gavagan-Fish bill was dropped, the *Crisis* commented that "next to jobs, security and fair treatment in the Army and Navy, the thing [African American] voters want most is for the federal government to outlaw mob violence and lynching."[143] This was recognition by the NAACP that, for all the symbolic importance of antilynching legislation, and regardless of the need for it, there were more practical matters that demanded attention. Antilynching did remain a priority for the NAACP, but as part of a widening agenda that increasingly included fair employment and anti–poll tax legislation. Nonetheless, the campaign successfully kept lynching in the public eye: a Gallup poll in 1937 suggested that 70 percent of Americans supported antilynching legislation, and even 65 percent of southerners were in favor.[144] Yet, even by 1940, antilynching legislation was, as Robert Zangrando notes, "an idea whose time had gone."[145]

White believed that FDR's silence and the administration's lack of cooperation was "the single greatest handicap" preventing legislation from being passed.[146] Yet the NAACP simply had nowhere else to go: the Democrats were too entrenched in Congress; the Republicans, numerically weak and dominated by conservatives such as Borah, Hamilton, and McNary, offered no real alternative. Antilynching bills always commanded more support in the House than in the Senate; throughout the 1930s antilynching bills would pass through the House with relative ease; it was the Senate where difficulties always arose. As Zangrando argues: "whatever advantages black voters possessed in northern and midwestern metropolitan centers when lobbying in the House were effectively cancelled by the more traditional state-wide constituencies with whom senators had to deal. Afro-American political leverage was an emerging but still limited force."[147] Few politicians, therefore, were prepared either to take risks for the African American community or to stand up to the South.

The forthcoming election and the fact that the African American vote had been ebbing away from the GOP for years perhaps explains the Republicans' sudden interest in antilynching legislation in 1940. It was apparent from the experience of 1936 that rhetoric was no longer sufficient to secure black support; politicians had to be seen to be doing something, or at least modernize their rhetoric, meaning that the election of 1940 offered the Republicans another opportunity to repair their fractured relationship with African Americans. The Republican strategy should, therefore, have been founded on two basic premises: first, the overwhelming vote for the Democrats in 1936 was an aberration; and second, African American loyalty was to Roosevelt and not his party. This latter point is especially important: at the beginning of 1940, Roosevelt had not announced his intention to break with tradition by running for a third term, and a possible successor was Vice President Garner. Nationally, African Americans had voted for Roosevelt, but locally the individual candidate, as White predicted, was becoming more important than the party. If a congressman was identified with antilynching legislation, regardless of how sincere or vigorous, this support was a potential vote winner in African American wards.

Antilynching legislation could have been passed, albeit with great difficulty, had there been any determination in either the White House or Congress to see it succeed. There were pragmatic reasons why the administration and, indeed, the Republican Party did not promote antilynching legislation. The administration recognized that conservative elements within Congress would seize upon any pretext to thwart the New Deal. Regardless of their sincerity, the Republicans' weakness in Congress throughout the 1930s precluded any attempt to take the lead in promoting antilynching legislation. The party maintained a notional commitment to antilynching in their platforms until 1952, but this had little impact upon their support among African Americans.

The Republicans' reluctance to become deeply involved in the antilynching campaign made poor sense politically. Had the Republicans endorsed antilynching legislation more vigorously, then they might have at least slowed, if not halted, African American defections to the Democratic Party. Republican support for the various bills put forward from 1934 to 1940 was consistent but unenthusiastic. The truth was that the GOP, and arguably the Democrats, took a superficial approach to antilynching legislation and African American aspirations generally. The failure of antilynching legislation was perhaps less critical than what these bills represented, as the crusade reflected the evolving allegiance and confidence of African Americans. Usurped on the issue, the Republican Party became ever more detached from African Americans.

3

The Darkest Horse

Several months after the 1936 election, D. W. Brogan, writing in the *Political Review,* argued that the Republican Party had to adjust to "an age which has at last forgotten Lincoln." Assessing the difficulties of the GOP, he declared: "the problem of Republican survival hangs on the ability of the party to realize that the old dog needs new tricks and on the ability of the old dog to perform new tricks."[1] The problems of the party were particularly acute as "the Democrats in the north were able, *without producing any serious hostile reaction in the south,* to win an overall majority of the Negro vote."[2] Provided it had learned its lessons, Brogan was fairly confident that the GOP would not cease to exist, although he warned that "if the party cannot raise money now or win seats in Congress in two years hence, it is indeed doomed."[3] Before the Republicans took their message to the people in 1938, there was some evidence that the "old dog" was prepared to at least try to learn a few new tricks.

The Republicans were thrown a lifeline in early 1937 when Roosevelt, in an effort to ensure passage of New Deal legislation, attempted to reform the Supreme Court. Republicans had long suspected, of course, that Roosevelt was trying to subvert the Constitution, and now they seemed to have evidence that this was indeed his intention. Landon's attitude, for example, illustrates the very real fear many Americans had about the power that was concentrated in the hands of Roosevelt: "he claims the greatest power any President has ever had, yet he will probably try to lay the blame for this depression [in 1937] on the fact that he doesn't have still greater powers."[4] The Republican response to the Court plan was perhaps surprising: for the most part, party representatives said nothing. This tactic made good political sense; not only did it heighten tensions within the Democratic Party, but a policy of silence meant that Roosevelt could not claim that only reactionaries opposed him. Landon went along with this policy, but Hoover and GOP chairman John Hamilton and many in the party, especially outside Congress, were critical of it. Interestingly, this tactic had the support of those Democrats who were also concerned about the direction of the New

Deal. Landon, for instance, met Democratic Senator Burton K. Wheeler of Montana to offer support to those Democrats resisting the New Deal provided they ran as independents.[5] There was a fear among Democrats who were against the Court plan that Republican opposition would galvanize the party behind Roosevelt; congressional Republicans thus remained dutifully silent.

In late July, efforts to reform the Court were abandoned, and it was only at this point that the Republicans began to attack the plans. The eventual defeat of the Court plan "shattered the myth of invincibility" surrounding Roosevelt and had long-term ramifications within the Democratic Party; victory in 1936 had, in reality, signaled the end of any pretense of Democratic unity.[6] While the Republicans could not claim much credit for the Court defeat publicly, it did represent a rare setback for Roosevelt. Nevertheless, this did not necessarily enhance the prospect of a renewed and united Republican Party: "it was just as well that the Republicans concentrated on fighting the Court bill," attests Mayer, "because they could agree on little else."[7] After the Court fight, many Republicans began to consider again the possibility of a political realignment against the New Deal, and there were at least some Democrats who were receptive to the idea.[8] Frank Knox, Landon's running mate, even suggested that the GOP rename itself the "Constitutional Party" to broaden its appeal. Despite this suggestion, as the election of 1938 loomed, many Republicans remained opposed to the idea of a formal realignment, as there was now increasing criticism of Roosevelt and a feeling that their cause would be better served if they acted independently.

After the 1936 election, Landon and Hoover battled for the soul of the Republican Party. Hoover, the only leading Republican to speak out during the Court fight, still had the support of many "Old Guard" Republicans in 1937; he felt that the disastrous defeat in 1936 meant that Landon had no claim to the party's leadership, and he sought to regain it himself. Friction was also generated between the two by the perception that Landon had failed to defend the record of the Hoover administration in 1936. Landon, in turn, felt that Hoover was a perpetual presidential candidate and continually seeking absolution for his defeat in 1932. He was not alone in feeling that any rehabilitation of Hoover would be disastrous for the GOP, but the ex-president persisted in trying to bring the party back to his way of thinking. In August 1937, Hoover announced that he wanted a special Republican convention to discuss the party's plans for the 1938 elections.

Landon feared that the party's Old Guard would dominate such a convention; he also felt that it would serve to expose the continuing splits within the party, and this made particularly poor political sense at a time when the Democrats were having problems of their own.[9] Capper, McNary, Borah, Martin, Vandenberg, and Knox were also opposed, as were most Republicans in Congress. Convinced that Hoover was trying to secure the 1940 nomination, Landon successfully blocked the convention, and prevented further public division in the process. As a compromise, a "program committee" under the chairmanship of Glenn Frank, former president of the University of Wisconsin and "a reputed liberal," was set up to examine the future direction of the party.[10] This two-hundred-member committee was to "ascertain as fully as possible the various views held by the rank and file of the Republican party."[11] This served the dual purpose of creating the illusion of unity and ending Hoover's quest to control the party machinery.[12]

From the outset then, the Frank Committee was at best an exercise in damage limitation. The committee had a broad remit but no power; there was no guarantee that any of its conclusions would find their way into the Republican platform of 1940. The committee, however, took the remarkably progressive step of asking Ralph Bunche, the eminent African American political scientist from Harvard and later UN mediator in Palestine, to write a report on the problems of African Americans. The appointment of Bunche may have suggested to African Americans that the GOP was trying genuinely to reassess its historic relationship with them. He was certainly an excellent choice for the role, but he was also a strange one—after all, the party might not like what he had to say. The GOP could have taken the safer option and appointed a party hack to trot out another condemnation of the New Deal, but this would have fooled no one. It may well be that Frank recognized the desertion of the GOP by African Americans in 1936, sincerely wanted to address the problem, and truly thought that his committee could make a difference.[13] Less charitably, it could be argued that the GOP wanted Bunche's name rather than his ideas.

The Republicans knew not only that Bunche was, in the words of Benjamin Rivlin, "one of the keenest students of race relations" in the country, but also that he was a liberal.[14] A Republican student at Harvard who believed that Bunche was an "ultra-liberal" endorsed his appointment regardless: "any survey he made would be scholarly and objective and un-influenced by his own political views."[15] Bunche set about his task with the best of intentions, telling Frank that he would contribute to the report as "a member of a disadvantaged minority group" who was "actively interested in any measures or policies leading toward the amelioration of the problems of my group."[16] He believed that the committee was "constructive and honestly designed to be of aid to the Negro people."[17]

The Republicans were shocked when Bunche submitted his 130–page report, in which he declared:

> Despite extended periods of power enjoyed by the GOP and the long-standing loyalty of the Race, the party has made no significant progress toward the realization of the fundamental political objectives of the Race; namely, enfranchisement in the South, protection of civil liberties, anti-lynching legislation, and the appointment of members of the Race to policy-forming and other responsible positions.[18]

The African American needed "everything that a constructive, humane, American political program can give him, employment, land, housing, relief, health protection, unemployment and old-age insurance, enjoyment of civil rights, all that a twentieth-century American citizen is entitled to."[19] He argued that the New Deal had improved the situation, but it still fell a long way short of the "minimal needs" of African Americans.[20]

Bunche concluded that the African American vote for the Democrats in 1932 and 1936 was a "bread and butter" vote—in other words, a vote for the economic benefits of the New Deal and not for the Democratic Party. Republican efforts to win southern lily-white support and their continued use of "socially unintelligent, inept and self-seeking" African American leaders had alienated many black voters.[21] If this was to change, then new black leadership was needed to replace "the old slogans, the shop-worn dogmas and appeals used so effectively in the past" with "concrete evidence . . . of a determination to fully integrate the Negro in American life."[22] The Republican Program Committee felt that Bunche's recommendations were too "impractical," "revolutionary," and, crucially, too similar to the prevailing ethos of the New Deal. Bunche's proposals were ignored, and the committee's 115–page report, eventually published in February 1940, contained precisely five paragraphs on the problems of African Americans. These echoed Landon's 1936 indictment of the New Deal and warned against "a progressive shunting of Negroes out of the normal productive enterprise into a kind of separate relief economy, leaving them, as it were, on permanent 'reservations' of public relief."[23]

Francis Rivers wrote to Walter White to explain aspects of the report.[24] If Rivers was looking for White's endorsement, it was not forthcoming. White asked Bunche for his opinion on Rivers's explanation, "which doesn't seem to me to explain very much"; he was also concerned about "the margin between what is in the report and what you among others recommended."[25] Bunche's reply illustrated just how disillusioned he had become with the whole process. First of all, he chastised White for suggesting, most likely in jest, that he had become a Republican: "I am not a Republican and never have been, and on the basis of what I've seen lately, never likely to be."[26] As far as the substance of the report was concerned, Bunche declared: "from what I have seen this report was written without any reference to the materials contained in my own report on the needs of the Negro." It appeared to Bunche that Rivers had condensed and turned the original report into an "extremely partisan report" that was "pretty gosh-awful." The Frank report, Bunche concluded, was "innocuous" as far as African Americans were concerned.[27]

The Frank Committee report did little to rehabilitate the GOP in the eyes of African Americans; in fact, it probably exacerbated African American alienation, as it was public knowledge that Bunche's findings had been ignored. Criticism of the report is undoubtedly justified, all the more so when the circumstances under which the Frank Committee was formed in the first place are taken into consideration. The committee itself was an exercise in window dressing, and its purpose was merely to create the illusion of unity at a time when the party seemed to have a chance to exploit rare problems for Roosevelt. The equivocation and vagueness of the report merely reinforced the perception of party weakness.[28] The *New York Times* commented: "the caution of the present report, once the generalities are left behind, tends to draw attention to the strong differences of opinion which actually exist in the party."[29] Both Landon and Hamilton endorsed the report despite it illustrating that the GOP was starting to drift ever closer to the New Deal. "Mr. Hoover may still belong to the Republican Party," smirked the pro-Democrat *Nation*, "but the Republican Party no longer belongs to Mr. Hoover."[30]

The fact was that the report did not represent the party, particularly in Congress, where, the *Nation* noted, "GOP congressmen were uniting to sabotage some of the New Deal projects which the report implicitly endorsed."[31] The report was also a manifesto without a candidate, made no reference to foreign policy, and was virtually ignored by the party convention in 1940. The Program Committee was conceived, certainly by Landon, as a way of preventing further internal strife; when it became clear that even this limited purpose was too ambitious, it was quietly forgotten. The report suggested that some Republicans were concerned enough about African American votes to ask a noted liberal his opinion, yet African Americans knew that the report had rejected something much more radical—indeed, Bunche's proposals were radical by most standards in the 1930s—unsubtly replacing it with a tirade against the New Deal. Overlooking African Americans would have been less damaging than patronizing them, and the eventual report served to reinforce the view that the GOP was either unable or unwilling to address, even rhetorically, the problems of African Americans.

"No Place to Go but Up"

Some Republicans were encouraged by Roosevelt's problems in 1937, despite the precarious position of their own party. "Perhaps," speculates Plesur, "part of the GOP's optimism stemmed from the fact that they had no place to go but up."[32] Landon felt that unity was essential, and that the party had to liberalize, give westerners more say in its affairs, check the continued influence of the party "Old Guard" in the East, and, crucially, regain the African American vote. Despite these difficulties, the Republicans, unlike the Democrats, were able to go into the 1938 elections at least publicly united. After the election of 1936, western Republicans became less likely to offer even qualified support to the New Deal (possibly because liberal Republicans often simply joined the Democrats), as they began to question the increasing tendency of the New Deal to centralize power. The result, however, was that western Republicans became more conservative at a time when easterners were beginning tentatively to embrace aspects of the New Deal.

Republican fortunes began to revive at the beginning of 1938 with polls showing the administration to be increasingly unpopular. Despite this upturn, divisions within the party remained. There was now, crucially, a realization of the significance of the urban vote, and this finally convinced eastern Republicans of the need to modify the party's appeals; in other words, the party had to become less conservative in the East and offer a tangible alternative to the New Deal. To this end, the GOP elected more liberal leadership in some northeastern states. The possibility of realignment in American politics along liberal-conservative lines had also receded by 1938 as the Republicans were less keen on a formal coalition now that their fortunes were reviving independently, while conservative Democrats suspected that the GOP was more interested in political gain than political principle. A new party would also be hampered by existing political structures such as primary laws, patronage, and the seniority system in Congress.[33] An informal conservative coalition, therefore, still made the best sense.

In 1938, the Republicans gained 8 senators, including the reelection of Warren Barbour in New Jersey and the election of Robert Taft in Ohio. In the House, Republican numbers rose from 89 to 169 without the loss of a single incumbent.[34] Significantly, many Republican victories were against liberal Democrats, including six liberal senators; furthermore, many defeated Democrats had been elected in 1932, 1934, and 1936. Forty-five of the Republican House victories came in the Midwest, with a further 27 in the Northeast; in fact, nearly one-third of all Republican gains in 1938 came in Pennsylvania (where the Democratic Party was deeply split) and Ohio.[35] Southern Democrats, unsurprisingly, were unaffected by the national shift to the Republicans. The GOP also won 18 of 27 gubernatorial contests, scoring significant victories in Massachusetts, Connecticut, Minnesota, Pennsylvania, Ohio, and Michigan.[36] The narrow defeat of renowned gang-buster Thomas Dewey in the New York gubernatorial race was a good reflection of the modification of the Republicans' electoral appeal, and similar appeals were made elsewhere in the Northeast.[37] It is also noteworthy that many of those Democrats who won reelection in 1938 did so as opponents of the New Deal. The most significant consequence of the election, therefore, was that Republicans and conservative Democrats could now prevent any further move to the left by Roosevelt. Interestingly, the *Crisis* reported that African American voters had moved away from the Democrats in Michigan, Ohio, and Pennsylvania.[38]

By 1938, there was no longer the same sense of emergency as there had been earlier in the New Deal. Moreover, the Republicans recognized the importance of the urban liberal vote and modified their appeals accordingly, and they were also able to exploit the self-inflicted problems of the Democrats, resulting in the GOP becoming a much more coherent force in Congress. Circumstances would change, but for a period after 1938 the Republicans could look forward to the 1940 election with some optimism: the party's fortunes were improving while Roosevelt, the scourge of the party for so long, would not, in theory, be running for reelection.

"The Town Whore Joins the Church"

The election of 1940 was in many ways extraordinary. It was fought against the backdrop of real battles in Europe as one by one democracies fell to the blitzkrieg while at home a president was seeking an unprecedented and, to many, a deeply disturbing third term. More extraordinary still, a crumpled amateur—and a Democrat as recently as 1938—stormed to the top of the Republican ticket in one of the most memorable conventions in American history. Utilities magnet Wendell Willkie had not run in the Republican primaries, but with carefully engineered publicity generated by the hundreds of "Willkie Clubs" that had sprung up all over the country, he was able to win the nomination at the national convention with no states backing him, no campaign headquarters, and little enthusiasm among the party's leaders. Indeed, shell-shocked Old Guard Republican leaders could only watch aghast as the "Miracle in Philadelphia" unfolded. The combination of a divided, largely isolationist Republican Party, a war in Europe, and catastrophic defeats in the previous two presidential elections facilitated the rise of Willkie. Willkie, described by Conrad Joyner as "a novelty, a sparkling prism and a thrilling entertainment," could not have emerged onto the political landscape, or risen so quickly, at any other time.[39]

To many African Americans, the impending demise of democracy in Europe was much less significant than the continued absence of democracy at home; to most, the third term was simply not an issue.[40] Roosevelt, losing ground with some of the Democratic Party's core supporters, remained stubbornly popular among African Americans, despite the lack of real progress on racial matters. In fact, elements within the NAACP were concerned that the Democrats were beginning to treat the African American vote with the same contempt the Republicans had shown before 1932.[41] Conversely, during the campaign the embers of Lincoln's legacy flickered briefly. The Republican standard bearer spoke to African American voters in a way that no other presidential candidate had ever dared; when Willkie talked of democracy, equality, and an end to discrimination, it was not mere campaign rhetoric. During the remainder of Willkie's tragically brief political career, through word and deed, he stayed true to his principles, campaigned on the basis of them, and ultimately sacrificed his political ambitions to them. Willkie was, as one contemporary proclaimed, "the only man in America who has proved he would rather be right than be president."[42]

In April 1940, a Gallup poll declared that the forthcoming election would be the closest since 1916. The Democrats were still in the lead, but it was a slender one in Missouri, West Virginia, Delaware, Indiana, Kentucky, and New York. The Republicans, meanwhile, were slightly ahead in Illinois, New Jersey, Michigan, Pennsylvania, and Ohio. The African American vote was, of course, crucial in all of these states, and a swing of less than 10 percent would see them shift from the Democrats to the Republicans or vice-versa.[43] The *Crisis* commented that both parties were ignoring this to avoid having "to pay a good price for the much-needed support of the black voter."[44] African Americans, therefore, could theoretically elect the next president. If a party wanted black support, the *Crisis* asserted, it would have to offer certain guarantees regarding the right to vote in the South, the poll tax, discrimination, federal appointments, segregation in the armed forces, relief, and equal citizenship.[45]

Prior to Willkie's emergence, African Americans cannot have viewed the potential Republican candidates in 1940 with any great confidence. Robert A. Taft, the son of President William Howard Taft and a newly elected senator from Ohio, was against the New Deal and would need the "rotten" southern vote as well as the Midwest at the party convention if he was to win the nomination.[46] Arthur Vandenberg, the veteran senator from Michigan, had periodically spoken out on racial issues, but had offended both labor and farmers and was, consequently, unlikely to win the nomination; he was seen as more liberal than Taft, but, again, opposed the New Deal. Thomas Dewey was the rising star of Republican politics and, at thirty-seven, was the youngest of the candidates, but he did not appear to have any firm views on African American issues.

Willkie had been a registered Democrat as recently as 1938 and was an outspoken critic of aspects of the New Deal and Roosevelt's leadership. The two had clashed throughout the 1930s over the running of power companies and the Tennessee Valley Authority (TVA). Willkie's stance against the New Deal and what he saw as its attempts to restrict business made him a potential recruit for the Republicans and a source of hope for those the New Deal had failed. He also saw big government as a threat to the American liberal tradition, a view that further endeared him to Republicans. Willkie was very popular with the public, as testified nationwide by hundreds of "Willkie Clubs"; these in turn built up Republican grassroots support, pressuring convention delegates to eventually select Willkie on the sixth ballot.[47] Veteran Republican senator Jim Watson perhaps summed up the feelings of many in the party when he told Willkie: "you know, Wendell, it's all right if the town whore joins the church, but they don't let her lead the choir on the first night."[48] Landon, however, spoke for many when he wrote to Willkie, declaring: "there is no doubt that you have caught the imagination of the American people."[49] Willkie became, according to his biographer Joseph Barnes, "a crusader for the common welfare with a few dangerously liberal ideas."[50] Nevertheless, it was the fact that Willkie was untainted by isolationism, not his "few dangerously liberal ideas," that made him an attractive proposition to many Republicans.

Superficially, there was little to recommend Willkie to African Americans, but he did have quite an impressive record of progressivism. He attended the Democratic National Convention in 1924 as a delegate from Akron, Ohio, where his mission was to challenge the Ku Klux Klan within the party and to urge support for the League of Nations. He said of the convention: "the fight against intolerance we won. I consider that there was an absolute repudiation of the Klan by this convention."[51] His brother later commented that "he practically dropped his law practice for a year to make speeches against them [the Klan] whenever and wherever he could get an audience."[52]

Willkie was a genuine believer in civil liberties for all Americans, even those, such as leftists, who were often perceived as being un-American. In 1939, he had condemned the Dies House Un-American Activities Committee; in March 1940, in an article entitled "Fair Trial," he outlined his position on civil liberties:

> Equal treatment under the law means exactly what it says, whether the man before the tribunal is a crook, a Democrat, a Republican, a communist or a businessman; whether he is rich or poor, white or black, good or bad. You cannot have a democracy on any other basis. You cannot preserve human liberties on any other theory.[53]

A presidential candidate holding these views should have given some hope to African Americans. In addition, unlike many Republicans, Willkie had openly endorsed much of the New Deal. In 1938, during the utilities battle with Roosevelt, he commented that "the New Deal has realized that the conditions of poverty and insecurity beyond the powers of the state to handle have created the need for social legislation in Washington."[54] He would not, therefore, necessarily be restricted by the concepts of states' rights or a decentralized federal government—the kind of conservatism that had, conceivably, cost the Republican Party African Americans votes—when determining his policies.

At the Republican convention, Willkie told African American delegates about his campaign against the Klan in Akron in 1924 and assured them that his company, the Southern and Commonwealth, had many African American employees, although "I don't how many . . . or in what categories but it's a hell of a lot of them."[55] After his nomination, he told the African American press: "I want your support. I need it. But irrespective of whether

Negroes go down the line with me or not, they can expect every consideration. They will get their fair share of appointments, their fair representation on policy-making bodies. They'll get the same consideration as other citizens."[56] The party also unveiled its strongest ever "Negro" plank, promising an economic and political "square deal," pledging to end discrimination in the civil service, federal government, and military. It also demanded that suffrage "be made effective for the Negro citizen" and a law to combat mob violence.[57] Willkie can take much of the credit for this more blunt approach to civil rights, although it made many Republicans uncomfortable. The Democrats, now nervous about the African American vote, included, for the first time, a "Negro" plank in their platform. This plank praised the achievements of the New Deal and dealt in generalities about striving "for complete legislative safeguards against discrimination" in government and the armed forces and promised equal protection under the law for all citizens.[58]

The *Crisis* remained wary. It had "little fault to find" with Willkie's acceptance speech in his home town of Elwood, Indiana, when he declared that he wanted an "America free of hate and bitterness, of racial and class distinction."[59] It did, however, question Willkie and the GOP's sincerity and willingness to act positively; there was little evidence, the *Crisis* argued, that Willkie's speech "indicates clearly that this is the kind of America he or it wants."[60] It also commented on a sign in Willkie's hometown that warned, "Nigger, don't let the sun go down on you." "This is the atmosphere from which Mr. Willkie springs," it noted, while conceding that "he may have outgrown it."[61]

Having won the nomination, Willkie made a genuine attempt to win African American support, motivated not simply by votes but by his sense of duty to all Americans. He claimed to have no "special plan" to win the African American vote but pledged to enact the Republican platform as far as he could.[62] The omens were not good: African Americans knew little about him, and he was running against the enormously popular Roosevelt. He was also hampered by the record of the GOP in Congress; it was true that the Republican platform's "Negro" plank was the strongest in generations, but the party in Congress had proved unreceptive to the needs of African Americans and, pertinently, to some of the pledges now enshrined in the platform. Accordingly, anything said by a senior Republican was likely to be regarded with a healthy degree of skepticism.

It was to Willkie's credit, therefore, that he still endeavored to reach out to African Americans by speaking in Chicago and Harlem (admittedly, he perhaps recognized that the South was unwinnable and he simply had nothing to lose by speaking to African American audiences). Although not recognized at the time, Willkie was, without doubt, the most racially progressive presidential candidate in American history. Subsequent events would show that his philosophy, at least partly outlined in Chicago, was born of genuinely held conviction, not expedience. On one level, the Chicago speech of September 1940 contained what one would expect of a candidate speaking before an African American audience, touching as it did on the themes of equality, relief discrimination, lynching, and Jim Crow. Yet Willkie went much further in an effort to address the problems of African Americans. "It is not right," he declared, "that America should continue a practice in which the Negro is the last to be hired and the first to be fired. The Negro has little hope if he must wait until the Whites [*sic*] have all been employed."[63] Willkie also promised to end discrimination in the federal government: "I say to you that under my administration there shall be no discrimination between people because of race, creed or color in the appointments to federal positions. That man who serves as my subordinate who makes any such discrimination shall be fired on the spot."[64]

The *Crisis* took some comfort from Willkie's Chicago speech but remained unconvinced: "[it] was not the historic document his followers would have us believe."[65] Willkie's claim to "abhor" lynching was compared to similar statements from other Republican candidates down through the years, all of which meant nothing without the political will to do anything tangible about the crime. Willkie was praised for recognizing the problem of employment discrimination and wanting to move African Americans from relief rolls to proper jobs, but this was tempered by the knowledge that the GOP was backed by the very industries that refused to employ African Americans.[66] Willkie's attacks on discrimination in the federal government were described as "bold" by the *Crisis*, and his promise to dismiss those guilty of discrimination was similarly praised as "straight talk." His problems were the persistent disappointment suffered by African Americans at the hands of the Republican Party and a concern about his purported sympathy for southern whites having to vote for the Democrats out of "necessity."[67]

"The Longer It Is Put Off the More Obvious It Becomes"

Willkie's pronouncements on the race question certainly stirred the Democrats into action, and the various concessions and efforts made by Roosevelt were a direct result of the threat he posed.[68] Roosevelt met African American leaders six times during 1940, but he was only prepared to make token concessions including the issuing of two commemorative stamps, one featuring Booker T. Washington and the other marking the seventy-fifth anniversary of the Thirteenth Amendment (albeit two months early). Furthermore, in October 1940, Roosevelt promoted Colonel Benjamin O. Davis to brigadier general, creating the country's first-ever African American general. Presidential secretary James Rowe, recognizing the political benefits of such a move, argued that "the longer it [the promotion of Davis] is put off the more obvious it becomes" that the promotion was politically motivated.[69] Davis, it should be noted, was six months from retirement and had been bypassed for promotion previously and would not actually command troops in combat during the Second World War.[70]

Selective service was also a potential headache for the president as, according to Rowe, it "raises the problem of segregation one week before the election."[71] Rowe suggested that the first selective service call be made without reference to race. He further advised that notable African American appointments to the preparedness effort should be made, including that of Judge William Hastie, who had "national status" and was "non-political," as assistant to Secretary of War Henry Stimson. "Stimson," Rowe continued, "should make the announcement rather than the White House, so as not to make it too obvious."[72] Roosevelt was advised to meet the editor of the "largest Negro newspaper in Chicago" (presumably the *Chicago Defender*), which was pro–New Deal and keen to "prepare a series of articles showing what the President has done for the Negro over the last seven years."[73] Rowe also urged Roosevelt to direct the Civil Service Commission to use fingerprints instead of photographs on application forms and attempt to calm the furor generated when the White House suggested that Walter White had endorsed segregation in the armed forces. The Democrats clearly felt that they had a fight on their hands if they were to maintain the African American vote, but continued to believe that it could be secured with largely symbolic gestures.

Willkie's commitment to civil rights did not necessarily endear him to the NAACP; even though the two would become firm friends after the election, Walter White pointedly refused to meet him before the election, fearing that it would be construed as an association endorsement.[74] Moreover, William Pickens, the NAACP's director of branches, caused controversy within the association after creating and agreeing to serve on the "Non-Partisan Colored Citizens Committee for Wendell Willkie." He was soon forced to stand down because of the association's nonpartisanship, although he believed that his Republicanism was the real issue. He later claimed to Willkie that White "got the Board to pass an ex–*post facto* resolution that I could not serve on the committee. Mr. White had quite other political plans then." This is further evidence of White and the NAACP linking the progress for African Americans with success for the Democratic Party.[75]

Willkie found himself dealing with what he described as "some of the most aggressive black leaders in the country" and under attack from African American Democrats.[76] In October 1940, the "Colored Division" of the Democratic National Committee linked Willkie's parents and his wife's parents to the Nazis and claimed that his sister was married to a German naval officer. This was all, of course, untrue (his sister was in fact married to an American naval attaché in Berlin) and strenuously denied by Willkie, but he was personally affected by the charges.[77] Attacks on Willkie's attitude toward African Americans continued throughout the campaign. Julian Rainey, the eastern head of the Democrats' "Colored Division," believed that Willkie's attitude toward African Americans was born of expedience as he "was unheard of by Negroes until two or three months ago" and had "no public record" on racial issues.[78] Rainey felt that Willkie's true feelings were to be found in his hometown of Elwood, Indiana, which "for many years" had a sign warning African Americans to stay out.[79] Rainey also pointed out that Willkie had many business interests in the South.

Emmett Scott, Booker T. Washington's former secretary, was in charge of the overall Republican effort to win African American votes, while Francis Rivers of New York and Sidney R. Redmond of St. Louis led the campaign in the East and West respectively.[80] African American Republicans followed many of the same tactics they had employed without conspicuous success in the election of 1936. Nevertheless, Rivers and Scott set about their task with vigor. Rivers assailed the New Deal, declaring that African Americans currently suffered more discrimination than at any time since emancipation. He accused the New Deal, with its "Negro hating" southerners and labor leaders, of trying "to put Negroes on relief and get them out of jobs in private industry."[81] The New Deal discriminated against and segregated African Americans at every level.[82] Scott also articulated the Republican argument that the New Deal was creating relief reservations for African Americans; citing the Republican platform in 1936 and the recent Frank report, he declared that his party would oppose relief "as a permanent substitute for employment. . . . Without a secure place in the private productive industry, Colored citizens are doomed."[83]

In October 1940, the Republican National Committee issued a pamphlet written by Rivers entitled "An Appeal to the Common Sense of Colored Citizens." This pamphlet represents perhaps the most strident and articulate contemporary indictment of the New Deal and its attitude toward African Americans. According to Rivers, the New Deal had done little for African Americans and had, in many instances, actually made conditions much worse. The pamphlet is, of course, highly partisan, yet an indication of its importance comes from Walter White, who could find little to fault in the document; in fact, his only complaint was that it characterized all southern whites as racist.[84] Rivers argued that the New Deal had, for instance, separate "Jim Crow" departments for African Americans that were actually designed to hinder the careers of African Americans and appease the South. Furthermore, African Americans were limited to advisory roles, and this had eliminated them as skilled workers in federal service.[85] In fact, federal agencies only employed 3.4 percent African Americans compared to 7.8 percent prior to Roosevelt's election.[86]

Rivers accused the New Deal of discriminating against African American workers or displacing them in favor of white labor. The best example of this was the case of cotton-gin workers who were recategorized as agricultural workers and therefore did not benefit from the provisions of the National Recovery Administration (NRA).[87] In addition, the Wages and Hours and Social Security laws did not cover agricultural or domestic workers and excluded some 70 percent of African American workers as a result.[88] Out of 115,000 field agents in the AAA, only 4 were African American.[89] The Public Works Administration (PWA) put African Americans in the lowest-paying and least-skilled jobs regardless of their qualifications.[90] Perhaps the most damning statistics published by Rivers concerned relief. Despite seven years of the New Deal, there were actually more African Americans on relief than ever, and African Americans constituted an even smaller proportion of the workforce than they had in 1930. According to Rivers's figures, in 1933 there were 2,117,644 African Americans on relief; in 1940, this had risen to 2,500,000. In 1930, African Americans made up 11.7 percent of the workforce; in 1937, they made up only 6.6 percent.[91] To make matters worse, the number of African Americans on work relief was actually dropping: in 1935, the figure stood at 906,356; in 1938, it was 275,000; and by 1940, it had dropped to 225,000. All of this was while African American unemployment was rising.[92]

Southerners held a disproportionate amount of influence in the New Deal, argued Rivers, and used this to discriminate against African Americans and to block antilynching legislation in Congress.[93] Rivers also claimed, with considerable justification, that Roosevelt was frightened of standing up to the South and only condemned lynching when the victims were white. He noted that segregation in government could be halted by executive orders, but this was unlikely to happen under Roosevelt as he had actually segregated government employees as assistant secretary of the navy in 1916.[94] Unless there was dramatic reform to help African Americans, asserted Rivers, then "the colored citizen has no chance to attain any of his major objectives under four more years of President Roosevelt and the New Deal."[95] Roosevelt, he claimed, did not have the political will to end segregation and discrimination, as he did not want to offend the South; and the South dominated the Democratic Party.

Under Willkie and the Republicans, Rivers stressed, African Americans would have fair treatment in agriculture and industry, equal treatment in federal service, relief without discrimination, desegregation of the military, an antilynching bill, and would take their place as full members of America's democracy. Rivers concluded that continuance of the New Deal meant "frustration and [a] segregated existence." By contrast, if Willkie won there would be "a justifiable hope for attaining all the major goals for which he has fought throughout the years."[96] Rivers predictably concentrated on the negative aspects of the New Deal for African Americans, and some of his assertions can certainly be challenged, but much of his criticism was valid. Rivers, needless to say, studiously avoided any mention of the Republicans' record prior to 1932 or in Congress since.

As the election neared and it became increasingly likely that Willkie would lose, Republican appeals to African Americans became more desperate. In his last press release to the African American papers prior to the election, Scott declared: "when Republicans are punished and lose, WE LOSE. When Republicans WIN, at least we keep what we have."[97] It was difficult to see from where his optimism sprang when he stated that "it is now apparent that Willkie and [his running mate Charles] McNary will receive an overwhelming majority of the Negro votes on Election Day," but he had a point when he argued that "Franklin Roosevelt has failed to give Colored people anything but honeyed words."[98] He also contended that a vote for Roosevelt and a third term would further strengthen the position of the South in the Democratic Party and lead to a dictatorship, noting "minorities suffer most under dictatorship."[99] This desperate plea was much too little, much too late for the Republicans.

Roosevelt won the election, but with a greatly reduced popular majority, winning 27,243,466 popular votes and 449 in the Electoral College to Willkie's 22,304,755 and 82, respectively. Willkie won more votes than any previous Republican candidate; he also restricted Roosevelt to the smallest winning margin since 1916. While Roosevelt's share of the African American vote either remained constant or rose, in every state where it was deemed to be important the Republicans made gains, including victories in Michigan and Indiana. In Illinois, Missouri, Ohio, Pennsylvania, New York, and West Virginia, the African American vote was perhaps the deciding factor, but Roosevelt could have lost all these states and still had a majority of 45 in the Electoral College.[100] It is clear, therefore, that the African American vote, while important, was not actually crucial to the victory itself.

Willkie's entreaties to African Americans had failed. This was at least partly because many African Americans still did not trust the Republicans and because Willkie, despite his pronouncements, was not viewed with any great confidence. Moreover, it could be argued that the seeming indifference of the GOP finally destroyed the party in the African American wards of Chicago and elsewhere, but it must be stressed that the black vote was won by Roosevelt and not lost by Willkie. The president's conciliatory gestures in the run up to the election and, more importantly, the tangible benefits African Americans had seen since he took office proved persuasive. What must also be remembered is that racial issues were peripheral in the election; the Depression was still the main concern of most Americans, the Second World War (which America would enter in a year's time) was also important, and Roosevelt's decision to run for an unprecedented third term all took precedence over civil rights.

"Imperialisms at Home"

After his defeat, Willkie became even more vociferous in his defense of civil liberties and minorities, his attacks on those who were racist, anti-Semitic, or intolerant of political minorities becoming a crusade when America entered World War II.[101] He believed that racism abroad had been a major cause of the war, and that racism at home, especially discrimination in the military, was a major barrier to American victory.[102] Willkie's espousal of African American rights was multifaceted and proved beyond any doubt the sincerity of his pronouncements during the election campaign.[103] Willkie also was critical of those who felt that "social experiments" should be postponed until the war ended, telling the Republican National Committee in April 1942 that guaranteeing the rights of African Americans under the Constitution and ending discrimination was "not in the realm of social experiment."[104]

Willkie spoke at the NAACP annual conference in Los Angeles in 1942, cementing his position as the foremost white champion of African American rights. He argued that the war was not about race or color but rather about freedom and tyranny, and he criticized what he saw as "race imperialism" within America. Things were changing, however, as many Americans realized that "we cannot fight the forces and ideas of imperialism abroad and maintain a form of imperialism at home."[105] Furthermore, he felt that the war was effecting a change in attitudes because "when we talk of freedom and opportunity for all nations, the mocking paradoxes in our own society become so clear they can no longer be ignored."[106] After the conference, White told Willkie that "it is no exaggeration" that his speech had "done more to lift the morale of Negroes than any other thing within the past year. They now see hope where before there was only despair."[107]

At last it seemed that African Americans had a genuine ally in the Republican Party, or perhaps more accurately, they had a genuine ally *despite* his membership in the Republican Party. Willkie was a supporter of the National Urban League, a trustee of the Hampton Institute (one of the largest African American universities in America), and helped in a campaign to force the navy, coast guard, and marines to accept black volunteers.[108] He was a supporter of the March on Washington Movement and served on the National Council for a Fair Employment Practice Commission.[109] He despised the poll tax, arguing that the spectacle of the anti–poll tax bill being held up by a few senators damaged America's position as the leader of the free world.[110] Willkie later asserted that all Americans should oppose the poll tax and the Democratic "white primary" because "any measure which deprives any group of citizens in our country from exercising the inherent rights as set forth in the Constitution is inimical to the interests of all citizens."[111] Willkie was also appointed special council to the NAACP to fight stereotyping in the film industry.[112]

The most serious threat to race relations during World War II was the Detroit riot of June 1943, in which thirty-four people, mainly African Americans, died.[113] While most politicians condemned it, or in Roosevelt's case remained silent, Willkie, in a coast-to-coast radio speech in the aftermath of the riot entitled "An Open Letter to the American People," tried to address the root causes of the problem.[114] He argued that African Americans remained alienated and on the periphery of American society, and that both parties were guilty of failing to examine their basic needs: "one party cannot go on feeling that it has no further obligation to the Negro citizen because Abraham Lincoln freed the slaves. And the other is not entitled to power if it sanctions and practices one set of principles in Atlanta and another in Harlem."[115] He believed that the rights of African Americans had to be guaranteed by legal equality and equal opportunities in education, health care, and the armed forces. He warned that the Detroit riot could be repeated in many American cities, and that such incidents reflected badly on America as "two-thirds of the people who are our allies do not have white skin."[116]

In a 1943 interview, he said that if elected president he would appoint an African American either to his cabinet or to the Supreme Court and added: "if I am elected, and if I do not do this, I want you to write a piece saying that . . . Wendell Willkie made such and such a statement to you, and that Wendell Willkie is a liar."[117] In an article on African Americans written for seven Republican newspapers prior to the GOP convention in 1944 (to which he was not invited), Willkie chided his party for embracing states' rights arguments and urged federal laws to eliminate the poll tax and lynching.[118] Ellsworth Barnard sums up Willkie's crusade succinctly: "his record from the end of 1940 until his death was one of absolute integrity."[119]

Willkie's last published work was entitled "Our Citizens of Negro Blood" and appeared in *Collier's* in October 1944. He again described the inequities suffered by African Americans in housing, education, employment, and the justice system as "America's greatest and most conspicuous scandal," and he again stressed that America's "ugly discrimination at home" had an impact abroad. America had to address the problems of African Americans, and he agreed that there were many, of which discrimination in the armed forces was "the most bitter and ironic."[120] Willkie then turned his attention to the Republican and Democratic platforms for the 1944 presidential election; both were "tragically inadequate," but the Democrats' platform was particularly evasive. He believed that African Americans would view the Republican "Negro" plank, which carried pledges on segregation in the armed forces, lynching, the poll tax, and a Fair Employment Practices Commission (FEPC), "as a device to delay, rather than to take effective action."[121] Of the Republicans' commitments, Willkie regarded the FEPC as the most important but was concerned by the actions of Dewey in blocking a state FEPC in New York, where he was now governor: "justly or not, Negro leaders were quick to point out that the Governor's action coincided with several Republican state conventions where a forthright position on the race issue might have harmed his candidacy."[122] Regardless of the truth of this claim, Dewey's support of similar legislation if elected president in 1944 was already tainted. Willkie condemned the Democrats for pandering to southern racists and believed that the Republicans were only marginally better. He demanded laws against the poll tax and lynching and an executive order to end segregation and discrimination in the armed forces.

Was Willkie the man to return the African American vote to the GOP in 1944? Walter White certainly felt that he had great potential. In April 1943, he declared that African Americans still chose Roosevelt as their preferred presidential candidate for 1944, but that their second choice was the increasingly popular Willkie. The African American vote was now "in the balance," according to White, due to the influence of southerners in the Democratic Party.[123] He told George Gallup: "if the candidates are Roosevelt and Dewey, 75 to 95% [of African Americans] would vote for Roosevelt. If the candidates are Roosevelt and Willkie, the percentage would be just the opposite."[124] A *Pittsburgh Courier* poll of ten thousand African Americans in the fall of 1943 found that 84.2 percent wanted Wendell Willkie as the Republican candidate for the presidency in 1944.[125] White was undoubtedly exaggerating Willkie's popularity, but a second candidacy for the man dubbed "the nation's number one patriot" and America's "foremost champion" by the African American press after his death would surely have been good news for African Americans.[126]

More than any other Republican, Willkie had a genuine empathy for African Americans, an empathy not tainted with expediency. He knew where the party had gone wrong, but his views were out of touch with the mainstream of the party on this and, indeed, many other issues. There was, however, a danger that Willkie's outspokenness on the race question would alienate white Americans. Pollster Elmo Roper warned that if there was a perception that Willkie "advocated an aggressive policy which might be regarded as truculent, I think he would most certainly be defeated at the polls."[127] Perhaps he remained a liberal Democrat at heart, but what is certain is that when he died of a heart attack on 8 October 1944, the Republican Party's historic championing of African American rights also, finally, died.

Willkie was a product of 1940; he simply could not have emerged as the leader of the Republican Party at any other time. During World War II, the only American civilian to have a higher public profile than Willkie was Roosevelt. But as Willkie's status among the American people rose, his position within the Republican Party itself, never particularly solid, became ever more tenuous. Willkie's liberalism was outlined in his book *One World*, which was based on his experiences traveling the globe and meeting world leaders, including Stalin and Churchill, in 1942.[128] This liberalism in both foreign and domestic policy was, however, alien to the mainstream of the GOP, and the popularity of, and critical acclaim for, *One World* further estranged him from many within the party. Here was the Republican presidential candidate of 1940 gallivanting around the world, at the hated Roosevelt's request, during potentially crucial midterm elections. "In the final reckoning," argues Milton Viorst, "Wendell Willkie was a maverick, a solitary figure, unwanted by his party, unmourned, and, as a political reformer, unsuccessful."[129] By 1944, therefore, a Willkie presidency, never a realistic prospect, became an impossibility for a man who no longer had a party.

It would be wrong to dismiss Willkie as a mere historical footnote: few defeated presidential candidates have generated so much and such positive interest.[130] Furthermore, Willkie's vision of a new world in the wake of the Second World War was in marked contrast to the course embarked upon by the United States and, in particular, the Republican Party. Moreover, in civil rights, it is no exaggeration to say that he was many years ahead of his time. Willkie was, however, an anomaly in Republican politics. A nominal Democrat until 1938, on his nomination he had exhorted "you Republicans" to follow him, thus giving the air of someone looking in on the Republican Party from the outside. His attitude toward African Americans, foreign policy, and domestic policy, including much of the New Deal, was at odds with much of the party. It is entirely possible that the Republican Party merely provided him with a platform; he is said to have suggested to Roosevelt, to whom he was actually quite close politically, that they should seek to realign American politics by forming a new party that would abandon southern Democrats and reactionary Republicans to their fate. The notion did receive an audience, but it was never given serious consideration.[131] Even with Willkie nominally at the helm of the GOP, the African American vote still remained the preserve of the Democrats, a fact that did not unduly concern most Republicans.

4

The Totally Political Man

Stung by another defeat, after the 1940 election the GOP embarked on yet another period of soul-searching. First and foremost, it was essential that the party make up its mind on foreign policy. Willkie's position was clear: America had to do all it could to help the Allies, in other words, Britain, in the fight against Hitler; he also urged the Republicans to engage in "loyal opposition" after their defeat. This made many Republicans uncomfortable; indeed, had the extent of Willkie's liberal internationalist sympathies been better known in the spring of 1940, it is unlikely that he would have been nominated. As early as February 1941, congressional leaders were disavowing Willkie's statements, insisting that he spoke for himself and not the party. Until the eve of Pearl Harbor, many Republicans, and undeniably many Americans, believed that America could avoid entanglement in the war and that the Axis powers did not threaten America's security directly. Everything changed on 7 December 1941. Isolationism, the mainstay of Republican foreign policy for so long, was immediately and fatally discredited, and the Republicans had to find a patriotic alternative quickly. Arthur Vandenberg, so long in the vanguard of the isolationist wing of the GOP, recalled that Pearl Harbor "ended isolationism for any realist."[1]

Some Democrats advocated the suspension of elections for the duration of the war, but Republicans were universally opposed; party chairman Joseph Martin expected the 1942 elections to go ahead as planned and announced that the Republican Party would be aiming to make gains. Attempts to reduce overt partisanship during the war failed. There was a suspicion among some Republicans that Roosevelt would use the war to increase his own power, and after Pearl Harbor, the GOP had to decide how critical it could be of the administration during wartime. Taft, for instance, believed that "the New Dealers are determined to make the country over under the cover of war if they can."[2] Moreover, it has been suggested that Republican partisanship, under the guise of patriotism, actually became more acute during the war.[3] The 1942 midterms would, therefore, see "politics as usual" in America.[4]

The main division within the Republican Party was between Willkie and Taft. Willkie, of course, wanted the total abandonment of the isolationism that had dominated GOP foreign policy since the end of the World War I; Taft was a critic of lend-lease and anything he saw as drawing America into an unacceptable postwar international organization. Once again the Republican Party was faced with an extraordinarily divisive issue, and once again the Republican solution was to appoint a committee. This committee would examine the question of the party's foreign policy, thereby bypassing any embarrassing public debate that could be detrimental at the polls. Martin appointed a seven-man subcommittee to avoid the divergent positions of Willkie and Taft in an effort to maintain the pretence of unity.[5] This subcommittee presented a sufficiently uncontroversial eight-hundred-word resolution in April 1942 that was just about acceptable to all sides; Willkie saw it as an abandonment of isolationism, but prewar isolationists knew that this was not the case.[6]

In October 1942, the GOP issued a ten-point manifesto, which was approved by 115 Republican representatives.[7] As expected, the manifesto accused Roosevelt of being more interested in personal political gains than the successful prosecution of the conflict. The Republicans, importantly, recorded their opposition to a negotiated peace and pledged to fight vigorously until "complete decisive victory was won."[8] The manifesto also stressed the importance of preserving the two-party system. Alluding to a postwar international organization, it asserted that America had "an obligation and responsibility" to promote "world understanding and [a] cooperative spirit" to maintain world peace.[9] Many Republicans felt that the statement was too strong, particularly on postwar arrangements, and withheld their endorsement, even though the document committed the party to nothing specific and was concerned more with the midterm elections than a postwar settlement.[10] In common with other statements of Republican intent, the ten-point manifesto was designed to foster party unity as much as define party policy.

Walter White believed that the Republicans had missed "a golden opportunity" in omitting African Americans from their ten-point declaration of policy and principle. Martin replied that "it was an oversight rather than an intention. We will try to correct it sometime."[11] White was not convinced of Martin's good intentions: "Joe has always been most friendly but, unhappily, he and other political leaders are too frequently given to overlooking the Negro and they need to be reminded so that they don't forget next time."[12] White sent Martin's letter, confidentially, to the editors of five African American newspapers and asked them to comment editorially on the Republican declaration.[13] The *Norfolk Journal and Guide* obliged, commenting that the "Republicans missed an opportunity to strike a blow for democracy."[14]

In the 1942 midterm elections, the Republicans won 44 more seats in the House, giving them a total of 209 compared to the Democrats' 222, 120 of which were held by southerners. In addition, the Republicans now had 9 more senators, while 29 of the 57 Democratic senators were southerners. The GOP also won gubernatorial contests in New York, Michigan, and California. Some Democratic liberals were defeated while some isolationist Republicans, especially strong in the Midwest, were reelected. The perceived isolationism of Republican incumbents did not prevent the vast majority of them (110 out of 115) being reelected.[15]

Isolationism versus internationalism was not the only issue in the election; the New Deal was increasingly challenged as the war and its hardships occupied the minds of Americans. Yet what hampered the Democrats most in 1942 was the extremely poor turnout; only 28 million Americans voted compared to some 50 million in 1940. Turnout, of course, always drops in off-year elections; in 1938, for example, 36 million Americans went to the polls.[16] Thomas Dewey, for example, won the New York gubernatorial election with a noticeably reduced turnout compared to 1938. Republican analysis of the returns recognized the low turnout but concluded that "the figures do not indicate any relation between Republican strength or weakness and the size of the vote cast."[17] Regardless of the underlying reasons for their success, the Republicans finally believed that they had an opportunity to rein in the hated New Deal; *Fortune*, for example, commented that many of the victorious candidates "think they have a mandate to repeal all New Deal reforms."[18] Significantly, some commentators reckoned that a majority of African Americans had backed the GOP for the first time since 1932.[19]

The Democrats learned a number of lessons from this experience: isolationism was not dead; America's war aims needed to be better defined; and the American public required Allied victories. Without all of this, there was a very real concern that the party could lose in 1944.[20] Republican strategists tended to agree with this synopsis, but believed that their attacks on inefficiency in war output and questions about the high command were also factors.[21] The midterms also drove the GOP toward the center of the debate on internationalism and away from the extremes of Willkie and Taft. The elections also provided a new generation of potential Republican leaders—most notably Dewey—who, the Old Guard hoped, could deny Willkie the

Republican nomination in 1944. Nonetheless, the gains again postponed party reform and prevented rational debate about foreign policy.

The elections also served to engender rare, if superficial, unity in Republican ranks; when the party met to discuss the new session of Congress on 8 January 1943, McNary commented, "the harmony was so thick it ran down my cheeks."[22] This threatened to be extremely short-lived unless the vexed question of foreign policy could be resolved successfully. Indicative of the stalemate over foreign policy was the replacement of Joseph Martin as party chairman with Harrison Spangler. Spangler, a committeeman from Iowa, was a compromise, as the election of either an isolationist or an internationalist would have split the party.[23] To further complicate matters, Willkie's internationalist treatise *One World* appeared in April 1943. Selling over 1 million copies, it quickly generated considerable support for American participation in a postwar international organization.[24]

It was absolutely essential that foreign policy be dealt with and removed as a possible source of division well in advance of the 1944 presidential election. Under the shrewd stewardship of Vandenberg at Mackinac Island in his home state of Michigan in September 1943, the Republicans agreed in principle to a postwar international organization.[25] Pointedly, there were no invitations for Hoover, Landon, or Willkie. Spangler privately conceded that the presence of Willkie, or indeed his refusal to attend, would have proved divisive.[26] Although many remained wary, the Mackinac agreement successfully eliminated foreign policy as an issue in the forthcoming presidential election, preserving a veneer of harmony between isolationists and internationalists on foreign policy and satisfying most in the party, including Willkie.[27]

"The Japs Done Declared War on You White Folks"

Unlike in World War I, when even W.E.B. Du Bois urged African Americans to set aside their grievances until the conflict was over, African Americans, though no less patriotic, were much more circumspect about their country's participation in World War II. Given the disappointments and violence suffered during and after the last conflict, there was no prospect of African Americans remaining silent or postponing progress this time. Some even questioned whether it was their war at all: "I hear the Japs done declared war on you white folks," remarked an African American sharecropper after Pearl Harbor.[28] Indeed, while African Americans recognized that their lot would be immeasurably worse under Axis powers, prior to Pearl Harbor there was little enthusiasm for any war that perpetuated British colonialism. Furthermore, there was acute resentment about the treatment of African Americans within the armed forces and the persistence of African American unemployment at a time when industrial output was increasing dramatically to meet the needs of the preparedness program.[29]

The African American response to the Second World War took a number of forms. In the summer of 1941, the March on Washington Movement (MOWM), led by A. Philip Randolph, whose support for the eventual war effort would remain highly qualified, threatened mass protest unless steps were taken to ameliorate conditions for African Americans, particularly discrimination in the war industries and the military. In the absence of compromise from Randolph, Roosevelt announced Executive Order 8802, which outlawed discrimination in the hiring of workers to do government contracts and set up a Fair Employment Practices Commission (FEPC).[30] The *Pittsburgh Courier*, articulating the qualified loyalty of African Americans, launched its "Double V" campaign, demanding "victory over our enemies at home and victory over our enemies on the battlefields abroad."[31] Within a month of Pearl Harbor, the *Crisis* announced, in contrast to Du Bois' stance in 1918, that "now is not the time to be silent," while the NAACP convention of July 1942 refused to postpone the quest for equality.[32] The war also saw the membership of the NAACP mushroom from 50,000 members in 355 branches in 1940 to 450,000 members in 1,073 branches by 1946.[33]

The executive order creating the FEPC remained the only wartime concession from Roosevelt and was largely ineffective.[34] It was apparent that African American aspirations would be low on the administration's list of priorities until at least the end of the war. Furthermore, the rising expectations of African Americans were not greeted with particular sympathy from the majority of whites, and racial tensions generated by the war finally culminated in riots in Detroit and Harlem in 1943. It has been argued that these riots stifled mass action and cooled the militancy of many African Americans, notably the NAACP, who moderated their demands, seeking the cooperation of liberal whites instead.[35]

By the early 1940s, there was, as noted, a fear among African American leaders that the Democrats were becoming as complacent as the Republicans about the African American vote. In November 1943, twenty-seven prominent African American leaders from twenty organizations, led by the NAACP, issued a "Declaration by Negro Voters." It was highly critical of both parties in Congress and their vacillation over civil rights issues, notably legislation to outlaw both lynching and the poll tax. It warned that

African Americans would not be swayed by "meaningless generalities" that were "promptly forgotten on election day."[36] Instead, African Americans, potentially holding the balance of power in seventeen states with a combined electoral vote of over 280, would vote for the party that guaranteed their rights. There was a feeling, or perhaps simply a hope, that the African American vote was becoming more fluid and would not be the exclusive preserve of the Democratic Party. The black vote, the declaration announced, "cannot be purchased by distributing money to and through party hacks."[37]

The declaration recognized that the successful prosecution of the war remained the primary concern of African Americans, but discrimination in the armed forces caused particular disgust and had to be addressed. It accused both parties of trying to "delude" African Americans with half-hearted support of legislation on lynching and poll tax. Black voters would no longer put up with excuses: voting against cloture would be regarded as opposition to the aspirations of African Americans and other minorities. The declaration demanded that the FEPC be continued and expanded during the remainder of the war and then in peacetime, and it asserted that any candidate wanting the African American vote had to support actively FEPC legislation. Signatories of the declaration included Mary McLeod Bethune, Thurgood Marshall, Channing Tobias, Hastie, White, Randolph, and Congressman Adam Clayton Powell and represented organizations with 6 million members.[38] Harrison Spangler, commenting on the declaration, claimed to be interested in the plight of African Americans as the New Deal "has sought to use all minority groups as pawns in its games of power politics," whereas the Republicans would "work to the betterment" of African Americans and all other minorities.[39] White wanted to know if the GOP was going to address the plight of African Americans; he was not hopeful, however, because "certain elements" of the party seemed to be keener on cultivating their alliance with southern Democrats, particularly over opposition to the soldier vote bill and cloture. "The Republican party," warned White, "has a very great task ahead of it to overcome the mistakes of distant and recent years."[40]

The declaration, despite its public bellicosity, masked the serious concerns of the NAACP leadership. At a special meeting of the board of directors in July 1944, NAACP cofounder Arthur Spingarn argued that attacking Roosevelt would only lead to the election of Dewey, while assistant secretary and *Crisis* editor Roy Wilkins conceded ruefully that "we are not organized to influence [the black] vote to any great degree." Hastie, who had resigned as Secretary of State Stimson's civilian aide over discrimination in the armed forces in 1943 and would campaign for the Democrats in 1948, feared that "the Democratic leadership psychologically is in the same position as the Republican leadership was in 1930."[41] It would appear, then, that despite the rocketing recruitment of the NAACP, the bravado of the "Declaration by Negro Voters," the MOWM, and the Double V campaign, African American political influence remained extremely limited.

Morale among African American Republicans deteriorated during the war. Throughout 1944, they complained publicly about the direction that their party was heading; in February, black Republicans from thirty-six states, led by Robert Church, met in Chicago to discuss the forthcoming Republican convention and the nature of the party's appeal to African Americans. They issued a "Declaration by Negro Republican Workers," which reminded the GOP that it had not won a national election since it lost the African American vote and warned that unless it was "courageous enough to rededicate itself to the principles upon which it was founded," it would not regain this vote.[42] They demanded an end to military segregation, a say in the postwar settlement, and inclusion of African Americans in policy-forming, rather than advisory, roles within the GOP and any future Republican administration. They also demanded legislation to prevent discrimination in employment, a commitment to full employment after the war, and federal housing. Other demands included the enactment of legislation on lynching, education, the Fourteenth and Fifteenth Amendments, the poll tax, and segregation on interstate travel; they also wanted the Atlantic Charter to be extended to apply to Africans and other exploited people. The Republican–southern Democrat alliance was condemned as "unholy and vicious," especially in relation to the federal education bill and the soldier vote bill.[43] The concept of states' rights was denounced, as were presumptions about the constitutionality of bills by members of the Congress. "[A]ll venal, parasitic, vacillating and reactionary politicians" were repudiated and full citizenship for African Americans was demanded.[44]

They stressed that the GOP's position was not irredeemable provided a Republican president and Congress fought the "malignant foes of democracy."[45] There was no formal endorsement of a candidate, but the preference seemed to be for Dewey, particularly as Willkie had withdrawn from the campaign by this stage.[46] Church challenged African American Democrats to follow their lead and issue a forthright statement about what they wanted from their party; if they did not, Church contended, then African American voters would know that they were "only looking for loaves and fishes." Church noted that William L. Houston, the national director of Negro Democrats, had remained silent about the racist Mississippi senator Theodore Bilbo.[47] The *Crisis* believed that the "Declaration by Negro Republican Workers" would make uncomfortable reading for many in the GOP, particularly Taft. It also demonstrated, according to the *Crisis*, that all African Americans, regardless of their political outlook, shared the same core objectives and linked the statement by African American Republicans to a statement made by African American editors to Roosevelt and also the "Declaration by Negro Voters."[48]

African American Democrats did meet to discuss the political situation, demanding decent wages, homes, education, equality, and social security, and, inevitably, praising Roosevelt. Segregation and discrimination were condemned, and demands were made for an anti–poll tax law, a federal soldier voting law, FEPC, an end to discrimination in Washington, D.C., federal aid to education, low-rent public housing, and policy-forming roles for African Americans. They also attacked the Republican–southern Democratic alliance that had abolished the WPA, passed antiunion legislation, and thwarted the federal soldier vote bill. They concluded by praising Vice President Henry Wallace and endorsing Roosevelt for reelection.[49] The *Topeka/Kansas City Plaindealer* reported that this was the first time that African American Republicans or Democrats had met publicly to discuss policy. "At least the smart political leaders of both major parties," commented the *Plaindealer*, "should know by now that it is going to take more than a lot of bunk, bull and high sounding vacuous oratory" to win African American votes.[50]

At best, the "Declaration by Negro Voters" represented a unity of purpose among African Americans, a unity reinforced by similar demands from African American Republicans and Democrats.[51] The declaration was a manifesto outlining the demands, aspirations, and grievances of African Americans, but behind its militant rhetoric was the painful recognition that little had changed or was about to change because of the war. The war momentarily galvanized many African Americans, but the streak of militancy evident in the MOWM had been diluted by the riots of 1943; African Americans were simply not in a position to make demands. Randolph signed the declaration, but the radicalism of his MOWM was absent; a more radical document would have urged mass demonstrations, a refusal of the draft, and a withdrawal of support for the war effort.[52] African Americans were undoubtedly restless, but their options were severely restricted. By 1944, the NAACP suspected that its closeness to the Democrats—recognized by African Americans, Republicans, and Democrats alike—threatened to jeopardize its hard-won, although still limited, political influence. Not only had the war further relegated African American concerns, but also the gains already secured under the New Deal were being imperiled. Democrat and, particularly, Republican African Americans were also disheartened by the lack of tangible progress, but all shades of African American opinion clung to the belief that the African American vote in pivotal states, in reality their only weapon, could be their salvation.

"A Self-Made Man Who Worshipped His Creator"

If Wendell Willkie was "the man who would rather be right than be president," then there were many who believed that Thomas Dewey was "the man who would rather be president than be right." Dewey's slight stature and ample self-belief provided an endless source of amusement for journalists, commentators, and cartoonists during his presidential campaigns of 1944 and 1948, generating some memorable quips of which the "bridegroom on a wedding cake" was one of the kinder. He was variously described as being able to "strut sitting down," as "a self-made man who worshipped his creator," and the "caricature of the totally political man."[53] Moreover, Dewey was not just a figure of fun. To many, not least African Americans, there were aspects of his character that caused serious concern, including a feeling that he lacked any real political principles, assiduously following public opinion and then acting accordingly. In 1944, Richard Scandett, a former Dewey supporter and a Republican for twenty years, declared: "the wind blows first, then Mr. Dewey points in its direction. . . . Sometimes it almost amounts to contortionism in the attempt to have both ears to the ground at once."[54] Furthermore, Dewey placed enormous faith in opinion polls; in 1940, he declared: "never argue with the Gallup Poll. It has never been wrong and I very much doubt that it ever will be, so long as George Gallup runs it."[55]

Having failed to secure the Republican nomination in 1940, Dewey again focused his attention on becoming the governor of New York. At the beginning of 1942, he backed the Double V campaign, attacking "intolerance, injustice and the tyranny of ignorance." Citing the "sacred memory" of Lincoln, he concluded that "only by guarding our hard-won rights as a free people can we hope to enjoy the blessings of peace when victory is finally won."[56] Dewey secured the GOP nomination for governor of New York in 1942 with the party's platform demanding equality of opportunity without reference to race and declared that discrimination was a "mockery of democracy."[57] He also condemned workplace discrimination in a number of speeches and vowed to enforce a number of civil rights laws already on the statute book.[58] Furthermore, he maintained that he would not attempt to roll back the state welfare program if elected.

He was also starting to sound like Wendell Willkie. Interviewed by the *Amsterdam Star-News,* Dewey reiterated his desire to challenge discrimination, promising to make current, ineffective laws work.[59] He told the *Star* that attacking discrimination abroad while maintaining it at home was "absurd" and argued that African Americans protest should not be halted because of the war. Dewey asserted that African American commitment to the war effort was "just as great as that of any other American."[60] Firms that refused to employ African Americans were damaging the war effort, and he cited the record of his own office, where black and white Americans worked together harmoniously. If someone in Dewey's administration was guilty of discrimination, he would "fire him on the spot."[61] As governor, Dewey declared that he "would tolerate no caste system. I believe that no job is too big or too good for a qualified Negro to fill."[62]

Toward the end of the campaign, Dewey twice spoke to African American audiences. At Union Baptist Church, he declared that America's diversity gave it strength, particularly in a time of crisis; he again recognized African American dedication to the war effort and maintained that one of America's war aims was to destroy "international discrimination." Dewey, revisiting a familiar theme, insisted that "it is absurd to talk about eradicating evils in other countries when we still have not wiped out those evils at home."[63] He criticized the token hiring of African Americans in war industries, especially when America needed manpower and stressed that African Americans did not want special treatment, just their rights as American citizens.[64] Prejudice, he affirmed, was a "blot on the American record" that he wanted "wiped out," and he believed that America had taken steps to achieve this.[65] This is, of course, precisely what Willkie had been saying since 1940.[66]

Dewey touched upon similar issues in his second speech, this time in Harlem, but he also attacked New York's Democratic administration. He assailed a "poll tax" imposed by the Democratic Party in Albany, citing the example of an African American whose tax assessment almost doubled when he registered as a Republican in 1940. Furthermore, in Albany, African Americans and whites did the same jobs for different pay, something he vowed to correct by making existing laws to combat discrimination effective. Ultimately, discrimination was "a betrayal of our war effort" and American ideals: "we cannot ask people to put their trust in a democracy that does not exist for them. . . . We must win the struggle for freedom at home as we win it throughout the world."[67] This was a candid assessment by Dewey, its frankness made all the more intriguing by his party affiliation, yet appearances by Dewey before African American audiences became an increasingly rarity.

Dewey duly became New York's first Republican governor in twenty years, counting Harlem among the wards in which he was victorious. Even though his victory was greatly assisted by divisions among the state's Democrats, it certainly increased the likelihood that he would be nominated by the GOP in 1944.[68] In Dewey's first term as governor, he was unable to live up to the ideals he had espoused during the campaign, but the undoubted highlight was the widely welcomed appointment of Francis Rivers as justice of the city court in New York in September 1943.[69] This made Rivers the highest-paid ("possibly [in] the nation") and highest-ranking African American ever employed by New York.[70] Rivers, a lifelong Republican and Dewey's most senior and loyal African American confidante, was initially appointed until December, but, having secured the support of the American Labor Party as well as the GOP, it seemed very likely that he would be elected to the post in November. The appointment of Rivers, together with the Democrats' refusal to select an African American to run against him, meant that some commentators felt there was now a possibility of the Republicans regaining African American votes.[71] The *Amsterdam Star-News* was suitably impressed by Dewey's efforts, describing it as "a bold stroke" by "a fearless and courageous public official."[72] Rivers was duly elected in November, securing the votes of both African Americans and whites. Channing Tobias, a Republican and head of the colored YMCA, told Dewey of his delight at Rivers's election, stating that "your courage, forthrightness and loyal support will not go unnoticed. They will be rewarded more generously in the future than they have been in the past."[73]

Within months of Rivers's victory, however, Dewey's relationship with African Americans had soured. In March 1944, the state legislature killed an antidiscrimination bill and replaced it with a new committee, the third in seven years.[74] Dewey was blamed for the failure of the bill and was criticized for not supporting the proposals of a committee he had appointed in the first place. Six members of the original committee, including Lester Grainger of the National Urban League and Tobias, resigned.[75] They asserted in their collective resignation letter that "the urgency and gravity" of the problems of discrimination meant that they were unwilling "to share with you the responsibility for the postponement of action."[76] The new committee would report its findings to the 1945 legislature.[77] Ironically, in the interview Dewey gave to the *Amsterdam Star-News* prior to his election, he was asked if he would appoint another commission. Dewey replied: "I don't like surveys where they simply serve to delay action. Certainly the Negro, more than any other group, needs action. I am a firm believer in sound investigation to get the facts. But I do not believe in investigation unless it leads to results. It is time for results."[78] To Dewey's critics, it seemed that results would have to wait until he had secured the presidential nomination; indeed, by the time the new commission presented its findings, Dewey could be in residence at the White House.

The NAACP registered its acute disapproval. Roy Wilkins declared: "the inescapable conclusion is that Governor Dewey is not interested in eliminating racial and religious prejudice," warning that he would "be viewed with suspicion by Negro voters."[79] Another critic accused Dewey of "using a pliant Republican majority in the legislature [to block] the passage of virtually every anti-discrimination measure" in 1944.[80] These measures included bills on housing, Jim Crow, a state civil rights bureau, and, especially, the New York State Commission on Discrimination. African American Republicans were concerned about the effect the failure of the bill would have on the party's prospects of regaining the African American vote, with Church telling Dewey that "the passage of New York State's Fair Employment Act by a Republican administration, would have a far-reaching effect on Colored citizens throughout this country."[81]

Dewey justified the killing of the bill, observing that "we are far short . . . of having established either a fundamental policy or a system of law which adequately meets the problem as a whole."[82] Dewey perhaps had a point: there was little to be gained from a law that, in his view, simply would not work. As far back as the gubernatorial campaign of 1938, Rivers was drafting speeches for Dewey that complained about the lack of enforcement of the laws against discrimination that already existed. So at least in this regard, Dewey was being consistent by blocking the antidiscrimination bill.[83] Tobias, hitherto a Dewey ally as well as a Republican, was incensed. He accused Dewey of failing to support the bill because he did not want to alienate southern Republicans before the party convention.[84] Tobias further alleged that when the bills were before the state senate, New York lieutenant governor Joe Hanley was in the South garnering convention votes for Dewey.[85] Tobias declared that "there was nothing complicated or highly controversial about the bills for those who are true believers in American democracy," and emphasized that he and other members of the committee had resigned because they believed that Dewey was "playing politics" and they refused "to continue as partners in futility."[86] Tobias not only resigned from the commission but also, as the 1944 election campaign began in earnest, even went so far as to endorse Roosevelt publicly.[87]

The *New York Post* was also critical of Dewey: "it is one of the oldest and sleaziest tricks of politics to block a program or kill a measure by calling for further study and consequent postponement of all action," noting that Dewey could be president by the time the new committee submitted its report.[88] Joseph V. Baker, in the *Philadelphia Inquirer*, attempted to explain why Dewey had killed the bill. He claimed that because the law had been proposed two weeks before the adjournment of the state assembly and would have probably been ineffective, Dewey had chosen to abandon the bill and take responsibility for its failure. Baker praised Dewey for his lack of opportunism:

> This man has a passion for thoroughness; and even before this measure showed its head, he had publicly sworn against loading the judicial docket with obviously unconstitutional legislation. And in that light, candidate or no candidate, wrath or no wrath, he asked for further study and a possibly better solution of a tough problem.[89]

Dewey biographer Richard Norton Smith agrees with this hypothesis, arguing that Dewey had not backed the bill because it was badly drafted and fundamentally flawed. Nevertheless, African Americans were not convinced, and Dewey's standing further deteriorated when Frank S. Columbus, of the lily-white Brotherhood of Locomotive Firemen and Enginemen union, was then appointed to the new committee along with a number of other people the NAACP felt were inappropriate.[90] Regardless of his motivation, the failure of the bill was a public relations disaster for Dewey.

"Anyone Who Joins Rankin Cannot Have the Negro Vote"

By 1944, there were over 9 million Americans in the military, some 5 million of whom were overseas, and their votes would be vital in the forthcoming presidential election. The Green-Lucas soldier voting bill, which was brought before Congress in 1943, attempted to address the main area of contention on this issue: namely, whether the states or the federal government should allocate the soldier vote. Dewey and most Republicans favored the former and Roosevelt the latter. The bill united conservative Republicans and southern Democrats in opposition, albeit for different reasons: Republicans did not want soldiers voting Democrat, while southern Democrats did not want southern African American soldiers voting at all. Even though reactionary southern Democrats had declared publicly that their objective in opposing the bill was the maintenance of white supremacy, Dewey did not change his position. Wilkins contended that Dewey's stance represented tacit support of the position taken by southern Democrats.[91] Dewey also endured patently unfair comparisons with notorious racists such as Mississippi senators John Rankin and James Eastland, with the *Crisis* announcing that "anyone who joins Rankin cannot have the Negro vote." This was a harsh assessment, but perhaps understandable given the GOP's predilection for alliances with southern Democrats, and, despite protestations by his staff, Dewey had once more been tainted on an issue of importance to African Americans.[92] Many Republicans proceeded to vote against the bill despite the blatantly racist motivation of southern Democrats, and the states' rights soldier vote bill passed the Senate by a margin of 42 to 37 in December 1943; in January 1944, the House, by a vote of 224 to 168, voted against replacing the Senate bill with a federal law. Wilkins warned that African American voters would punish "collaborators with the Rankin-Eastland bloc."[93] Notwithstanding the controversies surrounding the soldier vote, some 4 million servicemen voted in 1944.[94]

The ongoing controversy over the poll tax was also a potential headache, and the NAACP was keen to make life as uncomfortable as possible for Dewey and the Republicans on this issue. Efforts to pass an anti–poll tax bill mirrored the crusade to pass an antilynching bill throughout the 1930s, particularly the frustration of the bills' advocates and the intransigence of their opponents. Filibusters, the failure of cloture, halfhearted support, and the need to pass "more important" legislation plagued efforts to pass an anti–poll tax bill (not to mention efforts to create a permanent FEPC during the 1940s). This was all depressingly familiar for veterans of the antilynching campaign. Periodic attempts did continue to be made to pass a federal antilynching law, but the focus of the efforts of civil rights groups, primarily the NAACP, shifted toward more tangible goals. This perhaps reflected the increasing public confidence of the association and its allies, but it did not make the prospects for success any brighter.

The poll tax was significant as it underpinned some of the most powerful men in Congress, men who had little mandate even within their own constituencies: in 1936, only a quarter of possible voters used their ballots in the eight poll-tax states; the rest were eliminated from the electoral process by their poverty.[95] In October 1939, Congressman Lee Geyer, a California Democrat, introduced the first unsuccessful anti–poll tax bill. Geyer established the National Committee to Abolish the Poll Tax (NCAPT) in 1941 as an umbrella group for organizations opposing the law. NAACP members were prominent, but the AFL, the Congress of Industrial Organizations (CIO), the YWCA, and the National Negro Congress also lent support.[96] In 1942, Claude Pepper, a Florida Democrat, and Wayland Brooks, a Republican from Illinois, added an amendment to the soldier voting bill suspending the poll tax for soldiers for the duration of the war.[97] The anti–poll tax bill eventually escaped from the House Judiciary Committee and made it to the floor of the House for a vote. George Bender, a Republican congressman from Ohio, was persuaded to take the lead in promoting the bill after realizing that more people voted in his congressional district than in the whole of Mississippi.[98] In another damning indictment of the tax, Rhode Island, then the smallest state in the union (with a population of seven hundred thousand), cast more votes than Alabama, Mississippi, Georgia, Virginia, and South Carolina (with a aggregate population of 11 million) combined.[99]

The bill passed in the House by 254 to 84 on 13 October 1942. George W. Norris (Nebraska), Barkley, and Pepper provided an articulate defense of the bill in the Senate, arguing that the poll tax was not a reasonable qualification for voting. The federal government, they insisted, had a duty to protect the right to vote. Barkley declared: "I know of no more opportune time to try to spread democracy in our country than at a time when we are trying to spread it in other countries and throughout the world."[100] It was, Barkley believed, a question of democracy, not of race: the federal government, therefore, had a right to protect the franchise. Opponents contended that voting was a privilege and not a right; they also declared that it was the sole preserve of the states to determine voting qualifications, and that any attack on this would undermine states' rights. Cloture on the bill predictably failed, and Roosevelt refused to speak out in its defense.[101]

In 1943, Bender, the chairman of the steering committee on the bill, told Dewey that he was "particularly gratified that the Republicans stood almost to a man for the passage of this legislation."[102] He felt, however, that it was important for Republican senators to vote for cloture and requested that Dewey support publicly efforts to pass the bill: "it is essential to pass such legislation in order to demonstrate [at home and abroad] our sincerity in the present war."[103] By 1944, the bill still had not passed. White urged Dewey to use his "strategic position" in the GOP to ask Republican senators to support cloture.[104] Dewey informed White that he had "always fought against the poll tax and every other device to deprive free people of their votes," but White was not convinced.[105] He felt that the governor was dodging the issue as he did not state whether he supported federal or local action or if he would support cloture: "to say one is against the poll tax but refrains from advocation [*sic*] of specific steps to abolish it is not enough."[106] Church attacked White, who had been "playing the New Deal and Roosevelt game since 1933," for attempting to blame the defeat of cloture on the Republican Party and Dewey. The real blame for failure, Church insisted, lay with Roosevelt, who "never fails to speak out on legislation in which he is personally interested."[107] Church suggested that White's "telegraphic barrage" be directed at the White House and the Democratic Party and asserted that "the Negro will not be deceived despite the peregrinations of Walter White's logic."[108]

The *Washington Post* commented that "it would obviously be a political blunder of first-rate magnitude for Governor Dewey to antagonize members of the Senate by injecting himself into the anti–poll tax fight."[109] There was a feeling that Dewey's chances of winning southern votes would be enhanced if he remained silent on the poll tax. If Dewey was cynical enough to kill an antidiscrimination bill in his own state to assuage the feelings of the South, as his critics believed, then there was little chance of him offending the region over the poll tax. The Republicans then decided that the best way to rid the nation of the poll tax was with a constitutional amendment, but this would require the support of three-quarters of both the Senate and the House to become law. If the amendment successfully negotiated Congress, it would then have to be approved by three-quarters of the state legislatures, which the *Crisis* argued could take "until Doomsday." "The senators," it continued, "are emulating Mr. Dewey on his state FEPC bill—stalling until after the election—but like Mr Dewey, they are too, too transparent."[110] White advised Dewey not to seek a constitutional amendment, reminding him that a constitutional amendment abolishing child labor had been passed twenty years previously but had been ratified by only twenty-eight states.[111]

It is possible to see why some saw the Republicans' proposal for combating the poll tax through a constitutional amendment as logical. After the GOP convention, Oliver Randolph, an African American Republican from New Jersey, offered a rejoinder to White over the party's platform, alleging that White had "become a New Deal partisan first and a champion of Negro rights second." Explaining the Republican stand on the poll tax, Randolph argued:

> There are 48 states in the Union. An Amendment to the federal constitution requires ratification by two-thirds of them, or 32 states. Forty states have no poll tax and it is logical to assume that they would favor the amendment. . . . With only 8 poll tax states, constitutional amendment seems the short way of correcting the national suffrage scandal.[112]

This argument may have carried some weight, and generated more debate, had it come from a senior Republican or the presidential candidate himself, but there is little to suggest it was either widely reported or was even the official Republican rationale for advocating a constitutional amendment; moreover, it did not explain the lack of satisfactory answers from the GOP to questions posed regarding civil rights. Dewey's presidential campaign had begun inauspiciously among African Americans.

No anti–poll tax bill was passed in 1944, but demands for legislation did not cease, as a further attempt to enforce cloture on the bill was defeated in the Senate at the end of July 1946 by 39 votes to 33. Those against cloture included seven Republicans from New Hampshire, Connecticut, Maine, Oklahoma, South Dakota, and Colorado.[113] By 1948, with another presidential election looming, an anti–poll tax bill was no nearer becoming law; another bill passed the House in February, but the Republicans continued to argue for a constitutional amendment to abolish the tax.[114] Even Irving Ives, a Republican state senator from New York and a Dewey ally, argued that this was a deeply unsatisfactory way of dealing with the problem.[115] A further attempt to introduce poll-tax legislation was eventually made during the special session of Congress called by Truman in the summer of 1948, but it was abundantly clear that Taft, the de facto Republican leader in the Senate, had no intention of breaking the southern filibuster.[116] Taft did state that he would use every possible parliamentary mechanism to pass the anti–poll tax bill, but if this endeavor failed, he would shelve the bill.[117] Needless to say, the bill did fail, and amid the recriminations Barkley questioned the motivation of the Republicans. Writing privately to White, he questioned "whether they [the Republicans] deliberately steered the Senate into the filibuster or had any semblance of good faith in trying to get action on the measure, it might be unwise for me to conjecture, but at any rate I hope that all those who are interested in this legislation will properly assess the maneuvers of the majority in regard to it."[118] The poll tax would not be finally abolished until the 1960s.

"No Time . . . to Be Ungrateful to True and Tried Friends"

The election of 1944 was a generally low-key affair with Americans preoccupied with the war. Few commentators thought that the Republicans had much chance of defeating Roosevelt, in spite of his health, his decision to run for an unprecedented fourth term, and the gains the Republicans had made in the 1942 midterms. The cast of characters seeking the Republican nomination was much the same as in 1940, with the addition of Governor Harold Stassen of Minnesota, a liberal reformer and internationalist World War II navy veteran; Governor John Bricker of Ohio ("an honest Harding," according to William Allen White); and, potentially, General Douglas MacArthur, a conservative. Dewey, Willkie, and Taft, however, were again the main hopefuls. Willkie's highly publicized "One World" trip in autumn 1942 made him the best-known and most popular Republican in the country, but this popularity was not, as noted, reflected within the party. Many leading Republicans resented not only Willkie's nomination in 1940 but also, crucially, his internationalist approach to foreign policy, and it was this that cost him the 1944 nomination. Willkie felt that he had to run in isolationist Wisconsin if he was to be regarded as a serious contender, a brave gesture but a major tactical error, and having won no delegates from the state, he withdrew from the race, remaining on the fringes of the party until his death.

The prospect of the GOP championing African American rights energetically was no brighter in 1944 than it had been in 1940. Harrison Spangler, the RNC chairman, told White that once the New Deal was defeated in the election, "the Republican party will again undertake its historic task of working for the betterment of the Negro people." White, recalling the southern Democrat–conservative Republican alliance in Congress, was highly skeptical.[119] Moreover, as the 1944 Republican convention approached, the African American press was largely hostile to Dewey. *The Weekly Survey of the Negro Press* reported "close to complete unanimity" in opposing a presidential bid by Dewey, attributed in the main to his apparent ambivalence toward civil rights, particularly the failure of antidiscrimination legislation in New York.[120] It seemed that even African Americans within the Republican Party would remain hostile to Dewey unless he explained why he had thwarted New York's antidiscrimination legislation.[121]

Willkie submitted an alternative platform to the convention that included an extensive section on civil rights. He recognized that Republican legislation guaranteed African American rights after the Civil War but felt that it was strange that the GOP so often retreated behind arguments about states' rights when civil rights were discussed. He argued that the poll tax had to be abolished by federal statute, and that a federal antilynching bill had to be introduced. African Americans, he asserted, did not accept "technical arguments against cloture" in the debates on anti–poll tax and antilynching bills.[122] Furthermore, he said that like all Americans, African Americans feared for their jobs and demanded the right to serve in the armed forces of the United States without discrimination, arguing that "there is nothing more democratic than a bullet or a splinter of steel."[123] Willkie maintained that African Americans did not necessarily trust the Democratic Party but that they were not prepared to abandon it on the strength of "vague assurances," "pious platitudes," or a "1944 version of states' rights doctrine."[124] He recognized that since the beginning of the New Deal, African American voters had become "a determined purposeful unit" while their leaders were "alert and educated and sophisticated" and now saw their plight as part of a worldwide struggle.[125] African Americans merely wanted the rights guaranteed to all Americans, which was "consistent with the very principles upon which the Republican party was founded."[126] African Americans, declared Willkie, should have full equality and their full rights as citizens. The fact that the Republican Party gave African Americans their freedom "makes them more resentful that it should join in acts which prevent them from obtaining the substance of freedom."[127]

This was ignored, and the 1940 candidate was not even invited to the convention, let alone allowed to address it. Even in the absence of their most vocal advocate of African American rights, the Republicans, having nominated Dewey, still managed their most extensive plank ever on "racial and religious intolerance." It advocated a congressional inquiry into segregation and discrimination in the armed forces, vowed to create a *federal* FEPC, pledged to pass a constitutional amendment outlawing the poll tax, and promised "sincere efforts" to end lynching.[128] Never before had a party made such wide-ranging commitments to African American Americans.[129] It was reported, however, that there were fewer African Americans attending the Republican convention in 1944 than in 1940.[130] Of pressing concern was the lack of African American delegates from many potentially pivotal states including New York, Pennsylvania, Ohio, Indiana, New Jersey, California, Oklahoma, Maryland, Tennessee, and Michigan. Indeed, southern states had usually provided the bulk of African American representation at GOP conventions, but southern apportionment had been reduced.

Walter White had at least some praise for the Republican platform, describing the section on an FEPC as "unequivocal and excellent." The rest of the plank garnered less praise: yet again, White wanted to know if the Republicans were advocating federal or state action on lynching; if they meant federal legislation, then "it was utterly futile" without enforcing cloture. As for the military, an investigation into mistreatment of African Americans in the armed forces would not be complete until the war ended. A constitutional amendment to abolish the poll tax was, however, the "most objectionable" aspect of the plank.[131] Even the normally loyal *Topeka/Kansas City Plaindealer* remained unconvinced about the merits of the Republican platform or the sincerity of the party, suggesting that its platform "might have been achieved by the New Deal had it not been blocked by a coalition between southern Democrats and stalwart Republican reactionaries."[132]

The Democratic plank, dismissed as a "splinter" by White, contained precisely forty words and promised only protection under the Constitution; it said nothing about the poll tax, an FEPC, or discrimination in the armed forces.[133] The Democrats also dumped liberal Vice President Henry Wallace in favor of Harry S. Truman, a fairly undistinguished Missouri senator with Confederate roots, as a concession to the South. This combination, the *Crisis* warned, rather hopelessly, could "toss Mr. Roosevelt out of the White House after twelve years."[134] The *New Republic* was similarly concerned that the Democrats' "evasive tactics" had done more to return the black vote to the Republicans than the GOP's "far-reaching platform promises."[135] Nevertheless, the Democrats were confident that the personality of Roosevelt and the record of the New Deal could deliver the African American vote.

Ultimately there was little in either party platform to appeal to African Americans.[136] The Republican platform was the better of the two; its advocacy of a permanent federal FEPC, the *Crisis* believed, gave the GOP a head start in the quest for the African American vote, contrasting with the Democrats' lack of commitment to continue the FEPC, even in its current temporary guise.[137] The *Crisis* expressed hope that the Democrats would do something to distance themselves from their "puerile" platform; if they did not, then many African Americans could be voting Republican. Neither party met the demands of a committee representing twenty-five African American organizations and led by White that appeared at the party conventions.[138]

Evidence from polls supported the contention that the African American vote could be a crucial factor in the outcome of the election. In mid-August, New York, Pennsylvania, Missouri, and Michigan were solidly for Roosevelt, while Kentucky, Illinois, West Virginia, and Indiana were pro-Dewey; New Jersey and Ohio were too close to call. In each of these states, African American voters could be the difference between victory and defeat. There was even speculation from the CIO's Political Action Committee (PAC) that the African American vote in from eight to ten large northern cities could decide the election. The CIO-PAC, working in collaboration with the Democratic National Committee, refused to name these cities, but the *Topeka/Kansas City Plaindealer* suggested that they were New York, Philadelphia, Chicago, Baltimore, Louisville, Detroit, St. Louis, Cleveland, Los Angeles, and Indianapolis.[139] *Look* magazine reported in September 1944 that a 4 percent increase in the Republican vote over 1940 in twelve states would see Dewey elected president.[140] Polls also indicated that the Republicans were losing ground among African Americans in Chicago and that Dewey was running well behind Willkie's showing in 1940.[141] Despite the growing and increasingly recognized importance of the African American vote, it appeared that the Republicans were neither trying nor expecting to make significant gains among African American voters. The Republicans, argued the *Plaindealer*, were doing very little to win this vote, whereas the Democrats "believe the Negro vote does matter in the election and they will have to win it."[142]

Herbert Brownell, Republican campaign manager, appointed C. B. Powell, the editor of the *Amsterdam Star-News* and a recent convert to the GOP, to lead the Republican campaign drive among African Americans.[143] African Americans from the Midwest were soon disappointed with Powell's efforts; they met Brownell in September to discuss reinvigorating the campaign and, if necessary, replacing Powell with Church. Powell was regarded as being too close to Rivers, who was, of course, very close to Dewey, and was being criticized "for his failure to cope with the vigor" of the Democratic National Committee and the CIO-PAC.[144] Powell, a Roosevelt supporter in 1940, was also quoted, on his first day in the job, as saying that the Republicans "have done nothing for Negroes." Deeply dissatisfied, African American Republicans wanted $150,000 to bolster their campaign.[145]

There was also a worrying lack of passion. S. D. Redmond contacted

Brownell in October 1944 after the National Colored Republican Conference in Chicago, reporting "not as much enthusiasm as I would like to have seen." Moreover, the Republican Party was not generating nearly enough support in the African American press, and Redmond suggested that "we should leave off the political and sentimental aspects and go after these papers in a cold-blooded business-like way, and bring their columns to Dewey and Bricker's interest." Concern was also expressed that there were only limited efforts from the western arm of the campaign, based in Chicago, to win African American votes. Redmond was told that in Chicago there were only two men and a sick typist handling African American matters, and he suggested that this was at least partly Brownell's responsibility as he had cut back campaign expenditure. Consequently, not enough was being done to win African American votes.[146]

The main issue in 1944 was the war, or rather, the peace, now that victory seemed to be at hand. Roosevelt's main priority was the successful prosecution of the war, and, having "reluctantly" accepted the nomination, he vowed not to campaign strenuously. This presented Dewey and the Republicans with a number of problems; the GOP had little to campaign against in 1944. Allied victories in 1944 made it, as Mayer points out, "pointless, if not dangerous" to attack Roosevelt's war record, particularly given the GOP's prewar isolationism. Moreover, attacks on the New Deal might encourage workers who had migrated to industrial centers to vote.[147] Perhaps the Republicans' frustration led to Roosevelt accusing them of appealing to intolerance. He even denounced the GOP for copying the propaganda tactics outlined by Hitler in *Mein Kampf*: "you should never use a small falsehood; always a big one, for its very nature would make it more credible, if only you keep repeating it over and over again."[148] The *Crisis* blamed the Republicans for the vitriolic nature of the 1944 campaign, noting, for example, the attacks the GOP made on Sidney Hillman, a Russian-born Jew and the leader of the CIO-PAC.[149] Notwithstanding this, the Democrats were not entirely innocent of injecting malice into the campaign; a Democrat pamphlet entitled *Win with FDR* declared that "US fascists want this man [Dewey] in the White House" and commented upon the Republican candidate's "Hitler mustache."[150] Senators Guy Gillette (Democrat, Idaho) and Warren Barbour (Republican, New Jersey) met to urge both parties to eliminate race hate from the campaign, a sentiment endorsed by Taft.[151]

As in 1940, and indeed every election since Reconstruction, civil rights was a fairly minor issue. Dewey made several references to equality for all and an end to discrimination during the campaign: "there can be—there must be—jobs and opportunity for all, without discrimination on account of race, creed, color or national origin."[152] He later reiterated this: "we need above all to renew our faith; faith in the goodwill of our fellow men regardless of race, creed or color; faith in the limitless future of our country."[153] In October, Roosevelt finally spoke out on an issue of importance to African Americans when he condemned the poll tax. "The right to vote," he declared, "had to be protected without tax or artificial restriction of any kind." Roosevelt also censured Dewey and the GOP over their stance on the soldier vote bill.[154] Speaking later in Boston, Roosevelt condemned all forms of intolerance: "there is no room in it [America] for racial or religious intolerance." America, he argued, was fighting for a world where "men and women of all races, colors and creeds can live and work and speak and worship in peace, freedom and security."[155]

This collection of well-intentioned generalities was as close as either candidate came to making a stand on minority rights. Presidential candidates had always paid lip service to these ideals, but in 1944, in the midst of the fight against fascism, they should have carried greater resonance. Each candidate was committed to the spirit of these principles, but applying them was a different matter. Willkie had perhaps shown in 1940 that taking a high-minded stand would win votes, and this, and more importantly the war, should have made the contest for the liberal center vital in 1944.

The words and actions of leading figures within the GOP were often at odds with the lofty ideals expressed in the party's platform. The NAACP viewed Taft and Vandenberg with suspicion because, among other things, they wanted to make the distribution of relief a state concern. In 1943, the conservative Republican–southern Democrat coalition thwarted a bill giving federal aid to education, the Republicans objecting to the concept of federal aid while the southern Democrats were against its nondiscrimination clause. This coalition was also against the FEPC and the WPA, the latter of which Roosevelt dissolved at the end of 1942. Once again, the actions of the Republicans fell far short of their rhetoric. Dewey's record as governor was at best mixed, but the record of congressional Republicans was almost universally bad.[156] There were, however, exceptions. In 1940, Hamilton Fish introduced a nondiscrimination clause to the selective services bill, which, while it did not end or seek to end segregation, did at least mean that African Americans would be selected impartially. In 1944, he petitioned Secretary of War Henry Stimson, a former Republican, about the failure to employ African American combat troops. Stimson replied that many African Americans were "of lower educational classifications" and "unable to master the techniques of modern weapons."[157] Fish made this response public in the House on 23 February 1944. An ardent isolationist, suspected anti-Semite, and no believer in social equality between whites and African Americans, Fish, ostracized by both Willkie and Dewey, lost his seat in 1944.

The Republicans had, once again, neither given African Americans reason to support them nor offered alternatives to Franklin Roosevelt and the New Deal. The knowledge of the crucial nature of the African American vote could not raise the Republicans from their stupor; they again employed the tactics that had failed in every election since 1932 in halfhearted attempts to regain their former constituency. Even the *Topeka/Kansas City Plaindealer* eventually endorsed Roosevelt: "to turn away from Roosevelt now would be regarded as in-gratitude [*sic*], and this is no time for Negroes of America to be ungrateful to TRUE and TRIED friends."[158] There was a danger, argued Gordon Blaine Hancock, of the Associated Negro Press (ANP), that Dewey would be "a rubber stamp President with a politically bankrupt party behind him," and that this "would be one of the direst political calamities the nation has ever known."[159]

Both parties recognized that the African American vote was increasingly important, argued the *Plaindealer* on the eve of the election, "but Dewey and his advisors hesitated to believe what they saw while President Roosevelt not only saw and believed, he and his crowd acted upon it."[160] If, therefore, Dewey lost the African American vote because he felt that championing states' rights was more important, then he had only himself to blame as he had been constantly warned that the African American vote could prove pivotal. This strategy would win few votes in the South but could potentially cost numerous black votes in vital northern states. Roosevelt, knowing that the South would remain loyal to the party if not to him, was able to appeal to African American voters in important areas of the North: "Roosevelt started out with the firm belief that he could not win without the Negro vote," whereas "Dewey started out with the sly hope that he could win without it and be proud of it." In other words, the Democrats were as forthright as the Republicans were evasive.[161]

The analysts were not proved wrong, with Roosevelt winning 25,602,504 popular votes and 432 in the Electoral College, compared to Dewey's 22,006,285 and 99, respectively. The Democrats won the ten largest cities with a plurality of over 2 million.[162] The GOP lost thirty seats in the House and gained only one in the Senate; even Taft was reelected by a mere 17,740 votes.[163] The gains made in 1942 had proved transitory, had been convincingly reversed, and demonstrated the absence of any real mandate for the party over the preceding two years. Ten of the states where the African American vote was considered crucial were carried by the Democrats with reduced majorities, putting the African American vote into perspective. These ten states contributed 190 Electoral College votes to Roosevelt; had they gone to Dewey, the Republicans would have had a majority of 47. The Republicans won only two states, Indiana and Ohio, where the African American vote was deemed important.[164] It would appear, therefore, that without the African American vote, Roosevelt could not have won the election.

Brownell's analysis of the 1944 election gave the Republicans at least some cause for optimism: outside the Solid South, the Democratic plurality was 1,227,849 out of 41 million votes cast. Furthermore, shifts of less than 5 percent, or 300,000 votes, in fifteen nonsouthern states would have given Dewey 274 electoral votes.[165] In Michigan, New Jersey, and Pennsylvania, a shift of less than 1 percent would have given the states to the Republicans; in Illinois and Maryland, the shift required was less than 2 percent.[166] The Republican Party's election postmortem identified a number of areas where the GOP needed to improve, with Brownell reporting that one of the groups neglected by the party was African Americans:

> There is a real need for national legislation which will improve the position of the Negro race and constructive proposals dealing with such matters as the poll tax, lynching laws, fair employment practices and other matters of concern to this important minority group must be studied and solutions to these problems must be found. We must remember that many of the questions are not capable of easy solutions and that passing laws is not enough. Our party must dedicate itself in fact and in spirit to the goal of helping our Negro citizens to create for themselves a lasting measure of prosperity.[167]

Brownell was one of Dewey's closest and most senior advisors; his assessment, therefore, should have removed any lingering doubts Dewey had about the future importance of securing the African American vote.

Newspapers sympathetic to Dewey attributed Roosevelt's victory to the soldier vote, but the concentration of the African American vote in urban areas enabled the Democrats to carry Illinois, California, Pennsylvania, Maryland, Massachusetts, and Missouri. Part of the problem the Republicans encountered with African American voters resulted from the fact that "the New York crowd ran the show, spent the money and left the old time

Republican leaders out of the picture." Particular resentment was directed toward C. B. Powell and his lackluster campaign to win the black vote.[168] The *Crisis* credited Roosevelt's victory at least in part to the CIO-PAC, and this provided a lesson to African Americans. It was absolutely crucial that, in the future, African Americans worked to get the vote out; the NAACP had made a start by distributing information on the records of congressmen, but this had to be built upon.[169] Gordon Blaine Hancock believed that Republicans had lost despite the fourth-term issue, the breakdown of American traditions brought about by the New Deal, the money showered upon the GOP by business interests, and the support of disgruntled Democrats. If they could not win with this kind of support, then "they simply cannot win at all."[170] In the 1930s, the Republicans could blame their electoral failures on the Depression, but it was now clear that there were simply more Democrats than Republicans in the country.[171]

Brownell had finally recognized what African Americans had known since 1932: black voters were an increasingly vital part of the American electorate, and politicians ignored them at their peril. What remained to be seen was whether or not the Republicans, furnished with conclusive proof of this, would do anything about it. The GOP was also reminded by the ever-dwindling band of African Americans loyal to it that it had lost every election since the African American vote defected to the Democrats. It was clearly time for the Republicans to live up to the distant memory of Lincoln and the more recent memory of their own platform pledges. Dewey, the party's titular leader and still the governor of New York, was young enough and well regarded enough within the party to be given a second chance in 1948. Over the next four years he would be continually reminded why he lost in 1944, but had he learned anything? Would he court the African American vote next time? And, crucially, would the Republican Party finally live up to its historic responsibility to African Americans?

5

Jockeying, Buck-Passing, and Double-Talk

A major impediment to Republican hopes of regaining the African American vote and, much more importantly, the White House disappeared when Franklin Roosevelt died in April 1945. Harry Truman's assumption of the presidency did little to inspire African Americans. The journeyman senator from the border state of Missouri—and the choice of southern Democrats in 1944—had replaced the most popular white politician among African Americans since Lincoln, and it was by no means certain that the black vote would stay with the late president's party.[1] With the defeat of 1944 still fresh in the memory, and Brownell's assertion that the black vote was vital to the future success of the GOP, the Republicans—and Dewey in particular—now had the opportunity to respond positively. In fact, no governor in the country could boast more racially progressive legislation than Dewey by the time of the 1948 election. Nevertheless, Dewey yet again failed to win the African American vote and yet again failed to win the presidency. It is essential, therefore, to attempt to reconcile his good record on civil rights with his failure to win or even court the African American vote in 1948. Dewey was repeatedly reminded of the importance of the African American vote but still took no action; this may seem superficially perplexing, but Dewey, confident of victory, did not think it necessary to court any special-interest vote.

By the 1940s, the focus of the NAACP had shifted away from the antilynching crusade toward abolishing the poll tax and creating a permanent FEPC. The controversy over the FEPC rumbled on during the spring and summer of 1945 and followed the frustratingly well-worn path trod by the antilynching and anti–poll tax campaigns. The agency was, of course, a temporary wartime measure, and a bill to extend its lifetime had languished in the Rules Committee since the Labor Committee approved it in February.[2] The FEPC had plenty of enemies; for example, the Russell Amendment of 1944, proposed by Senator Richard Russell of Georgia, meant that FEPC appropriations had to be approved by Congress, effectively destroying the autonomy of the agency.[3] As always, southern Democrats were vocal in their opposition, and, by the end of June 1945, the Senate Rules Committee proposed giving the agency $125,000 to wind up its affairs. Mississippi's Theodore Bilbo vowed to hold the floor of the Senate until the end of the fiscal year to prevent fellow Democrat Dennis Chavez of New Mexico, a prominent supporter of the legislation, from presenting an amendment to give the FEPC $450,000.[4]

The newly installed president worked behind the scenes for FEPC legislation during the spring of 1945, and by the summer was publicly backing a permanent agency, but by this stage any prospect of passing legislation was gone.[5] The debate in the House on the FEPC threatened to delay other measures, particularly a $771 million appropriation for other war agencies.[6] Southerners eventually sought a compromise, not only fearing that the FEPC could become permanent but also concerned about the possibility of thousands of war workers going without pay if the deadlock continued.[7] There were suggestions that there was sufficient support for Chavez's bill, but eventually Barkley sought a compromise and won a $250,000 appropriation for the agency, which in turn freed funding for other agencies. It was suspected that Barkley did not want to see the Republicans claim the credit for prolonging the life of the FEPC, and not everyone was satisfied with the new appropriation.[8] Liberal Republican Wayne Morse of Oregon protested, but it was apparent to him that the situation was hopeless.[9] The *New York Times* called the outcome a "qualified victory" for the FEPC but argued that such a debate should not be going on during a war.[10] Neither side, therefore, wanted to be seen to be hampering the war effort with partisan bickering.

In August, Republican senators Joseph Ball (Minnesota) and Harold Burton (Ohio) declared that they would insist upon the creation of a permanent FEPC in the fall and could rely on the support of other Republican senators. Seeing an opportunity to embarrass the administration, they noted that the Democrats had left the FEPC out of their program.[11] Truman soon rectified this, and in September an FEPC became part of his twenty-one-point program. He told Congress that "substantial progress" had been made during the war to eliminate discrimination, and that efforts would continue during the postwar period with the creation of a permanent FEPC.[12] Yet by the end of the month, the House had blocked an FEPC bill.[13]

By the end of 1945, the FEPC, ordered by Congress to cease operating in June 1946, appeared doomed. Truman had made it clear that he wanted to see an end to discrimination in the federal government, but it was equally apparent that a peacetime FEPC would be immensely controversial. He issued Executive Order 9664 in December 1945, further reducing the status and power of the FEPC to the extent that it became a mere fact-finding agency. Chavez remained bullish, vowing to reintroduce an FEPC bill during the next session of Congress.[14] Most of the FEPC's offices had been closed and most of its funding withdrawn, but by the start of 1946 Truman wanted it to do a survey of discrimination against minorities after the war. "Thus," sighed the *Crisis*, "we are back where we started; making surveys to find out what everyone already knows, namely that there is brutal prejudice [against minorities]." More research would simply make it more difficult than ever to pass legislation creating a permanent FEPC.[15]

By February 1946, it was apparent that the bill for a permanent FEPC was going to be filibustered to death in the Senate; yet again, a tiny minority of senators was conspiring to thwart a piece of legislation that the majority, at least publicly, wanted. On 9 February 1946, 48 senators (22 Democrats, 25 Republicans, and one Progressive) voted for cloture; 36 (28 Democrats and 8 Republicans) did not.[16] Once more the will of the Congress and the American people was being obstructed by a small group of southern Democrats, although the FEPC bill was effectively killed by the refusal of those supporting it to back cloture.[17] The *Crisis*, calling the three-week spectacle in the Senate a "sham battle," alleged with some justification that each party was "striving to make a record without actually passing this bill." It also noted that every congressman was up for reelection in November, and that African American voters would exact vengeance on those who had not supported the bill.[18] Roy Wilkins vowed that, henceforth, the NAACP was going to use its influence to defeat those senators who voted against cloture or "willfully absented themselves from the session at which voting occurred."[19] The *Crisis* was prepared to acknowledge, however, that Barkley had given the bill his full support, whereas Taft "contributed nothing . . . but parliamentary guile."[20] By the time of the midterm elections of 1946, an FEPC law was no closer.

"Let's Wake Up Republicans"

The faith of African American Republicans in their party continued to ebb after the defeat of 1944 as the party persistently failed to keep even its most basic promises. Robert Church took the lead in demanding publicly that the GOP pay more attention to the requirements of African Americans and the necessity of winning their votes, while Francis Rivers did so privately.

Between 1944 and 1948, the Republicans were continually reminded of just how important African American votes were and the extreme folly of ignoring this almost universally accepted fact. No one was more aware of this than Herbert Brownell, yet he refused to meet African American Republicans in early 1945, despite them coming to New York at their own expense. Church then lambasted the Republican campaign of 1944 and specifically Brownell's tactics. Brownell's decision to appoint C. B. Powell, "one of Charley Michelson's Colored Democrats," to lead efforts among African Americans in the East was again criticized, as was the black leadership that had been chosen without consulting African American Republican leaders.[21] Church believed that without the "unpopular" appointment of Powell, the Republicans may well have won the three hundred thousand votes in fifteen nonsouthern states needed to put Dewey in the White House.[22] The GOP's approach to African Americans was, Church attested, backward-looking and politically unsustainable; the Republican National Committee, unlike the Democratic Party, the CIO-PAC, and even the Communist Party, did not have a single African American in any policy-forming position. "Every major political organization has seen the light but us," complained Church. It was also imperative that any African Americans appointed be "from voting states," a clear effort to curtail whatever influence Perry Howard and his ilk still clung to.[23]

Church, his concerns ignored, called a meeting of African American Republican leaders in August 1945 to awaken Republicans from their "lethargy towards the largest single minority" and demand more African Americans in the RNC and in policy-formulating positions.[24] He again reminded Republicans that since they had lost the black vote they had not won a presidential election and were unlikely to do so until they regained it. Church asserted that "the time has now come for us to corral our forces and by specific demand point out the way for the Republican party to recapture the Negro Vote."[25] Later that month, African American Republicans convened, under the chairmanship of Church, as the Republican American Committee and issued a "Declaration to the Republican Party." The declaration was fairly wide-ranging, but the bulk of it dealt with familiar themes, for instance, its assertion that, if it were to recapture the White House, the party's "entire attitude and strategy must be completely changed as it affects colored citizens." The committee was alarmed at the exodus of African Americans from the party and the party's lack of commitment to equal rights. It also demanded that African American Republicans be allowed to appoint their own leaders: "We do PROTEST the imposition of HAND PICKED

LEADERS not of our choosing by the Republican National Committee." It noted that there was no African American organization within the party until a few weeks prior to elections, and that African Americans were excluded from policy-formulating positions. Furthermore, they demanded that Brownell meet Church, challenging the party chairman to confirm that the GOP would serve African American interests by seeking legislation for full employment, a civil rights bill for Washington, D.C., and antilynching and anti–poll tax laws. The lack of an FEPC also perturbed the committee, especially as it had been part of the party's platform in 1944. The GOP, therefore, had to vote for cloture on the FEPC bill and endorse adequate state FEPC laws based on New York's state antidiscrimination law.[26]

The *Baltimore Afro-American* commented after the Republicans' victory in the midterm elections of 1946 that perennial claims that they did not possess the votes to pass civil rights legislation were no longer valid; indeed, "if the GOP means business . . . it now has the best opportunity in years to prove it."[27] In January 1947, the *Afro-American* received a reply from Joseph Martin that was astonishing in its honesty. The Republican Speaker of the House of Representatives, who had apparently taken the lead in endeavoring to regain the African American vote in 1936, told a group of African American leaders that the party would not be pursuing an FEPC bill:

> The FEPC plank in the 1944 Republican platform was a bid for the Negro vote, and they did not accept the bid. They went out and voted for Roosevelt. I'll be frank with you. We are not going to pass an FEPC bill, but it has nothing to do with the Negro vote. We are supported by New England and Middle Western industrialists who would stop their contributions if we passed a law that would compel them to stop religious as well as racial discrimination in employment. I am not saying that I agree with them, but that is the situation we face, so we may as well be realistic. We intend to do a lot for the Negroes, but we can't afford to pass the FEPC bill. . . . We have a number of mavericks in our party who may not go along with us on needed labor legislation, so we may need some voters from the other side until this issue is taken care of. After the labor legislation is out if the way, we may be able to pass the poll tax bill.[28]

This startling admission encapsulated the Republican attitude toward civil rights. It can only have further eroded the ever-fading hopes of loyal African Americans that the party would take positive action on civil rights, and it also illustrated that the GOP was still very much the party of business, and that where business interests and civil rights clashed, the party hierarchy would side with business. It was a frank admission that the FEPC plank in 1944 had been a political gambit, and it was an equally frank admission that the gambit had failed. As always, bigger issues took precedence, in this case the impending Taft-Hartley Labor Act, and politics rather than sentiment would continue to dictate Republican policy. The best thing that could be said of Martin's statement was that at least it was honest.[29]

In August 1948, the Republican American Committee issued a press release, expressing its disappointment that the first Republican-controlled Congress in sixteen years had not, despite platform pledges, taken any action on civil rights and economic problems. The GOP faced serious problems unless this was rectified, and "the colored voter will not be deceived by legislative jockeying, buckpassing and double talk." The committee restated its demands and urged the party to "nurture and cultivate the noticeable trend of colored voters back to our party" in 1946, but to do this, the "entire attitude and strategy" toward African Americans had to change. The committee again resolved that antilynching and anti–poll tax bills had to be "must" legislation; moreover, the party had to appoint a special committee to examine the relationship between African Americans and the GOP. Finally, party principles had to be enshrined in a bill of rights.[30]

This was militant stuff from the Republican American Committee, but it was telling Brownell nothing new. In addition to his analysis immediately after Dewey's defeat in 1944, in late 1945 Brownell urged Republicans to take a more considered approach to winning votes, including appeals to special-interest groups. Again, he stressed the importance of African American voters and "the need for a careful and accurate presentation of the Republican point of view" to them.[31] Close contact, he argued, had to be maintained between the party and African American voters; the creation, in November 1945, of the National Council of Negro Republicans, chaired by Joseph V. Baker, was a step in the right direction. Brownell published a further report in April 1946, which recognized that since 1936 the African American voter had become increasingly important in at least thirteen states and was "an integral part of the electorate and his influence is strong in all close congressional districts where he resides."[32] Brownell declared:

> The Republican Party should support unequivocally the rights of Negroes to full citizenship in the whole of the United States. . . . The Democratic Party is so constituted that it must deny those rights. . . . I cannot impress upon you too strongly my belief that the National

Committee should increase its efforts among the Negro voters of the country.[33]

This was a potentially radical departure for the GOP, and, at this stage of Truman's presidency, its criticisms were perfectly valid.

Brownell, perhaps in an effort to placate Church, appointed an African American, Valores "Val" Washington, as executive assistant to the campaign chairman of the Republican National Committee to establish a minorities division in April 1946.[34] In another, undated, memorandum that he wrote as party chairman, Brownell once again stressed the importance of the African American vote, urging the GOP to "take a definite stand of true liberalism" toward African Americans and noting that the "loss of that voting bloc can be directly attributed to our own carelessness."[35] Brownell reminded Republicans, erroneously, that one of the founding objectives of the party was the freeing of the slaves, and that, had "the immortal Lincoln" not been assassinated, then "the complete emancipation of the Negro would have been accomplished."[36] He recognized that African Americans were becoming increasingly vocal in demanding their constitutional rights and "if the Republican party has the moral fortitude to sincerely uphold the law of the land I am very certain that the Negro voter will return to the Republican party to which he so justly should still be a part."[37]

In October 1947, the party's monthly publication *The Republican* recognized the need to regain the African American vote. In an article entitled "Wake Up, Republicans," J. N. Wagner, a Chicago lawyer, asserted that there was much to be gained by courting African Americans as they held the balance of power in up to seventeen states.[38] He believed that the Democratic Party had enticed black voters with the FEPC, and that the GOP needed to regain their trust. The party had to mount a "militant campaign . . . to prove to the Negro that his welfare was of vital importance to the Republicans." For a start, Republicans needed to plan better "not six weeks before the coming election." Wagner believed that up to a half million African American veterans could be voting in the South, and that they should be cultivated instead of southern lily-whites. The GOP should also seek to deny representation to southern states denying the vote to African Americans.[39] Wagner maintained that African Americans voted Democratic because they received more, and better, representation in that party. Could African Americans really continue to see the GOP as "their" party, he wondered? He concluded that "if Republicans will only befriend the Negro today, that Negro will vote Republican tomorrow. Let's wake up, Republicans."[40] In this same issue of the *Republican*, the demands of Church's Republican American Committee, first aired in 1945, were repeated, demonstrating how little had changed in the intervening two years.[41]

External African American pressure was also put on the Republican Party. The NAACP wrote to the Republican National Committee at the end of March 1946 with its perennial demands for an FEPC, an antilynching bill, an anti–poll tax law, a housing bill, and the repudiation of the conservative Republican–southern Democrat coalition. The association again noted that although an FEPC was advocated in the GOP platform in 1944, the party's record on the issue was decidedly mixed. If, for example, the Republicans voted for cloture, then an anti–poll tax law could be passed in weeks. The association warned that African Americans would pay very close attention to the Republican stance on these issues in the elections of 1946 and 1948.[42]

As the 1948 GOP convention approached, the "Continuations Committee of Negro Organizations," representing twenty-one organizations with 6 million members, outlined what African Americans wanted from the party of Lincoln. The committee was not approaching the Republican Party with high expectations as the GOP, despite its success in the 1946 midterms, had still not implemented any of its 1944 platform commitments. The Continuations Committee pointed out that an antilynching bill had failed as had an amendment to the selective service act exempting military personnel from the poll tax. One of the main reasons for African American realignment, it declared, was "the cavalier treatment" of African Americans by Republican leaders. It was reiterated that African Americans were no longer tied to any party, would refuse to be persuaded by the platitudes of Republican platform writers, and would demand that the GOP "live up to its pledged word."[43] It is abundantly clear, therefore, that Dewey had ample evidence, from some of his closest allies, from voices within and outside of the Republican Party, of the vital importance of the African American vote long before the election of 1948. What remained to be seen was how he responded as he sought the presidency for a second time.

"I Mean Business on This Thing"

Defeated in his bid for the presidency in 1944, Dewey returned to Albany to continue as governor of New York. Launching his new legislative program in January 1945, he advocated the passage of an antidiscrimination bill. Dewey, of course, had been blamed for the failure of an earlier effort to pass similar legislation, and this renewed effort was not without considerable opposition; the idea of a state government acting as an enforcer of minority rights was a radical departure. As well as those who simply opposed the bill on ideological grounds, there were those who claimed that legislation against discrimination, on both the local and the national level, would actually exacerbate the problem. Nevertheless, Dewey emphasized the need for legislation against discrimination in his speech to the New York State Legislature in January 1945. He recognized that legislation alone would not solve the problem but stressed that "action should be taken to place our state in the forefront of the nation in the handling of this vital issue."[44]

At the end of January, the State Commission Against Discrimination (SCAD), chaired by Republican state senator Irving Ives, published its report. Ives had been appointed by Dewey in the wake of the failure of the 1944 bill and was supported by Democratic state senate leader Elmer F. Quinn. The *New York Times* predicted that the antidiscrimination bill could be "one of the most controversial" bills of the new session, but Ives steeled himself for the battle ahead, declaring, "I mean business on this thing."[45] A new commission, with an annual budget of $300,000, would protect the right to employment without discrimination on account of race, creed, color, or national origin. It would seek to do this through "conciliation, persuasion and conference" in the first instance but could seek redress through the courts and could prosecute offenders if necessary. The bill viewed discrimination as "un-American" and punishable by a fine of $5,000 or a year in prison, but stressed that the problem was not insurmountable as those employers who integrated their workforces during the war were "now generous in their praise" of minority workers.[46] Dewey, initially taciturn about the bill, soon declared it "one of the great social advances of our time."[47] He also apparently told a delegation demanding the passage of the bill, including Francis Rivers and the NAACP's Thurgood Marshall, that he wanted it passed without amendments.[48] The *New York Times* believed that Dewey's endorsement would convince wavering Republicans to back the SCAD; indeed, he met with opponents of the bill in an attempt to enlist their support.[49]

At the end of February, the SCAD, or Ives-Quinn, bill passed the New York Assembly by 109 to 32 without amendment.[50] The bill then passed the Senate by a vote of 49 to 6 and was signed into law by Dewey on 12 March 1945.[51] The *Crisis* was fulsome in its praise: "successful passage of the measure is striking evidence of what can be accomplished when the forces of fair play are properly organized to combat discrimination in employment."[52] The passage of the bill clearly demonstrated Dewey's skill as a chief executive as well as firmly establishing him as the leading progressive force within the Republican Party.

Dewey may have been slow to endorse the Ives-Quinn bill, but he was quick to praise it. He told the New York NAACP: "it has been a matter of deep gratification for me that we have made such great progress in our state this year in inter-racial relations."[53] In a radio address, he reassured New Yorkers that the new law was not designed to "tell you who you may have in your home as domestic help or guests or roomers, or that it may tell employers who they may hire and who they may not hire." The law, he stressed, merely upheld the Constitution.[54] Democratic state chairman Paul Fitzpatrick attacked Dewey for claiming credit for the Ives-Quinn law, suggesting that it "was forced upon him and the Republican party." "Public opinion," continued Fitzpatrick, "was far ahead of him and he caught up with it only as a matter of political expediency."[55]

There is evidence that the governor was not as enthusiastic about the Ives-Quinn law as he appeared publicly; in a conversation with Ives, he reputedly exclaimed: "For God's sake, Irv, you really care about this thing. Why?" Ives apparently replied, "For God's sake."[56] Dewey's ambivalence did not prevent him from taking credit for the law; but in doing so, he tended to stress the "undramatic" approach that it took. Dewey emphasized this to the Negro Labor Committee:

> Most gratifying of all, to me, is the widespread acceptance of the spirit of our new law. We have, indeed, a new approach, through sober, constructive leadership. We seek to educate, to convince, to break down bars, to open doors, to create where hostility existed, a cordial welcome. We look to the day when, truly, no man shall be deprived of equal opportunity because of race, religion or national origin.[57]

The law rid New York of Jim Crow trains and saw four times as many African American women employed in sales and clerical work. It also set precedents for other civil rights legislation during Dewey's tenure as governor. On 5 April 1948, for example, he signed the New York State Fair Education Practices Act, outlawing racial and religious discrimination in higher education. Sponsored by Elmer F. Quinn and Lewis Olliffe, a Republican, it became law in September.[58] By 1950, a similar law prohibited discrimination in public housing. Dewey biographer Richard Norton Smith sees Dewey as an effective proponent of African American rights because he "stressed education over headlines and reconciliation over the sound and fury of post-war America," something he did without shocking the GOP at large or imitating the Democrats.[59] The question that remained was whether Dewey could translate his record into votes on a national level.

The Ives-Quinn law could have provided the template for legislative action by the Republican Party on civil rights on the national level as it demonstrated what could be done with a thoughtful approach to the problem of discrimination.[60] Here was a successful law that commanded bipartisan support and was untainted by overt expediency on the part of its advocates. Clearly, there were those elements in New York's Republican Party who were deeply opposed, and their concerns would have been shared by other Republicans nationally, but a coalition of moderate Republicans and liberal Democrats could have mirrored their New York counterparts and championed similar legislation in the Congress.

"An American Charter of Human Freedom"

When Roosevelt died, many commentators wondered if the African American vote would remain loyal to the Democrats or become truly independent. On the eve of the 1948 presidential election, Henry Lee Moon, a senior NAACP member who was involved in the CIO-PAC, wrote that African Americans had voted for Roosevelt and not his party, expressing his suspicion that they would not vote as a bloc as they had done in previous elections. He stressed, however, that their support remained the vital factor in those states that had been crucial to Roosevelt's victory in 1944; echoing, or rather promoting, NAACP doctrine, he noted that the influence of African Americans came from the "strategic diffusion" of their votes in marginal states.[61] Walter White, dusting off the argument he had been expounding for nearly twenty years, agreed: "no person and no organization can deliver the Negro vote."[62] It appeared for the first time that the African American vote would have to be truly earned. Although the memory of Roosevelt was fresher than that of Lincoln, there was a feeling that Truman could squander his predecessor's legacy. Neither party, therefore, could confidently rely on history, distant or recent, to deliver the African American vote.

In the early days of the Truman presidency, 87 percent of Americans felt that the unassuming Missourian was doing a good job.[63] Within eighteen months, this had changed dramatically. He was ridiculed in the press and was viewed as the most incapable incumbent since Andrew Johnson succeeded Abraham Lincoln. Worse still, with an election looming, he had alienated both labor and farmers, two constituencies utterly indispensable to the Democrats' electoral coalition.[64] Economically, the predicted post-war depression never materialized; unemployment was low and business thrived, but the cost of living had risen, and there was a shortage of housing, consumer goods, and even meat. Americans' other concerns in the postwar world revolved around reconversion to a peacetime economy and the threat posed by the Soviet Union.[65]

Truman accepted the advice of Bob Hannegan, the Democratic Party chairman, not to involve himself in the 1946 midterm elections. Most Democrats running for office neither mentioned him nor sought his endorsement; some even played recordings of Roosevelt's speeches to bolster their chances. For many, it was not enough. As predicted, the Republicans won both houses of Congress, for the first time since 1928. In the House, Republicans now outnumbered Democrats by 246 to 188; in the Senate, the margin was 52 to 38. The Democrats also lost Chicago, Detroit, New York, and Jersey City, while the Republicans now occupied a majority of the country's governor's mansions.

Many Republicans believed that their new mandate meant the end of the New Deal. The Republican congressional leadership, which fell into the hands of conservatives such as Taft and Martin, certainly thought so as they set about trying to dismantle the Roosevelt legacy. There was a sharing of labor between Taft and Vandenberg in the Senate: Vandenberg took charge of foreign affairs while Taft dealt with domestic policy. Nevertheless, the divisions that had plagued the party for a generation still remained; a schism remained over foreign policy, and there was reluctance among more liberal elements to utterly destroy the New Deal. As with the midterms of 1942, the GOP mistook a protest for a mandate.

The attitude of African Americans in 1946 is difficult to gauge with any accuracy. The Republican National Committee estimated that the party had won about half of the African American vote, gaining the majority of it in Illinois and making substantial gains in Pennsylvania.[66] Nevertheless, as many other traditionally Democrat voters had voted for the Republicans, this should not have necessarily been seen as a repudiation of the Democrats by African Americans. Yet the Democrats had reason to be concerned. African American leaders believed that the African American vote would desert the Democrats due to the party's "Bilboism," the death of Roosevelt, and the apparent sidelining of Eleanor Roosevelt. There was also concern about the party's indifference toward an FEPC and the continuing influence of southerners. This must have made worrying reading for Democrats. The Republicans' analysis of the results suggested that their success was no mere protest vote, arguing instead that it was the GOP's program and disgruntlement about excessive bureaucracy that had attracted voters.[67]

For the first eighteen months of the Truman presidency, the low expectations of African Americans were justified. Truman limited himself to gestures such as, for example, supporting the FEPC bill when it had little chance of passage and urging the end of the poll tax without enforcing the Supreme Court's "white primary" ruling of 1944.[68] Yet Truman needed to demonstrate to liberal elements in his party that he could be a decisive leader; in the fall of 1946, civil rights provided such an opportunity. Mob violence against African Americans escalated throughout 1945 and 1946, and, after a number of particularly vicious lynchings, Truman finally met the National Emergency Committee to End Mob Violence on 19 September 1946.[69] This group, led by Walter White, gave the president shocking details about attacks on African Americans and warned him that this was hurting America's image abroad. As a direct result of this meeting, Truman formed the President's Committee on Civil Rights (PCCR). He had actually already decided to form a committee to investigate civil rights abuses but chose this meeting as the ideal time to make it public. "Here was," argues William Berman, "an ingenious solution that would serve Truman's political needs by allowing him through symbolic action to improve his standing among northern liberals while, conversely avoiding the alienation of the South."[70]

There was a very deliberate shift in Truman's attitude toward African Americans and civil rights after the 1946 congressional elections. Henceforth Truman realized that he needed the African American vote if he was to remain resident in the White House after 1948.[71] Truman, under attack over strikes, rising prices, as well as the sacking of Henry Wallace as secretary of commerce, deemed it wise to wait until December 1946 before issuing Executive Order 9808 to create the PCCR. NAACP influence on the PCCR was plain to see. Four of White's recommendations—Frank P. Graham, Franklin Roosevelt Jr., Dorothy Till, and Channing Tobias—were appointed to the committee. Two other members of the fifteen-strong committee, Sadie T. Alexander and Morris L. Ernst, were also NAACP allies. The NAACP could expect, therefore, to have, at the very least, indirect input into the committee.[72]

The PCCR symbolized White and Truman's interdependence. If Truman were genuine, then the NAACP could secure a number of its aims; if he were not, then the association's credibility would suffer in African American communities and it would also be isolated on the national political stage by being so closely identified with the Democratic Party.[73] An indication of the importance of the new alliance between Truman and the NAACP came in June 1947, when Truman became the first president to address the association's annual conference. While this was of huge symbolic importance, Truman did not make any specific promises.[74]

In October 1947, the recommendations of the committee were announced and proved to be more wide-ranging than Truman had expected; nevertheless, the commission's report, *To Secure These Rights*, became the blueprint of the civil rights agenda.[75] Truman commended the report as "an American charter of human freedom" but refused to say how much of it he was prepared to implement.[76] As he had encouraged the committee, he had to endorse at least some of its findings, which he did by early 1948. The recommendations of the PCCR required congressional approval, meaning that this was not, therefore, a presidential crusade for civil rights, and Truman continued to believe that, like Roosevelt, he could keep African Americans and white southerners relatively happy. When it became apparent, however, that southern opposition was going to be more militant than at first expected, he shelved plans for a civil rights bill; at this stage, Truman was disinclined to stand up to the South.

In January 1948, the Republican Policy Committee announced its intention to pass antilynching, anti–poll tax, and FEPC legislation in the current session. Antilynching would be given priority, while the other two measures would be dropped if a long filibuster seemed likely.[77] This may have been in response to *To Secure These Rights*, but it was almost certainly an attempt to preempt Truman on civil rights. In February 1948, Truman proposed a ten-point legislative program, including measures to end lynching and Jim Crow and the establishment of a permanent FEPC. The omnibus civil rights bill, as it became known, was the first-ever special message to Congress on civil rights and was, in fact, the strongest civil rights program ever proposed. Barkley, who had not been consulted, knew that southerners would be outraged by the bill and refused to sponsor it.[78] The *Washington Post* suggested that Truman would do little to see civil rights legislation passed, arguing that his real motivation was to embarrass the Republicans and the Eightieth Congress by making it apparent to African American voters that the GOP had no interest in civil rights.[79] Gary Donaldson agrees: "clearly, the February 2 message was . . . steeped in the political necessities of the election of 1948."[80]

The Republicans continued their own tentative steps in the civil rights arena. On 6 February, the Senate Labor and Public Welfare Committee voted 7 to 5 to release Irving Ives's bill to create a permanent National Committee Against Discrimination in Employment, in effect, an FEPC law.[81] A decision on the priority of civil rights bills was to be made by a conference of Republican senators. The Republican Policy Committee would then make recommendations, but Taft emphasized that the Marshall Plan would take precedence (although Senate and House policy makers were cautiously optimistic that a filibuster on the antilynching bill could be broken).[82] The Republicans clearly believed that there was political capital to be made from civil rights. Chairman Carroll Reece, in a letter to party activists, claimed that the Democrats had done "nothing tangible" on civil rights. He defended the GOP's record, declaring that civil rights legislation had always been passed in the House "with overwhelmingly Republican support."[83] He claimed that the reason these efforts had failed was because of the use of the filibuster by southern Democrats, and he reminded readers that the Democrats had controlled Congress since 1932 without passing any civil rights legislation, whereas the recent Republican record at the state level, particularly in New York, New Jersey, and Connecticut (both of which had followed the Empire State's example), was excellent.[84]

By March, Truman abandoned efforts to pass the omnibus civil rights bill due to greater than expected southern resistance.[85] In April, after a secret vote, Republican senators decided to support the antilynching bill ahead of the anti–poll tax bill; Taft argued that the antilynching bill stood the best chance of success, but this meant, in effect, that other civil rights bills were being set aside indefinitely.[86] Before long, however, even the antilynching bill was threatened as Congress was giving priority to military matters due to the escalation in Cold War tensions.[87] The motivation behind this momentary Republican concern for civil rights was undoubtedly dictated by political necessity and the desire to make things awkward for the Democrats; civil rights was, after all, potentially the final full stop in Truman's political obituary.

6

Dewey Defeats Truman

As the election of 1948 approached and the prospect of a Truman defeat grew ever more likely, the president and his advisers decided to actively seek the northern African American vote. A secret memorandum written by James Rowe entitled "The Politics of 1948" recognized that the African American vote, Democratic, he argued, since 1932, had been a major factor in the Democrats' victory in 1944.[1] The "balance of power" theory, Rowe ventured, explained Dewey's "assiduous and continuous cultivation of the New York Negro vote" and the passage of the SCAD.[2] New York Democrats believed that Dewey would carry New York in 1948 because he commanded the support of African Americans and Italians.[3] Moreover, thanks to Walter White and other leaders, the African American voter had become a "hard-boiled trader" who was deeply concerned by the dominance of southerners in the Democratic Party and their efforts to block civil rights legislation. Republicans were well aware of this and, therefore, had nothing to lose by championing civil rights legislation: if it succeeded, they could take the credit; if it failed, they could blame the Democrats. To counter this, the Democrats had to emphasize the improvement in the economic conditions of African Americans since 1932, although this strategy had "worn a bit thin." New tactics, rather than mere gestures, were needed to ensure that African Americans did not vote Republican in the key states of Illinois, Ohio, and New York.[4]

Rowe maintained that the Republicans would advocate an FEPC and measures against the poll tax and lynching at the next session of Congress. The president should, therefore, respond by "recommending measures to protect the rights of minority groups." Crucially, he believed that "the South can be considered safely Democratic" and "can be safely ignored." The South's only importance stemmed from its representatives in Congress, and alienating it was "the lesser of two evils."[5] Truman, he felt, had to deliver specific measures to specific constituencies—Jews, African Americans, and farmers, for example—and directly address potentially controversial issues that affected these constituencies. A memorandum from Oscar Ewing of the DNC supported this analysis:

> There is no danger of losing the South. It will neither go Republican nor vote for Wallace. In any event, however, it takes a considerable number of southern states to equal the importance of such states as New York, Pennsylvania and Illinois. . . . A split in the southern wing of the party will do no harm politically. . . . There is, therefore, everything to be gained and nothing tangible to be lost by making the most forthright and dramatic statement on the issue [civil rights] and backing it up with equally dramatic and forthright action. Every attempt to compromise loses the votes that count.[6]

Truman accepted these recommendations in part, and, although his conclusions proved prescient in most respects, Rowe (and Ewing) seriously underestimated southern opposition, causing the president to delay putting forward civil rights measures, and overestimated the GOP's commitment to civil rights.

By June 1948, Truman was being urged to recall Congress because "this election can only be won by bold and daring steps."[7] This would have had a number of benefits, including highlighting the record of the Eightieth Congress ("the glass jaw of the Republican Party," according to *Harper's* columnist Elmer Davis) and forcing Dewey to defend it.[8] This was likely to embarrass Dewey and would split the GOP on a number of issues including housing, foreign policy, and social security; these tactics would also allow Truman to be portrayed as a crusader for ordinary people. Yet this strategy remained potentially hazardous. Of particular concern was the possibility that the Republicans would introduce civil rights legislation and cause a southern filibuster. It was again emphasized that "the election will be won or lost in the northern, Midwestern and western states. The South cannot win or lose the election for the Democratic Party." Truman could claim credit for civil rights legislation only as long as Democrats, not Republicans, introduced it.[9] Democratic strategists also reckoned that if Truman could win the West and the labor vote, he would emerge victorious even if Dewey managed to win New York, Pennsylvania, Illinois, New Jersey, Ohio, and Massachusetts.[10]

By the time of the Democratic National Convention in July 1948, Truman's priority was to be renominated, and as a result he downplayed civil rights. Having been renominated, he was then forced to accept a more far-reaching, Americans for Democratic Action (ADA)–sponsored, civil rights plank than he had wanted.[11] This in turn caused many southern delegates, although not as many as feared, to leave and eventually form the States' Rights Democratic ("Dixiecrat") Party.[12] Ironically, the Dixiecrats could have done more to thwart civil rights had they remained within the party; the southern bolt, therefore, made poor political sense and lifted any further obstacles to the embrace of civil rights by the party.[13] Dixiecrat posturing, therefore, insulated Truman from his party's racists and helped ensure continued backing from northern African Americans.[14]

Regardless of the pressures on Truman, the consequences of the Dixiecrat walkout were immediate and positive. Two weeks after the convention, Truman issued Executive Orders 9980 and 9981, establishing a Fair Employment Board and creating the Committee on Equality of Treatment in the Armed Services. African American leaders were privately unhappy with the limited scope of these measures but publicly supported Truman.[15] The following day, the special session of Congress started. It is clear that, faced with the dual threat of former vice president Henry Wallace's liberal challenge on the Progressive ticket and the Dixiecrat revolt, Truman had little choice other than to court the African American vote. Prior to the convention, Truman, despite his advisers' attempts to minimize the importance of a southern revolt, had shown no real stomach for outright defiance of Dixie; by the time the convention had finished, he had no alternative but to follow Rowe and Clifford's strategy.

The executive orders, together with the Dixiecrat revolt, convinced many African Americans that Truman was sincerely committed to civil rights, although his continued reticence was demonstrated by the fact that he made no further comment on the subject for two months. Truman remained, therefore, reluctant to campaign overtly for African American votes. The research division of the Democratic National Committee recognized the importance of the African American vote in the West and recommended that Truman make brief references to civil rights in speeches in Los Angeles, Chicago, and Omaha. Truman, however, remained circumspect; he referred to civil rights briefly in Chicago but not at all in Los Angeles. Nevertheless, by endorsing civil rights in the Democratic platform and issuing Executive Orders 9980 and 9981 on discrimination in the military and the federal government, Truman recognized that he was taking a calculated risk.

"A Bold Record of Downright Fairness"

A reinvigorated GOP approached the election of 1948 with considerable confidence. Franklin Roosevelt, for so long the nemesis of the party, was dead, and the Republicans controlled both houses of Congress. It seemed that Truman's sojourn in the White House would be brief. Moreover, according to Hugh Gloster in the *Crisis*, the Republicans were preparing to take advantage of Democrat splits by endorsing legislation on lynching, the poll tax, and an FEPC.[16] The campaign for the Republican nomination saw a few new hopefuls. Governor Earl Warren of California, who had turned down the vice-presidential berth in 1944, was now a contender, as were the Speaker of the House of Representatives, John W. Martin, and Harold E. Stassen, the former governor of Minnesota. Notwithstanding the appearance of new challengers, the main contenders were again Dewey and Taft, and there was little doubt who African American voters preferred. Taft had opposed the New Deal, sought to give relief apportionment to the states, and, throughout his career—despite being from the pivotal state of Ohio with its large black population—had done little to recommend himself to African Americans. The *Cleveland Call and Post*, a Republican newspaper, remarked that the senator "seems to be hell-bent to eliminate the Negro vote" and was "doing more to drive hundreds of thousands of Negro voters away from the party than anything the New Deal has ever done."[17] Taft, for example, opposed school desegregation; in 1943, he declared that "it occurs to me that once the federal government goes into the question of white and colored schools, we will never stop. We shall go on until we require every state to permit colored and white children to go to the same schools as we do in Ohio."[18]

The sense among African Americans was that Taft was against fair employment legislation and for states' rights; his stance may have been ideological rather than racist, but it was nonetheless deeply disturbing to African Americans.[19] There was also a suspicion that Taft was keen to court the white southern vote and would need the South's rotten boroughs to secure the nomination; while visiting South Carolina in 1948, Taft declared that the GOP was "very hopeful of carrying several southern states." He told his audience that he deplored discrimination against African Americans in employment but argued, "there is probably more of this in the North than the South." He spoke in favor of an antilynching law and the abolition of the poll tax but again opposed the proposed FEPC bill as it encouraged "federal interference."[20] Taft also reassured southerners that the GOP was the party of states' rights.

Dewey, on the other hand, had an excellent record on African American appointments. Aside from Francis Rivers, Dewey appointed Bertha Diggs to the Department of Labor, three African American assistant attorneys general, and a number of other African Americans to notable positions.[21] Joseph Ferguson of the *Philadelphia Inquirer* claimed that Dewey was "without a peer" where minorities were concerned, and that this was "based upon a bold record of downright fairness in the use of official prerogatives where race and religion have been concerned."[22] Dewey's failure to utilize his record and the advice of trusted allies remains one of the greatest errors of the campaign of 1948.

A confident, cheerful, if not exactly united, Republican Party met in Philadelphia, where, despite the efforts of Taft and Stassen, Dewey was unanimously renominated.[23] Dewey thus became the first defeated Republican presidential candidate to be renominated.[24] He was in virtual control of the convention and was just about acceptable to both conservatives and liberals within the party.[25] The general feeling was that only Dewey stood any realistic chance of defeating the president: Truman led Taft in every hypothetical poll prior to the conventions.[26] Brownell became campaign manager.[27]

Warren, who, like Dewey, had the dubious distinction of being dubbed "the new Calvin Coolidge," won the vice-presidential nomination, giving the ticket an East-West balance and a liberal look, "accentuat[ing] the changed nature of the party," according to Conrad Joyner.[28] Warren's record on minority rights was mixed. He had a liberal reputation and practiced nonpartisan politics in his own state, receiving both the Democrat and Republican nominations for governor. He had, however, infamously sanctioned the internment of Japanese Americans during World War II, but this admittedly serious black spot aside, his record was otherwise reasonably progressive. He grew up in integrated surroundings, but does not seem to have particularly endeared himself to California's African American population. He lost in the African American districts of Los Angeles and San Francisco in 1942 and, overwhelmingly, in 1946. In 1947, there was not a single African American among twenty-five judicial appointments, although he did integrate the state National Guard, increase minority employment in the civil service, and fight against the Klan as district attorney.[29] Warren accepted the vice-presidential nomination because Dewey would give the office cabinet status and because he said he "felt an obligation to the party."[30] *Time* commented:

"barring a political miracle, it was the kind of ticket that could not fail to sweep the Republican Party back into power."[31] "The Warren nomination," asserts Jules Abels, "seemed to be a bull's eye at the time, but Warren soon turned out to be a monumental disappointment to Dewey." He concludes that "Warren had no hand in strategy decision."[32]

The Republican civil rights plank of 1948 largely mirrored that of 1944, which the Republican-controlled Congress had, of course, pointedly failed to pass. The 1948 version recognized that "constant and effective insistence on the personal dignity of the individual, and his right to complete justice without regard to race, creed or color, is a fundamental American principle."[33] It demanded antilynching legislation (again without specifying whether this would be on the state or federal level), the abolition of the poll tax and military desegregation, although endorsement of a permanent FEPC was abandoned at the behest of conservatives.[34] According to the *Topeka/Kansas City Plaindealer*, the civil rights plank, described as the "usual ambiguous document," was written without African American input.[35] Despite this, there was an apparent "air of confidence" among African American Republicans attending the convention due to the nomination of Dewey and his private pledges on civil rights.[36] It was nevertheless suggested that Dewey had been advised to moderate his support for civil rights if he wanted to win the election. The *Plaindealer* maintained, however, that a Dewey victory would mean that African Americans had a friend in the White House.[37] Walter White presented the demands of the Continuations Committee of Negro Organizations, and the 6 million people they represented, to the convention but generated little enthusiasm.[38] The party's civil rights subcommittee, the NAACP complained, "consistently evaded or expressed disapproval" of the recommendations of the Continuations Committee.[39]

The *Crisis* rebuked the Republicans over their failure to enact civil rights legislation despite their platform commitments in 1944 and control of the Congress for almost two years: "the Republican candidate for the presidency will have to make it on his own. His party in Congress has produced a big, round zero as far as the Negro is concerned."[40] The *Baltimore Afro-American* agreed, asserting that Dewey and Warren were "still only the front men for a motley collection of mediocre performers whose actions in Congress have been something less than lousy."[41] McCoy and Ruetten put this problem more succinctly: "Dewey had to run on Taft's record."[42] If the Republicans wanted African American votes, therefore, it was down to Dewey to win them. White, pausing momentarily during a tirade against

Henry Wallace, condemned the "beautiful pledges" of the GOP's 1948 platform, accusing the Republicans of joining forces with reactionary southern Democrats to defeat FEPC, antilynching, and poll tax measures.[43]

"Maximum Efforts to Achieve Positive Legislation"

There was a degree of internal Republican pressure for action on civil rights in the aftermath of the convention. "The Politics of 1948" memorandum is justly famous and is correctly seen as the catalyst for Truman's embrace of civil rights in 1948. Had Truman not acted upon at least some of Rowe's recommendations, then the outcome of the election might have been very different. Students of the Republican Party could be forgiven for wondering why the GOP was not offered similarly sage advice. The truth of the matter is that Francis Rivers, Dewey's closest and most loyal African American ally, was extremely concerned about the black vote during the summer of 1948 and urged Dewey to take positive action. Dewey would once again be warned about the importance of the black vote, and again the warning would go unheeded.

Rivers, having consulted Jack Blinkoff, urged the GOP to take advantage of the special session of Congress and strenuously advocate civil rights legislation.[44] "The best strategy," he told key Dewey adviser Charles Breitel, "requires maximum efforts to achieve positive legislation rather than a program of only defense and counter-offensive to Mr. Truman's moves."[45] It appeared that A. Philip Randolph was ready to urge African Americans to refuse the draft unless the armed forces were desegregated; if this threat was carried out, then "civil rights will be a burning discussion in America at the height of the special session" due to prosecutions of those refusing the draft.[46] It was imperative, therefore, that during the special session of Congress, Republicans be seen to be doing all they could to defeat the filibuster of the antilynching bill. "This would occur," Rivers believed, "at the same time that Mr. Truman would appear in the light of failing to live up to his pretension in refusing to cause an end to draft resistance by issuing an executive order to ban Jim Crow in the armed forces."[47] Randolph wanted to meet Dewey to urge the governor to oppose segregation in the armed forces publicly.[48] Unfortunately, within the week Truman had signed Executive Order 9980, neutralizing Randolph's threat.

Rivers enclosed a thirteen-page examination of the situation, written with the aid of Blinkoff, with his letter, offering three reasons why the Republicans should promote civil rights legislation: principle, legislative efficiency, and expediency. As far as principle was concerned, there needed to be "belated recognition" that political equality was essential in a democracy. There was also a Cold War dimension: if America was to be "the exemplar and inspiration to the world," then it had to address genuinely the plight of its African American citizens. Rivers and Blinkoff argued that the difficulties the party might encounter with controversial or complicated legislation (the legislative session would be too short to pass complex bills) would not emerge if it embraced civil rights. Antilynching and anti–poll tax bills, they stressed, would not, and should not, divide the GOP.[49]

The embrace of civil rights by the Republican Party could be done with little political risk as it was in accord with the founding principles of the party and the current party platform; the only voters it would alienate were those in the South who would not vote Republican anyway. "On the contrary," they argued, "the Republican Party can use the adoption of civil rights legislation for legitimate political capital among minority groups in pivotal states, whose importance to Republican victory cannot be overestimated." Republicans, however, had to be very wary of any alliance with "the worst elements of the Democratic party," as this "would permit Mr. Truman to appear as the champion of idealism." Conversely, endorsing civil rights would incur the wrath of southern Democrats and "the Republican Party would reveal itself to the American electorate as being uncompromising on [civil rights]." Explaining GOP support for civil rights, Rivers and Blinkoff offered a draft of a statement in an attempt to turn Truman's slurs about a "do-nothing" Congress against the president, arguing that it was the final desperate act of a discredited president determined to cling to power at any cost.[50]

They believed that it was extremely important that the Republicans receive due credit for any legislation passed during the special session. One way of doing this would be to have Dewey consult congressional Republicans very publicly during efforts to pass civil rights legislation. Republicans could introduce the bills, with Dewey's endorsement coming once southern filibuster had been provoked. Truman would soon become embroiled in the dispute and be identified with southern reactionaries. Regardless of the success or failure of civil rights legislation, Dewey would benefit. Paralleling Democratic analysis, Rivers and Blinkoff argued that civil rights legislation would be "passed due to Dewey–Republican leadership" or fail "because of lack of Truman leadership."[51] Rivers and Blinkoff conceded that there would not be sufficient time in the special session to deal adequately with the Ives bill to prevent discrimination in employment and bills to end segregation in the armed forces. It was also essential that the anti–poll tax and antilynching bills not be watered down to appease southern senators as this "would only arouse bitter opposition from the minority groups whom it is intended to benefit and lead to charges that the Republican Party is evading its responsibility and is insincere."[52]

Rivers's analysis made a good deal of sense, but it did not suggest anything that Dewey could do independently of the congressional party. It did not advise Dewey to talk directly about civil rights to African American audiences, and it ignored the decent record of Dewey, both in terms of legislation and appointments, as governor of New York. Rivers also relied on the good faith of Republican congressmen, something not very much in evidence throughout the period, and their ability and willingness to turn the recall of Congress to their advantage. These concerns are, however, immaterial as Dewey ignored Rivers's advice. This was almost certainly due to his confidence that he would prevail over Truman, but it could also be a reflection of his own exasperation with Republicans in Congress. This memorandum really should have been sent to the likes of Taft and Vandenberg as well, since Dewey had little influence over the Republican legislative program in Congress. The GOP was, therefore, offered a positive and workable response to Truman's recall of Congress, but it required the party to demonstrate some uncharacteristic political shrewdness. Unfortunately, much of Rivers's analysis proved perceptive: Truman did indeed pass an executive order prohibiting discrimination in the armed forces; he was able to come across as "a champion of idealism" while the Republicans became associated with the "forces of reaction."

Brownell's appointment of Val Washington as executive assistant to the campaign chairman of the Republican National Committee in 1946 had been an attempt to appease African American Republicans. Washington was a graduate of the University of Indiana, a Willkie supporter in 1940, and a former general manager of the *Chicago Defender*; he was appointed by Governor Green to the Illinois Interstate Commerce Commission in 1941, and he was the only African American in the country to hold such a position.[53] Washington argued that African American fraternal organizations provided the best way of communicating with African American leaders, a strategy that may have garnered support among the black middle class, but that was unlikely to galvanize the mass of African Americans.[54]

In August 1948, Brownell argued that the appointment of Washington demonstrated that the GOP was "the unswerving enemy" of discrimination.[55] Washington stated that the 1948 Republican campaign among African American voters would be conducted on the basis of Dewey's record as governor of New York. "The Republican Party," asserted Washington, "has the best platform, the best candidates and the best record," and African Americans knew that a GOP victory would greatly benefit them. He argued that the Democrats were still the party of the South, and it was southerners who controlled many of the most important congressional committees. He noted that Truman's conversion to the cause of civil rights happened during a Republican Congress but was absent when the Democrats controlled both houses. Furthermore, Truman had the power to end discrimination in the military, but the president preferred to delay action; in fact, Truman had "never really had any intention of doing anything about civil rights." The PCCR and Truman's message to Congress were, Washington claimed, gambits to win the African American vote. Dewey's record, by contrast, "assures vigorous prosecution of all violations of civil rights under existing Federal civil rights statutes."[56]

Washington, an NAACP member, was setting about his task enthusiastically, but he soon became embroiled in a feud with Walter White over the latter's alleged bias toward the Democrats.[57] Considering the record and motivation of the Republicans in Congress between 1946 and 1948, and the fact that they were either not astute enough or not interested enough to promote civil rights, it is perhaps not surprising that the NAACP sought sanctuary with the Democrats. Whether a Republican Congress serving President Dewey would have been any more forthcoming on civil rights is a moot point. The principle behind the FEPC, for instance, would have remained anathema to many conservative Republicans. Nevertheless, it was increasingly apparent that White was positioning the NAACP alongside Truman, and that he viewed a Democratic victory as vital to the continued advancement of civil rights.

Multiple warnings about the importance of the African American vote, both private and public, would go unheeded by the GOP. The PCCR and Truman's pledges on civil rights together with the Dixiecrat secession meant that the Republicans would need to wage the most dynamic campaign ever if they were to prise the African American vote away from the Democrats. In 1936, the party was unelectable. In 1940, its presidential candidate's liberalism was viewed with unjustified skepticism; in 1944, the party ran a passionless campaign with a candidate who was tainted by both his own political record and that of his party in Congress. In 1948, the stakes could not have been higher. The GOP had again chosen Thomas Dewey, and he was better placed than any contemporary Republican to regain the African

American vote; indeed, no Republican candidate since "the immortal Lincoln" had as palpably positive a record on African Americans as Dewey.

"If the Republicans Are Smart, They Will Enact This Program"

Some contemporary commentators felt there was a sense of desperation about Truman's embrace of civil rights. The *Commonweal* warned in August 1948 that the military and the civil service might delay action on Truman's two executive orders in the hope that the Republicans would prove victorious; the executive orders, therefore, served only to reemphasize the hopelessness of Truman's position.[58] In October, *Commentary* examined what progress had been made on civil rights in the year since *To Secure These Rights* was issued. In a thoughtful and well-argued article, it concluded that there had been "pitifully little accomplished," and that the Eightieth Congress had done nothing.[59] Civil rights, it suggested, could save Truman from a defeat similar to that suffered by Landon. In contrast to the Republicans, Truman had "exhibited intrepid statesmanship" on the issue while among Republicans there was "little passion for the [civil rights] program and [they] did not believe its enactment vital to their success."[60] Indeed, Taft actually indulged the opponents of civil rights: "it seems slightly implausible that so little was accomplished by so many."[61] Optimists had hoped that *To Secure These Rights* would have compelled the Republicans to take action, but the GOP sensed victory in 1948 and was, therefore, not interested. This perception was reinforced after Henry Wallace announced his candidacy as there was a belief he would split the African American vote and give marginal states to the Republicans.

Dewey was a reluctant campaigner. With victory seemingly inevitable, he was loath either to repeat the mistakes of 1944 or exacerbate splits within the party; the less he said, the fewer people he would alienate. His main tactic, therefore, was to emphasize unity, and his priority appeared to be maintaining his core support rather than attracting estranged Democrats.[62] Dewey had good reason to be confident: just about everybody in the country, with the possible exception of Harry Truman, believed that the Republicans would win. Dewey's faith in opinion polls was well known, and in 1948 he was ahead in just about every poll. The Crossley Poll of 15 October, for example, put Dewey ahead in twenty-seven states, including many of those with significant numbers of African American voters.[63] In September, an Elmo Roper poll said that Dewey's lead over Truman had "an almost morbid resemblance to the Roosevelt-Landon figures of about this time in

1936." Roper went so far as to declare that he would be devoting himself to other things as the election was a foregone conclusion.[64] There appeared, therefore, little need for Dewey to embroil himself in civil rights or, for that matter, any controversy.[65]

A problem for Dewey was that while his record as governor of New York was undoubtedly good on civil rights, African Americans elsewhere in the country knew very little about him.[66] Efforts by the Republican National Committee to promote him with advertisements in the African American press were hindered by his apparent refusal to make more than passing reference to civil rights during the campaign.[67] He mentioned the topic in Pennsylvania on 11 October and New York on 21 October. In New York, Dewey, speaking at memorial dinner for the late Al Smith, demanded "justice and equal treatment for all" and stated that he had "found it possible to find peaceful, honest solutions" to the problems of minorities.[68]

Dewey's failure to speak out on civil rights was compounded by Taft's tactlessness. Taft was sent to the South to campaign, to neutralize him as potential handicap on the national scene rather than as part of a realistic attempt to win the region; his pronouncements owed more to 1928 than 1948.[69] In South Carolina, he declared that the GOP was "far more in accord" with the South than the Truman administration; in a later speech, he announced that "substantially there is no difference between the Republican Party and the Southern Democrats" on the race issue.[70] This encouraged some southerners to believe that Dewey would not be a forceful advocate of civil rights, and if elected, would, in fact defer to Taft on the subject. Dewey largely avoided speaking in the South; therefore, the only notable Republican voices heard below the Mason-Dixon Line belonged to Taft, Stassen, and Carroll Reece, the Tennessean former chairman of the party.[71] Taft may have been running a fool's errand in the South, but, consciously or otherwise, he had further undermined GOP prospects in crucial northern African American wards.

The Wallace candidacy caused considerable unease among Democrats, and early in the campaign the former vice president was identified as a greater threat to the Democrats' hold on the African American vote than the Republicans, notably in New York City, Chicago, and Los Angeles.[72] Wallace's main concern was foreign policy, but he was unequivocal on civil rights, even campaigning to integrated audiences in the South, a tactic specifically designed to win northern black votes. Wallace attacked both parties on civil rights, arguing that Truman did not believe in civil rights while the "Republicans remember the name of Abraham Lincoln but willfully forget the principles of Abraham Lincoln."[73] Walter White realized that African American votes for Wallace could guarantee a GOP victory, and the NAACP unleashed a campaign against him.[74] White declared that he had been asking Wallace for years to appear at the NAACP's annual conference, while William Hastie, speaking at the Democratic Party's headquarters, called the Progressive Party "a political puppet securely tied to the communist party line" and described its standard bearer as "notoriously disinterested" in civil rights while vice president and in the cabinet.[75] Despite some support from African Americans for Wallace as late as September, the discrediting of the Progressives by the Democrats and the NAACP had succeeded to the extent that by the time of the election, this support had evaporated.[76] The association's attacks on Wallace confirmed that it was far from neutral in the election. Noted conservative black columnist George Schuyler asserted that those who believed the NAACP was nonpartisan "should have their heads examined."[77]

After persuasion from Clifford, and only a week before the election, Truman made a speech in Harlem in front of sixty-five thousand people. This speech, on the first anniversary of the issuance of PCCR's *To Secure These Rights*, was the only one he made addressing civil rights directly, and in it he defended his record and condemned the "do-nothing" Congress for not passing his proposals. The Harlem speech was, however, probably too late in the campaign to influence many voters.[78] Truman's overall strategy was to attack congressional Republicans rather than Dewey in order to associate his opponent with the "do-nothing" Congress. These attacks, which were clearly unfair to Dewey's record, went unchallenged. Dewey could have countered by defending his achievements and attacking the equally bad record of Democrat congressmen, but he chose not to. When asked why Republicans had not enacted the legislation requested by Truman, given the similarities between it and the Republican platform, Brownell replied that it was designed to be enacted by a Republican president. "Obviously," he declared, "this cannot be done at a rump session called at a political convention for political purposes in the heat of the campaign."[79] Other Republicans even felt that their record would actually be an advantage and attempted no effective defense of it. The GOP stance during the special session was a sign of the party's overconfidence, but it also mirrored that of Roosevelt during the 1932–33 interregnum; neither was about to do anything to help a seemingly "lame-duck" president desperately seeking self-justification.

Throughout the campaign of 1948, there was a perception that congressional Republicans were only interested in civil rights legislation as a way to embarrass and split the Democrats. In August, K. M. Landis II, writing in the *Chicago Sun-Times*, bemoaned the Republicans' stance. "One of these days, by some accident," sighed Landis, "a real civil rights program will pass, and it may then be too late for anybody to believe in the good faith of the party of Lincoln."[80] Landis had a point, but it is clear that it was not only the Republicans who were "playing politics" with civil rights legislation. Truman never truly believed that any civil rights legislation would be passed during the special session, and it was obvious to Republicans that the issue was being used to embarrass them before the election.[81] They decided, therefore, to respond in kind in an effort to increase Democrat divisions; after a week of token debate, the anti–poll tax bill was removed from the Senate's agenda.

In September, paralleling 1936, the Republicans won in Maine. Brownell soon declared publicly that the victory virtually ensured a GOP victory in November, announcing that the success confirmed unofficial reports that Dewey would be elected with an "overwhelming majority." Dewey, however, was more circumspect and warned against overconfidence.[82] On the eve of the election, Taft, ignoring Dewey's appeal, predicted a majority of 5 million for the Republicans.[83] Yet Truman had successfully turned the campaign into a battle between himself and the Republican-controlled Congress rather than a contest between the candidates, and this was beginning to cause consternation within the Dewey camp. Dewey sent Brownell to Washington to meet Republican congressional leaders to discuss the situation, suggesting that they pass a progressive program, but both Taft and Vandenberg refused to budge.[84] Dewey and Brownell decided to keep this meeting secret as it would further expose splits within the party and the trepidation that belied their public confidence.

In the latter stages of the campaign, reports began to reach Brownell that Truman was closing the gap, especially in California and Illinois.[85] This was beginning to trouble another of the inner circle, Edwin Jaeckle, who was concerned too many of Dewey's advisers relied on polls and were assuming that the election was won.[86] Brownell met Republican state chairmen to discuss whether Dewey should change his tactics; they decided, virtually unanimously, that Dewey should not alter his strategy. They were also, Brownell would recall, later highly critical of the campaign Dewey ran.[87] To make matters worse, Elmo Roper now suggested that the election was far from the foregone conclusion he had earlier predicted, as Dewey was not attracting disenchanted Democrats, who were either supporting the Dixiecrats or the Progressives, were undecided, or were abstaining. Worse still,

Dewey's support was no larger than it had been in 1944.[88] A survey done by the Associated Negro Press predicted that not only would the vast majority (seven out of ten) of African American voters be voting Democrat, but also that Truman would emerge triumphant.[89] Democratic chairman Howard McGrath, having checked with state Democratic organizations, believed the signs pointed to a Truman victory.[90]

"The Only Way a Republican Is Going to Get into the White House Is to Marry Margaret Truman"

Truman scraped home with 24,105,812 popular votes and 303 electoral votes to Dewey's 21,970,065 and 189, respectively. The polls had miscalculated again; their misjudgment was not on the scale of the infamous *Literary Digest* poll of 1936, but, as the *Chicago Daily News* noted dryly, "the pollsters may say that the error was not great but when a man breaks into a dance after he has been pronounced dead, the doctor can expect to lose a few patients."[91] Groucho Marx joked that "the only way a Republican is going to get into the White House is to marry Margaret Truman."[92] The most accurate poll was, apparently and improbably, carried out by the Staley Milling Company's informal Pullet Feed Poll in Kansas City.[93] A swing of only sixty electoral votes would have meant a Dewey presidency. The significance of the black vote is starkly illustrated by Truman's slim majorities in California, Ohio, Kentucky, Illinois, Missouri, and West Virginia, some 112 electoral votes. Although Truman lost New York, he won 108,000 votes in Harlem compared to a paltry 34,000 for Dewey, who did only marginally better than Wallace's 29,000 votes. Dewey actually managed to poll fewer African American votes in the Empire State than in 1944.[94] In direct contests in New York between African American Democrats and Republicans, the Democrats won.

If Dewey had won Ohio (Taft's state), California (Warren's), and Illinois, he would have become president with 267 electoral votes. A shift of 3,500 votes would have given Ohio to Dewey; with a shift of 16,500 votes, he would have won Illinois. In fact, Truman's 130,000 majority in African American areas of Chicago was four times his Illinois majority.[95] Indeed, when Democratic strategists in the state realized that Truman was catching up to Dewey, Jack Arvey, of Governor Adlai Stevenson's campaign, stated that "we put extra money in all the Negro wards."[96] State Democrats clearly recognized that the African American vote was likely to be the difference between victory and defeat. Truman ran ahead of Dewey by three to one in

Chicago and Ohio's African American wards.[97] A shift of 9,000 would have given Dewey California. In all, a shift of only 30,000 votes out of 10,661,000 cast in three pivotal states would have given Dewey overall victory.[98] Republican analysis agreed that the African American vote was important in Chicago, New York, and Philadelphia and conceded that it was "a potent influence" in California, Illinois, and Ohio.[99] Despite carrying Delaware, Indiana, and Maryland with African American votes, the Republicans did not win the majority of the African American vote in any state.[100]

While forecasts of a Dewey victory may have discouraged many Republicans from voting, the analyst Samuel Lubell determined that the contrary was true: "far from costing Dewey the election, the [Democratic] stay-at-homes may have saved him almost as crushing a defeat as Landon suffered in 1936."[101] Without Wallace and the Dixiecrat Strom Thurmond, Truman could have won a further 85 electoral votes, giving him a landslide. The GOP was aided by the Wallace vote in New York, New Jersey, Michigan, Maryland, Pennsylvania, and Ohio, and it might have been helped in Illinois had Wallace been allowed on the ticket there; Truman was also assisted by the comparative loyalty of the South.

Different groups, particularly the farm lobby and labor, wanted credit for Truman's victory. Brownell and Republican analysis concluded that it was the farm vote that had determined the election.[102] So convinced had Brownell been that the farm vote would prove crucial that he had threatened to resign when Dewey refused to heed his advice to campaign for it.[103] Dewey would later admit to knowing little about farming concerns, and by the end of 1948, he was also attributing his defeat to the farm vote.[104] Other analysis supports Brownell's view that the farm vote was the vital factor, especially in Wisconsin, Ohio, Illinois, and Iowa; indeed, Dewey's vote in ten midwestern states had dropped by 585,000 from 1944.[105] Yet Truman could have lost in Minnesota, Iowa, Wisconsin, Wyoming, and even his home state of Missouri—a total of fifty-five electoral college votes—and still scraped home, suggesting that the farm vote was not the absolutely vital factor that many have claimed.[106]

Speaking in Kansas City following the election, Truman declared that "Labor did it," and he still maintained in his memoirs that this was the case.[107] While there is merit in this argument, it neglects the fact that Truman lost major industrial states such as New York, New Jersey, Michigan, Indiana, Connecticut, and Pennsylvania (although congressional Democrats emerged victorious in these states) and polled a third fewer labor votes than Roosevelt had in 1944.[108] Nevertheless, Truman's victories in Ohio and Wisconsin (won by the Republicans in 1944) and Illinois and California were owed at least in part to a major campaign by the labor movement to persuade people to vote.[109] Labor remained unconvinced about Truman, but determined to defeat both Wallace and the Republicans; it had little choice other than to back him.[110]

The African American press came to a different conclusion. The *Pittsburgh Courier* asserted that Truman's victories in California, Ohio, and Illinois were due to the black vote and that African Americans had supported the Democrats despite the black press's backing for Dewey.[111] The *Chicago Defender* suggested that 5 million African Americans had voted and between 80 and 85 percent of them had supported Truman.[112] The NAACP believed that African Americans had voted for Truman by a margin of three to one, which it attributed to the president's civil rights program, his defiance of Dixie, the Taft-Hartley Labor Act, and the failure of the Eightieth Congress to enact civil rights legislation.[113] In Dewey, the Republicans had picked the best possible candidate from an African American point of view, yet African Americans, like whites, "did not warm to him, did not trust him." Furthermore, he failed to speak out on major issues, meaning that "they did not know where he stood on their special interests and on general black problems."[114] One Harlem editor asserted that African Americans "felt if they didn't support Truman no other politician would ever defy the southerners again."[115] The *Crisis* concluded that, ultimately, few African Americans had voted for Wallace, attributing this to the growing influence of Communists in the latter stages of his campaign.[116]

Brownell later recalled that "we thought Dewey would be elected, and we based our predictions not so much on the Republicans' strength as on the Democrats' weaknesses."[117] They believed that the splits in the Democratic Party would ensure a Republican victory. Brownell would credit Clark Clifford for formulating the Democratic strategy in 1948, believing that Truman, on Clifford's advice, exploited the differences between Dewey's moderate internationalism and the conservative isolationism of the congressional leadership.[118] Clifford contended that everything the Democrats did was geared toward labor, the farmer, African Americans, and the consumer.[119]

Truman had not only rebuilt the Roosevelt coalition, but he had also received more African American votes than his predecessor had ever managed. African Americans responded to Truman's policies as poor people as well as a minority group, believing that his stance on social welfare, as well as civil rights, would benefit them.[120] Truman was a genuine believer in civil rights, if not the actual prospects for the success of his own program (nor what he termed "social equality" between the races). He was also blessed by a team of advisers who were both sympathetic to the cause of civil rights and saw the political benefits of promoting it. Moreover, African Americans had voted in greater numbers than ever before: in the North, the African American population had grown by 40 percent during the war, and 80 percent of them voted for Truman.[121] Without the African American vote, Truman would not have won the election. Truman contained the threats from Wallace and Thurmond, while Dewey's supposed liberalism did little to endear him to African American voters.

The African American vote in 1944 had, on reflection, been vital to Roosevelt's success, but even armed with this fact, the Republicans did not respond positively in 1948 and had clearly learned little from the experience. They seemed to believe their own propaganda: the election was already won and they did not have to court interest groups. Furthermore, they seemed oblivious to their abject failure to regain the African American vote; Brownell, it spite of all the evidence he had uncovered to the contrary, declared in his memoir that "Dewey's success in attracting the support of black and ethnic voters was one of our sources of inspiration."[122] Brownell's commitment to civil rights was utterly genuine, as he would demonstrate as Eisenhower's attorney general, but his analysis in this instance is fatally flawed. Despite winning in Harlem in 1942 and 1946, Dewey lost there in 1944 and 1948, and this represents a categorical, if perhaps undeserved, rejection by African American voters.[123] Dewey also ignored Brownell's admonishments to broaden the Republicans' appeal.

Contemporary Americans were no wiser about where New York's governor stood on racial matters: 20 percent believed he would support federal civil rights legislation; 24 percent felt that he would leave it to the states to decide; and a further 20 percent thought he opposed both state and federal action.[124] This reflected the perception that Dewey had "no apparent interest in general ideas" and "no sign of an underlying philosophy."[125] George Mayer believes that in 1948 the Republicans had "everything to gain and little to lose by spearheading the fight against discrimination" because they had no southern constituency and, therefore, little to lose by courting African Americans. He continues: "it required nothing more than a reactivation of a historic position that had been abandoned out of sheer apathy."[126] It has also been suggested that Dewey failed to win the African American vote because he hoped to make gains in the South, but this was never a realistic proposition.[127]

More generally, Jules Abels states that "the Republicans couldn't agree on whether they had been chastised because Dewey was too far on the left or the Eightieth Congress was too far on the right."[128] Many Republicans felt that the reason they lost was because the party was too keen to appropriate aspects of the New Deal; others believed that the influence of the Old Guard and reactionaries had caused their defeat. The majority of party members adhered to the view that the party offered "me too" policies to the voter rather than more conservative alternatives. Dewey was philosophical in defeat, but there was residual bitterness from Republican congressmen over his coolness toward them during the campaign. What was abundantly clear was that Dewey would never again be entrusted with the Republican nomination.[129]

Dewey was lambasted by conservative Republicans. Among the most vitriolic criticism was that of Budington Kelland, a member of the Republican National Committee from Arizona who felt that the "Albany group" had too much influence on the campaign, which "consisted in sending a train around the country to give the good people a chance to see the next president of the United States." He continued: "the Albany group provided the candidate with smug, shallow, insincere speeches," which served to "stir up an avalanche of apathy." Kelland believed that it was a "bland and selfish campaign conducted solely for the benefit of the candidate" and that ignored Republican members of Congress.[130] Kelland, however, had earlier agreed with the strategy of saying nothing controversial.[131] Dewey conceded that he had been guilty of overconfidence but stated that he would remain the titular leader of the party. The result was another disaster for the Republican Party; it had immortally "snatched defeat from the jaws of victory."

7

The Elephant and the Skunk

The *Chicago Defender* announced confidently that white supremacy had been "struck a death blow" by Truman's victory, and asserted that, minus the Dixiecrats and Wallace, Truman had a clear mandate and would keep his promises.[1] Henry Lee Moon agreed, arguing that even though it contained a hard core of reactionaries, the Eighty-first Congress would be "considerably more liberal" than its predecessor, and that "victory for the forces of liberalism is in sight."[2] As America prepared for the new Congress to begin, this optimism was quickly tempered by concerns about Republican sincerity on civil rights.[3] An embittered Republican Party, whose resentment was sharpened by his persistent criticism of the "do-nothing" Eightieth Congress, confronted Truman. The *New York Times* reported on Christmas Eve of 1948 that the Republicans would use the new session of Congress to embarrass the Democrats over civil rights by making a slight change in the filibuster rule.[4] Truman was painfully aware that his mandate was limited by a wafer-thin plurality (he won only 49.5 percent of the popular vote), the divisions within his party, and the constant threat of the Dixiecrat-Republican alliance; despite the election, little had actually changed in American politics.[5] That Truman lacked Roosevelt's skill in manipulating Congress, while Democratic leadership in both houses was largely unexceptional, added to his problems still further. Nevertheless, in his State of the Union address, Truman reemphasized his desire to see enacted the civil rights program he had sent to the previous Congress.[6]

Even Arthur Krock, a supporter of retaining the filibuster and a skeptic about "civil rights"—a term he invariably set off with quotation marks or prefaced with "so-called"—believed that a change in the filibuster rule was likely in the current session of Congress, and he attributed this to the GOP's keenness to regain the African American vote.[7] Walter White provided America with another reason for abolishing the filibuster, arguing that "idiotic notions of racial superiority" aided Soviet propaganda, and this linkage to the Cold War would become a recurrent theme in the civil rights struggle in Congress.[8]

The hope that had accompanied Truman's victory was to be extremely short-lived. A NAACP study demonstrated how important African Americans had been to Truman's victory, and the association believed that this gave it political leverage. The board of directors called upon the Senate to amend Rule 22 (the filibuster rule), while Wilkins conceded that "there is little hope for enactment" of civil rights legislation without this change. White was soon expressing concern about "a pattern of evasion" that was already evident among congressmen, having been told by one senator that other bills were more important.[9] Moon suspected that Democrats in Congress would not stand up to Dixiecrats who had deserted the party ticket, fearing that they would join forces with the Republicans.[10] African American faith in Truman's ability to secure civil rights legislation, if not his sincerity, had therefore dissipated almost as soon as his second term began.

Five Republican senators—Morse, Ives, Everett Saltonstall (Massachusetts), Homer Ferguson (Michigan), and William F. Knowland (California)—soon challenged the filibuster.[11] Ferguson and Ives wanted the two-thirds rule abolished but recognized that this would be virtually impossible to achieve; the *Crisis* concurred, but suggested that the Republicans were "playing smart politics."[12] Morse, along with Democrat Whip Francis Myers of Pennsylvania, introduced a resolution that would permit cloture on all motions by a majority of those present rather than the current two-thirds.[13] No Democrat made any effort to support cloture, and Morse's plan, unsurprisingly, was rejected.[14] One potential political danger for Truman came predictably true on 31 January 1949, when southern senators announced that if he pursued civil rights legislation, his entire program would be jeopardized. The Republicans, keen to see the Democrats squirm, duly demanded that civil rights be the first item on the Senate's agenda.[15] Nevertheless, optimists maintained that the filibuster could finally be abolished.

White remained cautious. In February 1949, he telegraphed Vandenberg, expressing his concern that the senator was soliciting Republican support to uphold his August 1948 ruling on cloture in the Eightieth Congress.[16] Vandenberg, then the presiding officer in the Senate, concluded that cloture could be used only for "pending measures" and not preliminary hearings. This was a "narrow and legalistic" interpretation, according to McCoy and Ruetten, which, unfortunately, coincided with the views of southern senators.[17] White feared that this would make the passage of civil rights legislation impossible. In addition, Taft had to deny that conservative Republicans had agreed to block civil rights legislation in return for Dixiecrat support to protect Taft-Hartley.[18] White had received "apparently authentic reports" that conservative Republicans were allying with Dixiecrats to uphold Vandenberg's earlier ruling. The sole outcome of this, warned White, was "only defeat—utter and crushing defeat—for those who want and insist upon honest and effective civil rights legislation."[19]

Administration senators tried to outmaneuver southerners by sending a cloture petition to the vice president and chair of the Senate, Alben Barkley. If Barkley felt that it was valid, his decision would be upheld by a majority of the Senate since, as Berman notes, "the existing rule did not provide for the application of cloture on filibusters directed against a motion."[20] Wherry, the Senate minority leader, and Carl Hayden (Arizona) sponsored Resolution 15 to alter Rule 22. They felt that the rule did not allow the Senate any real chance of thwarting filibusters because, since senators could filibuster a motion to take up a measure, they could, therefore, filibuster the same piece of legislation twice.[21] The Hayden-Wherry Amendment sought to end debate on a motion with two-thirds of the vote present, and this could be passed if Republicans and northern Democrats united against southern opposition; Senate Majority Leader Scott Lucas could then secure cloture to bring the measure to a vote. This maze of procedure simply had to be negotiated; otherwise, Truman's civil rights program would be becalmed.[22] Some Republicans were reluctant to support the cloture petition sent to Barkley as it would undermine Vandenberg's earlier ruling. On 2 March, however, Vandenberg urged Republicans "to vote the way in which they think is right." Taft agreed: "this is not a party matter. . . . I don't know how one can ask them to vote against their convictions." Taft declined to say how he intended to vote.[23]

The following day, Truman carelessly mentioned that he wanted a simple majority of a Senate quorum to allow cloture (the position of the ADA and the NAACP), undermining northern Democrats in their efforts to enlist Republican support for the minor change to Rule 22 and redoubling southern senators' determination to oppose change in the process.[24] Taft argued that "this made the position of southern senators more unyielding"; indeed, southern senators attributed increased support for their position to Truman's statement.[25] Wherry initially refused to sign Senate Majority Leader Scott Lucas's cloture petition because of Truman's tactlessness, but he, Taft, fifteen other Republicans, and seventeen Democrats eventually signed on 10 March. Barkley, in turn, ruled to limit the threat of filibusters by allowing cloture on the motion even though it was not a pending measure.[26] On 11 March, Vandenberg announced that while he favored the Hayden-Wherry Amendment, the Barkley ruling was "an affront to due legislative process" and had to be rejected to maintain the Senate's integrity.[27] Barkley's ruling was overturned 46 to 41, with 23 Republicans and 23 mostly southern Democrats voting against.[28] White believed that Vandenberg had given an "aura of respectability" to opposition to Barkley's ruling. Wilkins later called it the "most crucial vote on civil rights in the last ten years."[29] The *Baltimore Afro-American* declared that "the Elephant has embraced the Skunk"[30]

Lucas, desperate for a resolution and concerned about the rest of Truman's program, was apparently prepared to offer major concessions to the South on Rule 22.[31] This allowed the Republican–southern Democrat coalition to agree to an amendment to Hayden-Wherry that would make southerners invulnerable both in the current session and in the future. The eventual "compromise"—worked out by Knowland of California and introduced by Wherry—determined that closure could only be invoked by two-thirds of the Senate, in other words, by at least sixty-four votes. The new rule kept the old two-thirds vote for cloture and also provided that cloture could be voted on motions to take up as well as on measures themselves.[32] There was one exception to the new rule, relating to filibusters themselves, which could continue as long as necessary if there was an attempt to alter the rules against filibusters.[33]

The compromise was passed by the Senate, with 34 Republicans joining forces with 29 Democrats in favor and 8 Republicans (Aitken, Langer, Morse, Ferguson, Lodge, Tobey, Ives, and Malone) joining forces with 15 Democrats against.[34] What was clear to all sides was that finding 64 senators to vote for cloture on civil rights legislation would be virtually impossible. Several Republicans viewed the compromise as a "sell-out"; Morse, for example, accused his GOP colleagues of entering "an unholy political marriage with southern reactionaries," declaring shortly afterwards that "a new de facto political party" had been created.[35] His suggestion was rejected that a filibuster be halted by a simple majority of those present as a long as a quorum—as few as 49 (requiring, therefore, only 25 votes to end a filibuster)—was present.[36]

Recriminations abounded. The *New York Times* was critical of Truman's "impromptu and somewhat imperious remark" in favor of a simple majority; the Republicans were, however, complicit as the Dixiecrats "couldn't have got to first base without . . . most respectable Republican help."[37] The net result of this was that the prospects for civil rights legislation were poor, while the filibuster illustrated the "helplessness of the Senate."[38] Lucas told reporters: "civil rights bills are practically dead for this session" and accused the Republicans of "abject surrender" to the South.[39] Taft, the chairman of the Republican Policy Committee, would have preferred a cloture rule based on two-thirds of those present, but insisted that there was "no practical difference" between this and the two-thirds requirement, provided there was effective leadership within the Senate. Vandenberg, echoing his stance on lynching in the 1930s, stated that it was "supremely important" not to put the Senate in a position where minorities could obstruct business in a "national emergency," although he clearly did not regard the Dixiecrats and their 2.5 percent of the popular vote in the 1948 election as a minority.[40] Both Taft and Vandenberg expressed the hope that Democratic leaders in the Senate would test the new rule by reintroducing civil rights legislation, while Wherry vowed to test the new rule.[41]

White, blamed by both black and white liberals for the debacle, recognized the magnitude of the setback. He was scathing about the Wherry Amendment, conceding: "we have taken a terrific beating at the hands of the Dixiecrat–conservative Republican coalition." What made the situation worse was that southerners had "privately admitted" that they would have failed had northern senators been sufficiently determined, "but the southerners never quit. They pulled [off] a spectacular victory."[42] The *Crisis* identified Vandenberg as the catalyst for the rule change, asserting that his "speech against the ruling influenced enough Republicans to cause defeat."[43] The new rule made "it almost impossible to stop a filibuster in the future, and . . . equally difficult to change the rules again. Then they had the gall to label this a 'compromise.'"[44] The *Crisis* argued that neither Wherry nor the Dixiecrats had any intention of allowing a vote on cloture, nor a further change in the rules, as it would require twenty-four-hour sessions to achieve either.[45] Lucas again blamed the GOP, saying that the party's leadership in the Senate "must assume the responsibility for striking the dagger into the heart of civil rights."[46] The *Chicago Defender* dubbed "the die-hard Negro-haters of both major parties" as "Republicrats."[47] Mary McLeod Bethune commented: "the loss of the battle while disappointing in itself was not so piercing a blow as the Republicans appear to have insulted our intelligence."[48] Robert Church's Republican American Committee condemned a "transparent sham."[49]

"The People of the South Need Have Very Little to Worry About"

Notwithstanding the failure to blunt the power of the filibuster, fifteen months after it had been originally announced, Truman's civil rights program—including fair employment practices, anti–poll tax and antilynching bills, and a civil rights act—was finally presented to the Senate in April 1949. The proposed civil rights act, which was the only fresh addition to the program, called for a five-member commission on civil rights within the executive department to make appraisals of policies. The commission would make an annual report, with recommendations, to the president. A joint congressional committee of fourteen members would also be set up and, in addition, the Department of Justice would be expanded to enforce the law. A new assistant attorney general would head a special civil rights division, while FBI staff would be trained to investigate civil rights cases. Among the punishments imposed on state or local officers violating civil rights would be a $10,000 fine and/or twenty years imprisonment. Perhaps foreseeing defeat, Truman did not make any special message to accompany the proposals.[50]

Administration leaders in the Senate argued that the new cloture rule made it impossible to limit debate on these measures, but the Republicans disagreed vehemently. If the proposals were to be successful, it would, as noted, require northern Democrats and Republicans to muster sixty-four votes twice, first to end the filibuster on the motion to consider the bill and then on the legislation itself. There was, however, a further potential subtext to the issue, with suggestions that Republicans from northern farm states would vote against civil rights if southern Democrats were to support killing the repeal of a margarine tax.[51] Joseph Martin denied that the GOP had made any deals on civil rights, maintaining that "a majority of our members are sure to vote for anti–poll tax and anti-lynching measures."[52]

Three weeks of hearings on the Fair Employment Practices bill, described by Ives as the most important part of the entire civil rights program, began in the House on 11 May 1949. A key fact that supporters of the FEPC wanted to stress was that it was not aimed specifically at the South. Secretary of Labor Maurice J. Tobin, for instance, assured Congress that enforcement powers would only be used as a last resort and stressed that "the people of the South need have very little to worry about."[53] Ives stressed that, in those states with fair employment legislation, the emphasis was on voluntary compliance and education, rather than punitive enforcement measures.[54] The House Labor Subcommittee approved the FEPC bill unanimously at the start of June.[55] Within a few days, the Senate Judiciary Committee approved an antilynching bill presented by Homer Ferguson, a diluted version of a bill offered to the Eightieth Congress, but based on sounder constitutional grounds.[56] Despite apparent progress, the NAACP was still critical of the administration and the unanticipated "faintheartedness" of Democratic congressmen.[57] Wilkins declared that the association, furious with Truman as well as Congress, would "try to defeat both Democrats and Republicans" who had hampered civil rights legislation.[58] In late July, the anti–poll tax bill was duly passed 273 to 116, but its success was tempered by the knowledge that it would probably not even reach a vote in the Senate; indeed, there was little satisfaction among the bill's supporters when it passed.[59]

On 7 July, Lucas promised that the FEPC would be at the top of the civil rights agenda, a move that pro–civil rights groups felt was poor strategy as it had little likelihood of success. Nevertheless, by 30 August, the FEPC was on a list of "must" legislation from Truman, even though the situation was bad in the House and virtually impossible in the Senate, particularly when Mississippi's James Eastland was appointed to head the Senate Judiciary Committee's subcommittee on civil rights.[60] To make matters worse, John Stennis, another Mississippian, was in charge of the House Rules Committee dealing with the anti–poll tax bill. Some of the most reactionary elements of the Dixiecrats were, therefore, in a position to delay all Truman's civil rights proposals.[61]

On 22 September, after a meeting of the Senate Republican Policy Committee, Taft expressed willingness to extend the congressional session to consider civil rights legislation, although he was equally happy to postpone the fight until January.[62] The administration's leaders in Congress finally abandoned any hope of passing civil rights legislation in the current session on 4 October 1949. Wherry alleged that Lucas and the Democratic leadership had deliberately selected the civil rights bills that "they know will be the hardest to pass." "They hope," he continued, "that they can go to the country and campaign in 1950 and claim that it was the Republicans who blocked it."[63] Lucas ignored a suggestion that, in future, antilynching take precedence over the FEPC bill, claiming that both Truman and "the principal minority groups" had agreed to abandon the struggle because there was a better chance of success in the new session.[64]

A year after Truman's triumph, the prospects for genuine advancement on civil rights looked as grim as ever. The Republicans and northern Democrats were keen to be seen to go on record as being in favor of civil rights, but both knew that their maneuvering was an exercise in futility. The Republicans' stance was particularly duplicitous as they had collaborated on a rule change that ensured that their civil rights program, which few of them actually truly believed in, could never be passed, while also allowing them to shift the blame for this, admittedly unconvincingly, onto the bogeymen of the South.

"A Mockery of Democratic Government"

Reflecting on the abject lack of progress in civil rights in 1949, a headline in the *Crisis* asked, "Does the Republican Party Want the Negro Vote?" Its correspondents Arnold Aronson and Samuel Spiegler argued that Republican success in 1952 relied upon "recapturing at least a major part of the Negro vote," particularly in the five states—New York, California, Ohio, Illinois, and Pennsylvania—with the largest number of electoral votes.[65] The Republicans' mixture of ambivalence and hostility toward FEPC legislation extended to the nation's state capitols as well. In a number of battleground states, the Republicans had deliberately torpedoed FEPC legislation. Earlier in the year in Illinois, it appeared that a state FEPC would be secured quite easily, but GOP leaders ordered party members to vote against the bill. One Republican told the state senate that he was voting against because he had been threatened with political, economic, and even social reprisals.[66] In Ohio, the state Republican platform in 1948 had advocated an FEPC law, but when a bipartisan bill was introduced, the GOP offered a weakened substitute, unwanted by FEPC supporters, which was subsequently defeated.[67] Similar stories played out in both Michigan and Pennsylvania. In Pennsylvania, for example, Governor Duff stated that the GOP had an "unmistakable obligation" to pass a fair employment law, but pressure from the Pennsylvania Manufacturers Association, led by a member of the Republican National Committee, opposed the measure, and the Senate and the House both bottled up FEPC bills.[68]

In Minnesota, Republican governor Luther W. Youngdahl was prevented from fulfilling a platform pledge on the FEPC by his own party. In Colorado, a Democrat-controlled House passed an FEPC bill that was then diluted to the point of worthlessness by the Republican-controlled Senate. In Indiana, Philip Willkie, son of the late Wendell, was the only Republican to support an FEPC bill.[69] The constant failure on fair employment could be blamed on the GOP's key supporters: manufacturing organizations and chambers of commerce had consistently opposed FEPC legislation, and, Aronson and Spiegler claimed, "the leadership of these organizations is, of course, frequently identical with the leadership of the state Republican organizations." These organizations supported the GOP financially, therefore, "Republican strategists chose to take the cash and let the votes go." Aronson and Spiegler wondered where these organizations would go if they stopped supporting the GOP if the party supported FEPC laws.[70]

The national debate on fair employment recommenced in January 1950.

Wherry declared that there was "an urgent need" for fair employment practices legislation, but he felt that a compulsory law could be counterproductive and lead to frivolous allegations of discrimination and, therefore, do more harm than good. A voluntary law, he insisted, offered the best chance of securing equality of opportunity. He maintained that the amendment that bore his name meant that there was now a mechanism for breaking a filibuster.[71] Truman recognized that he had suffered politically over the failure of civil rights, especially in crucial northern states and, because of this, rather than in spite of it, braced himself for another futile, sham battle with Congress, rather than allow the Republicans to exploit the situation further. In his State of the Union address of 4 January 1950, he duly urged that his civil rights program of February 1948 be enacted, while on 9 January the administration's budget message to Congress called for an FEPC.[72] At the same time, forty-seven Democratic senators met and agreed not to provoke a filibuster on civil rights legislation, a concession that civil rights might arise and disrupt the session's schedule.[73]

The president also met a delegation from the National Emergency Civil Rights Mobilization, led by Wilkins. The NAACP's acting secretary began to read a statement but was interrupted by the president, who stated: "you don't need to make that speech to me, it needs to be made to Senators and Congressmen."[74] While the FEPC would continue to be the main civil rights test, bills on lynching, the poll tax, and an "omnibus" civil rights bill would again be considered, even if none of these measures was likely to succeed; moreover, Democrat representative Brooks Hayes of Arkansas urged compromise on the FEPC bill, suggesting that the administration abandon plans for "forcing" legislation. Truman refused to endorse this so-called "Arkansas Plan."[75] Truman did, therefore, resist southern pressure to weaken his civil rights program, although this was largely symbolic as by mid-January the prospects of enacting civil rights legislation were already faint.[76] As Berman observes, Truman "was reluctant to invest much executive capital in a legislative enterprise that could bankrupt the rest of his program."[77]

At the beginning of January 1949, the House had voted to restrict the power of the House Rules Committee by allowing any measure bottled up for twenty-one days to go to the floor rather than remain in committee indefinitely. In January 1950, an effort by conservative Republicans and southern Democrats to restore the old rules failed at least partly because a vote for reversion could be construed as a vote against the FEPC.[78] This represented a major victory for Truman, despite 89 (33 percent) southern Democratic congressmen supporting a return to the old rule. For once, the

Republican–southern Democrat coalition did not succeed.[79] The reform of the 21–Day Rule was lauded as the "worst Confederate defeat since Appomattox" by one liberal writer.[80] Truman's victory did not, however, notably improve the chances of the FEPC bill passing in the Senate.[81] On 23 January, Sam Rayburn, the Speaker of the House, a Texan unsympathetic to civil rights, sidetracked the FEPC bill (which most Republican representatives opposed in its current form anyway) after a prolonged session, in favor of a bill for statehood for Alaska and Hawaii. On 17 February, the FEPC bill was again delayed due to southerners provoking seven time-consuming roll calls (members were answering their names and then leaving the chamber, requiring further roll calls).[82] It would now be 27 February at the earliest before it could be brought up again.[83]

A voluntary FEPC now began to gain support in the House, mainly among Republicans uncomfortable with a compulsory bill. This resulted in the McConnell Amendment, which removed the bill's enforcement powers but retained wide powers to support its search for discrimination, as well as allowing the issuing of contempt of court penalties.[84] Perhaps 80 percent of Republicans were backing McConnell's substitute bill; indeed, there was even the possibility that southern Democrats would support it as a way of thwarting the administration.[85] Jacob Javits and Clifford Case were among those Republicans vowing to resist the voluntary measure, maintaining that the FEPC had to have an enforcement provision to be effective.[86] Nonetheless, the McConnell bill, backed by Republicans and southern Democrats, was passed 221 to 178 after an all-night session in the House.[87]

The *Crisis* conceded that although the McConnell bill was "weak," it at least served to keep the issue alive and it also forced the Senate to act. The "friends" of the FEPC were the congressmen who voted against it (128 Democrats and 49 Republicans).[88] Adam Clayton Powell called the McConnell bill "a fraud, a sham and a hypocrisy," which "most reactionary Republicans will be glad to vote for."[89] The *New York Times* concluded that the "bill has been so diluted that very little is left of it but an expression of good intentions." Moreover, this "toothless measure" brought a permanent FEPC no closer, while "the prospective filibuster awaiting FEPC in the Senate only adds to the hollowness of the entire procedure."[90] The bill was, however, associated with Republicans and southern Democrats, and this had potential electoral benefits for the northern Democrats in November.[91]

On 11 April, attention reverted to the Senate where Truman, Barkley, and Lucas postponed action on the FEPC, instead pressing for a vote on Marshall Plan appropriations as a filibuster against the FEPC could delay the president's European Recovery Program (ERP).[92] Republican leaders in the Senate demanded immediate action on the FEPC, stating, with a nod to November, that the repeated postponement of taking up the measure "cast doubt upon the good faith" of the administration on the matter.[93] Wilkins telegraphed the White House regarding the wider political implications of postponement, asserting: "continued delay and evasion on the part of the Democratic leadership not only forestalls enactment of this [FEPC] bill, but imperils the entire Fair Deal program." Wilkins also spoke about African Americans' "increasing resentment" against the Democrats.[94]

The FEPC stood little chance of even being debated by the Senate; administration sources expected to be five to eight votes short of enforcing cloture.[95] Homer Ferguson claimed that if there was a conspiracy to thwart civil rights, it was between northern and southern Democrats, not Republicans and southern Democrats.[96] The motion eventually fell twelve votes short, representing the "death blow" to the legislation, with each party blaming the other for its failure.[97] Lucas censured Wherry for passing the two-thirds rule in the first place, and Wherry responded that even with the old rule, there would not have been sufficient votes and noted that only nineteen Democrats (36 percent) had voted for cloture, and that Truman had remained mute on the topic.[98] The *New York Times* accused the thirty-two senators who voted against cloture of "making a mockery of democratic government" and noted that the votes of Democrats had defeated the proposal.[99] The *Crisis* believed that the Republicans "should have and could have done better, but they did put the Democrats in the shade"; however, overall, "neither the Republicans nor the Northern Democrats can blame the Dixiecrats."[100]

Truman, speaking in Chicago, said that he would pursue the issue into the next Congress if necessary.[101] Taft responded by declaring that "every kind of civil rights measure is promised by the President. At the same time he knows that half his party bitterly fights his program."[102] Taft insisted that the antilynching bill was a better test case for cloture, but conceded that the only way of passing civil rights legislation would be to face down the southern filibuster over a period of weeks, and there simply was not the time to do this. It was readily apparent, however, that civil rights was going to be a factor in the forthcoming election.[103] Clear evidence of this fact came from one of Truman's administrative assistants, Stephen J. Spingarn, son of Joel and nephew of Arthur. Spingarn was acutely aware of the significance of the FEPC struggle: "we cannot win the FEPC cloture fight in *this* Congress but . . . it will be pretty important in November *how* we lost it."[104]

In July 1950, administration leaders in the Senate announced their intention to prevent a southern filibuster. Seventeen Democrats and forty-four Republicans, including heavyweights such as Wherry, Taft, Knowland, Ferguson, Lodge, Saltonstall, and Ives, supported the idea, but it still failed to receive the required sixty-four votes.[105] Truman's civil rights program was thus marooned. Morse blamed the Senate's reformed cloture rule, but Wherry again countered that even under the old rules, cloture would not have been attained. RNC chairman Guy Gabrielson, spying the election on the horizon, argued that minorities had "been betrayed by the Democrats and their false promises on civil rights. . . . Those who hope and pray for civil rights action can only look toward a Republican Congress for results."[106]

"The Croaking Voices of Reaction"

By the end of January 1949, there were moves to oust RNC chairman Hugh Scott, seen as Dewey's man, and end Dewey's ostensive leadership of the party.[107] At a policy meeting of the RNC in Omaha, Scott announced, or rather confirmed, that Dewey would not seek the nomination in 1952.[108] Budington Kelland, vitriolic in his criticism of Dewey in the aftermath of the election, took the lead in trying to remove Scott, and saving the party from "the Albany gang."[109] Scott managed to keep his job at this stormy meeting by a margin of 54 votes to 50 and survived a proposal to declare the position of chairman vacant "in the best interests of the party."[110] The closeness of the contest ruled out harmony in the near future, while Scott had to accept a new executive committee and the deposing of several of his supporters. The *New York Times* noted that the "debate exposed to view many of the skeletons in the Republican closet," and that "no one had a good word to say for Messrs. Dewey or Brownell."[111] Brownell, seen to have usurped Scott, was blamed for the recent defeat, but to his opponents, Scott remained "a symbol of Dewey misrule."[112] In essence, the Omaha meeting was an opportunity for Republicans to come together and criticize Dewey, Brownell, and Scott for their handling of the 1948 campaign, particularly their failure to defend the reputation of the Eightieth Congress.[113]

Against this backdrop, the GOP in the House of Representatives announced a complete reorganization of its policy-making machinery. The brainchild of Minority Leader Martin, the party named a nine-member campaign committee to moderate between the liberal and Old Guard factions of the party and respond to what many in the House perceived as Dewey's lack of support in 1948.[114] The GOP was already looking to the midterms of 1950 with some trepidation, knowing that Truman's Fair Deal, essentially a continuation of the New Deal, was as entrenched as ever; moreover, many of those Republican congressmen up for reelection were in marginal seats. Notwithstanding a failed effort to overthrow him as leader of the Republican Policy Committee and replace him with Henry Cabot Lodge Jr. of Massachusetts, Taft's position remained secure.[115] Whatever the GOP's weaknesses in the House, in the Senate it could always revive its alliance with southern Democrats to block the Fair Deal.[116]

Dewey bullishly defended his record and his campaign. In his Lincoln Day speech in Washington, he declared: "I find that I have been reelected . . . to that somewhat mythical office known as titular head of the Republican Party."[117] Dewey noted the "dismal record" of the GOP over the last twenty years, but insisted that he was not seeking "scapegoats or excuses." The main problem was that the Republican Party had been "split wide open for years," but "we have tried to deny it to ourselves." It was time to confront the party's problems rather than harking back "wistfully to the miscalled 'good old days' of the nineteenth century." To continue along this path would be to "bury the Republican party as the deadest pigeon in the country."[118] Conversely, Dewey urged the GOP not to "out-promise" the Democrats, because "they will promise anything to anybody to get a vote." "Only a progressive forward-looking Republican party," he continued, "can provide the leadership this country needs."[119] Dewey knew that the social advances of the last twenty years could not and should not be sacrificed, but he asserted that the federal government had to be "more efficient, more economical and better managed." "This is," he concluded, "the historic role of the party of Lincoln. . . . Our party was formed in the hot fires of a struggle to advance the cause of human liberty. . . . It is time we returned to our historic role."[120]

The party could agree on nothing except, as Arthur Krock wryly observed, that "Republicans ought to be in office instead of the Democrats." The GOP's problems were exacerbated by the fact that even if it did agree on a program, it was in no position to enact it due to congressional weakness, and could only hamper Truman's program with Dixiecrat assistance. Despite their lack of unity or a program, many Republicans believed, with good reason, that Truman was fundamentally weak, and they were prepared to exploit Democratic differences over civil rights and cloture in preparation for the elections of 1950 and 1952.[121] Scott emphasized this point: "let's take its much-publicized civil rights program as an illustration. Anyone with a rudimentary knowledge of how things operate knows that that program will never be enacted so long as the Southern Democrats in the Senate retain their power to filibuster."[122]

Scott maintained that his battle to retain his post at Omaha was actually beneficial for the party, but by the summer he was under renewed pressure.[123] He vowed to remain as GOP chairman unless there was agreement among the factions upon a replacement who could bring harmony and cohesion to the party. He also condemned a "small group" that was "seeking to stir up party dissension," a reference to a "secret" meeting in Chicago at the beginning of July designed to oust him. Further meetings of malcontents were held in Washington, hosted by R. B. Creager of Texas, another Dewey critic, and there remained powerful figures in the party, including important donors, who wanted Scott removed. Taft did not publicly call for Scott's head, but his lack of an endorsement was telling.[124]

Scott limped on before finally resigning in late July. There was speculation that the new chairman would come from the West as many of the main party offices were held by easterners; the main candidates included Guy Gabrielson and A. T. "Bert" Howard, the Nebraska state chairman.[125] Conferring by telephone, Dewey and Taft were keen to avoid a public squabble about the chairmanship, but this could only be achieved if the two men agreed on a candidate. Gabrielson, a member of the New Jersey state legislature in the 1920s, seemed the likely choice, having met Dewey's people and impressed elements within the Taft camp. Howard had the advantage of being from the Midwest, which was where the GOP felt that the 1952 election would be won or lost. Both Taft and Dewey faced potentially tricky contests in their respective states in November (although at this stage Dewey was not seeking reelection), and both wanted the issue of chairman sorted out as quickly and as painlessly as possible before hitting the campaign trail.[126]

Opposition to Gabrielson was strong but disorganized; even so, he was only elected chairman of the party by a bare majority, winning 52 votes to the 47 received by latecomer Axel J. Beck of South Dakota and to Howard's single vote.[127] His support came primarily from backers of both Taft and Stassen, and his victory ended Dewey's perceived domination of the RNC.[128] The election did little, however, to heal intraparty differences, but Gabrielson pledged to be "an impartial presiding officer" who would practice "complete neutrality in word and spirit." With this in mind, and in an effort to draw a line under the 1948 defeat, Gabrielson declared that "the only campaigns we can win are those in the future."[129]

Also in July 1949, Republicans from twenty-seven states, under the banner of the National Coalition Committee, had held a two-day meeting in Chicago to assail the "me-tooism" of their own party and the "socialistic trend" of the Democrats.[130] As part of its fourteen-point program, the meeting declared that federal aid to public housing and education was tantamount to socialism. It also called for a "grass-roots convention," the habitual Republican response to avoid solving the party's problems, to be held before the 1950 elections.[131] The Republicans returned to Chicago in October, when state chairmen and vice chairmen from fifteen midwestern and Rocky Mountain states assembled for a two-day meeting to discuss strategy for 1950. A statement released by the meeting declared with grand overstatement and unflinching paranoia that the GOP was "the only bulwark between hopeless debt and servitude under an eventual system of socialism engendered and still being engendered by the Democratic party."[132] Although this faction was unrepresentative of the wider party, it was still a striking departure from Dewey's brand of Republicanism.

Gabrielson addressed the meeting and outlined the GOP's plans for the next two elections. His main emphasis was on organization, particularly the recruitment of more young people as activists to go into the precincts to campaign for those Republican senators who were up for reelection in 1950 and also in those areas lost by less than 10 percent in 1948.[133] The RNC planned to start a school to teach its activists political techniques to influence voters and win elections, including courses on how to win the black, white-collar, and farm votes. Gabrielson admitted that this was a response to, and modeled on, the CIO's successful (and hated) PAC system, and he even expressed hope that it would create a faction of Republican-minded union members.[134]

In February 1950, six Republican governors, attempting to strike a more conciliatory tone than that expressed in Chicago, drafted a program for the party. They demanded that it abandon its "backward-looking" attitudes and proposed a twelve-point "progressive" program, arguing that any Republican program "should not be imitative but neither should it be cold and negative." The party had to demonstrate that it had a social conscience and cared about the needy, the old, and the unemployed. The governors concluded:

> In short, our Republican party should be an organization that is broad and not exclusive, a party of service and not of privilege, a party that is hard-hitting and not timid, a party of faith in the future and not

backward looking, a party that is progressive and not backsliding, a party that is constructive not petty.[135]

Gabrielson pronounced the statement "excellent."[136] The RNC, in "separate and closed" meetings with committees from the House and Senate, soon announced support for a "strong policy against the spread of Communism or fascism at home and abroad," which met with approval from both Wherry and Vandenberg. On civil rights, it pledged: "the right of equal opportunity to work, to vote, to advance in life and be protected under the law should never be limited in any individual because of race, religion, color, or country of origin. Therefore, we shall continue to sponsor legislation to protect the rights of minorities." The GOP's slogan for the 1950 election was to be "Liberty Against Socialism."[137]

Yet again, however, the party failed to secure any semblance of unanimity on its program. Hopes that the RNC statement would foster unity were dashed when a progressive group including Lodge, Ives, Javits, and Margaret Chase Smith made their disapproval public, a direct challenge to the conservative leadership being asserted by Taft, Wherry, and Martin.[138] The progressive impulse in the congressional party may not have been large (it carried more weight in the party nationally), but it was determined to be heard.[139] Javits also warned that the two-party system was "doomed" if elements of the GOP persisted in allying with Dixiecrats.[140] The governors' pledge on civil rights was not enough for Javits, who demanded that the party declare its "forthright determination" to pass civil rights legislation in the current Congress and to break the filibuster if necessary. He was also disappointed that the party, announcing its principles on Lincoln's birthday, "did not declare unequivocally for FEPC, anti-lynching and anti–poll tax legislation in the best Lincoln tradition." Lodge felt that the slogan "Liberty Against Socialism" was alarmingly simplistic, as Truman and his administration might have been "opportunists" but they were by no means socialists.[141] Javits soon expressed concern that there was "a grave danger" that congressional Republicans were opposing the administration simply for the sake of opposition and "improvising coalitions with Southern Democrats," which he again asserted was a threat to the two-party system. Furthermore, much of party policy was defined in negative terms, rather than as workable alternatives to the Fair Deal.[142]

The liberal counterattack against the interim platform was continued by Dewey and the New York GOP. He responded robustly to criticism of Republican tactics, including his own, in recent presidential elections, declaring that heeding the "croaking voices of reaction and isolationism" would be a catastrophe for the party. Ironically, according to Dewey, the voices of complaint came largely from those party officials who could not even win their own states and were often those extreme conservatives or isolationists. To Dewey, it was important that voters knew that the GOP "did not intend to repeal the twentieth century." He continued: "we refuse to be against the Ten Commandments just because the Democrats say they are for them." He reminded listeners that New York led the way in the fight against discrimination, "and just because Mr. Truman now comes along and says he is for it, I refuse to turn against it to avoid the epithet 'me too.'" He condemned "these impractical theorists" who "want to drive all moderates and liberals out of the Republican party and then have the remainder join forces with the conservative groups of the South." If this were to happen, the GOP would never win another election.[143]

Ives now urged the GOP to return to the "realism" of Abraham Lincoln if it was to check what he claimed were the socialistic tendencies evident in the current administration. He believed that the party had to have a constructive program of its own, accepting that "our party's record, especially in the field of civil rights . . . has failed miserably to conform to promise or tradition." He further warned that unless platform pledges were made sincerely, voters would not trust the party.[144] The progressives soon offered their own ten-point plan, which included "smashing the filibuster on civil rights."[145] The failure of the interim platform to give a forthright commitment to fair employment practices was seen as weakening the party's chances of retaining control of New York in the forthcoming elections. Ives and Lodge both condemned the platform's "weasel words" on civil rights.[146]

The NAACP watched the situation with interest, but without any genuine expectation of change. Wilkins was, however, quick to praise Ives, agreeing that the civil rights section of the statement was "weasel worded and totally inadequate" and expressing the hope that liberals in the party would be able to return it to its former position as "an advocate of civil rights legislation." He described Ives's statement as "most heartening" and as demonstrating that there were still liberal elements within the party.[147] "If the Negro voter ever entertained any illusions about Republican 'principles,'" remarked the *Crisis*, "they certainly vanished with issuance of the 'Republican statement of principles.'" The party's stand on civil rights was "vacuous," with Republicans preferring to "join hands" with southern Democrats to "jam through the Wherry Amendment," making cloture virtually impossible. The main conclusion that could be drawn was that the GOP "no longer regards itself as the 'friend' of the Negro."[148]

Also using civil rights as their focal point, a number of Republicans, including an unspecified number from both the House and the Senate, Javits among them, wanted to create an equivalent to the ADA to "liberalize, modernize and humanize" the party. One of the principal figures behind the move was Russell Davenport, Willkie's former speechwriter, who was then working at *Fortune* magazine. On civil rights, stated Davenport, it was the "duty of the party to proceed uncompromisingly," while the alliance with the Dixiecrats constituted "treason to the principles of republicanism."[149] Javits and Davenport eventually founded "Republican Advance" in July 1950.[150]

Dewey seemed to have realized belatedly that the African American vote was crucial, even if most of his party had not. This division again reemphasized the differences between the party in large industrial states and Congress, as well as the struggle for control of the party's machinery between the Northeast and the Midwest. Despite this belligerence, it was apparent that Dewey's defeat in 1948, the removal of Scott, and the rise of Joseph McCarthy and his brand of virulent anticommunism had shifted the balance of power in the party towards the Midwest and conservatism.[151] Liberal Republicans were talking a good game, but they were very clearly in retreat.

"Liberty Against Socialism"

The key issues in the midterm elections of 1950 were the war in Korea, communism, and corruption in the Truman administration.[152] Dewey, having reversed his earlier decision not to seek reelection, recounted to an African American audience in New York the efforts of his administration to fight discrimination and contrasted it with Truman's "every promise" on civil rights being "cynically broken." He blamed the Democratic Congress for "refusing" to pass legislation on fair employment, antilynching, and anti–poll tax: "at every chance the Democrat Congress votes down every law against racial and religious intolerance." Demonstrating a belligerence markedly absent from his presidential campaigns, he declared that "the Democratic party is the party of Jim Crow, of Bilbo and of Rankin," whereas "the Republican party is the party that brought liberal progress to New York and led the way in the nation against every form of discrimination"[153]

The *Chicago Defender*, concerned about voter apathy, warned that "all the yammering about racism, all the righteous indignation and the militant resolutions of our leadership will go for naught unless we go to the polls and vote. . . . Negroes who don't vote, particularly where there are no bars to voting, are literally cutting their own throats." It suggested that the Republicans were "still confused on the issues that are closest to our hearts," and that their alliance with the Dixiecrats had "scuttled" Truman's civil rights program and "succeeded in gagging and diverting every serious attempt to match the promises with performances."[154] The *Defender* declared that "Truman has been unyielding" in contrast to the GOP, which had "danced away every opportunity to take civil rights leadership in the Congress" but was now "bombarding the colored electorate with pamphlets which aim to show how the Democrats raped civil rights."[155] It concluded: "the Republicans . . . pose as defenders of fundamental human rights in one breath, and make love to the Dixiecrats with the other." They would continue to suffer in northern districts because of this.[156]

The Republican Party made gains in the Midwest and Far West, and some of the Democratic Party's most prominent figures, including Lucas and Myers, were not reelected. Taft, despite the attentions of the labor movement, was reelected easily, winning 1,642,550 votes and a 430,900 margin.[157] The GOP had also made gains in Philadelphia, Chicago, and Los Angeles, but the Democrats retained control of both houses. Furthermore, there were more African Americans elected to public office than "at any time in our memory."[158] The midterm elections were a "moral victory" for the GOP, and although the crushing nature of Taft's reelection illustrated a swing to the right, there was no consistent pattern across the country.[159] When civil rights was not subsequently among Truman's five "must" pieces of legislation, it was patently clear that the prospects for legislation in the new Congress were even less bright than they had been in the old.[160] The *Chicago Defender* wrote that the election indicated the "dangerous extent to which fascism is spreading in America," warning, "after a while it won't be safe to be known as a supporter of democracy lest you be called a subversive influence against the American ideal."[161] After these encouraging results, Taft declared that, in 1952, the Republicans "can beat Santa Claus." He challenged the GOP to win back the black and "nationality" votes, and urged party leaders to start to do something about this.[162] Gabrielson's analysis, gleaned from 524 party leaders, suggested that it was "failures" in foreign policy and the lack of preparedness that had cost the Democrats. These were "fortunate" issues, Taft noted, that may not be around in two years' time.[163]

Clarence Mitchell wrote to White in the aftermath of the elections to assess the prospects for civil rights in the new Congress. He noted that fifty senators who had voted for cloture remained, and that nine new senators would probably support it. In the House of Representatives, 149 supporters of the FEPC were still in office, but the overall makeup of the House would not alter radically. The main problems the NAACP faced would be in the committees in both houses and also the Senate leadership. Mitchell felt that the association should endeavor to prevent Dixiecrats gaining key positions and suggested that Republican congressmen should be pressured into supporting a compulsory FEPC.[164] White maintained optimistically that African Americans could elect the next president. He was concerned, however, that with the defeats of a number of key allies, the election of 1950 could have dealt a "death blow" for civil rights legislation for the next two years. He expressed the hope that the Republicans had learned lessons from 1946 and 1948 elections about the value of the African American vote, but came to the worrying conclusion that the most influential party in the forthcoming Congress would be the Dixiecrats.[165]

"Stop This Foolishness on Civil Rights"

Despite the admonishments of liberal Republicans about the need to embrace civil rights, it was apparent that congressional conservatives were more interested in courting Dixie. In February 1951, Everett Dirksen, the vanquisher of Scott Lucas in Illinois, announced the GOP's intention to run in the South in 1952, while Senator Karl Mundt, a conservative isolationist from South Dakota and an unabashed advocate of marriage with the Dixiecrats, was appointed vice chairman of the Senate Republican Campaign Committee, as "part of a long-range program to build up Republican strength in the South," according to the *New York Times*.[166] Alarmist claims in the *Baltimore Afro-American* suggested that Dixiecrats and Republicans had held a secret meeting in Washington, D.C., in March 1951 to discuss forming a new party. The speculative ticket consisted of Taft for president and Harry F. Byrd as vice president, or an Eisenhower-Russell ticket. Among those allegedly invited were: Senators Mundt, Bricker, Brewster, and Millikin and Representatives Clarence Brown (Ohio), Halleck (Indiana), and Gwinn (New York). The *Afro-American* had not, however, been able to determine how many senators actually attended.[167]

If this was slightly hysterical speculation, what could at least be verified was that the RNC had set up a committee to try to create an effective two-party system in the South, but a spokesman said that there was no connection between this and the Washington meeting. The invitations to this meeting were sent by Fred V. Virkus under the auspices of the National Coalition Committee, a group exploring the possibility of a Republican-Dixiecrat alliance. Recent speeches by Mundt on the topic had been well received, and the National Coalition Committee had been formed to pursue the idea further. Virkus believed that the GOP "had everything to gain" by a merger, while another defeat could threaten its existence.[168] Lapsed New Dealer Raymond Moley asserted that northern supporters of the Republican Party wanted the GOP "to stop this foolishness about civil rights," stating that legislation was not the way to solve racial problems. He noted that despite Dewey's strenuous and successful efforts in passing the SCAD bill in New York, "Harlem does not vote for him." Moley believed that there was no longer a two-party system in America, and asserted that "what we need is a coalition of conservative Republicans and Southern Democrats."[169]

The advantages and disadvantages of a hypothetical Dixiecrat-Republican merger were debated by GOP spokesmen in the pages of *Collier's*. Mundt believed that the Republicans and the Dixiecrats should formally unite as it would end the trend toward a powerful centralized government and the socialism he saw as inherent in the New Deal and Fair Deal, while sustaining the fight against communism. Republicans tried forming alliances with minority and pressure groups without success; in fact, argued Mundt, they had tried everything but an alliance with the South. Presciently, he declared that the South was "the natural and logical source of new strength for the Republican party." If it was not for the "informal, unorganized, undirected alliance" of Republicans and southern Democrats, Mundt declared, America would be much closer to communism. This coalition, he asserted, would guarantee victory in 1952.[170]

Clifford Case, a congressman from New Jersey and a noted liberal, disagreed vehemently with Mundt's thesis as it would "destroy the Republican Party and bring disaster to our nation." He asserted that "sooner or later . . . legally sanctioned discrimination will be ended in the South, and in the South of the future there is a permanent place for a political party which really believes that the Negro is not an inferior person." "The Republican party," he argued, "can be that party. Its traditions require that it should be. The Democratic party in the South can never be." Case believed that it was "tacitly assumed" that any Republican-Dixiecrat merger would be the end of civil rights. A merger was also unlikely for practical reasons: southerners would not wish to cede their cherished seniority in Congress and would no longer be able to "wag the dog." Furthermore, votes won by this coalition in the South would cost it traditional GOP votes in the North—for example, in

New York, Michigan, and Connecticut, where Dewey triumphed narrowly in 19489—and it would have little or no chance in Illinois, California, Ohio, and Massachusetts.[171]

Mundt soon announced that the bipartisan Committee to Explore Political Realignment had been created by one hundred delegates from seventeen states. These were, according to Mundt, "likeminded Americans" from both parties who wanted to find "a working formula for combining their voting strength to stop the encroachment of socialism and the all-inclusive centralized superstate." Mundt did not confirm it, but it seemed that five southern governors had attended the conference. Mundt's aim was to transform the conservative coalition in Congress against "socialistic legislation" and "bureaucratic tyranny" before the presidential election of 1952. In fifteen years, claimed Mundt, this alliance had decided the outcome of thirty-five different measures.[172]

While Mundt was whistling at Dixie, Gabrielson's business dealings with the Reconstruction Finance Corporation (RFC) came under scrutiny. It emerged that his company, Carthage Hydrocol, had received an $18.5 million loan and was allowed to defer payment for a year, and a number of Republican senators believed that Gabrielson should resign.[173] Ironically, at the same time as pressure was being put on Gabrielson, his Democratic counterpart William Boyle was being investigated by the Senate, and heavily criticized by the GOP, regarding three loans totaling $645,000 from the RFC.[174] Gabrielson defended the loan to his company while maintaining unconvincingly that the RFC should be abolished, claiming that private industry would have funded his company had there been no RFC. Gabrielson refused to countenance resignation and was given a vote of confidence by Republicans attending a twenty-two-state eastern and southern regional conference.[175]

It also emerged that Gabrielson had attempted to make the head of the RFC, Harvey J. Gunderson, president of the New York Stock Exchange. Gunderson did not get the job, but many Republicans were still outraged by Gabrielson's actions. Richard Nixon, a member of the subcommittee investigating the claims, believed that the evidence pointed to "an act of impropriety." Gabrielson said that the first part of the loan was made in 1946 before he joined the company, and the last two parts in 1948 and 1949 before he became chairman of the GOP.[176] Unconvinced, Nixon urged both Gabrielson and Boyle to resign. Neither had done anything illegal, he conceded, but there was "the paramount need in the country today . . . to restore public confidence in the integrity of our national leaders and government officials."[177] Boyle resigned on 13 October, but Gabrielson remained in his post despite "mounting rumors" that he would be "eased out" when the RNC met in January in favor of "someone less tangibly oriented toward the candidacy of Senator Robert A. Taft."[178]

While the controversy was raging, Gabrielson found the time to announce a three-pronged GOP strategy to launch the 1952 election campaign, consisting of a speaking tour in five southern states in November; a meeting for the leaders of 22 million ethnic Americans, who held the balance of power in many key states; and, finally, a goal of at least five thousand Lincoln Day rallies. Gabrielson declared that a genuine opportunity had arisen to crack the Solid South, particularly because of southern concerns about states' rights, a term that was essentially code for opposition to civil rights.[179] He also declared that American voters "want a change in 1952" and the end of Truman's "corrupt administration." The recent election of a Republican mayor in Little Rock, Arkansas, "indicates that the once solid South is eager for a two-party system."[180] The importance of these states' delegates to Taft at the forthcoming Republican convention, and Gabrielson's increasing association with Taft's candidacy, strongly indicate that he was doing the Ohioan's bidding below the Mason-Dixon Line.[181]

Speaking in Atlanta, Gabrielson restated his desire to see a two-party South and expressed his belief that the region was ready for this change. "The purpose of my trip," he readily conceded, "is to really develop a two-party system." The Republican policy in the region would be based on "the states running their own affairs and the cutting down of federal bureaucracy."[182] Gabrielson described the South as a "great frontier" for the GOP and announced that the party would be organizing in the region and targeting a number of congressional seats. He also stressed that the Republican Party would not abandon its commitment to civil rights, declaring, "we must do away with second-class citizenship in this country and make everybody, regardless of race, color, or creed, equal."[183]

Clarence Mitchell was also in the South. Speaking in Birmingham, Alabama, he urged Truman to punish those who had bolted from the party in 1948, and threatened to "dry up" federal funds for the South if discrimination was not ended.[184] He restated the NAACP mantra that African Americans would vote for the party that delivered civil rights legislation in the current session of Congress, and he warned that the Democratic Party did not have "a ninety-nine year lease on our support." Mitchell also urged black voters to let Taft know that "we do not like the kind of campaign he is making throughout the South" in his appeals to Dixiecrats. "That kind of campaign might make him the darling of the Confederates in Alabama, but it will never help him to carry New York, California and Pennsylvania." Mitchell, carefully insulating Truman from criticism, condemned the "weak and spineless" advisers who surrounded the president and endeavored to "water down his stand on civil rights." If Truman had "punished the rebels" of 1948, they would not currently be in possession of the key chairmanships in Congress.[185]

It was patently obvious that the GOP would be heading into Dixie in 1952 with hopes of at least denting, if not ultimately cracking, the Solid South. The party had shown little real interest in the region since the days of Herbert Hoover, yet a new dynamic, attributable largely to Truman's civil rights stance, had emerged, making gains in the region appear both feasible and strategically worthwhile. This was a mission now rooted in hope rather than mere expectation, as GOP conservatives had demonstrated that their sympathies lay increasingly on the side of states' rights, and they, like many southerners, resented what they regarded as the creeping centralization and "socialism" of the Truman administration. The states' rights position in the South was, of course, a smokescreen to shroud opposition to civil rights, and there can be little doubt that those Republicans who wrapped themselves in the cloak of states' rights knew this. It was also apparent that the South, or rather the skeletal Republican organizations in the region, would be essential to Taft's nomination, and he, like the Dixiecrats, was prepared to use an unashamedly antidemocratic mandate to achieve his ambitions. More generally, the dwindling band of Republican liberals saw its influence diminish as the party realized that the route to electoral success lay in the embrace of McCarthyism and anticommunism, rather than any progressive impulse.[186] Ascendant conservatism within the GOP, in alliance with the Dixiecrats in Congress, behind a likely presidential nomination for Taft, was very bad news indeed for liberal Republicans, civil rights, and African Americans.

8

The Unfinished Business of America

At the beginning of 1952, Robert Taft seemed destined finally to secure the presidential nomination he craved. His reelection in 1950, Henry Moon asserted, made him the "triumphant symbol of resurgent conservatism." Taft was not inclined to disagree, seeing his success as a repudiation of Truman and his "socialistic-planned economy" and failed foreign policy; labor attributed his victory to scaremongering about communism.[1] Despite maintaining, without much conviction, that he had no interest in running, it was readily apparent that Taft's reelection made him not just a potential presidential candidate, but the man most likely to secure the Republican nomination.[2] Leaving as little to chance as possible, in December 1951 Gabrielson filled the key convention posts with Taft supporters.[3]

The prospects of a Taft candidacy filled African Americans with dread. Taft had, of course, courted the South in 1948, revisited in 1951, and was the de facto leader of the GOP in a Congress that had pointedly failed to pass any civil rights legislation. Taft reaffirmed his hostility to an FEPC with enforcement powers in April 1952, stating that this was "primarily the duty of the states," although he did suggest a commission to study the problem as an alternative.[4] The *Chicago Defender* condemned his "brazen courtship" of Dixiecrats and "his failure to crack the party whip on civil rights."[5] The *Crisis* concurred: "Taft's record on issues vital to Negroes is one of double-talk, obstructionism and opportunism."[6] Speaking in early 1952, Walter White found "no widespread enthusiasm" for the GOP among African Americans, reinforced by a unanimous preference for "anybody but Taft." White warned, however, that alienation from the Democrats could see black voters supporting a good Republican candidate.[7] Just before the GOP convention, White reiterated his opposition to Taft's candidacy, declaring: "if Taft is the nominee, a great many Negro voters will stay at home."[8] Clarence Mitchell continued the NAACP's attack, claiming that the senator "sounded like a candidate running for the governorship of Mississippi."[9]

Yet Taft attracted some grudging respect, although rarely affection, in the country at large. Arthur Schlesinger commented that "even his enemies respect his intellectual honesty and his reasoning powers, if not his conclusions."[10] Moon disagreed:

> His immense prestige stems from nothing positive in his political career and is, indeed, based upon a myth diligently cultivated by his supporters and widely accepted by those who confuse bluntness with honesty. . . . Certainly nothing in his record justifies his reputation for singular honesty and superior intellect.

Moon also noted that Truman's association with the Pendergast machine in Missouri was never forgotten; Taft's past in the similarly corrupt Cox-Hynicka machine in Ohio was rarely mentioned.[11] Taft's career was also sullied by his reliance on southern delegates ("Dixie zombies") at Republican conventions and support from "the anti-Negro and anti-Semitic political underworld" including Gerald L. K. Smith.[12] Taft also demonstrated an "utter incapacity to comprehend the forces shaping the world in which we live. It reveals a nineteenth-century mind. . . . In short, it is the record of a politician of very mediocre caliber."[13] Gloster Current of the NAACP claimed that Taft was "more interested in gaining the support and approval of the Dixiecrats than of Negro voters, organized labor and liberals."[14]

Taft's supporters took a different view of his attitude toward civil rights. A "Taft for Senate Committee" pamphlet aimed at black voters claimed that he "doesn't promise one thing in his campaign and another in Congress," noting his support for cloture against filibusters, but ignoring his role in writing a liberal civil rights platform at the convention in 1944, complete with FEPC, and then disregarding it while in control of Congress.[15] The "Citizens' Committee of the South Central District to Elect Senator Taft" noted that, as the first Republican majority leader in twenty years, he had led the fight to oust the infamous Mississippi bigot, Senator Theodore Bilbo. Taft, it continued, "has not 'kidded' Negroes about civil rights"; on the contrary, he had "stood up for first-class citizenship," "advance[d] our civil rights by intelligent voting," and would defy the "Dixiecrats-Democrats."[16] Taft was at least consistent on the thorny issue of the FEPC, maintaining that his opposition to an agency with enforcement powers had remained unaltered for five years. He believed that the wartime FEPC had "accomplished a great deal by persuasion" and claimed that he had attempted to set up a peacetime version of the agency. He felt that a compulsory law would encourage frivolous cases, and he did not want the federal government "to intrude into all kinds of personal relationships."[17] Taft at least pledged to appoint an African American to his administration if elected.[18]

"Cure All the Evils in Men's Hearts"

The lack of a suitable moderate standard bearer strengthened Taft's position, and Dewey genuinely believed that Taft's presidential ambitions had to be checked to prevent the party from lurching further to the right and the virtual guarantee of defeat it would bring. To do this, Dewey needed a candidate who could rally the party's progressives and, most importantly, secure victory in 1952. As early as April 1949, Dewey began the process of trying to persuade General Dwight D. Eisenhower to seek the Republican nomination.[19] When the two men met in July 1949, Dewey initially suggested that Eisenhower succeed him as governor of New York, and stressed that he had a "duty" to seek elected office. Eisenhower, however, was skeptical.[20] Dewey, according to Norton Smith, saw Eisenhower as "a hero rather than a politician, a diplomat-soldier whose vague ideas on domestic policy were all the more salable for their mystery."[21] When Eisenhower was appointed to head NATO, Dewey felt that this made him an even more attractive prospect. Dewey was, nevertheless, acutely aware that Eisenhower risked being seen as his puppet and, therefore, refused to endorse the general publicly.

Eisenhower remained recalcitrant, privately pledging not to run if Taft agreed to broaden America's international commitments, but the Ohioan refused, and this, together with Dewey's warning that MacArthur could seize the nomination, persuaded him finally to resign from NATO in April 1952 and begin campaigning formally in June.[22] It was abundantly clear to the Taft faction, and indeed, the party at large, that the Eisenhower candidacy was being underwritten by Dewey. One anti-Dewey Republican remarked: "the face is the face of Eisenhower, but the political brain is the brain of Tom Dewey and his henchmen." Taft agreed that there was "no doubt" that Dewey was directing the Eisenhower campaign.[23]

Eisenhower was born in Texas and raised in Kansas and could only be described, according to Piers Brendon, as a racial liberal in "a southern context."[24] Much of Eisenhower's career was spent in the South, and this was the source of most of his negativity toward African Americans in the military.[25] Eisenhower referred to "darkies" while serving in North Africa in 1943, despite the War Department banning the term in 1942; he reportedly chuckled at a training film showing African American soldiers carrying weapons, professing that he had never seen this while supreme allied commander, but he did at least desegregate USO and Red Cross clubs in Britain.[26] During the Battle of the Bulge in late 1944, he famously issued a call for troops "without regard to color or race," but he was forced to rescind this order by General George C. Marshall; indeed, his efforts to integrate units during the battle were criticized by his friends, which led him to conclude that he was reasonably liberal on race. Eisenhower said of African American troops at the Battle of the Bulge, some of whom had never held a rifle before: "they fought nobly for their country and I will never forget."[27] At the end of the war, he discovered that many Americans had developed different ideas about what constituted racial liberalism.[28]

White derided southern Democrats' "ludicrous" efforts to nominate Eisenhower for the presidency in 1948, stating that the general was "a man of integrity and deep conviction." White recalled speaking to Eisenhower for three hours shortly before the invasion of Normandy, and he agreed that the continuation of segregation was a cause of friction between black and white troops. The general was "implacable in his opposition" to segregation, and "we confined our discussion to practical means of abolishing it as swiftly as possible." He received a promise from Eisenhower that segregation would be abolished as soon as "circumstances permitted."[29]

White's faith in Eisenhower's "integrity and deep conviction" was short-lived. At Senate hearings regarding segregation in the army in April 1948, the general was questioned by Everett Saltonstall. Eisenhower stated that the army was one of many "mirrors" on American society, and that there was "race prejudice in this country." He noted that in the fall of 1944, the army did not make the best use of its 600,000 black soldiers in Europe; nevertheless, 2,400 volunteered for frontline service and were organized as platoons and distributed among white troops as there was no time to train them to work independently in larger forces and also because "they do not seem to gain a self-confidence among themselves when used in larger units." From that point on, Eisenhower advocated the organization of African American soldiers in units no larger than platoons. Eisenhower feared that, because African Americans were not as well educated as "his brother citizen that is white," they would be relegated to all the minor jobs in an integrated force, which could result in, for example, a lack of African American NCOs. African Americans would, therefore, progress better in separate units. He hoped that things would change due to education and mutual respect, but in his statement that "I do believe that if we attempt merely by passing a lot of laws to force someone to like someone else, we are just going to get into trouble," he was expressing a view he would maintain throughout his presidency. He did not, however, favor a return to the "extreme segregation" of the army he had joined nearly forty years earlier.[30]

White privately admitted that he had blundered in his praise of Eisenhower, but felt that he should not appear apologetic over it.[31] Nevertheless, he had to issue a statement admitting that he had misjudged Eisenhower prior to his testimony. He conceded that he had been "naïve" and noted "that white and Negro soldiers fought ably and without friction during the critical Battle of the Bulge seems to have faded from the General's memory."[32] Eisenhower later told E. Frederic Morrow, the first African American to serve in the cabinet, that all his field commanders opposed integration, and it was not until later that he realized that they were all southerners; indeed, Eisenhower had many southern friends and was also interested in southern military history.[33] He had, furthermore, commanded poorly performing African American troops early in his career, but it did not occur to him that their performance was due to poor training or indifferent officers, and he admitted that this had had a negative impact upon his view of black troops and African Americans more generally.[34] He summed up his experience with African American Illinois National Guardsmen with the assessment, "they just couldn't do anything."[35]

When he was president of Columbia University, Eisenhower described Ralph Bunche as "one of the greatest statesmen this country has produced today" for his work at the United Nations. Eisenhower was concerned, however, about inviting Bunche, due to accept an honorary degree, to his house.[36] Also during his tenure at Columbia, he praised the progress of African Americans in a visit to Harlem. No other people in the history of mankind, he declared, "have come so far on the road to understanding citizenship and culture in eighty-five years as has the Negro race."[37] As the momentum behind Eisenhower's bid for the Republican nomination increased at the beginning of 1952, so too did the pressure from African Americans. Civil rights advocates were particularly interested in the general's attitude toward an FEPC. In an undated response to a query about the FEPC, Eisenhower, who described it as a "shotgun question," declared his support for equality and fairness for all Americans and the involvement of the federal government as far as it was constitutionally allowed. He did not believe, however, that legislation was the answer and felt that more could be done through leadership.[38] White sought clarification of this statement, and asked the general to reconsider his view.[39] Wilkins took a more realistic view of Eisenhower's attitude, telling White, "I don't think that anybody with even a little knowledge of how things are going expected Eisenhower to come out for FEPC."[40] Eisenhower had adopted a similar position to Taft, although he was disturbingly closer to the views of southern Democrats than those of the senator.[41]

Eisenhower's stance was a boon for the Democrats as it meant that they could weaken their own civil rights stance without necessarily widening party splits on the issue; it also meant that they could offer African Americans less, but still more than the Republicans. Eisenhower and the Republicans were, in effect, letting the Democrats off the hook on the extraordinarily divisive issue of civil rights. The implication was that supporters of civil rights really had nowhere else to go but the Democratic Party, and that there was, furthermore, no need for the Democrats to do anything that might further antagonize southerners. Clarence Mitchell was quick to accuse Eisenhower of surrendering to Dixiecrat sympathizers within the GOP, warning that "unless the general changes his views on this subject, many of his key supporters in Congress may be defeated in November."[42]

Eisenhower, asked about reform of Rule 22, replied: "I don't know what I would do." Pressed again about the FEPC and informed that thirty-seven states had no fair employment practices laws, thus fueling Kremlin propaganda, he agreed that there was "no question" about this, but maintained that it was something "we have reserved to the states specifically." He maintained that he was not willing to support a "punitive" law.[43] A few days later, he reiterated his states' rights stance but had no objection to setting up a federal commission to investigate the problem, provided it had no enforcement powers.[44] Eisenhower asserted: "my own belief is this: no true American, no American worthy of the name, would want deliberately to exclude another American from full opportunity to enjoy every guarantee under the Constitution. . . . Equality is the basic concept of our whole Government—we must never forget it."[45] The *Chicago Defender* complained that Eisenhower's attitude made "Taft look like an advanced thinker. . . . The general is clearly against sin, but he doesn't plan to do anything about it."[46]

Eisenhower had "dashed the hopes of the liberal wing of his party" by coming out against an FEPC, stalling on segregation in education and the elimination of segregation in the military.[47] He stated his "unchangeable and unalterable" support for equality and would do whatever the federal government could do, but, ultimately, he said, "I do not believe that we can cure all the evils in men's hearts by law."[48] While he did not know that segregation made schools in the South more expensive, he did at least declare that "we can no longer afford to hold on to the anachronistic principles of race segregation in the armed services."[49] White believed that Eisenhower's views on the FEPC were to the right of Taft and even of Senator Russell of Georgia.[50] This, White felt, contrasted with his record as supreme allied commander and the hopes of his supporters that he would be "another Wendell Willkie." White saw his stance as "backtracking" and criticized his "verbosity and doubletalk."[51] It was clear that whomever the Republicans nominated, he was not going to be a champion of civil rights.

"Is the Elephant Capable of Remembering?"

A strident African American voice within the Republican Party fell silent in April 1952 when Robert Church died at the age of sixty-seven while attending a state GOP meeting at Nashville.[52] The *Chicago Defender* wrote that "the Republican Party lost its conscience as far as Negro GOP leadership is concerned." Church was "enlightened enough to see the grave shortcomings of his party for the Negro and was astute and courageous enough to hold the party's feet to the fire for failure to hew a liberal line" and refused to be "the stooge of the vested interests." In the spring of 1951, for instance, when Mundt was talking about a Republican-Dixiecrat merger, Church wrote to GOP chairman Gabrielson demanding that he disavow this notion publicly. When Church died, "a mighty oak fell in the Republican Party."[53]

With the election six months away, the *Defender* accused politicians of "still operating in 1952 on a set of facts that made political sense in 1932" with regard to the relative importance of the African American vote in the North and the southern white vote.[54] The *Crisis* agreed: "the man who gets into the White House next November is going to need Negro votes" and will only get them with a "forthright civil rights platform." African Americans knew that the Republicans had offered only "sanctimonious phrases and empty promises" and were allied with southern Democrats. It warned the GOP that "you can't keep on appeasing Negro voters with plums and platitudes." The Democratic record was "not much better" but at least boasted the presence of Truman.[55]

As the conventions approached, African Americans could muster scant enthusiasm for either party. White, whose quadrennial analysis of American politics had altered little in twenty years, wondered if "the elephant [is] incapable of remembering as well as forgetting?" The Democrats, moreover, had "no outstanding candidate." The election hinged, he believed, on "not which party is the wisest and bravest but on which is slightly less stupid than the other."[56] White and other African American leaders were keen to remind the two parties of the significance of the black vote in 1948 and the increasing numbers of African Americans registered to vote in the South. "What the Negro Wants in 1952," a statement by twenty leading African American organizations, noted that 70 percent had backed Truman despite "the fact that his leading opponent was an able Republican whose civil rights record was well established."[57] The minimum program acceptable to African Americans would have to include an end of filibuster and reform of Rule 22; an FEPC; antilynching legislation; the protection of the right to vote; the end of discrimination in the military; the abolition of segregation in interstate travel; and forbidding federal money from being used to support segregation. Furthermore, African Americans would oppose any candidate who was not "explicit and uncompromising" on civil rights.[58]

The NAACP claims that the African American vote could swing an election were supported by Elmo Roper. Speaking on NBC, he reported that 45 percent of African Americans respected the views of the NAACP and asserted that African Americans voted on the "single issue" of civil rights, concluding that "the Negro vote in the North can, indeed, be a marginal difference between one party or the other." The NAACP, he continued, was the most important black organization and "cannot be ignored" by politicians.[59] The NAACP, which he noted was nonpartisan, was trusted by more African Americans than actually voted, meaning that "the protest sentiment has not yet been fully converted into a protest at the polls." This was probably because they were not well organized enough politically and were prevented from voting in much of the South, while in the North those who had moved from the South had to wait to vote due to residency requirements.[60]

Roper discussed the "paradox" of the Solid South and the northern black vote, and their relative importance to the Democratic Party. His research demonstrated that African Americans leaned toward the Democrats: 14 percent were independent, 24 percent were Republicans, and 62 percent were Democrats and had voted that way over the preceding twenty years. A much smaller percentage of African Americans (31 percent) voted than other groups (52 percent), although this figure was skewed due to the situation in the South, where about two-thirds of black Americans lived.[61] In large northern cities, perhaps as many as 63 percent of African Americans had voted, meaning that around 2 million voted in the North and 1 million in the South. In the North, the Democrats had a plurality of about 750,000 among black voters, which made them crucial in key northern states where the overall plurality of the Democrats was less than 500,000 in the last three or four presidential elections.[62]

The Democrats stood to continue to be the recipient of African American votes, provided the party did not stray from Truman and Roosevelt's civil rights commitments; if they did, the Republicans could benefit.[63] He concluded, to the delight of the NAACP and the particular satisfaction of White, that "it is a fact and not a myth that the Negro vote can swing it [a presidential election] either way."[64] By suggesting that African Americans were solidly wedded to the Democratic Party, this analysis, though thoughtful and undoubtedly accurate, amply demonstrated that African Americans were essentially dependent on a Democratic victory, and a narrow victory at that. A Republican triumph with a miniscule proportion of the black vote—and therefore with no political debts owed to African Americans—could spell disaster for progress on civil rights.

"A Lot of Explaining"

The Republican convention promised to be controversial. Many delegates felt—and statistical evidence appeared to support their view—that Taft could not be elected, and questions were asked about his methods in trying to secure the votes of southern delegates.[65] Taft, supported by Gabrielson, wanted the disputed delegates from Texas, Louisiana, Mississippi, Georgia, Virginia, and Puerto Rico (hardly Republican strongholds) to be able to vote on each other's credentials.[66] Eisenhower supporters, led by Henry Cabot Lodge Jr., believed that Taft was trying to rig the convention, and that the nomination could hinge on the outcome of the dispute.[67] The Credentials Committee asked that pro-Taft delegations from Texas and Georgia not be seated, even though they had already been approved by the National Committee.[68] White, claiming "highly reliable sources," had alleged that delegates to the Republican National Convention from the South, notably Mississippi, Texas, Georgia, South Carolina, and Louisiana, were being bought for $2,500; although he declined to speculate whether they were being bought for either Taft or Eisenhower, the implication that they were destined for the former was obvious.[69] The convention duly unseated the pro-Taft delegations from Georgia and Texas, and it was clear that Taft could only secure the nomination with what Arthur Krock called "a tainted certificate."[70]

In 1952, it was the Republicans' turn to have an embarrassing and divisive convention controversy on civil rights, although it was by no means on the scale of the Democrats' Dixiecrat hullabaloo of 1948.[71] Together with the issue of the rotten boroughs of the South, there was dissatisfaction among

African Americans in the New York delegation, where Harold C. Burton (of the "Crispus Attucks Republican League") and Charles S. Hill were threatening to back Taft if Eisenhower did not alter his stance on the FEPC. They stated that Eisenhower's "civil rights stand is suicide in Harlem."[72] Burton and Hill later told Dewey that Eisenhower's "position [was] worse than that of Senator Russell of Georgia." Their loyalty was first of all to their race, rather than the state or national Republican Party, and, despite his position being flawed, they had come to the somewhat depressing conclusion that Taft offered more to African Americans.[73] One of these delegates, presumably Burton, was warned by Dewey that his job with the New York Board of Elections would be under threat if he did not support Eisenhower.[74] Burton and Hill's defection to Taft was brief. They were soon arguing that while the two potential candidates' views were very similar, Eisenhower's advisers were altogether more liberal on the issue. Burton also contended that unless the civil rights plank was "as good or better" than the one adopted in 1948, he would, supported by around twenty African American delegates, instigate a floor fight.[75] Hill asserted: "we are doomed to failure because the subcommittee and the Resolutions Committee is controlled by the old guard Republicans who are supporting Senator Taft."[76]

Northern and southern Republicans clashed again on civil rights in subcommittee, with the threat of taking the issue to the convention floor. There was also the possibility of taking another draft of the plank—the fourth—to the full Platform Committee for a showdown, although it was abundantly clear that there would be no endorsement of a compulsory FEPC regardless of which faction emerged triumphant. Civil rights was the last plank of the platform to be completed, after a proposal that the 1948 plank be readopted was rejected.[77] When the finished civil rights plank finally emerged, it came out against the poll tax and vowed to make lynching a federal crime, but it rejected a compulsory FEPC (although it implied that Congress would have the final say). In addition, it rejected a southern proposal that the matter of civil rights be left to the states, although it stated that civil rights was primarily their responsibility.[78] Morse urged Eisenhower to reject the "weasel-worded" civil rights plank if the GOP "is to win the support of the civil rights groups" and "keep faith with Lincoln"; parts of the platform, he declared, were "entirely too reactionary."[79]

The faltering morale of African American Republicans and the strong-arm tactics of Dewey were amply demonstrated when the Burton group not only sided with Eisenhower but also felt compelled to abandon plans for a floor fight after being warned by Ives and New Jersey governor Alfred E.

Driscoll (the architect of his state's New York–inspired civil rights legislation of 1949) that this would aid Taft's bid for the nomination.[80] Worse still, Lodge warned that Eisenhower would not accept the nomination if the platform included a compulsory FEPC.[81] The party duly adopted the proposed platform without a dissenting vote. Burton announced rather hopefully that the platform could be construed as advocating a compulsory fair employment practices law and seconded the move for its adoption, although he soon conceded ruefully that the civil rights plank would "take a lot of explaining" to African Americans.[82]

Burton later claimed that Eisenhower had assured him that a fair employment practices law "could be" enacted if he became president. Burton also confirmed that he abandoned the idea of a floor fight on civil rights on the advice of Driscoll and Ives, who warned that it would only benefit southern elements.[83] Burton blamed Hobson Reynolds of Philadelphia for the civil rights plank and claimed that he had asked Perry Howard for assistance, to which the Mississippian replied: "I'm not interested in the FEPC and the Negroes. I'm interested only in nominating Taft and stopping Eisenhower."[84] Burton further alleged that when he saw the plank, he said: "I'm not satisfied at all. We'll have a hell of a time explaining it." He decided that he would lead a floor fight on the plank, and "all the Negro delegates still agreed to carry the fight with me," but the following morning Reynolds presented a new plank and the African American delegates decided to substitute this for the one created by the Resolutions Committee.[85]

Martin had given Burton five minutes to speak to the convention, but ten minutes before he was due to speak he was called to the meeting with Ives and Driscoll, where he was told that they would not be able to get the amended plank passed by a majority vote. Reynolds told Burton not to address the convention as "the Negroes will soon forget it." Burton then attended a meeting with Javits, Driscoll, and Ives to discuss the FEPC, before speaking to the convention.[86] The *Chicago Defender* published the civil rights plank that Burton was supposed to present to the Republican convention, which advocated a simple majority to enforce cloture, "federal legislation prohibiting discrimination in employment," and "establishment of a federal agency empowered to enforce that prohibition."[87] The debacle over the civil rights plank demonstrated once again the weakness of African American Republicans, but, more tellingly, it also revealed that even their staunchest supporters were prepared to be brutally pragmatic about civil rights.

One final effort to persuade the GOP to alter its course came from Chicago city councilman and AME minister Archibald Carey. "I trust it is not immodest to point out," he declared, "but is it significant that the Republican Party has not won a national election since it lost the Negro vote?" He continued: "the Republican party became great when it launched the fight for human freedom. The Republican party will be greater when it widens freedom's borders." "We cannot tolerate expediency," he warned; "we cannot compromise with righteousness." To those who felt that "the time was not ripe," he declared that "no man can enjoy his civil rights posthumously." When asked what African Americans wanted, he always replied, "nothing special." Quoting "My Country 'tis of Thee," with its plea to let "let freedom ring," he declared:

> That's exactly what we mean—from every mountain side, let freedom ring. Not only from the Green mountains and the White mountains of Vermont and New Hampshire; not only from the Catskills of New York; but from the Ozarks of Arkansas, from the Stone Mountain in Georgia, from the Great Smokies of Tennessee, and from the Blue Ridge Mountains of Virginia—Not only for the minorities of the United States, but for the persecuted of Europe, for the rejected of Asia, for the disenfranchised of South Africa and for the disinherited of all the earth—may the Republican party, under God, from every mountainside, LET FREEDOM RING.[88]

The Republicans "ignored Carey's eloquent challenge."[89]

The *Defender* concluded: "we can't see how any Negro in 1952 can give blind support to a political party that brazenly flaunts [sic] their basic rights as American citizens."[90] The African American press was virtually unanimous in its condemnation of the Republican plank. The *Baltimore Afro-American* declared that "the Republican party appears to have written off as lost forever the traditional support of colored voters."[91] The *Crisis* opined that the conventions had "left an uneasy feeling, both as to candidates and platforms," with the Republicans opting for states' rights, which had "come to mean that states may cheat, discriminate against, segregate, beat, maim, murder and otherwise mistreat their dark citizens without interference from the Federal Government," and that this "double-talk" had left African American voters angry.[92] It appeared that the party was more interested in courting the southern white vote.

Roy Wilkins, who had telegraphed the GOP urging a "realistic and practical demonstration of good faith on civil rights," predictably echoed the *Crisis* line, asserting that the Republicans had approved "essentially a states' rights plank."[93] Referring to Elmo Roper's findings that the GOP would not win the election without the African American vote, White predicted that because of the "shameless and shameful platform surrender of civil rights," the GOP would not regain the black vote.[94] In late July, New York NAACP member Roderick Stephens wrote to Arthur Vandenberg Jr. of Eisenhower's campaign team, warning that the general's integrity was being risked, as "he can't be for white supremacy and against second class citizenship," nor could he woo the South without losing support in the North. Eisenhower, he believed, had to lose the support of those who believed in segregation and discrimination if he was to win the election.[95]

On the vexed issue of the party's election machinery, the Republicans at least managed to avoid controversy. Party Chairman Gabrielson, "a fervent supporter of Taft" according to the *New York Times*, was replaced by Arthur Summerfield of Michigan unanimously and without a hint of dissent.[96] The *Times* declared with undue optimism that this represented the "passing out of the Old Guard."[97] Summerfield also took over as Eisenhower's campaign manager to allow Lodge to concentrate on his Senate reelection campaign. Brownell, meanwhile, who had acted as the general's convention manager, made the symbolically important step of returning to his law practice, thus ending any insinuation that Dewey was directing Eisenhower's campaign.[98] Lodge and Brownell's departures from Eisenhower's team meant that the GOP's national campaign had lost two of its key spokesmen on civil rights, and, although two Dewey aides remained with Eisenhower, it would become increasingly clear that, while Eisenhower may have been Dewey's anointed successor, he was definitely not Dewey's puppet; indeed, it would be Taft's influence that would prevail on the candidate.[99]

"America Deserves a Better Fate"

Had Truman chosen to stand for the presidency again, he would have been an utter liability in the South. In March 1952, a Gallup poll had him trailing Eisenhower by 62 percent to 30 percent; even the apparently unelectable Taft led him by 46 percent to 42 percent in the region.[100] That same month, the president who had done more than any other for civil rights announced that he would not be reseeking his party's nomination.[101] This was a stunning blow to African American hopes; quite simply, no candidate from either party approached Truman's commitment to civil rights. Among the

Democratic hopefuls, Adlai Stevenson—the Illinois governor and Truman's preference—was potentially acceptable to African Americans, but in early 1952 he still had not confirmed his intention to run.[102] Moreover, even if Stevenson did decide to run, he maintained that the question of the FEPC should be dealt with by the states in the first instance, before the federal government became involved. By May 1952, there were "hints of desperation" among African American leaders about the Democratic nomination.[103]

White declared that the nomination of Senator Richard Russell of Georgia would "ensure the election of almost any Republican and virtually destroy the Democratic party." Russell had no chance of winning the nomination, but he was determined to prevent Truman's renomination and adoption of a strong civil rights plank. The Dixiecrats, White speculated, wanted to throw the election to the House of Representatives.[104] The *Chicago Defender* asserted that Democratic compromise on civil rights would "be the signal for Negro voters to return en masse to the Republican party."[105] The withdrawal of Truman from the contest was welcomed by the Dixiecrats, who saw a chance to destroy the Democrats' civil rights program and reassert control of the party, even at the cost of electoral defeat.[106] The Dixiecrats had to be resisted, the *Defender* concluded: "We must do our part to keep such shysters from seizing the reins of power in our great republic. America deserves a better fate."[107]

The Dixiecrats, led by Byrnes, were once again threatening to bolt and form a third party, but Truman refused to cut a deal.[108] In fact, he was, if anything, more strident on civil rights than ever. Speaking to the ADA (whom he had described as "crackpots" due to their militant stand on civil rights in 1948), he attacked the "dinosaur wing" of the GOP and urged enactment of civil rights legislation; at Howard University on 13 June 1952, he declared that advances in civil rights were the "trumpet blast outside the walls of Jericho." He urged an end to the poll tax, an antilynching law, and an end to restrictive covenants, and he praised advances in the courts. It was, McCoy and Ruetten believe, the "most impressive speech of his career," but it made a compromise at the Democratic convention more difficult than ever.[109]

Truman and his staff attempted to offer a stronger civil rights plank, and some concessions were secured in the Resolutions Committee.[110] This resulted in a plank that northern liberals did not contest, southerners could not contest, and Truman found acceptable.[111] White called it "a distinct advance" over 1948 and a "signal victory for the forces of liberalism in the party."[112] It did not meet all the criteria set down by the NAACP-led

Leadership Conference on Civil Rights (LCCR), although it "substantially embodie[d]" its recommendations. "For the first time," White announced, "a major party has asserted that it will undertake the task of curbing the filibuster and removing the roadblock of the rules committee in the House."[113] That White managed to draw such a positive conclusion from such a meager morsel indicated that, once again, he was banking on a Democratic victory.

The only reason that the plank did not result in the Dixiecrats stampeding for the exits was because Truman was not heading the ticket. The eventual nomination of Stevenson was palatable, particularly as, in an attempt to foster unity, he had selected Alabama senator John Sparkman as his running mate. Despite the façade of unity, many Democrats remained concerned about the northern African American vote; Adam Clayton Powell, for example, refused to campaign.[114] The *New York Times* noted that "it is a curious cynicism of American politics that the Democrats should expend so much heat on the precise wording of the civil rights plank inasmuch as the Southern Democrat contingent in the Senate will do everything to block such legislation no matter what the Democratic platform may say about it."[115]

The Republicans were quick to seize on the nomination of Sparkman, whose record, according to White, was one of "consistent opposition to the civil rights objectives of the Democratic party."[116] Lodge believed that it demonstrated that the Democrats were neither serious nor sincere about passing civil rights legislation in the next Congress. This gave the GOP an opportunity to capture segments of the African American vote in traditionally Democratic states such as New York, Illinois, Pennsylvania, and California—states that were crucial to Republican ambitions. Assessing their performance in 1948, Republicans now recognized that they had been let down not only by Dewey's overconfidence but also by their failure to win either the farm or, crucially, the black vote.[117] After their own insipid convention performance on civil rights, Sparkman's nomination was a gift to the Republicans.

An editorial in the *Chicago Defender* entitled "Democrats Slay the Dixie Dragon" optimistically declared that white supremacy had been "slain, embalmed and buried" by the Democrats.[118] The paper also suggested that Sparkman was not a liability as he had supported the civil rights plank, but it did concede—with an extraordinary generosity rarely extended to foes of civil rights—that "as a practical matter" he had voted against the FEPC and cloture, maintaining that he was not a typical southern racist and was liberal on other issues.[119] Stevenson drew praise from the *Crisis*, which described him as "a good man" who "leans perceptibly toward liberalism." Yet Stevenson remained vague on specifics. He saw the need for an FEPC but refused to go into details about how it should be achieved; he wanted a change to the filibuster rule, but he did not outline how this would be secured.[120]

"Making Equality of Opportunity a Living Fact for Every American"

As the campaign began in earnest after the conventions, the *New York Times* noted that the Republicans had carried eight states in 1948 by a margin of less than 5 percent, and that these states had provided Dewey with 149 of his 189 electoral votes. If the GOP were to win in 1952, then it had to retain most, if not all, of these states; furthermore, in eleven marginal states the African American vote held the potential balance of power.[121] On top of this, the Republicans were trying to crack the Solid South, but "Eisenhower leaders" had apparently decided that, because the Democrats had the area "sewn up," they should strengthen their bid for the northern African American vote, a task made easier by the nomination of Sparkman.[122] Stevenson's strategists, however, believed that Eisenhower's stance on the FEPC made it difficult for the general to win much of the northern black vote. Thus the Democrats remained confident that even if they did not meet the demands of African Americans, they still came much closer than the Republicans. They felt that Eisenhower was making a mistake in concentrating in the South instead of the urban North, and they believed that they could hold both the northern urban African American vote against any late Republican appeals and the farm vote in the West.[123] Conversely, the Republicans were heading for potentially their best showing in the South since 1928, with even a win in Texas possible. Nevertheless, it appeared likely that the legacy of the New Deal and the Fair Deal would be enough to secure the black vote for Stevenson.[124]

On 4 August 1952, Lodge and fifteen Eisenhower supporters stated that a Republican victory would help the passage of an FEPC with "adequate enforcement powers" that would not interfere "in states where adequate laws are in effect" and would instead work in cooperation with the state governments.[125] Eisenhower initially made no comment. Senator Herbert Lehman of New York immediately denounced the statement as "a fraud on the American people."[126] Javits rebuffed the criticism: "the fundamental issue . . . is the effort of the Democrats to make a strictly partisan issue of federal civil rights legislation. To appropriate the issue for campaign purposes or to throw dust in the people's eyes by the cry of fraud is only to put further obstacles in the way of Federal civil rights legislation."[127]

Concurrent to the statement of pro–civil rights Republicans, an African American delegation—speaking for a group of black leaders who had been Republicans in the past, and including officers of organizations with a combined membership of 3 million—met Eisenhower in Denver. They announced that his election would "greatly advance civil rights progress in America." Bishop Ward Nicholls of the African Methodist Episcopal Church (AMEC) admitted, however, that Eisenhower was not yet willing to concede to a compulsory federal law. The delegation found Eisenhower to be "sincere and honest" with "deep convictions" about equality; moreover, Eisenhower "was impressed" by the statement of sixteen Republicans calling for a compulsory FEPC and would study it carefully.[128]

Eisenhower's tentative wooing of African Americans continued when he told Archibald Carey that he favored "complete integration" of the military and would also work for "first-class citizenship" for all Americans.[129] Carey stated that Eisenhower "had confided to him that he had not been given the facts of the true nature of the FEPC," implying that Eisenhower was prepared to be more flexible on civil rights.[130] Yet at the same time that Carey was making this statement, Eisenhower was in the South campaigning, a trip that included a meeting with Eugene Talmadge, the arch-segregationist governor of Georgia. The *Chicago Defender* suggested that Eisenhower was using spokesmen on civil rights "whom he might repudiate."[131]

With the nomination of Sparkman, the GOP finally had something substantial on civil rights with which to attack the Democrats. Because most of the black press was supporting Stevenson, however, its criticism of the Alabaman remained tepid.[132] Sparkman may have helped to draft the civil rights plank and prevent a revolt by southerners, but this did not mask his consistent opposition to civil rights in the Senate over the previous ten years.[133] Val Washington, assistant to the chairman of the RNC, issued a nine-hundred-word statement calling Sparkman a "Bilbo," perhaps the most damaging insult imaginable to a white politician seeking black support.[134] He also restated and slightly updated the ritual Republican appeal to African Americans, declaring that Eisenhower had "the Republican tradition for implementing the welfare of the Negro minority behind him; he has a party platform reaffirming the Republican interest in Negro welfare" and "carried the Republican platform to Dixie."[135]

Dewey also condemned nomination of "Jim Crow" Sparkman: "so long as Senator Sparkman is on that ticket, this is a Jim Crow ticket." Sparkman, he continued, had voted against civil rights legislation on at least twenty-three instances, and "anybody who would crush one minority would crush the rest of us."[136] Dewey soon accused Stevenson and Sparkman of running under a "white supremacy" label in Alabama, where the 1948 state ballot included the slogan "white supremacy." Dewey noted that this was the motto of the Klan, and it meant that "one heartbeat away from the president, [is] a man who proudly waves the old-time Ku Klux Klan banner of hate under your noses." The "white supremacy" motto continued to appear on Alabama's absentee ballot in 1952. "While Governor Stevenson offers up honeyed words about the rights of minorities in one part of the country," Dewey asserted, "he advocates that you elect as his running mate and possible successor a man who has spent his whole public life fighting to suppress the rights of American citizens."[137]

Driscoll, speaking in Harlem to an audience of one thousand, accused the Democrats of hypocrisy concerning civil rights, alleging that "the hands that control the Democratic party are those of Sparkman and other professional Southerners." He claimed that the Democrats' strategy in Congress was to propose civil rights legislation to keep northern liberals and African Americans happy, and to thwart it to keep the South happy.[138] Even Taft entered the fray, calling Truman an "effective demagogue" and accusing the Democrats of appealing to black voters while having "done nothing for them," noting that southern Democrats had blocked "every piece of beneficial legislation."[139] To emphasize this point, the RNC released the voting records of Republicans and Democrats in Congress from 1933 to 1952, demonstrating that the GOP had consistently supported civil rights measures. The RNC declared: "despite all the ballyhoo of Democrats, the truth is that if proportionately as many Democrats as Republicans voted in favor of civil rights legislation in Congress, then civil rights legislation could be passed."[140] GOP liberals were also keen to create a positive impression of the party's FEPC stance; Ives, for instance, told the State Republican Committee that the national platform advocated a compulsory FEPC. As the *New York Times* noted, with a healthy dose of understatement, his "interpretation of the Republican national platform plank on civil rights is at odds with the meaning generally ascribed to it at the time it was adopted."[141]

Sparkman stated that these attacks showed "how desperate the Republicans are" and attempted, neither convincingly nor successfully, to defend himself.[142] He asserted that the press was "distorting his position on civil rights," a statement White declared "unbelievable," given that it was indisputable that Sparkman had voted against civil rights on twenty-three out of twenty-three opportunities.[143] Sparkman was in some respects more progressive than his GOP counterpart, although on civil rights there was not a great deal to differentiate the two. Nixon declared that he wanted a federal antilynching law and the abolition of the poll tax; he opposed the filibuster and supported the limiting of debate upon the votes of forty-nine senators. He opposed, however, a compulsory FEPC: "I believe that each state should deal with this problem . . . in the first instance if possible." He was concerned that "a compulsory FEPC would set the cause of good race relations [in the South] back fifty years." Nixon had "consistently opposed segregation" and wanted home rule and desegregation for Washington, D.C. (where he, like Sparkman, had signed a restrictive covenant when buying a house), and he stated that "one of the first moves" of a new Republican administration would be to bring this about. He expressed concern that "much of the talk about civil rights has been political talk," and that this was "particularly true of the party in power," which made "promises about civil rights with no thought of ever carrying out those promises."[144]

In an interview with Wilkins and Theodore Spaulding, called at the request of Sherman Adams, Eisenhower confirmed his opposition to a compulsory FEPC and his preference for a commission to study the facts about segregation.[145] Wilkins said that fair employment was the "number one concern" for African Americans, but Eisenhower felt it was unfortunate that he was to be judged solely on his attitude to the FEPC. He reiterated that he was "vigorously in favor" of the desegregation of Washington, D.C., and would eliminate discrimination anywhere the federal government had jurisdiction. Furthermore, he would stand by Republican platform pledges on antilynching and anti–poll tax legislation and was opposed to filibusters, but he could not promise to do anything to change Rule 22. Wilkins described Eisenhower as "sincere and honest" but noncommittal on civil rights; his attitude toward FEPC legislation remained a cause for particular concern.[146] In his autobiography, Wilkins claimed that, far from the forty-five minutes that had been publicly claimed, he had spent only fifteen minutes with Eisenhower, and that the general was "tense," referred questions to his aides, and "knew very little about racial matters."[147] Eisenhower was, Wilkins concluded, "a good man" but only "slightly acquainted" with African American problems and clung to the "West Point, Old Guard view of race relations."[148]

By the end of August, Stevenson was finally urging a change to Rule 22, stating that he would use his influence in the Senate if elected.[149] Lodge promptly accused Stevenson of engaging in a "pious, insincere piece of double-talk" on civil rights. Lodge noted that he would be the chairman of the Senate if the Republicans won and would push through a change to Rule 22. "I will fight filibusters as long as it takes to end filibusters," he said. "I guarantee to get action on the filibuster question. I am red hot for this." He also felt that there was a good chance that Eisenhower would approve a bill eliminating discrimination in employment, although the source of this optimism was not immediately clear.[150]

Eisenhower headed south in early September as only the second Republican presidential candidate, after Herbert Hoover in 1928, to entertain serious hopes in the region. Speaking in Little Rock, Eisenhower dealt with civil rights cautiously and quickly, urging southerners to protect the rights of African Americans; in Birmingham, he made no mention of civil rights, but in Tampa he quoted the Declaration of Independence to the effect that all men were created equal. The crowd listened in silence to his comments about civil rights, cheering only when he attacked the Democrats.[151] Byrnes announced his support for Eisenhower based on Stevenson's stance on Taft-Hartley, fair employment practices, and the filibuster.[152] Within two weeks of securing this endorsement, Eisenhower was greeted by his "close and long-time friend" Byrnes and a crowd of thirty-five thousand in South Carolina. He praised the South, assailed the administration, but also stated that he wanted to "move forward rapidly to make equality of opportunity a living fact for every American," a statement, though not specifically referring to race, that was greeted with silence.[153] By October, fifty-six southern newspapers were supporting Eisenhower while twenty-nine backed Stevenson, which offered proof enough for at least some African American commentators to conclude that Sparkman was not a Dixiecrat.[154]

The *Greenville Piedmont* urged its readers to vote for Eisenhower because he supported states' rights and opposed desegregation, claiming that civil rights legislation could cost 20 percent of Greenville's whites their jobs. The *Greenville News* stated that Stevenson was Truman's stooge and had been "endorsed by labor racketeers, John L. Lewis, the discredited left-wing ADA, and the NAACP."[155] White telegraphed Eisenhower to ask for a repudiation of statements made in South Carolina's newspapers.[156] Sherman Adams, replying on Eisenhower's behalf, told White that the general had "no control" over particular advertisements placed in newspapers, and that "he most certainly does not subscribe to its content."[157] Not satisfied by this response, the NAACP asked Eisenhower to repudiate publicly the South Carolina advertisement.[158] White then sought permission from Adams to quote the repudiation contained in his earlier letter.[159]

"Walking between the Raindrops"

After the meeting with Eisenhower, Wilkins met Stevenson and then presented his assessment of the candidates to the NAACP board of directors. Stevenson told Wilkins he would support a change in Senate Rule 22 and "looked with favor" on the Humphrey-Ives FEPC bill. Stevenson made a very favorable impression on Wilkins, who described the Illinois governor as "a charming person, brilliant, witty and keenly analytical" and as someone who understood civil rights issues. Wilkins was unconvinced by Stevenson's assertion that the South would "go along" with a civil rights program and warned the governor to be wary of any compromise suggested by southerners. Wilkins also spoke briefly about Sparkman, noting his voting record on civil rights; Stevenson limited his comments to stating that Sparkman was a "liberal Southerner" and had a decent chance of steering legislation through the Senate.[160] In contrast with the brevity of the Eisenhower meeting, the interview with Stevenson lasted two hours.[161]

In September, the NAACP board considered a draft statement on the forthcoming election demanding that "political opportunism be abandoned by both parties and their candidates." It also urged African Americans to register as the election "promises to be one of the closest in American history," asserting once again that black votes held the "potential balance of power."[162] This reflected the level of unease within the association about the future of civil rights, the prospect of a Republican victory, and the perceived closeness of the organization to the Democrats. When the board announced its assessment of the candidates, and in anticipation of inevitable criticism, it stressed that "the NAACP is politically non-partisan. But it has responsibility to express its judgment." It credited Stevenson with taking the "most forthright" stand on civil rights and commended "the clarity and courage of his pronouncements," for example, his attitude toward the filibuster, Rule 22, discrimination, and an enforceable FEPC. The association was impressed by the sincerity of Eisenhower and praised him for vowing to abolish discrimination in Washington, D.C., but "regretted" his position on the FEPC and the abolition of Rule 22. Of the vice-presidential candidates: "we can only view with grave concern their presence" on the tickets. The association would reconsider its analysis if the candidates changed their positions on key civil rights issues.[163]

The RNC quickly and predictably challenged the NAACP's assertions, particularly the comparison of Nixon to Sparkman. Val Washington accused the association of being influenced by the ADA, and pointed out the relative records of the two vice-presidential candidates in the Senate, including Nixon's support of the FEPC.[164] Further criticism came from within the association. David E. Langley, the vice chairman of the Richmond Republican Committee and a NAACP member, wrote to Wilkins, stating: "I personally resent the Association going on record as endorsing any particular candidate or party," and asserting that "not all Negroes . . . are Democrats." He went so far as to accuse Wilkins of using the NAACP "to foster your own political ambitions."[165] Wilkins replied that "we have on our Board of Directors a number of Republicans and others who are supporting General Eisenhower" and noted the "highly emotional and partisan climate" of the campaign. When the association did make any kind of statement on an election, Wilkins ventured that both sides "are quick to accuse us of 'entering' politics."[166] Wilkins privately conceded that he intended to "walk between the raindrops" as far as an endorsement of either side was concerned.[167]

At a meeting of branches in Ohio, White again stretched the concept of nonpartisanship when he blamed the Republicans for African American support of the Democrats, asserting that "four million Negro voters today ask the Republican party to stop forcing the Negro to vote as a block in opposition to the Republican ticket."[168] African American voters did not want to be the "chattel" of the Democrats, but segregation and discrimination had caused them to vote as a bloc. The rejection of Taft for Eisenhower by liberal Republicans appeared to offer hope to African Americans, but Eisenhower had embraced Jenner and McCarthy in his own party and southern Democrat reactionaries Talmadge and Byrnes. This would mean, asserted White, 1 million African American votes for Stevenson. "Every four years," he continued, "the Republicans succumb to the illusion that they can crack the solid South." It would be a "miracle" if they were to win Texas, Florida, Virginia, and Louisiana and their 56 electoral votes, but this would be a pyrrhic victory, White believed, alienating as it would northern African Americans in eight pivotal states with 221 electoral votes.[169] Unusually, this year there was even the possibility of the African American vote being as important in Texas as it had been in California, Illinois, and Ohio in

1948. White was publicly hopeful about the election: "never in history have those who fight and abhor race prejudice been so advantageously placed to do something about the evil" as in the eight pivotal states identified by *Newsweek*. White believed that "all signs point to one of the closest races in American political history" and wondered "how long will it be before the Republicans wake up?"[170]

White, writing in *Look* magazine, claimed that the destination of the African American vote was by no means certain. Stevenson, who was no Truman in the eyes of African Americans, needed to be much more forthright. White conceded that the selection of Sparkman could lead to the "*temporary* desertion" (White's italics) of African American voters (who apparently remained undecided) in key states as the Democrats had surrendered to the Dixiecrats at their convention, in the belief that the black vote was "in the bag" and could be ignored.[171] White had, therefore, downgraded the Democratic platform he had described as a "signal victory for the forces of liberalism in the party" in July to its current status as disappointing, even if it remained superior to the "woefully weak and meaningless" platform of the Republicans.[172] White predicted that the Republicans would try to capitalize on Eisenhower's enormous personal popularity in the South in an effort to win the region.[173] "The answer for both parties is simple," he concluded; "neither can have both Southern conservative and Negro support."[174]

Other NAACP members were becoming wary about the association's tacit support for the Democrats. Board member Daisy Lampkin, a lapsed Republican who had been instrumental in the Parker campaign in 1930, switched back to the GOP after twenty years as a Democrat due to the nomination of Sparkman. Lampkin was concerned about the NAACP's apparent endorsement of the Stevenson ticket and the impact that this could have on the association's nonpartisanship.[175] Moreover, Sparkman symbolized everything she had fought for during her eighteen years as a field secretary for the NAACP, and, after twenty years in office, the Democrats had failed to live up to their pledges on civil rights. She concluded that an Eisenhower victory "would be in the interest of Negro rights as well as in the interest of American welfare, and world peace."[176]

This thorny issue of nonpartisanship soon reemerged publicly, and conveniently for White, when Lampkin was accused of using the NAACP mailing list to aid the GOP.[177] White telegraphed Lampkin about the matter, but she emphatically denied the allegation, saying that she used the *Pittsburgh Courier*'s mailing list, and that the paper was openly backing Eisenhower.

She warned: "I think that it is very wise that some of us are backing the GOP ticket. It would be tragic if the GOP wins with no Negro support. We would be in a very bad bargaining position," suggesting that her support of the GOP was less about Sparkman and the failure of civil rights legislation than the political realities of a Republican victory. She stressed her belief in the association's neutrality: "you know that I am opposed to the NAACP being used in any partisan, political way."[178] White thanked her, and noted that there were those who were construing her association with the NAACP as support for the GOP. He concluded, "you and I know it [is] impossible to make all persons understand [the] full facts but [I] believe it very desirable you make clear you speak for yourself and [the] *Courier* but not for NAACP."[179]

Having been accused of supporting Stevenson, and fending off criticism of Lampkin, White was soon disavowing another alleged endorsement, this time of the GOP. He wrote to RNC chairman Arthur E. Summerfield, complaining that his criticism of Sparkman was being interpreted as support for the Republican ticket on GOP campaign literature. "I request and insist that Republican literature purporting to show that I endorse any candidate be withdrawn and no more of it circulated."[180]

"Bid for Negro Vote Reaches New Peak"

Shortly before the election, it was reported that, because the GOP was not going to carry a single southern state and the fact that 90 percent of northern African American voters would be backing Stevenson, Republican strategists had decided upon an about-face on civil rights. This would involve Eisenhower appearing on Walter White's radio show to announce his support for a compulsory FEPC. This was all the more significant as, thus far in the campaign, Eisenhower had refused to do interviews and had, of course, consistently and repeatedly opposed a compulsory FEPC. The NAACP, conveniently citing its nonpartisanship, did not want White to interview Eisenhower unless it could interview Stevenson as well, which was deemed impossible to arrange before polling day.[181] This was a good example of the NAACP using its nonpartisanship to the advantage of the Democrats as White's radio show was no more an NAACP vehicle than his *New York Herald-Tribune* or *Chicago Defender* columns. More importantly in the wider civil rights struggle, if the rumors of an Eisenhower U-turn were true, it was a wasted opportunity to commit the Republican candidate publicly to the idea of a compulsory FEPC.

Truman continued to campaign vigorously, reprising his whistle-stop tour of 1948 in late September, and speaking more forcefully on civil rights (as well as praising Sparkman) than he had in the previous campaign.[182] Making a triumphant return to Harlem, Truman claimed Eisenhower would "turn back the clock" on civil rights. He called the Republicans' civil rights plank "the lousiest plank you ever read."[183] Crowd estimates ranged from 20,000 to 100,000, with as many as 1,750,000 seeing the president on his way to and from the rally. The crowd interrupted the speech with applause thirty-six times as he reminded them of his record and vowed to continue the fight for civil rights.[184] Truman accused the Republicans of always providing "just enough votes to insure the defeat of civil rights measures" and alleged that they were "not interested in civil rights." Stevenson, unlike Eisenhower, "had the courage to say the same thing about civil rights in New York and Richmond."[185] Truman was, of course, being utterly disingenuous. The *New York Times* accused him of "distortion," particularly in the implication that the Democrats "were innocent of responsibility" for the defeat of civil rights measures. Ultimately, it was "manifestly absurd for Mr. Truman to try to conceal the part that a large segment of his own party has had in the defeat of civil rights legislation."[186]

Stevenson was as good as Truman's word in Nashville, where he declared that he "would never be found guilty of talking in one way in the South and another way elsewhere. So I must say to you tonight that I stand on the platform of the Democratic party."[187] Alonso Hamby states, however, that in Richmond Stevenson "all but waved a Confederate flag."[188] On 10 October, an African American journalist accompanying the Stevenson campaign was denied accommodation in a New Orleans hotel, causing considerable embarrassment for the Democratic candidate. In Dallas, Stevenson slept on his train to avoid a repetition of the incident, commenting privately, "why can't they [African American journalists] go somewhere else? Are they trying to embarrass us?"[189]

Eisenhower reiterated his commitment to equality of opportunity in Los Angeles in October, calling it "the unfinished business of America. There can be no second-class Americans"; and he continued to state his belief in equality in speeches in New Jersey.[190] In Newark, for example, he condemned the "systematic political exploitation of minority groups in America" and attacked the poll tax, particularly Truman's attitude to it as a senator. He noted that civil rights legislation had been pioneered in Republican states, and he would urge other states to follow suit. Referencing the Cold

War context, he declared: "this is a kind of loss we can ill-afford in today's world."[191]

Under the headline "Bid for Negro Vote Reaches New Peak," the *New York Times* reported that both parties were "wooing the Negro vote in some of the hardest-hitting literature ever featured in a national political campaign." The Democrats had issued a "slick picture book" that was "obviously not intended for circulation in the South" as it branded Talmadge as "Negro-hating" and noted Byrnes's support of Eisenhower. The GOP had been "flooding heavily populated Negro areas of the northern cities with similar propaganda," including restatement of "white supremacy" allegations against Sparkman.[192] This was, however, likely to be to no avail: the *Kansas City Call* remarked that "if there is going to be a wholesale swing of colored voters to the Republican column this year, it will go down as the best kept secret of the century."[193]

The Republicans returned to Harlem in the final throes of the campaign, with Ives and then Eisenhower visiting the district in quick succession.[194] Eisenhower recalled the 2,500 African American soldiers who volunteered to bridge the gap in the lines in the fall of 1944, giving up their relative safety away from the front line. He also pledged a "crusade" to eliminate discrimination, particularly in Washington, D.C., and "wherever the Federal Government has responsibility."[195] Crowd estimates varied with police reckoning 100,000 were in attendance, and other sources suggesting no more than 25,000.[196] Two days after Eisenhower, Stevenson arrived in Harlem to "one of the most tumultuous receptions of the campaign" as he was greeted by 125,000 people. He devoted only a small proportion of his speech to civil rights, but he began by observing that "it is a little strange that a candidate can get cheers simply because he does not change his philosophy to suit his geography."[197] Three days later, Stevenson accused Eisenhower of talking like a lion on civil rights in New York and like a kitten in the South.[198]

Morse, "one of a very few Republican Senators whose civil rights record is unequivocal," according to White, was growing increasingly agitated with the GOP.[199] He told the AFL in mid-September that Taft was leading the GOP to defeat and confirmed that he would not be campaigning for the party during the election.[200] His enthusiasm for Eisenhower had waned after the general's meeting and public display of unity with Taft on 12 September.[201] Morse pledged his loyalty to the "Republicanism of Abraham Lincoln" and refuted claims that he was about to leave the party.[202] On 25 October, he resigned from the party, asserting that it had strayed too far from the principles of Lincoln and was "dominated by reactionaries running a captive general for president." He was becoming an "independent Republican" and was endorsing Stevenson, despite being the first senator to come out for Eisenhower, because the Republican candidate was "taking support from any source no matter how reprehensible," while a vote for Stevenson would be a vote against reaction and for "statesmanship."[203] From an African American perspective, the GOP, seemingly heading for victory, could ill-afford to lose such an important liberal voice.

"One of the Greatest Personal Majorities in American History"

Once again, the pollsters got it wrong. Having predicted a landslide in 1948 and been delivered the closest election in American history, in 1952 the pollsters opted for a close election and were rewarded with a landslide. More voters, 62 million, participated in the election than ever before, and Eisenhower won thirty-nine states to Stevenson's nine and 442 Electoral College votes to 89 for the Democrat; the popular vote saw 33,937,252 Americans (55.4 percent) turn to Eisenhower, compared to 27,314,992 for Stevenson, a plurality of 6,622,260. In fact, Eisenhower polled 11 million more votes than any previous Republican candidate.[204] In the aftermath of the election, Elmo Roper, chastened by the outcome in 1948, denied that he had predicted a close race or that his figures had suggested such. The role of public opinion research, he argued less than convincingly, was to determine what was going on, not to make predictions, and he suggested that predictions "served no useful purpose," doubtless noting the irony of such a statement from a pollster.[205] In 1948, he had believed that polls could be accurate, whereas in 1952, the closest he came to a prediction was when he said that either an Eisenhower landslide or a very slim Stevenson victory was possible.[206] Henry Lee Moon had some sympathy for Roper, arguing that "no one, not even the Republican politicians, seemed to anticipate the proportion of the Eisenhower triumph."[207]

The NAACP's analysis demonstrated that African Americans had voted for Stevenson and the Democrats by huge margins. In California, for example, 68.5 percent of African Americans voted for Stevenson and 24.7 percent for Eisenhower. This pattern was replicated across the nation: in Chicago, Stevenson outpolled Eisenhower by 70 percent to 30 percent; in New York, he won 77 percent of the vote in predominantly African American wards. In Michigan, Stevenson won a whopping 91 percent of the African American vote (in one slum area of Detroit Stevenson romped home by a ratio of 21 to 1). The total African American vote in forty-seven cities was 956,535 (73 percent) for the Democrats and 347,600 (27 percent) for the Republicans. Ironically, it was the African American vote in southern and border states that saved Stevenson from an even greater mauling, with association analysis suggesting that it was vital in keeping Arkansas, Kentucky, Louisiana, North Carolina, and West Virginia in the Democratic column.[208] A preliminary survey from the NAACP suggested that Eisenhower had failed to carry any predominantly black district in thirteen cities.[209] Moreover, the African American vote was three to one for the Democrats in forty-six black districts across twenty-one states; Eisenhower only won a majority of the African American vote in one district, Marshall, Texas (51 percent). Moon conceded that "the Negro vote was not a decisive factor" in the election; furthermore, except among African Americans and some Dixiecrats, "civil rights does not appear to have been an important factor."[210]

Republican analysis, completed almost a year after the election, was largely in agreement with that of the NAACP, with one proviso:

> NAACP surveys were very largely restricted to cities. The Republican percentage of the Negro vote for the country as a whole was very likely higher both in 1948 and 1952 than the NAACP survey indicates due to the fact that Negro voters in small towns and rural areas generally supported the Republican ticket in greater proportion than in the cities.[211]

The RNC noted that African Americans were the only group that did not shift toward the Republicans in 1952. It also recognized that while the South was the only area that the Republicans failed to carry, the party's vote went up by 14.4 percent in the region, carrying Florida, Texas, and Virginia for the first time since 1928.[212] For the most part, Eisenhower ran ahead of the Republican ticket in Senate, House of Representatives, and gubernatorial contests.[213]

Archibald Carey articulated his concern to Wilkins about perceived NAACP closeness to the Democrats in the immediate aftermath of the election. Carey, recognizing the predicament of the association, believed that as far as the election was concerned, Wilkins was "horribly biased and prejudiced." Carey felt that Wilkins believed that the Democrats were being honest about civil rights whereas Republican opposition was "sinister and venal." Carey argued that when it came to voting on civil rights, rather than just talking about it, the Republicans largely supported it while the Democrats were primarily opposed. Carey did not think that the Republicans were "angels," but he felt that using the terms "phoney" and "double-talk" to describe them was unfair, especially when suggesting the records of Nixon and Sparkman were the same. Carey did not predict that Eisenhower would lead a crusade for civil rights, but "I honestly believe we will have something creditable to show in the way of achievement when his term is done."[214] Wilkins attempted to clarify his position, arguing that while there had been consistent Republican support for much civil rights legislation, they had "never delivered the vote in the crucial instances," especially the Barkley Ruling to reform Rule 22. He stressed that he wanted African Americans to be members of both parties.[215]

Eisenhower's victory hinted at other modifications to the American electoral landscape. He carried seventeen of thirty-five cities with populations over three hundred thousand, including Los Angeles, San Francisco, Minneapolis, Seattle, and Denver (Dewey carried only four in 1948), reducing the Democrat plurality in urban areas by more than 1 million.[216] The suburban vote remained heavily Republican, often negating the still predominantly Democratic vote in the cities.[217] The rural and farm votes, the "material cause" of defeat in 1948 according to the RNC, returned to the GOP, and large gains were even made with the labor vote; although the majority still backed the Democrats. (Eisenhower carried eighteen of the twenty-eight major industrial districts, compared with five for Dewey in 1948.)[218]

Moon drew parallels with 1932, when the nation, except African Americans, moved to the Democrats. Where the Democrats' share of the African American vote fell, it was attributable to the presence of Sparkman on the ticket. Eisenhower's personal popularity was important to most groups (as were communism, Korea, high taxes, and prices) except African Americans.[219] The *Crisis* credited Eisenhower with "one of the greatest personal majorities in American history," but cautioned that "the Republican party achieved no such landslide." In the House, the Republican majority was tiny (three); in the Senate, the GOP had a majority of one, excluding Morse.[220] Despite their utter lack of support for the party of Lincoln, African Americans still had very specific expectations of the new administration, particularly for the reform of Rule 22, and would remind the Republicans that they could no longer blame the Democrats for the failure to pass civil rights legislation. The *Crisis* emphasized this final point: "when the Democrats were in power, the Republicans blamed their temporizing on civil rights on the southerners. Now they will not have that excuse and Negro citizens are expecting the GOP to redeem its civil rights pledges."[221]

After the election, the NAACP tentatively began trying to build some bridges with the GOP, issuing a statement noting the "obligation for the Republican party to put into effect its pledges regarding civil rights." It reminded the Republicans of their platform pledges and, struggling to remain upbeat, pledged "its full support" to the president-elect and the new Congress in their efforts to "implement the acceptable parts" of the party platform and campaign promises.[222] The association thus strived to make the best of a very serious tactical setback. White admitted to feeling "quite humble" after the election. Nevertheless, he noted that "enormous sums" were spent on advertising in southern newspapers, "whipping up fear of the Negro vote." White believed that predictions of a genuine two-party system in the South were premature, but feared for civil rights in a Congress dominated by Taft and presided over by Nixon.[223] Meanwhile, the *Chicago Defender* soon urged readers, in a perhaps unfortunate choice of words, to "close ranks" behind Eisenhower.[224]

Eisenhower, responding to a request from White, met with a four-strong NAACP delegation on 28 November and promised to do everything in his power to eliminate segregation and injustice. The meeting lasted for fifty minutes and was attended by White, Arthur Spingarn, Theodore Spaulding, and Channing Tobias. The new president "showed neither awareness nor resentment" that African Americans had heavily supported Stevenson, quipping, "I've got more friends in the Democratic Party than in the Republican Party." A well-briefed Eisenhower demonstrated a now-solid grasp of Rule 22 and stated that he would endeavor to see it abolished, although he conceded that this remained a matter for the Senate.[225] He also had made, according to White, "many statements off the record which indicate considerable growth" in his philosophy since he appeared before the Senate Armed Forces Committee in 1948.[226] White said that the delegation "left the meeting with the feeling that General Eisenhower wants to do the right thing." Eisenhower had clearly done much research on the race question, but he did not realize "the extent to which Southern Democrats and many members of his own party will go to prevent the implementation of his undoubtedly strong convictions."[227] Wilkins echoed White's sentiments believing that "before we accuse them [the Republicans] of bad faith we should give them time to act."[228]

An internal NAACP report on the meeting confirmed Eisenhower in this new and positive light. He "emphasized again and again the moral and spiritual aspects of the question of race and religion both as they create disunity at home and impair our prestige abroad."[229] Eisenhower soon pledged to appoint a committee to "get the facts" on discrimination in the United States and expressed "amazement" that African Americans still could not stay in all of the nation's hotels.[230] The *Chicago Defender* asserted that "Eisenhower's stock had gone up dramatically" in the eyes of White and the NAACP since the association had published its assessment of the presidential candidates in September.[231]

In a letter to Arthur M. Carter, the managing editor of Afro-American Newspapers, Wilkins tried to put as positive a gloss as possible on the Republican victory. He felt that, although the Republicans now had slim majorities in both houses of Congress, the prospects for the passage of civil rights legislation had not altered appreciably (in other words, they were still bad), and that the best barometer of future progress on civil rights would be the attitude of the Senate toward Rule 22. He maintained some faith in the president—a faith that had been conspicuously absent when he had met Eisenhower in August—stating that "it is my opinion that President-Elect Eisenhower will try very hard to do something on civil rights"; for example, despite being on record as opposed to a federal FEPC, he hoped "to do something about fair employment without having Congress pass a law." Indeed, he did not believe that Eisenhower and the Republicans "would retract on the civil rights issue," but it could take months, or even a year before action began. Eisenhower's opposition to a compulsory FEPC, he suggested, might actually serve to weaken the Republican-Dixiecrat coalition.[232]

The election was more than simply a setback for civil rights advocates; it exposed the weakness of the NAACP's entire political strategy. For twenty years, Walter White had expounded the balance of power theory, and, although it had proved salient in the close election of 1948, it was exposed as fundamentally worthless in a lopsided election, especially one in which African Americans had so overwhelmingly backed the loser. The harsh political reality for White and the NAACP was that they were faced with a new administration that, frankly, owed them nothing, and given the attitude of the NAACP and elements of the black press toward the GOP and the party's well-established congressional indifference, progress on the key elements of the association's program and civil rights more generally was highly unlikely. The Republicans had demonstrated that they could win a presidential election without the black vote, and the process of African American realignment begun during the Hoover years was now virtually complete.

Ironically, despite Eisenhower's reticence throughout his presidency, more would be achieved in his term of office in civil rights than at any time since Reconstruction, though he could claim little credit for much of it. In 1952, the party of Lincoln had again proved incapable of reconnecting with African Americans, but this failure proved irrelevant as the party swept back into power after twenty long, frustrating years of opposition.

CONCLUSION

The Deck or the Sea?

Even at the conclusion of the Civil War, the Republican enthusiasm about African Americans and their rights was minimal. Legend had it that the GOP was formed to rid America of slavery, fought the Civil War to achieve this end, and then protected the newly enfranchised former slaves in its aftermath. This was a powerful legend to African Americans living through the dark days of Redemption in the South, and it was a legend that many took north with them in the early twentieth century. The abolition of slavery was, however, only one of a number of considerations that motivated the party's founders. The amendments to the Constitution that freed the slaves, made them citizens, and gave them the vote were indeed Republican amendments; nonetheless, the Republicans who sought to protect African Americans were a minority in the party even in the 1860s.

During Reconstruction, certain traits that would later become synonymous with the party had begun to emerge—namely, that it was pro–big business and anti–big government, a path it would follow for the next half century. The Republican Party, concerned with making America rich in the 1920s and then trying to rebuild the party from the wreckage of the Great Depression in the 1930s, failed to react to the increasing political sophistication of African Americans. As late as the 1930s, many Republicans still believed that because they had given African Americans freedom they were owed black allegiance in perpetuity.

Why then did the Republican Party lose the African American vote? Herbert Hoover's role is central. Hoover may have had more pressing matters to deal with in the aftermath of the stock market crash in October 1929, but it is difficult to imagine him doing any more damage to the party's relations with African Americans if he had deliberately set out to alienate them. His southern policy was impractical and short-sighted; the southern vote for the Republicans in 1928 was a protest against the candidacy of Al Smith, not an endorsement of Hoover, and mistaking a protest for a fundamental change in voting habits was an error the GOP would commit repeatedly.

Hoover gambled on the South in 1928. He gambled that he could break the Democratic stranglehold on the region, he gambled that he could make the Republicans a national party, and he gambled that he could do this without alienating the burgeoning African American vote in the North. It was a gamble that initially seemed to pay off. In an uncanny premonition of the legendary "Roosevelt Coalition," Hoover briefly commanded the support of African Americans and white southerners. Yet he lacked the personality and the political dexterity demonstrated by Franklin Roosevelt to keep such an alliance intact. From the outset, Hoover's southern policy was built upon shaky foundations. Most southerners felt about as at home in the Republican Party as African Americans did in the Democratic Party. To many southerners, the GOP was still the party of Reconstruction, black rule, carpetbaggers, scalawags, and, of course, Abraham Lincoln. Even if the Republicans managed to surmount all of these problems, the party was essentially a paper organization in the South: it existed solely to send delegates to national conventions and receive patronage from Republican presidents.

Many Republicans in the 1920s and early 1930s felt that they had more to gain by breaking down the Solid South than they did by courting the northern African American vote. Simple arithmetic and grade-school history revealed this to be an inherently hazardous venture. The strategically placed African American vote in the North was potentially more important than the rotten boroughs of the South. Yet the Republicans persevered with this strategy to the extent that there was even a suggestion that Dewey preferred not to court the African American vote in 1948 in case he might alienate the South. He won neither the African American vote nor the South and lost the election as a result.

African Americans were less outraged that Hoover wanted to reform the party in the South—the need for reform was self-evident—than that he seemed determined to do this on a lily-white basis. Rather than attempting to create a two-party system in the South by enfranchising African Americans, who were natural Republicans, Hoover chose to embrace white southerners, to whom Republicanism was an anathema. Hoover's supporters argue that African American disenfranchisement was merely an unfortunate by-product of his southern reform, yet efforts to prosecute African American Republicans in the South, notably Perry Howard, without similar action against corrupt whites, expose Republican southern reform as a racist sham.

Hoover's actions as president reveal, at best, insensitivity toward African Americans and, at worst, a blatant and callous disregard for their aspirations. There was a persistent perception that Hoover simply did not care. By 1932, even Hoover's staunchest allies among African American Republicans were losing patience with him. The Parker episode confirmed to many African Americans that the Republican Party and Hoover could no longer be trusted, while the campaign against pro-Parker senators illustrated to African Americans that they could wield political power and reinforced the notion that the ballot was their most effective political weapon.

A number of factors coincided to deprive the Republican Party of the African American vote. The Hoover presidency is, of course, pivotal, but this does not fully explain it. Had the Depression not occurred, there is the likelihood that the switch of the African American vote would have been delayed, although perhaps not ultimately prevented. Furthermore, the Hoover presidency and the Depression coincided with increasing numbers of African Americans living and voting in the North. This in itself would not necessarily have been significant but for the concentration of the African American population. This meant that African American votes, although relatively few in number, assumed a greater importance with each election. African Americans also, for the first time, had an effective and articulate political outlet in the shape of the NAACP.

The New Deal is crucial to understanding African American realignment. Without the Great Depression, there would have been less need and little support for mass federal intervention. The kind of economic intervention required to help African Americans was unprecedented and would have been politically impossible to implement without the seriousness of the crisis that engulfed all Americans in the 1930s. The social change fostered by the New Deal could not, therefore, have taken place under "normal" circumstances. Any inclination toward progressive reform or genuinely reaching out to African Americans from 1920 to 1932 would have been extremely unpopular, reflecting the underlying racism within America. Under these circumstances, the lack of a reformist impulse in the Republican Party is understandable; besides, the Republican Party of the 1920s had little interest in the lowest echelons of American society, regardless of their race.

The loss of the African American vote by the Republicans can, therefore, be explained relatively straightforwardly. The alienation that African Americans felt from Hoover was compounded by the onset of the Great Depression. The Depression, in turn, led to the election of Roosevelt, and the benefits his New Deal brought to African Americans persuaded them to vote Democrat. The nature of Republican attempts to regain these votes, why they failed, and why they did not do more are, however, much more complicated. The Republican Party was held largely responsible for the Depression and subsequently spent twenty years in opposition; it had no cogent response to the New Deal and spent the period split over it, isolationism and World War II, and then foreign policy after the war, threatening to disintegrate as it lurched from one crisis of confidence to the next. This does not justify the party's neglect of African Americans, but it does put it into context.

What then did the GOP do to reach out to this formerly loyal group of supporters? The simple answer in the early 1930s is, not very much. The shock of the Great Depression, magnified by resounding defeats in 1932 and 1934, left the party in turmoil. It was clear that the party had to change, but it was unclear what change would involve or which faction of the party would dictate reform. With the Republicans preoccupied with survival, it comes as little surprise that they paid scant attention to African Americans during the early New Deal.

In the early 1930s, many Republicans saw the need to change the nature of their appeal, and some of the most vocal demanded that the party become more liberal. At the forefront of this was William Borah. He outlined frequently, articulately, and passionately the reasons why the party needed to reconnect with the American people. Yet this was the same William Borah who stubbornly opposed antilynching legislation and in doing so alienated his party from the group of voters most in need of GOP liberalism. Borah's presidential bid in 1936 may have been testament more to his considerable ego than his vote-winning ability, but, the Scottsboro case aside, it roused African Americans like no issue since the Parker nomination. The NAACP claimed, and frankly deserved, much of the credit for the torpedoing of Borah's presidential ambitions. As with the Parker nomination, the association had brought pressure to bear on the Republican Party and won. Borah's statements perhaps exaggerated the gap that had developed between the GOP and African Americans, and while his views did not reflect the party as a whole, he was the sole Republican opposing antilynching bills, and he did so with far more vigor than any Republican who supported them.

The Republicans could have embraced antilynching without alienating their supporters. Some, like Borah, linked it to states' rights and the extension of federal power, and it was this old fear of the growth of federal power that facilitated the rise of the conservative Republican–southern Democrat coalition by the late 1930s. This coalition was then able to thwart other legislation that would have been beneficial to African Americans, such as anti–poll tax laws and the creation of a permanent FEPC. The conservative nature of Republican politics in this period, and subsequently, meant that the GOP had very little substantive policy, notably economic and social policy, that was attractive to African Americans.

The 1936 election did see a change in the GOP's attitude toward African American voters, but now crucially, it also saw a change in attitude of African American voters toward the GOP. African Americans voted overwhelmingly for Hoover in 1932, of that there is no doubt, but it was unenthusiastic support borne of political impotence. In 1932, African Americans had a choice between the party of the South or the party of Lincoln; in 1936, they could chose between the party of the New Deal and the party of the Great Depression. For the first time, therefore, they had genuine alternatives. The Republicans certainly had a point when they warned that relief was not the solution to African Americans' problems, but it was difficult to argue with food and jobs, particularly as this was more than twelve years of Republican rule had offered. Republican candidate Alfred Landon had a decent record on race relations in Kansas, but, particularly when he vowed to give control of relief payments to the states, there was little he could do in the face of the tangible benefits brought by Roosevelt. Landon's commitment to African Americans extended beyond electioneering in 1936, but it also coincided with the waning of his, never great, reputation. Landon would forever be the man who led the GOP to the most humiliating defeat in its history, and, however well-intentioned, his influence would always be duly circumscribed.

The GOP's internal efforts at reform during the 1930s were haphazard and superficial, designed to create an illusion of unity rather than address the fundamental problems of the party. Perhaps the best example of this was the Frank Committee, set up after the debacle of 1936. The appointment of Ralph Bunche to examine the needs of African Americans suggested sincerity on the part of the GOP, but his findings were far too radical for the party and were guilelessly replaced with a harangue against the New Deal. African Americans refused to be fooled, particularly as it was common knowledge that Bunche's recommendations had been ignored. An opportunity for the GOP to recommit itself to African Americans had been carelessly discarded.

It is ironic that it took Wendell Willkie, a former Democrat, to try genuinely to reconcile the Republican Party and African Americans. Many, including Walter White, dismissed Willkie's commitment to African Americans during the election of 1940; they had heard too many promises from too many Republican candidates in the past. Nevertheless, Willkie demonstrated throughout his remaining four years that he meant every word he had said on civil rights. For the first time, a major political figure, a potential presidential candidate again in 1944, spoke out on civil rights and disregarded the consequences. There is nothing to suggest that Willkie was motivated by expedience or was covetously looking toward the African American wards of Chicago, New York, and Philadelphia and their crucial votes. The evidence categorically proves that Willkie supported civil rights vocally because he genuinely believed that it was the right thing to do. Willkie recognized that America could not fight a war for democracy abroad while denying 13 million of its own citizens their basic democratic rights at home. Willkie, the grandson of political refugees, knew that democracy in the United States could not exist separate and unequal; it had to be a living reality for all Americans, regardless of color, creed, or political ideology. The myths so often attached to Lincoln were briefly embodied in Willkie.

Many Republicans soon regretted their impetuous choice of presidential candidate in 1940, seeing Willkie as an opportunistic, divisive influence who was barely even a nominal Republican. His notion of "loyal opposition" during World War II, which he embraced with the noblest of intentions, was characterized by his "One World" trip, which coincided with the 1942 midterm elections. Many Republican activists felt that his priorities were wrong; that the president was using him; and that his enthusiasm for internationalism was dangerous for party and country. In the Wisconsin primary in 1944, they told him so. He understood the message and, true to his word, withdrew from the contest. The party did not even bother inviting Willkie to the 1944 convention. He was never able to make good his vow to not only to be nominated in 1948 but also to win the election.

Willkie was undoubtedly the presidential candidate most committed to civil rights that either party had ever seen. His defeat in 1940 and subsequent alienation from the party's hierarchy suggest that, even if he had lived, a Willkie presidency was an idle fantasy. Willkie did not, therefore, represent renewed idealism within the GOP, nor did he foreshadow a genuine commitment to civil rights. Pockets of racial liberalism remained in the party throughout the 1940s—Irving Ives, Jacob Javits, Herbert Brownell (all New Yorkers), and Wayne Morse stand out—but the party could not shake off the perception that its assurances on civil rights did not extend beyond tokenism, that they had little conception of the problems faced by African Americans, and, as such, that they echoed the thinly veiled racism that permeated American society.

In 1948, Thomas Dewey had the best record on civil rights of any governor in the United States. New York's State Commission Against Discrimination (SCAD) was the first of its kind to combat discrimination against minorities in employment. It provided an example that other states and, eventually, the federal government would follow. Dewey's public support of the law demonstrated that Republicanism and social justice were not mutually exclusive. Despite the SCAD and measures against discrimination in higher education, Dewey still could not win African American votes. In 1944 and 1948, African Americans rejected him; in 1948, this rejection cost him the presidency.

The blame for this lay with Dewey himself. In 1944, leading a party tainted by isolationism, he had the near-impossible task of challenging the enduringly popular Roosevelt, who had been further buoyed by Allied victories that brought the end of the war into sight. The American people clearly felt that the experienced Roosevelt was the man to guide them to victory and in the postwar world. On civil rights, Dewey was tarnished by his rejection of a prototype of the SCAD, but in 1948, he had no excuses. Republican analysis after 1944 indicated that the African American vote in crucial states could dictate the outcome of a relatively close presidential election. The fact that this research was carried out by one of Dewey's closest political allies, Herbert Brownell, demonstrates that he was aware of just how important the African American vote would be if he sought the presidency again. In 1948, Dewey failed to translate an enviable record on civil rights into African American votes. The most plausible explanation for Dewey's failure to court the African American vote in 1948 seems to be perhaps understandable overconfidence; rarely can an incumbent have gone into an election with Harry Truman's problems.

The Republicans were utterly outmaneuvered by Truman and consequently lost one of the closest elections in American history. One of the many reasons for this defeat was the fact that Truman won 80 percent of the African American vote, a greater percentage than even Roosevelt had managed. Overwhelming African American support for Truman would have been understandable if Dewey had had a reputation as a civil rights obstructionist, but Dewey was hamstrung by his refusal to campaign on his record. Dewey assiduously avoided controversy, and, in 1948, civil rights was controversial; thus his own supporters did not know where he stood on civil rights. African Americans, even in his own state, assumed the worst.

Republican ambivalence toward African Americans must be compared to the attitude of the Democrats during the same period. The Democrats, for example, only introduced a "Negro" plank into their platform in 1940, and this was even vaguer than the habitually woolly efforts of the Republicans. It is also worth reemphasizing that although Roosevelt was extremely popular among African American voters, and they, arguably, voted for him and not his party, he never championed their cause. Civil rights only finally became a national issue in 1948, when Truman's initial reticence evolved from genuine concern to political necessity. Truman's advisers recognized that he needed the support of African Americans, and other special interest groups, if he was to be elected. Political calculation was, therefore, clearly a major factor in his championing of civil rights.

Harry Truman gave the credit for his victory in 1948 to the labor and farm votes, certainly important factors, but there may have been more to Truman's assertion than is immediately obvious. Clearly, one of Truman's priorities in his new administration would be the repeal of the Taft-Hartley Labor Act, and labor was going to be his main ally in this endeavor. Truman could risk being associated with labor and, indeed, farmers as they were both extremely powerful interest groups, but African Americans were different. They received little credit for the Democratic victory outside of African American circles, and, by effectively ignoring their contribution to his victory, Truman could refuse to accede to any of their demands. He made it very clear to Walter White in the aftermath of the election that he would not be pushing civil rights and implied that the African American vote was not an important factor in his election success. Truman's reticence is understandable: African Americans were not nearly as useful allies as labor and farmers, particularly if the South were to be rehabilitated. This again calls into question Truman's earlier pledges on civil rights and reinforces the impression that he used the issue expediently, demonstrating just how limited his electoral mandate actually was. With the South more loyal than expected, one of Truman's aims was to reintegrate the region back into the Democratic Party, and this was not going to be done by fulfilling pledges on civil rights.

In the 1950s, civil rights would go through periods of activity and stagnation, and this coincided with the African American vote being seen as independent: while Stevenson matched Truman in 1952, over half of African

Americans voted for Eisenhower in 1956 before switching to Kennedy in 1960. The election of Kennedy ushered in the most important period in civil rights history, and as a legacy of it, the African American vote remained solidly Democratic. In the 1950s, when the solidarity of the African American voters had momentarily fractured, action on civil rights on a federal level was, at best, fragmented and grudging. It was always the hope of Walter White that the African American vote would not remain what he termed the "chattel of any one party," and would vote along class and economic lines as other Americans did. The reality was, however, that African Americans had to vote as a bloc if they were to exert any influence. White's pragmatic hope for the African American vote, therefore, proved to be a pipe dream. To make any progress, African Americans had to sell their vote to the highest bidder; if the vote was not solid, it could not dictate the outcome in key states and, consequently, the result of a presidential election. And there lay African Americans' best hope for equality.

Landon, Willkie, and Dewey all had liberal reputations in race relations, were altogether more progressive than their counterparts in the 1920s, and arguably had better records in that area than Roosevelt. Part of the difficulty in the 1930s and 1940s was that conservative congressional Republicans were often at odds with their progressive presidential candidates on specific and important areas of policy. This congressional conservatism is best illustrated by the failure of antilynching and fair employment legislation; of course, the main blame for failure lies with southern Democrats, but there was more that the Republicans could have done.

Perhaps African American Republicans of the period held an unrealistic view of what their party actually represented; it had, after all, paid little or no attention to their needs since Reconstruction. African American Republicans are often dismissed as old-fashioned and clinging to a mythical past, which certainly holds true for people such as Perry Howard and perhaps Emmett Scott, but for Robert Church and others like him, protection by the GOP was essential. Church was much too experienced a politician to view the GOP nostalgically. His increasingly desperate pleas for action in the 1940s reflect not only the extremely limited options for southern African Americans, but also the disenchantment of a loyal party member exasperated at what the GOP had become. There was also a growing number of professional politicians among African American Republicans in the North, epitomized by Francis Rivers and Val Washington, who had established themselves within the party's hierarchy.

Rivers was the public and successful face of African American Republicanism. His suggestions for the party were constructive but private; equally, his criticisms of the Democrats were articulate and valid. To some African Americans, however, his closeness to Dewey was a disadvantage, and he was seen as being too influential in the development of policy toward African Americans. Nevertheless, Rivers's achievements both as a judge and a Republican were considerable. Church, marooned in Memphis, had few of Rivers's advantages. His predicament perhaps reflects his and, by definition, other southern African Americans' desperation, but it also illustrates that he still regarded the GOP as the main, if not the sole, protector of African American rights in the South. From Church's perspective, if the Republicans were not prepared to protect African American rights, then no one would, and, as a result, he sought to cajole, threaten, and shame the party into action. Within the party, the perception remained that there was little to be gained from the rescue of beleaguered southern African Americans, together with the tantalizing prospect of breaking the Solid South. In the 1930s and 1940s, this never approached the efforts of Hoover in 1928, but it still preoccupied some Republican strategists in 1948 and, more overtly, 1952.

African American Republicans, then, attempted to use their influence from within and outside the party's structures to bring it closer to African Americans and to bring their votes back to it. The record makes it abundantly clear that these efforts failed. The ignoring of Church's exertions and exhortations reinforced the impression that the party was not interested in African American problems or rights. Rivers's criticisms of the New Deal and the Democratic Party were valid but ineffectual without a genuine, coherent, and feasible alternative. By the 1930s, the party's broader principles and problems took precedence over an archaic and largely sentimental commitment to African Americans. Equally, African Americans maintained an emotional rather than an ideological attachment to the GOP. Economics more than social policy wedded African Americans to the New Deal, and the economic conservatism of the Republicans alienated them from African Americans in the same way it alienated them from other elements of the working class. In fact, the African American presence, as the poorest section of American society, was incongruous in a party of businessmen and conservative middle-class whites. The Republicans simply did not and could not espouse the liberal economic policies needed to improve the position of African Americans. African Americans were, therefore, Republicans due to the lack of realistic options.

It is vital to recognize that civil rights was a fairly minor campaign issue until 1948 (and again until 1960). The Depression dominated the elections of 1932 and 1936, and it was still a major factor in 1940. The war was the preeminent issue in 1940 and 1944, while the foreign policy and the domestic record of Harry Truman came under scrutiny in 1948. In 1952, some Republicans, including, finally, Thomas Dewey, recognized the importance of the African American vote and, among other things, strenuously attacked the choice of John Sparkman—who was associated with "white supremacy"—for the Democrat ticket. Yet the Republican candidate Dwight D. Eisenhower made little effort to disguise his opposition to a Fair Employment act, now the cornerstone of African American demands, and had scant interest in black concerns more generally. This apathy enabled the Democrats to lessen their commitments to civil rights (which had, of course, split the party in 1948), and this had the effect of devaluing the political currency of the African American vote. As would be demonstrated throughout his presidency, Eisenhower had a very limited appreciation of the plight of African Americans. In fact, his outlook was essentially "southern," and he was incapable of making any commitments to African Americans beyond his limited interpretation of the parameters of federal power as laid down by a very narrow interpretation of the Constitution. Moreover, due to the overwhelming nature of his victory in 1952 and the equally overwhelming support of African Americans for his opponent, he was essentially free of any partisan commitment to this constituency.

To make matters worse, the GOP repeatedly fashioned ad hoc alliances with the Dixiecrats, the worst elements of American politics, throughout the period. The Dixiecrats were antidemocratic and unashamedly racist, lacked any real mandate, were utterly contemptuous of northern (and, indeed, world) public opinion, and were answerable only to themselves. They successfully blocked civil rights legislation by employing the filibuster in the Senate and racist scaremongering throughout Dixie. Yet, such was the nature of American politics that these racist reactionaries, due to their entrenched positions within Congress, were much more important politically to both the Democrats and the Republicans than African Americans, regardless of the strategic importance of the black vote in the North. African Americans were extremely badly let down by both parties.

The plight of African Americans remained peripheral throughout this period, but it did at least continue to grow in importance. It saw African Americans recognize their electoral influence; eventually the national parties realized this and, in the case of the Democrats, acted upon it. Even at the height of the New Deal, the Democrats, as the party of Bilbo and Byrnes, still did not constitute an alternative to the GOP. Most African Americans were still registered as Republicans in 1936, yet most voted Democrat, despite the uncomfortable truth that Democrats' espousal of civil rights was often no more genuine than that of Republicans.

The Republicans appeared temperamentally incapable of reaching out to African Americans. In the 1940s and early 1950s, much of the blame for this lies with Robert Taft. Taft, bereft of any real empathy for those occupying society's lowest economic strata—by definition African Americans—and motivated by a hatred of Roosevelt and the New Deal, effectively controlled Republican domestic policy. He had little interest in legislation of benefit to African Americans, being, at best, lukewarm about anti–poll tax and antilynching measures and downright hostile to fair employment legislation. Taft was also rightly perceived to be the Republican most sympathetic to the South and most in need of its rotten boroughs at convention time.

In some respects, it is difficult to understand why the Republican Party did not make more of an effort to regain the African American vote. The GOP was repeatedly warned that this constituency could determine the outcome of a presidential election, yet it repeatedly failed to respond positively. Expediency, pragmatism, and electoral arithmetic suggested that the Republicans should court the African American vote. African Americans were wedded to the New Deal by economics, but this did not necessarily prevent the GOP from advocating antilynching and anti–poll tax bills. These were two issues, one symbolic and one practical, that could have demonstrated Republican goodwill, but that proved instead symptomatic of the Republican failure of African Americans.

Lynching and the poll tax were both extinct in the North and, therefore, would not have roused opposition from traditional Republicans in the region. There was also a very practical benefit if an anti–poll tax law was passed with GOP support as many southern African Americans still saw themselves as Republicans. This was a potential opportunity for the Republicans to finally break the Solid South. This would, of course, have required rebuilding the party in the region, but the benefits could have been enormous. The fact that the Republican Party either did not recognize this or was simply not interested points to an absence of idealism and a lack of good sense.

The Republican attitude to African Americans from 1928 to 1952 was characterized by ignorance, conservatism, ambivalence, tokenism, and perhaps a lack of political judgment, but it was not characterized by open hostility or overt racism. Unlike in the Democratic Party, there were no public racists in the GOP. The political survival of no Republican member of Congress depended upon racist appeals to white constituents, yet too few were prepared to make even a perfunctory stand on civil rights. The party clearly could have done more. It could have advocated antilynching and anti–poll tax legislation and genuinely tried to pass it. It could have listened to the concerns of its own African American members. It could have attacked the blatant hypocrisy of the Democrats on civil rights. But it did none of these things.

Lincoln had bequeathed the loyalty of African Americans to the Republican Party, but between 1928 and 1952, this legacy was lost.

Abbreviations

AAA	Agricultural Adjustment Administration
AFL	American Federation of Labor
ANP	Associated Negro Press
BAAS	British Association for American Studies
CD	*Chicago Defender*
CIO	Congress of Industrial Organizations
ER	Eleanor Roosevelt Papers
ERP	European Recovery Program
FDR	Franklin Delano Roosevelt
FDRP	Franklin D. Roosevelt, Papers as President
FDRP-PSF	Franklin D. Roosevelt, Papers as President, President's Secretary's Files, 1933–1945
FEPC	Fair Employment Practices Commission
GOP	Grand Old Party
HH	Herbert Hoover Presidential Papers
HH-CC	Herbert Hoover, Presidential Papers, Subject File, Colored Correspondence
HH-RNC	Herbert Hoover, Presidential Papers, Subject File, Republican National Committee
LLS	Lewis L. Strauss Papers
MOWM	March on Washington Movement
NAACP	National Association for the Advancement of Colored People
NCAPT	National Campaign for the Abolition of the Poll Tax
NRA	National Recovery Administration
NYT	*New York Times*
OWI	Office of War Industries
PAC	Political Action Committee

PCCR	President's Committee on Civil Rights
PRP	Papers of the Republican Party
PWA	Public Works Administration
RAC	Republican American Committee
RNC	Republican National Committee
SCAD	State Commission Against Discrimination
SCHW	Southern Conference on Human Welfare
TED	Thomas E. Dewey Papers
WPA	Works Progress Administration

Notes

Introduction. The Mantle of Lincoln

1. President Bush, address to the NAACP Annual Convention, Washington Convention Center, Washington, D.C., 20 July 2006, http://www.whitehouse.gov/news/releases/2006/07/20060720.html.

2. *Guardian* (Manchester), 31 July 2000.

3. *Chicago Defender* (henceforth *CD*), 12 July 1952.

4. *Topeka and Kansas City Plaindealer* (henceforth *Plaindealer*), 18 February 1944.

5. Sherman, *McKinley to Hoover*; Burk, *The Eisenhower Administration*. The only work dealing specifically with this period is Rees's *From the Deck to the Sea*, a very general overview of the Republican Party and African Americans from the Civil War to the 1980s that is based entirely on secondary sources and lacking any real analytical edge.

6. See Sitkoff, *New Deal for Blacks*; and Weiss, *Farewell to the Party of Lincoln*. Sitkoff suggests that Roosevelt moved actively to embrace civil rights, whereas Weiss argues much more convincingly that economic factors were what wedded African Americans to the New Deal. Regarding the tie with the Republican Party, Weiss declares that "blacks who were suffering most from the Depression had the least to lose by leaving the Republican Party. And they stood to gain most from the tangible assistance of the New Deal" (216). Weiss is more interested, ultimately, in why African Americans said hello to the party of Roosevelt than why they bade farewell to the party of Lincoln.

7. See, for example, Sullivan's excellent *Days of Hope*; and Norrell's *The House That I Live In* and *Reaping the Whirlwind*. Other interesting studies of African American life in the South during the interwar and immediate postwar period include Payne and Green, *Time Longer Than Rope*, a good collection on grassroots organizing in the South prior to 1950; and Chafe, Gavins, and Korstad, *Remembering Jim Crow*, a participant memoir. Also well worth examination are Daniel's *Lost Revolutions*, which looks at life from the perspectives of both African American and white southerners, and *Standing at the Crossroads*, which looks at, among other things, the impact of the Second World War on the South.

8. Discussion of Eleanor Roosevelt's contribution is to be found in many of the biographies of her and her husband as well as specific texts on civil rights in the period, including those of Weiss, Sitkoff, and Janken, as well as Walter White's autobiography. For the Supreme Court and civil rights, look no further than Klarman's recent, voluminous *From Jim Crow to Civil Rights*. There are several good texts on the Great Migrations including Goodwin, *Black Migration in America from 1915 to 1960*; and Trotter, *The Great Migration in Historical Perspective*.

Chapter 1. The Lily-White House

1. Sherman, *McKinley to Hoover,* 259.

2. For Harding's condoning of lynching earlier in his career, see Downes, *Rise of Harding,* 51. There were rumors that Harding had black ancestry; see Downes, "Negro Rights and the White Backlash" 100–107. In fact, there are even allegations that he was a member of the Klan. Sean Dennis Cashman is in no doubt that "Warren Harding belonged to the Klan and disgraced the White House by being inducted there" (*America in the Twenties and Thirties,* 77). For information on race and his campaign in 1920 and lily-whites in the southern Republican party, see Berg, *Ticket to Freedom,* 47.

3. Murray, *Harding Era,* 402–3.

4. Berg, *Ticket to Freedom,* 48.

5. *New York Times* (henceforth *NYT*), 7 September 1924, cited in Sherman, "Republicans and Negroes," 27, 72.

6. McCoy, *Quiet President,* 329.

7. The Klan was influential in the GOP in Colorado, Ohio, and Indiana, according to Berg (*Ticket to Freedom,* 48). Condemnation of Coolidge is by no means universal. During the Coolidge years, Elbert Lee Tatum argues, "the Negro had very little against which to register complaint": they were better off, race riots and lynchings were declining, and most of the black press supported Coolidge (*Political Thought of the Negro,* 98). Donald McCoy challenges this assertion: "black Americans only shared incidentally in the prosperity of the decade, as no attempt was made to give them or smaller racial minorities a fair share" (*Coming of Age,* 127).

8. Lichtmann, *Prejudice and the Old Politics,* 151.

9. Mayer, *Republican Party,* 406.

10. *Collier's,* 82 (20 October 1928): 13, cited in Tatum, *Political Thought of the Negro,* 102.

11. See *Cleveland Gazette,* 30 June 1928, Lewis L. Strauss Papers (henceforth LLS), box 9.

12. *CD,* 20 October 1928, cited in Lichtmann, *Prejudice,* 156. Nancy Weiss states that Smith was also the preferred choice of Marcus Garvey (*Farewell to the Party of Lincoln,* 9–10).

13. It should be remembered that it was not only African Americans who were being neglected by the Republicans; immigrants and the working classes were similarly ignored.

14. Lichtmann, *Prejudice,* 156.

15. *Rope and Faggot* was published in 1929. White was, in fact, one-thirty-second black.

16. Perry, *Belle Moskowitz,* 203.

17. O'Dell, "Blacks, the Democratic Party and the Presidential Election of 1928," 1, 5. For greater detail on White's flirtation with the Smith campaign, see Janken, *Biography of Walter White,* 127–35.

18. O'Dell, "Blacks, the Democratic Party and the Presidential Election of 1928," 5–6.

19. Weiss, *Farewell to the Party of Lincoln*, 8–9. Belle Moskowitz, Smith's publicity director, later told White that Smith regretted not issuing this statement as it may have swayed African American voters in pivotal northern and border states with whose support he might have won the election (White, *A Man Called White*, 101; also cited in Weiss, 11). See also Berg, *Ticket to Freedom*, 50.

20. *Crisis* 35 (November 1928): 381; also cited in Sherman, *McKinley to Hoover*, 232.

21. It seems that at least some African Americans took this advice as the Republicans' own survey of the election reported that in New York: "the colored vote was very strong for Hoover in practically all the districts. This is particularly so of the Republican districts, where Hoover's majority was much larger than the rest of the ticket" ("Survey: Election of 1928, New York State." LLS, box 15). This assessment gives some credence to the view that the Democrats were making inroads locally in the North, but it also confirms that African Americans were still reluctant to help to put a Democrat in the White House.

22. Lichtmann, *Prejudice*, 157.

23. O'Dell, "Blacks, the Democratic Party and the Presidential Election of 1928," 9. Twenty percent of African Americans had voted Democrat in Baltimore, Missouri, Ohio, and Indiana (ibid.).

24. Allen to Hoover, 28 August 1928 (cited in Lichtmann, 154).

25. Interview with Alfred Kirchhofer by Raymond Henle, April 1969, Herbert Hoover Oral History, 8.

26. Edward Anthony, who was the associate publicity director for the 1928 campaign, argued that most of the anti-Catholic literature was anonymous (interview with Edward and Esther Anthony by Raymond Henle, July 1970, Herbert Hoover Oral History). Lichtmann is in no doubt that Hoover not only approved of the southern strategy but was also intimately involved in its planning and execution. He cannot, however, offer firm proof directly linking Hoover to the southern campaign other than evidence "that can be reliably attributed to Herbert Hoover and his close associates" (*Prejudice*, 147). Gould agrees with this hypothesis, commenting, "behind the scenes . . . Hoover quietly encouraged attacks on Smith and the skilful exploitation of anti-Catholic sentiments" (*Grand Old Party*, 251).

27. Gould also identifies Willebrandt as the main culprit (*Grand Old Party*, 251). GOP literature suggested that Smith had encouraged interracial marriage in New York (ibid., 252).

28. Weiss notes that the Democrats won 17 percent of the African American vote in Philadelphia, 27 percent in Cleveland, and 28 percent in Harlem. The figure for Harlem was the same as it had been in 1924 but had gone up from only 3 percent in 1920 (*Farewell to the Party of Lincoln*, 10).

29. See Garcia, "Herbert Hoover's Southern Strategy," 2; and Lisio, *Hoover, Blacks and Lily-Whites*, 71. Incidentally, Garcia and Lisio were both based in Iowa, Hoover's home state.

30. Lichtmann, p159.

31. According to Paul Lewinson, *Race, Class and Party*, 167, 176. The exception to this was in the border states. Elsewhere in the South, apart from Virginia and North

Carolina, Republican state parties were not "active as vote-getting organizations, save in presidential years" (ibid., 179). Hanes Walton Jr. concurs, noting that Joseph Tolbert's South Carolina black and tans, for example, "emerged every four years to go to the National Convention" (*Black Republicans*, 68). Areas of the South, including East Kentucky, East Tennessee, West Virginia, North Georgia, and even northern Alabama had functioning lily-white organizations dating back to the Civil War.

32. *NYT*, 17 March 1929, Herbert Hoover Presidential Papers, Subject File, Republican National Committee (henceforth HH-RNC), States Files, box 257, Georgia.

33. *World*, 22 April 1929, Herbert Hoover Presidential Papers, Subject File, Colored Correspondence (henceforth HH-CC), box 105.

34. Church to Hoover, 6 November 1929, HH-CC, box 105; also cited in Garcia, "Herbert Hoover's Southern Strategy," 128.

35. Howard was very unpopular among African Americans, particularly with figures such as Du Bois, Walter White, and Ralph Bunche, yet even Du Bois rallied to his cause when he was put on trial. For a largely sympathetic account of Howard's trial and more general career in the GOP, as well as efforts by Mississippi's white editors and politicians to prevent his prosecution, see McMillen, "Perry W. Howard." For a contemporary account of the attempts to prosecute Howard, see "GOP Negroes in Party Revolt," *World*, 22 April 1929, HH-CC. For more detail on the Howard case, see Lisio, *Hoover, Blacks and Lilywhites*, 129; Lewinson, *Race, Class and Party*, 181; and Garcia, "Herbert Hoover's Southern Strategy," 63.

36. "Hoovercrat" was the name given to those southern Democrats who backed Hoover in 1928.

37. Garcia agrees, arguing that the southern strategy was "poorly conceived and badly implemented ("Herbert Hoover's Southern Strategy," 165).

38. Viorst, *Fall from Grace*, 164–65.

39. Day, "Hoover and Racial Politics," 12. De Priest once declared that "before man made me a Republican, God made me a Negro" (file memorandum, 23 March 1931, undated newspaper clipping: "De Priest Says He Will Use Power," Herbert Hoover Presidential Papers [henceforth HH], Secretary's File, box 528).

40. Henry Anderson to Lewis Strauss, 19 December 1929, LLS, box 9.

41. *Chicago Tribune*, 21 June 1929, HH-CC, "De Priest Incident," box 107; also cited in Lisio, *Hoover, Blacks and Lilywhites*, 140.

42. Kenneth Goings argues that race was the pivotal factor in the campaign against Parker. Goings, *NAACP Comes of Age*. It should be noted, however, that Berg argues that Goings "tends to exaggerate" the African American role in the defeat of the nomination (*Ticket to Freedom*, 275).

43. Faith in Parker's ability was by no means universal. Associate Judge Harlan Fiske Stone believed that he lacked the experience and the intellect to be attorney general.

44. *New Republic* 62 (2 April 1930): 177–78, cited in Watson, "The Defeat of Judge Parker," 216.

45. *Charlotte Observer*, 18 April 1920, cited in Goings, *NAACP Comes of Age*, 23. For some of Parker's comments about African Americans, see Sherman, *McKinley to*

Hoover, 240–41. Similar comments appeared in the *Greensboro Daily News*, 19 April 1920, cited in Watson, "The Defeat of Judge Parker," 218.

46. *CD*, 5 May 1930, cited in Tatum, *Political Thought of the Negro*, 122.

47. A worker signing a "Yellow Dog contract" was forbidden to join a union.

48. White, *A Man Called White*, 106.

49. It is worth noting that the AFL had a membership of 3.5 million, while the NAACP had 100,000 members (figure for NAACP membership from *Crisis* 37 [May 1930]: 161). African American and labor votes were important in Kentucky, Illinois, West Virginia, New Jersey, Kansas, Ohio, New York, Missouri, and Indiana.

50. Goings, *NAACP Comes of Age*, 27. Ironically, one of the senators who voted against the Parker nomination was William Borah from Idaho. His bid for the presidency in 1936 would meet with a similar fate to Parker's nomination to the Supreme Court.

51. Moton to Walter Newton (Hoover's political secretary), 18 April 1930, cited in Lisio, *Hoover, Blacks and Lilywhites*, 217.

52. Watson, "The Defeat of Judge Parker," 222.

53. Vandenberg to R. K. Smathers, 28 April 1930, cited ibid., 232. There were, in fact, only around 13 million African Americans in the United States.

54. Vandenberg did not oppose Hoover lightly. He met with the president shortly after the Parker defeat, and Hoover made it clear that he bore the senator no malice: "he wanted me to know that my vote meant absolutely nothing in respect to our friendship and that we should proceed together as closely as ever. . . . I repeat that the hardest job of my life was voting against his nominee" (Tompkins, *Vandenberg*, 56).

55. In the Senate, Republican Simeon Fess questioned the role of the NAACP and said that Du Bois was a "Bolshevist," that William Pickens of the NAACP was a Communist, and that Felix Frankfurter was a defender of radical revolutionaries (Goings, *NAACP Comes of Age*, 46). For more of Fess's comments on Parker's opponents, see Watson, "The Defeat of Judge Parker," 227.

56. *Baltimore Afro-American*, 30 May 1930, HH, Secretary's File, box 430. See also *Congressional Record*, 71st Cong., 2nd sess., 8033–37, cited in Goings, *NAACP Comes of Age*, 42.

57. Associated Negro Press, "Parker Fight Shows up Some Negro Friends," press release, 7 May 1930, cited in Goings, *NAACP Comes of Age*, 29.

58. Goings, *NAACP Comes of Age*, 34.

59. Ibid., 35. A number of other factors were important to this "insurgency," according to Goings, including the impact of the Great Migration, the influence of radicals such as Garvey and the trade unionist A. Philip Randolph, lynchings, southern lily-white Republicans, the legal activities of the NAACP, and the increasingly vocal African American press (ibid., 38).

60. A similar explanation can be offered for the failure of a Mississippi court to convict Perry Howard of corruption. It seems unlikely that an all-white jury would have found him innocent under any other circumstances.

61. *NYT*, 8 May 1930, cited in Sherman, *McKinley to Hoover*, 244–45.

62. This comment was attributed to Hoover by Washington businessman and banker R. M. Hardy. Meeting with the president in May 1930, Hardy reported that he "could talk of nothing but the Parker case, and the part Negroes had played in having him defeated" (*CD*, 31 May 1930, HH, Secretary's File, box 430; also cited in Lisio, *Hoover, Blacks and Lilywhites*, 232).

63. It was in the aftermath of the Parker fight that Walter White christened Hoover "the man in the Lily White House" (*Crisis* 37 [July 1930]: 244).

64. *Crisis* 37 (July 1930): 225–27, 248. This quotation is also cited in Goings, *NAACP Comes of Age*, 54–55. The selection of editorials quoted by Du Bois in this article gives some credence to Goings's view that it was the NAACP rather than labor that was the prime mover in having the nomination rejected.

65. Kelly Miller to Walter White, 13 November 1930, cited in White, *A Man Called White*, 111. It should also be noted that the NAACP actively supported those it considered to be allies, including Arthur Capper (Republican, Kansas), George Norris, and J. M. Robison (Democrats, Kentucky). See also William Pickens, "Aftermath of Anti-Parker Fight," ANP press release, 14 May 1930, cited in Goings, *NAACP Comes of Age*, 57. Samuel M. Shortridge, from California, was targeted and defeated even though he had been a sponsor of the Dyer antilynching bill.

66. William Pickens was sent to Kansas to assist the campaign against Allen. For an account of this campaign, see *Crisis* 37 (October 1930): 338, 356.

67. Ibid. (November 1930): 373–74. In this article on the campaign against McCulloch, White contends—as he would continue to do throughout the 1930s—that the African American voter was "coming of age." Bulkley was glad of the assistance and pledged to support a federal antilynching bill, equal public school funding, and the enforcement of the Fourteenth and Fifteenth Amendments. He even attended an NAACP-sponsored anti-McCulloch rally. Berg argues that Allen and McCulloch were fairly easy targets for the NAACP (*Ticket to Freedom*, 55).

68. NAACP press release, 30 October 1930, NAACP branch file G-60, cited in Goings, *NAACP Comes of Age*, 70. White declared that "the infamous Klan has honeycombed political parties and especially the Republican Party in Indiana" (ibid.).

69. *Crisis* 40 (December 1934): 364; also cited in Goings, *NAACP Comes of Age*, 73.

70. Goings, *NAACP Comes of Age*, 38.

71. Lisio, *Hoover, Blacks and Lilywhites*, 189.

72. Requests for a message from the Republicans to the NAACP conferences in 1929 and 1930 appear to have been turned down. On 24 May 1929, James Weldon Johnson wrote to Hoover asking for such a message. French Strother (a Hoover aide), asked for Hoover's opinion, enclosed a handwritten note stating, "no answer." The same request was made on 19 June and received the same internal response. When Johnson inquired again in 1930, his letter again had "NO" handwritten upon it. It is unclear whether a formal rejection was sent or whether the request was simply ignored (HH, Secretary's File, box 755).

73. *Nation* 131 (July 1930), cited in Sherman, *McKinley to Hoover*, 248.

74. Sherman, *McKinley to Hoover*, 248.

75. *Crisis* 37 (November 1930): 389.

76. Furthermore, in October 1930, Dr. T. J Woofter Jr.'s report *The Economic Status of the Negro* appeared. Shortened from its original length of thirty-eight pages to a mere three pages, its recommendations were ignored by Hoover (*The Economic Status of the Negro*, HH-CC, box 106).

77. Weiss believes that it is important to remember the actual voting strength of African Americans when considering the attention given to them. In 1930, they constituted 10 percent of the total population of the United States, but two-thirds of them lived in the South or Washington, D.C. The reality was, therefore, African Americans who could actually voted accounted for only about 3 percent of the electorate, and for this reason, she writes that it was "not realistic to expect more attention" (*Farewell to the Party of Lincoln*, 23).

78. *Pittsburgh Courier*, 22 November 1930, "Republican Party General Political Survey, April 1931," pt. 2, sec. 5, p. 49, HH, Subject File, box 273A.

79. For further editorial comment from the African American press, see ibid., 48–54.

80. Ibid.

81. Ibid.

82. Ibid.

83. The 6 November 1930 *New York News* commented: "in the rock-ribbed Harlem district they voted nearly two to one Democratic" (ibid.). While the election of African Americans on the Democratic ticket in New York is significant, it is also worth noting that the electoral boundaries in Harlem were gerrymandered to ensure that the district would have African American representation (*Crisis* 37 [November 1930]: 377, 393). It was a Republican bill, drafted by Francis Rivers, that redrew the electoral boundaries in Harlem. From 1929 to 1974, only one African American Republican was elected from Harlem (E. Lewinson, *Black Politics in New York City*, 67).

84. Lisio, *Hoover, Blacks and Lilywhites*, 249.

85. For more detail on the disbandment of the Tenth Cavalry, see HH-CC, box 106. This contains the original order changing the status of the regiment as well as correspondence involving Walter White, Douglas MacArthur, Emmett Scott (of the Republican National Committee's Colored Division), Secretary of War Patrick Hurley, and Acting Secretary of War F. H. Payne, as well as NAACP press releases.

86. *Opportunity* 10 (April 1932): 115; also cited in Garcia, "Hoover's Southern Strategy," 144. The survey in *Opportunity* suggests that disaffection with the Republican Party among African Americans was actually much less pronounced within the higher social strata. Physicians, teachers, and clergy were overwhelmingly pro-Republican, as were a majority of social workers and lawyers, whereas the vast majority of students, laborers, domestics, and civil servants were pro-Democrat, suggesting that African Americans were beginning to vote along conventional class lines ("Opportunity Presidential Candidates Poll," *Opportunity* 10 [April 1932]: 115). This poll of 2,680 people also showed that the Democrats were supported by a majority of African Americans (1,344 to 1,186), and that Roosevelt was the preferred choice for the Democratic nomination.

87. Robert L. Vann, "The Patriot and the Partisan," speech made in Cleveland on 11 September 1932, cited in Weiss, *Farewell to the Party of Lincoln*, 15; and Buni, *Robert*

L. Vann, 194. Buni asserts that Vann's break with the Republicans led to the creation of Democratic organizations in Pennsylvania's African American districts. Pennsylvania was, arguably, the first northern state to see the transfer of African American allegiance to the Democrats. Having joined the Democrats, Vann was appointed special assistant to Attorney General Homer Cummings, but he was soon disillusioned by his new role (see *Robert L. Vann*, 198–211).

88. For some information on Roosevelt's perceived racial attitudes at this time, see Weiss, *Farewell to the Party of Lincoln*, 18–19.

89. The *CD* commented on 19 December 1931 that despite Hoover's record, "four more years of [Hoover] as a Republican will be better than a possible eight years of any Democrat" (cited ibid., 15).

90. In an interview with the ANP, Garner was generally evasive about issues pertaining to African Americans. He did not approve of lynching and said that he would, if elected, seek to enable African Americans in the South to vote but was reluctant to answer questions about the Fourteenth and Fifteenth Amendments (*Plaindealer*, 4 November 1932). See also Weiss, *Farewell to the Party of Lincoln*, 24–25.

91. *Opportunity* 10 (November 1932): 336.

92. *Crisis* 39 (August 1932): 247.

93. For percentages, see Weiss, *Farewell to the Party of Lincoln*, 30–31

94. See figures provided by Weiss, ibid., 33. The shift of other ethnic voters to the Democrats was much more pronounced than the minimal shift of the African Americans.

95. *Opportunity* 10 (November 1932): 19, 28.

96. Sherman, *McKinley to Hoover*, 257.

97. Ibid., 252.

98. Lisio, *Hoover, Blacks and Lilywhites*, 275–76. Lisio argues Hoover has been pilloried unfairly over his treatment of African Americans, and he attempts to redress this. Lisio, no apologist for Hoover, endeavors to insulate him as much as possible from the charges that he was a lily-white, a racist, and a bigot, arguing instead that he was a victim of his own reticence, bad advice, second-rate advisers, and an extreme dislike of those he saw as mere "politicians." Nevertheless, he concedes that Hoover had no consistent approach to, or understanding of, the plight of African Americans and was incapable of addressing their needs.

Chapter 2. Abraham Lincoln Is Not a Candidate

1. Schattschneider, *The Semi-Sovereign People*, 86, cited in Jones, *Republican Party*, 9.

2. Mayer, *Republican Party*, 428.

3. Mayer notes that many Republicans standing for reelection were being urged to support the New Deal by their constituents and "secretly cursed the national committee" (ibid., 432).

4. Weed, *Nemesis of Reform*, 45.

5. The election of 1934 meant that there were now 104 Republicans in the House and 25 in the Senate.

6. Senator David Reed to Herbert Hoover, 24 November 1934, cited in Weed, *Nemesis of Reform*, 46.

7. *NYT*, 9 November 1934.

8. Ibid.

9. Ibid.

10. Ibid., 2 December 1934.

11. Ibid.

12. Ibid.

13. Weed, *Nemesis of Reform*, 5.

14. Mayer, *Republican Party*, 436.

15. Borah believed that reform was crucial to Republican prospects in 1936. "In my opinion," he declared, "there must be a complete and bona fide reorganization of the Republican party . . . if we expect to have any showing in 1936" (*NYT*, 24 April 1935).

16. Ibid., 3 February 1935.

17. Ibid., 28 March 1935.

18. Ibid.

19. Ibid., 1 June 1935. Despite the desire not to discuss potential candidates, Landon was again being talked of as the most likely nominee.

20. Ibid., 8 June 1935.

21. Ibid., 7 July 1935.

22. Ibid., 10 July 1935. See also "The Cleveland Conference," ibid., 11 July 1935.

23. *NYT*, 18 December 1935. For more information on these and other regional conferences, see Weed, *Nemesis of Reform*, 68–72.

24. For a brief account of the primary campaign and nomination, see Mayer, *Republican Party*, 439–44. For the nomination, see *NYT*, 4 June 1936.

25. The *Literary Digest* poll had come within 1 percent of predicting the popular vote in 1932 and forecast a victory for Landon throughout the 1936 campaign. A Gallup Poll in September 1936 predicted that Landon could win anything between 99 and 272 electoral votes (Weed, *Nemesis of Reform*, 104–5).

26. *Crisis* 44 (October 1936): 305; *Baltimore Afro-American*, 17 October 1936, cited in McCoy, *Landon of Kansas*, 312.

27. *NYT*, 10 November 1935.

28. More generally, Landon was hampered by conservatives in the GOP, especially his running mate, Frank Knox, and the Republican National Committee chairman, John D. M. Hamilton.

29. Memorandum from Walter White, 1 January 1936, NAACP Papers (henceforth NAACP), pt. 11, ser. B, reel 22, frames 303–4. A similar sentiment is expressed in *Crisis* 44 (February 1936): 56–57.

30. *NYT*, 4 October 1936.

31. *Crisis* 44 (February 1936): 46–47. This article includes a *Literary Digest* poll from December 1935. White cites election data from 1924, 1928, and 1932 from marginal states, together with the potential African American vote, to reinforce his argument about the pivotal nature of the African American vote. White wanted African Americans to be politically independent, but by the end of the decade it seemed that African

Americans were becoming as entrenched in the Democratic Party as they had been in the Republican Party.

32. For the increasing importance of the African American vote, see *Time*, 17 August 1936, cited in Sitkoff, *New Deal for Blacks*, 91; and Ward, *Nation* 143 (1 August 1936): 119–20.

33. *Crisis* 44 (February 1936): 46–47.

34. Walter White to William Borah, Eleanor Roosevelt Papers (henceforth ER), reel 19, frame 0196; also quoted in *Plaindealer*, 29 November 1935.

35. Ibid.

36. Ibid.

37. NAACP press release, 3 January 1936, NAACP, pt. 11, ser. B, reel 22, frame 299.

38. *Plaindealer*, 21 February 1936.

39. Ibid.

40. Ibid.

41. Hamilton Fish Jr. to Walter White, 3 March 1936, LLS, box 51E. For Fish's efforts to defend Borah, see *Plaindealer*, 6 March 1936.

42. For more on Borah's record, see Redding, *Crisis* 44 (March 1936): 70–72, 82. In this article, which the NAACP reprinted for supporters, Borah's record on lynching, the Brownsville riot of 1908, and the link between female and African American suffrage were examined.

43. Undated *Chicago Tribune* editorial cited in the *Plaindealer*, 29 May 1936.

44. NAACP press release, 15 May 1936, NAACP, pt. 11, ser. B, reel 24, frame 124.

45. Walter White to William Borah, 18 May 1936. ER, reel 19, frame 0271.

46. Ibid., 0272. White's hostility toward Borah extended beyond the issue of lynching. White's research on the senator discovered that in April 1908 Borah had referred to African American soldiers as traitors: "if this doesn't alienate every Negro vote in the country, I'll eat my oldest hat" (Walter White to Lewis Strauss, 22 November 1935, LLS, box 51E). Borah's comments were made in relation to the actions of the Twenty-fifth Infantry in the Brownsville riot of 1906 (*NYT*, 21 April 1908).

47. *Norfolk Journal and Guide*, editorial, 30 November 1935, NAACP, pt. 11, ser. B, reel 24, frames 302–3. Not all of the African American press condemned Borah outright. The Republican-leaning *Plaindealer* believed that the senator's stance on antilynching legislation was based on principle and not prejudice, arguing that he had been "honest, sincere, frank and courageous." The *Plaindealer* maintained, however, that this was not the point, and that African American voters had demonstrated in the primary elections that they wanted someone in the White House who would stand up for their rights (22 May 1936).

48. It was not only the African American press that was critical of Borah. The *Chicago Tribune* took the senator to task for prejudging the constitutionality of the antilynching bill: "it was well understood that the South would not voluntarily raise the Negro to the full status of an American citizen." The *Tribune* noted that under the terms of the Fourteenth Amendment Congress had to provide citizens with equal protection under the law and there was no reason to believe that antilynching legislation would

necessarily be unconstitutional. The editorial concluded by accusing Borah of thinking "that no legislation against lynching can be appropriate. That is a large assumption" (undated editorial, *Chicago Tribune*, cited in *Plaindealer*, 29 May 1936).

49. *Crisis* 44 (July 1936): 209.

50. *NYT*, 4 and 7 June 1936.

51. Ibid., 10 and 11 June 1936.

52. Walter White to Lewis L. Strauss, 8 June 1936, NAACP, pt. 11, ser. B, reel 24, frame 377.

53. A similar gesture at the Democratic convention two weeks later precipitated a walkout by "Cotton Ed" Smith. Smith of South Carolina said that he would not support "any organization that looks upon the Negro and caters to him as a political and social equal," and asserted that the Democratic Party did not need the African American vote (*NYT*, 25 June 1936). Paul Ward of the *Nation* felt that Smith's walkout actually benefited the Democrats in the eyes of African American voters "Wooing the Negro Vote."(*Nation* [1 August 1936]: 119–20).

54. *Crisis* 44 (August 1936): 241. Also cited in Weiss, *Farewell to the Party of Lincoln*, 184. In the course of the Democratic convention, the "two-thirds rule," which had given a disproportionate amount of power to the South by requiring a two-thirds majority to pass resolutions, was abandoned. This lessened the power of the South within the party while potentially enhancing the position of African Americans. The abandonment of the two-thirds rule was also part of the reason for Smith's walkout. See also the undated NAACP press release, "FDR Told Omission of Lynching Is Disappointment," NAACP, pt. 11, ser. B, reel 24, frame 446; and a telegram from Walter White to Roosevelt, ibid.

55. *Crisis* 44 (August 1936): 241. See also NAACP press release, 12 June 1936, NAACP, pt. 11, ser. B, reel 24, frame 395.

56. *Crisis* 44 (August 1936): 241

57. Ibid. (July 1936): 209.

58. Ibid.

59. Ibid.

60. Johnson and Porter, *National Party Platforms*, 369.

61. David, Goldman, and Bain, *National Party Conventions*, 247.

62. Republican National Committee press release, 3 August 1936, cited in Weiss, *Farewell to the Party of Lincoln*, 186.

63. *NYT*, 18 October 1936.

64. McCoy, *Landon of Kansas*, 56. For a sympathetic appraisal of Landon, see Roy Garvin (editor of the *Kansas City Call*), *Crisis* 44 (May 1936): 139, 142. Garvin later informed White: "I am told by those who know him better than I that he is all right on the colored question" (Garvin to White, 20 October 1936, NAACP, pt. 11, ser. B, reel 22, frame 615). See also a letter from Harry Davis, an African American Republican, to White after the announcement of the Republican platform. Davis implied that Landon would go beyond the constraints of the platform to help African Americans (Harry Davis to Walter White, 15 June 1936, NAACP, pt. 11, ser. B, reel 22, frame 397).

65. 27 December 1934, ER, reel 18, frame 1041–42.

66. NAACP, pt. 11, ser. B, reel 22, frames 381–84. This followed a letter sent to all potential Republican candidates on 5 March 1936, asking for their views on issues relating to African Americans (ibid., 324–25).

67. *NYT*, 11 October 1936.

68. *Topeka Capital*, 2 October 1936, cited in McCoy, *Landon of Kansas*, 312.

69. *CD*, 17 October 1936, cited in McCoy, *Landon of Kansas*.

70. *Baltimore Afro-American*, 26 September 1936, cited in McCoy, *Landon of Kansas*, 311.

71. *Crisis* 44 (October 1936): 296. Also cited in Harrell, "Negro Leadership," 553. For further details on the Republican Party's efforts to undermine the New Deal among African Americans, see *Balance of Power*, a booklet issued by the Republican National Committee, Alfred M. Landon Papers, box 61, folder 7. An NAACP press release also promoted the balance of power argument, stating that "in no other presidential campaign has the Negro vote been so seriously considered as in 1936" (4 September 1936, NAACP, pt. 11, ser. B, reel 22, frame 502).

72. Weiss, *Farewell to the Party of Lincoln*, 197.

73. *NYT*, 6 October 1936.

74. Many states, including several in the South, had antilynching laws, and they were rarely effective. Georgia, for instance, had introduced an antilynching law in 1893, but between its introduction and 1934, there had been 403 lynchings in the state, again proving to African Americans the need for a strong, enforceable federal law. In addition, state antilynching laws may have been used to preempt or prevent federal action.

75. NAACP press release, 9 October 1936, NAACP, pt. 11, ser. B, reel 22, frame 579.

76. *Crisis* 44 (November 1936): 337.

77. NAACP press release, 9 October 1936, NAACP, pt. 11, ser. B, reel 22, frame 579.

78. This accounted for about 30 percent of the total African American population of the United States (Harrell, "Negro Leadership," 560).

79. Telegram from White to Landon, 14 October 1936, made public 16 October 1936, NAACP, pt. 11, ser. B, reel 22, frames 593, 599. See also NAACP press release, 16 October 1936, ibid., frame 599.

80. *Crisis* 44 (November 1936): 337.

81. Roosevelt had made a number of significant African American appointments, including former Republican Mary McLeod Bethune to head the Negro Division of the National Youth Association (NYA). Other significant appointments included: Ida De A. Reid, an Atlanta University sociologist, who joined the WPA; Eugene Kinkle Jones of the National Urban League was appointed to the Commerce Department's Division of Negro Affairs, while Robert C. Weaver joined the Public Works Administration (PWA). See Harrell, "Negro Leadership," 554. For a detailed appraisal of African Americans within the Roosevelt administration, see Kirby, *Black Americans in the Roosevelt Era*, chap. 6.

82. Weiss, *Farewell to the Party of Lincoln*, 119. Ickes was responsible for the PWA, which was popular with African Americans.

83. Ibid., 156. Ickes's speech would have been more forthright had it not been cen-

sored by Roosevelt's secretary, Stephen T. Early, a southerner. For the text of Ickes's speech to the NAACP conference in 1936, see Harold Ickes, "The Negro as a Citizen," *Crisis* 44 (August 1936): 230–31, 242, 253.

84. *Kansas City Times*, 30 October 1936, cited in McCoy, *Landon of Kansas*, 332–33. On 23 October, while visiting Detroit, Landon had met Henry Ford, who was known for his anti-Semitic views, a move strongly criticized by William Allen White, who felt that it would alienate Jewish voters (Weed, *Nemesis of Reform*, 110). Landon felt that there were attempts by the Democrats to depict him as a racist (*Topeka Capital*, 2 October 1936, cited in McCoy, *Landon of Kansas*, 311).

85. Weiss lists the *Chicago Defender*, *Cleveland Gazette*, and *New York Age* as being pro-Landon, while identifying the *Pittsburgh Courier*, *Atlantic World*, *Norfolk Journal and Guide*, *New York Amsterdam News*, *St. Louis Argus*, and *Chicago Metropolitan News*, among others, as Roosevelt supporters (*Farewell to the Party of Lincoln*, 203).

86. Ibid., 201.

87. Walter White received numerous offers to serve on political campaigns in 1936, including one from the National Allied Republican Council, which urged him to help "Save America from the Roosevelt-Bolshevik-Fascistic-Anarchistic-Communistic and Socialistic administration." Needless to say, he turned this, and other offers, down (E. W. Martin, vice chairman of the National Allied Republican Council, to Walter White, 30 April 1936, NAACP, pt. 11, ser. B, reel 22, frames 354–56).

88. Calvin Service Flash, "Head of NAACP to Make Eight Speeches for Roosevelt," 10 October 1936, ibid., frames 0585–86. Some members of the association were outraged by Spingarn's stance. The Cleveland, Ohio, branch was particularly vocal, stating that 98 percent of its members were backing Landon and expressing the view that the "national office has gone for Roosevelt" (telegram from Chester A. Gillespie, of the Cleveland NAACP, to Walter White, 17 October 1936. ibid., frame 601). They also pointed out that news items about Spingarn always emphasized his links to the NAACP. Another member of the branch accused the national office of double standards: "people here remember the fight on Borah . . . and Roosevelt's silence on lynching" (telegram from Charles H. White of the Cleveland NAACP, to Walter White, 17 October 1936, ibid., frame 605). This was particularly galling to Republican members of the association, given White's attacks on Landon over lynching and relief.

89. *NYT*, 3 September 1936.

90. Ibid., 26 October 1936.

91. *Pittsburgh Courier*, 10 October 1936, cited in Kenneally, "Black Republicans," 122. Owens confessed: "they paid me a lot. No, I won't say how much, but a lot" (ibid.).

92. Weiss, *Farewell to the Party of Lincoln*, 206.

93. *Crisis* 44 (December 1936): 369.

94. McGinnis, "Republican Party Resurgence," 3.

95. Walter White to Chester C. Bolton, 5 November 1936, NAACP, pt. 11, ser. B, reel 22, frames 700–701. Bolton seemed to agree: "I still believe that the action you and I sought could well have been taken and no doubt would have had a salutary effect [on the black vote]" (Bolton to White, 19 November 1936, ibid., frame 743). An NAACP press release expanded upon the notion that African Americans were now indepen-

dent and had not become a "chattel of the Democratic party" (NAACP press release, 6 November 1936, ibid., frame 714).

96. The most notable attempt to pass antilynching legislation was sponsored by Leonidas Dyer, a Republican congressman from Missouri, in 1922. For more detail on this effort to pass antilynching legislation, see, for example, Dray, *Persons Unknown*, 258–72.

97. Zangrando, *Crusade*, 102.

98. It should be noted that the number of lynchings always fell during campaigns for antilynching legislation. The NAACP's decision to embark on a campaign for antilynching legislation was not, however, entirely altruistic. Publicity generated by the campaign would not only help to reduce the number of lynchings, as southerners wanted to avoid federal legislation, but it would also generate much needed funds for the association.

99. Ironically, the NAACP privately queried the constitutionality of the Dyer bill. Furthermore, Dyer's ability to successfully guide the bill and even his sincerity in sponsoring it were called into question. For a detailed discussion of these issues, see Zangrando, *Crusade*, 51–72.

100. At the start of the court-packing crisis, Minority Leader Charles McNary told Vandenberg and Borah: "let the boys across the aisle do the talking. We'll do the voting" (Patterson, *Congressional Conservatism*, 107).

101. When Roosevelt finally met White in January 1936, he told him that there was no chance of passing Costigan-Wagner. Thomas Corcoran, a Roosevelt adviser, said of the president: "he does his best with it [antilynching legislation], but he ain't gonna lose his votes for it" (Weiss, *Farewell to the Party of Lincoln*, 119). Eleanor Roosevelt would later tell White: "the president feels that lynching is a question of education in the states . . . so that the localities themselves will wipe it out" (Eleanor Roosevelt to Walter White, 19 March 1936, ER, reel 19, frame 0241). Also cited in Weiss, *Farewell to the Party of Lincoln*, 118.

102. *NYT*, 2 January 1934. The main provisions of the bill included fining a county $5,000 if a lynching took place within its boundaries or a five-year prison sentence for any official involved in a lynching (ibid., 5 January 1934). White, appearing before the Senate Judiciary Subcommittee in February, presented statistics on lynching. He noted that of 5,053 reported lynchings since 1882, 3,513 of the victims were African American, and in only one-sixth of the cases was rape even the alleged justification. There had been 277 lynchings in the preceding twelve years, illustrating that southern states were not dealing with the problem. White stated that the lack of action on lynching made African Americans susceptible to communism (Zangrando, "Federal Anti-Lynching Bill," 107). Costigan was actually born in Virginia. The NAACP had originally hoped to have the bill sponsored by southern representatives.

103. Walter White to Eleanor Roosevelt, 20 April 1934, ER, reel 18, frame 0933.

104. *NYT*, 22 July 1934. By June, there had already been ten lynchings in 1934.

105. Zangrando, "Federal Anti-Lynching Bill," 110. Zangrando cites an eight-page pamphlet entitled *The Lynching of Claude Neal*. Lynchings fell from twenty-eight in 1933 to sixteen in 1934, and White attributed this to the threat of antilynching legislation (*NYT*, 1 January 1935).

106. *Crisis* 42 (January 1935): 10–11, 29. White listed the various organizations that had endorsed antilynching legislation and asserted that they had a combined membership of 42 million (ibid.). White had made a similar claim the previous year (*NYT*, 22 July 1934).

107. *NYT*, 17 April 1935. See also Edward P. Costigan, "Open and Boastful Anarchy," *Crisis* 42 (March 1935): 77–78; *NYT*, 17 April 1935. Krock believed that a filibuster was inevitable and stated, without irony, that it would be conducted by the "ablest men in the Senate."

108. See *Crisis* 42 (January 1935): 10–11, 29; and ibid., 42 (February 1935): 42–43, 61. The Democrats who supported the bill were predominantly from northern states but also included both senators from West Virginia, Neely and Holt. In the House, members from Minnesota, Illinois, Tennessee, Missouri, New York, Massachusetts, California, and Indiana offered support for the bill (ibid.). In February 1935, the *Crisis* listed another thirty or so senators and representatives who had replied to the NAACP's request for comments on the antilynching bill (ibid.).

109. Walter White to Eleanor Roosevelt, 20 April 1935, ER, reel 19, frame 008.

110. *NYT*, 2 May 1935.

111. Southerners actually began their filibuster even before the antilynching bill had been submitted by delaying the passage of the Bankhead Farm Tenancy Bill, a clear signal to the administration about the potential consequences of a prolonged antilynching fight (ibid., 24 April 1935).

112. Ibid., 17 April 1935.

113. Ibid., 2 May 1935.

114. Ibid.

115. *Crisis* 42 (June 1935): 177; italics in original. Organizations backing the NAACP's campaign now, apparently, had an aggregate of 50 to 53 million members (*NYT*, 19 April 1935).

116. *Crisis* 42 (June 1935): 177. For a list of those senators who voted for adjournment, inevitably including Borah, see ibid., 184. Notable Democrats also voted for adjournment, including: Barkley, (Kentucky), Black (Alabama), Dieterich (Illinois), Truman (Missouri), and Wheeler (Montana).

117. Gavagan was a congressman from New York whose constituency included Harlem. Costigan had resigned due to ill-health. White told the readers of the *Crisis* that 251 congressmen had either signed a pledge to support the bill or would endorse the bill when it came to the floor of the House (*Crisis* 44 [January 1937]: 15). For a list of many of those who had pledged to support this renewed effort to pass an antilynching bill, see *Plaindealer*, 20 November 1936.

118. *New York World Telegram*, cited in Zangrando, *Crusade*, 140. In January 1937, the NAACP issued a leaflet entitled *Stop Lynching*, which gave updated statistics about the crime (ER, reel 19, frame 0347).

119. *Crisis* 44 (January 1937): 15.

120. Ironically, Wagner introduced the bill the day after a Democratic senatorial "harmony dinner" (Patterson, *Congressional Conservatism*, 156). Frederick Van Nuys was a Democratic senator from Indiana. The Gavagan-Wagner–Van Nuys bill now

covered all instances of mob violence and not just those where the victim had been seized from custody. It also sought to impose much harsher penalties. See Zangrando, *Crusade*, 141–42; also cited in Weiss, *Farewell to the Party of Lincoln*, 242.

121. Walter White to Lewis Strauss, 22 April 1937. LLS, box 86. Unfortunately, White did not name those Republicans involved. Strauss was a former aide to Hoover and, it would seem, a contributor to the NAACP.

122. *Crisis* 44 (May 1937): 138–39.

123. Patterson, *Congressional Conservatism*, 157. For the comments of those senators supporting the bill, including Wagner, Van Nuys, and Capper, see ibid.

124. Jack, *History of the NAACP*, 40. Senator Theodore Bilbo of Mississippi told the Senate that if a secret vote were taken on the bill, it would have trouble finding ten supporters (ibid, 41).

125. *Crisis* 45 (February 1938): 49.

126. Jack, *History of the NAACP*, 44.

127. In late January, only 37 senators voted for cloture, and 51 were against; in mid-February, they met with slightly more success (42 for and 46 against), but it was clear that the bill was not going to pass. According to Taylor Merrill of the *Christian Century*, Arthur Capper was the only Republican to vote in favor of cloture, but he does not specify whether this was on the first or second occasion on which it was proposed (Merrill, "Lynching the Anti-Lynching Bill," 240).

128. NAACP press release, undated but probably February or March 1938, ER, reel 19, frame 0402. In June, Senator John Connally of Texas reportedly said that a proposed filibuster against the wages and hours bill would fail because it would not have Republican support. The *Crisis* asserted that this called into question the Republicans' commitment to antilynching legislation. This would not have surprised many African Americans and, if true, would validate White's criticism of the GOP in the aftermath of Gavagan-Wagner–Van Nuys ([June 1938]: 181).

129. Walter White to Lewis Strauss, 7 March 1938, LLS, box 86.

130. *Crisis* 45 (December 1938): 398.

131. Ibid. (March 1938): 84. This quotation also appears in an NAACP press release, undated but probably February or March 1938, ER, reel 19, frame 0403.

132. White to Fish, 5 March 1936, LLS, box 51E. White also referred to "that great 'liberal' Hamilton Fish" during the campaign (Walter White to Lewis Strauss, 6 March 1936, ibid.).

133. Borah died on 19 January 1940. Fish's decision to embark upon an antilynching bill would have been taken prior to Borah's death.

134. Emmett J. Scott, "Heavy Republican Support Passes Anti-lynching Bill," Republican National Committee press release, 18 January 1940, ER, reel 19, frame 0613.

135. Ibid., frame 0611.

136. Ibid., frame 0612.

137. *Plaindealer*, 8 March 1940.

138. Ibid., 29 March 1940.

139. "Fascist Activities of Hamilton Fish," File: 7 Confidential, Congress, 1941, Frank-

lin D. Roosevelt, Papers as President, President's Secretary's Files, 1933–1945 (henceforth FDRP-PSF), pt. 4, reel 7, frame 0395. Writer not specified.

140. *Plaindealer*, 18 October 1940.

141. Ibid.

142. Zangrando, *Crusade*, 164.

143. *Crisis* 47 (September 1940): 279.

144. *Washington Post*, 31 January 1937, ER, reel 19, frame, 0355. Also cited in Zangrando, "Federal Anti-Lynching Bill," 115. In March 1937, the *Crisis* reported the findings of the American Institute of Public Opinion on lynching, which found that 70 percent of the nation was in favor of an antilynching bill (44 [March 1937]: 81).

145. Zangrando, *Crusade*, 165.

146. Ibid., 128. White resigned from the Advisory Council to the Government of the Virgin Islands in June 1935 in protest of the lack of support antilynching legislation received from the White House. In his resignation letter, he told the president: "I cannot continue to remain even a small part of your official family" (*Crisis* 42 [June 1935]: 175, 183; quotation on 129).

147. Zangrando, *Crusade*, 146.

Chapter 3. The Darkest Horse

1. Brogan, "Future of the Republican Party," 186.

2. Ibid.; italics in original.

3. Ibid., 193.

4. Landon to Frank Altschul, 7 September 1937, cited in McCoy, *Landon of Kansas*, 361.

5. McCoy, *Landon of Kansas*, 356.

6. Mayer, *Republican Party*, 447. Brogan, writing in early 1937, felt that there was a very real possibility of a Democratic split ("Future of the Republican Party," 188).

7. Mayer, *Republican Party*, 448.

8. McCoy, *Landon of Kansas*, 357. Vandenberg was open-minded about political realignment and potentially abandoning the Republican name, particularly if the Republicans lost again in 1940 (Tompkins, *Vandenberg*, 152).

9. McCoy, *Landon of Kansas*, 366.

10. Plesur, "Republican Congressional Comeback," 533.

11. McCoy, *Landon of Kansas*, 373.

12. Weed, *Nemesis of Reform*, 192. For information on the structure of the Program Committee, see Cotter and Hennessey, *Politics without Power*, 194. See also Mayer, "Alf M. Landon," 331. Mayer is very sympathetic to the efforts of Landon to keep the Republican Party together in the years after 1936, believing that there was a stark contrast between the responses of Hoover and Landon to electoral defeat.

13. Weiss comments that Republican sources are "silent" on this issue; indeed, most literature pertaining to the Republican Party pays little attention to the Frank Committee (*Farewell to the Party of Lincoln*, 268).

14. Rivlin, *Ralph Bunche*, 8.

15. Ibid.

16. Ibid., 9.

17. Ibid.

18. Ibid.

19. Ralph J. Bunche, "Report on the Needs of the Negro (for the Republican National Committee)," 1 July 1939, Schomberg Center for Research in Black Culture, cited in Weiss, *Farewell to the Party of Lincoln*, 269.

20. Ibid.

21. Ibid.

22. Ibid.

23. *A Program for a Dynamic America: A Statement of Republican Principles*, report of Republican Program Committee submitted to Republican National Committee, 16 February 1940, 91–92, cited in Weiss, *Farewell to the Party of Lincoln*, 270. This passage is also quoted in a letter from Francis Rivers to Walter White (21 February 1940, NAACP, pt. 18, ser. C, reel 129, frames 27–29).

24. Ibid.

25. White to Bunche, 27 February 1940, ibid., frame 32.

26. Bunche to White, 28 February 1940, ibid., frame 34. Bunche reminded White that he had been employed as a nonpartisan expert by the Republican Party. White later told Bunche that he had described him as a Republican in jest, but he apologized nevertheless. For more on Bunche's political outlook, including his involvement in the National Negro Congress and his attitude toward the NAACP, see Kirby, "Ralph J. Bunche," 129–41.

27. Ibid.

28. For comment on the report, see Johnson, *Republican Party and Wendell Willkie*, 42; and Plesur, "Republican Congressional Comeback," 534.

29. *NYT*, 20 February 1940, cited in Johnson, *Republican Party and Wendell Willkie*, 42.

30. *Nation*, 9 March 1940, 325, cited in Johnson, 43.

31. Ibid.

32. Plesur, "Republican Congressional Comeback," 542.

33. Weed, *Nemesis of Reform*, 200.

34. Plesur, "Republican Congressional Comeback," 543.

35. Ibid., 544.

36. For a detailed appraisal of the 1938 election from a Republican point of view, see: "Summary of Salient Facts of the 1938 Election," Papers of the Republican Party (henceforth PRP), Part II, Reports and Memoranda of the Research Division of the Headquarters of the Republican National Committee, 1938–1980, reel 1, 0002–10. The conclusion drawn here was that states with 221 electoral votes could be considered "safely Republican," while New York, Illinois, Montana, and Idaho, with a total of 84 electoral votes, were too close to call. The Republicans were, therefore, looking forward to the election of 1940 with some optimism (ibid., frame 0006).

37. Weed, *Nemesis of Reform*, 192. Dewey's opponent Democrat Herbert Lehman only won in New York with the votes of the American Labor Party (Plesur, "Republican

Congressional Comeback," 546). Some Republican victories were due to the taking of a more liberal stance, but in others it was entirely down to local factors.

38. *Crisis* 45 (December 1938): 393.

39. Joyner, *Republican Dilemma*, 51.

40. There were exceptions; Roy Wilkins was exasperated to discover that there were those middle- and upper-class African Americans who felt that the third term would bring dictatorship and that the New Deal was too wasteful.

41. See, for example, the speech by Walter White to the NAACP Annual Conference, Philadelphia, 23 June 1940, ER, reel 19, frame 0654.

42. Remarks of radical labor leader Harry Bridges after Willkie had successfully prevented the deportation of William Schneiderman, a Communist, in 1943 (S. Neal, *Dark Horse*, 270).

43. See figures prepared by the NAACP (NAACP, pt. 18, ser. C, reel 23, frame 0071).

44. *Crisis* 47 (May 1940): 145.

45. Ibid.

46. For more information on the Taft candidacy, see *New York Herald Tribune*, 19 May 1940, FDRP-PSF, pt. 4, reel 20, frame 0274. Perry Howard backed Taft, and Taft would, like Hoover, become associated with the rotten boroughs of the South in his bids for the presidency (*Plaindealer*, 23 February 1940).

47. For a brief account of the convention, see Mayer, *Republican Party*, 456–57. Willkie had been identified by Arthur Krock of the *New York Times* as early as August 1939 as "the darkest horse" for the 1940 Republican nomination (Barnes, *Willkie*, 149).

48. Schlesinger et al., *Presidential Elections*, 7, 2925. For some reason, Willkie's campaign attracted comparisons with the vice industry. So chaotic and disorganized was the Willkie campaign that another contemporary commentator described his campaign train as resembling "a whore house on a Saturday night when the madam is out" (Moos, *Republicans*, 415; also cited in Reinhard, *Republican Right*, 7).

49. Landon to Willkie, 9 July 1940, Willkie MSS, Correspondence [Courtesy, Lilly Library, Indiana University, Bloomington, Indiana]. After his defeat, Willkie thanked Landon: "you were great during the whole campaign. You did everything you could for me and I am indebted to you" (Willkie to Landon, 20 November 1940, ibid.).

50. Barnes, *Willkie*, 149.

51. Ibid., 37–38. The resolution to condemn the Klan had, as noted, failed by the smallest margin in convention history. The Democrat split in 1924 ensured a Republican victory in the subsequent election.

52. Barnard, *Wendell Willkie*, interview with Robert T. Willkie, 66.

53. Wendell Willkie, "Fair Trial," *New Republic* 102, no. 12 (18 March 1940): 371. The *New Republic* later claimed that the Brooklyn KKK was supporting Willkie (ibid., 103, no. 16 [14 October 1940]).

54. Comments to the *New York Herald and Tribune* forum in October 1938, cited in Barnes, *Willkie*, 155.

55. Barnes, *Willkie*, 180. In fact, 1,086 out of 12,658 (about 9 percent) of Willkie's southern employees were African American according to a Republican pamphlet.

Francis Rivers, *An Appeal to the Common Sense of Colored Citizens*, distributed by the Republican National Committee (henceforth *Common Sense*), 26, NAACP, pt. 18, ser. C, reel 29, frame 90.

56. Moon, *Balance of Power*, 32. Willkie also told African Americans at the convention: "I am deeply appreciative of your support, but my views on civil liberties and citizenship would not be changed even if you voted against me. You will know this if you ever study my record" (*Plaindealer*, 5 July 1940).

57. Johnson and Porter, *National Party Platform*, 393. Russell Davenport, an early champion of Willkie's candidacy, was at least partly responsible for the writing of the "Negro" plank.

58. Ibid., 387.

59. *Crisis* 47 (September 1940): 279.

60. Ibid.

61. Ibid.

62. *Plaindealer*, 23 August 1940.

63. "'Wendell Willkie Speaks to Negroes,' Address at Rally of Colored Republicans, Chicago, Illinois, September 13, 1940, distributed by the Republican National Committee," 3, Willkie MSS, Speeches, 1940; also cited in *Common Sense*, 27, NAACP, pt. 18, ser. C, reel 29, frame 93.

64. Ibid., 4; also cited in *Common Sense*, 27, NAACP, pt. 18, ser. C, reel 29, frame 93. Mary Earhart Dillon claims that there were eight thousand African Americans inside the American Giants' baseball park, and they greeted this speech with little enthusiasm (*Wendell L. Willkie*, 202). Johnson suggests that there were fifteen thousand at the rally (*Republican Party and Wendell Willkie*, 135). This was one of ten speeches Willkie made in Chicago that day.

65. *Crisis* 47 (October 1940): 311. The *Crisis* reprinted the speech as released by the Republican National Committee (ibid, 321).

66. Ibid., 311.

67. Ibid. Willkie is also reported to have been fond of saying, "you can't do this to me—I'm a white man," when under pressure (Johnson, *Republican Party and Wendell Willkie*, 148).

68. Sitkoff, "Willkie as Liberal," in Madison, *Hoosier Internationalist*, 74–75.

69. James Rowe Jr., "Memorandum for the President: Negroes," 22 October 1940, FDRP-PSF, pt. 3, reel 5, frames 0269–70. Rowe would later write the famous "Politics of 1948" memorandum for Harry Truman, urging him, among other things, to seek actively the African American vote.

70. Robert R. Moton of the Tuskegee Institute, where Davis was professor of military science and tactics, had written to Roosevelt in September 1936, urging the promotion of Colonel Davis and arguing that "such action, I am sure would please the colored people" without costing the War Department too much money as Davis was keen to retire (Moton to Roosevelt, 16 September 1936, FDRP-PSF, pt. 4, reel 45, frame 0679). For further comment on the Davis promotion, see *Opportunity* 18 (November 1940): 323. For additional information on military desegregation as an election issue in 1940, see Dalfiume, "Military Desegregation."

71. James Rowe Jr., "Memorandum for the President: Negro Problem," 23 October 1940, FDRP-PSF, pt. 3, reel 31, frames 0846–48; underlining in original. Rowe listed eight things that the president should do to placate African Americans. For the announcement of Colonel Davis's promotion, see *Plaindealer*, 1 November 1940.

72. Rowe, Memorandum, 23 October 1940, FDRP-PSF, pt. 3, reel 31, frames 0846–48. Stimson was a Republican who had been appointed, along with Frank Knox, to Roosevelt's cabinet immediately prior to the Republican convention in 1940.

73. Ibid.

74. White was asked to meet Willkie in October 1940; he sought the advice of senior members of the association, but no record of their deliberations is available (memorandum from White to Roy Wilkins, Thurgood Marshall, E. Frederic Morrow, George Murphy, and William Pickens, NAACP, pt. 18, ser. C, reel 15, frame 0691). For the view that the meeting could be seen as an endorsement, see Janken, *Biography of Walter White*, 267. See also the letter that White wrote to Willkie in mid-1941 suggesting that the two get to know each other better (White to Willkie, 14 July 1941, Willkie MSS, NAACP correspondence, 1940–42). In 1944, the two were approached by the Viking Press about collaborating on a book about civil rights. Willkie was keen to do the book but could not see where he would find the time. See Robert Ballou, Viking Press, to Walter White, 15 August 1944, ibid.; Willkie to White, 23 August 1944, ibid. For more detail on the Willkie-White friendship, see White, *A Man Called White*, 198–205.

75. William Pickens to Willkie, 8 August 1942, Willkie MSS, Correspondence: Pickens, William.

76. Barnes, *Willkie*, 191.

77. Similar charges were, of course, made against Landon in 1936. Some Democratic strategists believed that this slur against Willkie cost them a number of midwestern states. Roosevelt was informed that the "asinine negative attack on Willkie's German ancestry . . . will probably result in defeat in Iowa and Minnesota, and may wipe out all Democratic representation in those two states" ("Fire Alarm," 11 July 1940, cited in FDRP-PSF, pt. 4, reel 9, frame 0557). Lowell Mellett, an administrative assistant, reported to Roosevelt that he had seen two "painstaking statistical studies" of the 1940 election one of which "prove[d] that the German vote gave Willkie his large block of middle western states" (memorandum from Mellett to Roosevelt, ibid., frame 0508).

78. *Plaindealer*, 13 September 1940.

79. Ibid. Bishop R. R. Wright of the African Methodist Episcopal Church and member of the Democratic National Committee followed a similar line of attack (ibid., 25 October 1940).

80. Ibid., 30 August 1940. Redmond was the son of S. D. Redmond, a prominent Mississippi Republican.

81. Ibid., 2 February 1940.

82. Ibid.

83. Ibid., 8 March 1940.

84. White to Rivers, 22 October 1940, NAACP, pt. 18, ser. C, reel 29, frame 60.

85. *Common Sense*, 4, NAACP, pt. 18, ser. C, reel 29, frame 68.

86. Ibid., 6, frame 70.

87. Ibid.

88. Ibid., 9, frame 73. Sitkoff and Weiss both put the figure at about two-thirds (Sitkoff, *New Deal for Blacks*, 55; Weiss, *Farewell to the Party of Lincoln*, 166).

89. *Common Sense*, 7, NAACP, pt. 18, ser. C, reel 29, frame 71. For more detail on discrimination against African Americans by the AAA, see ibid.; Sitkoff, *New Deal for Blacks*, 54–56; and Weiss, *Farewell to the Party of Lincoln*, 55–56.

90. *Common Sense*, 10, frame 74. African Americans received about 31 percent of the PWA's payroll in 1936. Of these, about 16 percent were skilled and 64 percent unskilled (Sitkoff, *New Deal for Blacks*, 68). For an appraisal of the PWA and African Americans, see Wolters, *Negroes and the Great Depression*, 196–203. The main benefits of the PWA for African Americans came with the construction of new homes and schools. Harold Ickes, the head of the PWA, endeavored, with mixed results, to improve conditions and wages for African Americans (Wolters, *Negroes and the Great Depression*, 196–203). See also Weiss, *Farewell to the Party of Lincoln*, 51–53.

91. *Common Sense*, 11, NAACP, pt. 18, ser. C, reel 29, frame 75.

92. Ibid. In 1937, using federal government statistics, the National Urban League estimated that the number of African Americans on relief had risen from 2,118,000 (18 percent) in 1933 to 3,030,000 (39.5 percent) in 1937. This is, of course, a good deal higher than Rivers's estimate but could suggest that the number of African Americans on relief peaked in 1937 and was dropping by 1940. It does, however, give some credence to Rivers's findings ("The Negro Working Population and National Recovery," National Urban League memorandum, cited in Parris and Brooks, *Blacks in the City*, 23). John P. Davis, writing in the *Crisis*, confirmed that in October 1933, 2,117,000 (17.8 percent) African Americans were on relief. By January 1935, two years into the New Deal, 3.5 million (29 percent) were on relief, and this was largely due to discrimination both in the North and the South (44 [May 1935]: 141–42, 154–55). The 1940 figure quoted by Rivers represented a substantial drop from 1935. Weiss provides figures suggesting a major fall in African American unemployment between 1931 and 1940 in New York, Philadelphia, Chicago, and Detroit (*Farewell to the Party of Lincoln*, 300).

93. *Common Sense*, 13–16, NAACP, pt. 18, ser. C, reel 29, frames 77–80.

94. Ibid., 16, frame 80.

95. Ibid., 20, frame 84.

96. Ibid., 32, frame 96. Republican attacks of this nature on the New Deal could be dismissed as predictable diatribes, but it is important to note that there were those on the left who had come to similar conclusions. See, for example, *Crisis* 42 (May 1935): 141–42, 154–55. Ralph Bunche was also critical of the New Deal.

97. *Plaindealer*, 1 November 1940.

98. Ibid.

99. Ibid.

100. The *Plaindealer* suggested that Roosevelt's victory could be attributed to the African American vote in crucial states (15 November 1940).

101. In December 1942, Willkie warned the National Conference of Christians and Jews about intolerance but pledged "to fight to the fullest extent against such intolerance. In the courtroom and from the public rostrum, I will fight for the preservation

of civil liberties, no matter how unpopular the cause may be in any given instance" (Barnes, *Willkie*, 228). Shortly before America entered the war, he was persuaded to represent William Schneiderman, a Communist who was facing deportation. He took the case at his own expense and, in spite of the potential political risk, felt that there was more at stake than the future of one man: "I am sure I am right in representing Schneiderman, of all the times when civil liberties should be defended it is now" (ibid., 322). The case was decided by the Supreme Court in Schneiderman's favor in June 1943.

102. Barnard, *Wendell Willkie*, 337.

103. Ibid., 339–40.

104. Confidential NAACP memorandum, 18 April 1942, Willkie MSS, NAACP file, 1940–42.

105. Text of the address of Wendell Willkie to the NAACP annual conference in Los Angeles, 19 July 1942, released 20 July 1942, Willkie MSS, Speeches, 1942. (Extracts from this speech are also to be found in: Willkie, *One World*, 138; Barnes, *Willkie*, 327; and S. Neal, *Dark Horse*, 273.)

106. Text of the address of Wendell Willkie to the NAACP annual conference in Los Angeles, 19 July 1942, released 20 July 1942, Willkie MSS, Speeches, 1942.

107. White to Willkie, 28 July 1942, Willkie MSS, NAACP 1942, July–December. Willkie noted that his audience in Los Angeles was "one of the warmest I ever had the pleasure of speaking before" (Willkie to White, 30 July 1942, ibid). White's letter is also cited in Barnard, *Wendell Willkie*, 341.

108. Willkie to White, 9 April 1942, Willkie MSS, NAACP correspondence, 1940–42.

109. A. Philip Randolph approached Willkie to speak at an MOWM mass meeting in 1942. Willkie was unable to attend but would have liked to (Randolph to Willkie, 4 April 1942, and Willkie to Randolph, 8 May 1942). See also MOWM pamphlet *The Story of Jim Crow in Uniform*; and Willkie to Randolph, 22 October 1943. Willkie accepted Randolph's invitation to serve as honorary chairman of the National Council for a permanent FEPC (Randolph to Willkie, 28 September 1943; Willkie to Randolph, 22 October 1943, Willkie MSS, Correspondence, Randolph, A. Philip).

110. Statement by Willkie at a meeting of the Newspaper Guild of New York, 19 November 1942, Willkie MSS, Speeches, 1942.

111. Willkie to Katherine Shryver of the National Committee to Abolish the Poll Tax, 8 December 1943, Willkie MSS, General.

112. Willkie to White, 25 November 1941, Willkie MSS, NAACP file, 1940–June 1942. For correspondence between White and Willkie on this issue, see White to Willkie, 25 November 1941, ibid.; White to Willkie, 30 December 1941, 21 January 1942; "Film Executives Pledge to Give Negroes Better Movie Roles," NAACP press release, 21 August 1942, ibid. For more details on this matter, see White, *A Man Called White*, 198–205; and Barnes, *Willkie*, 328. Willkie and White traveled to Hollywood several times, and they did receive some vague promises, but White later wrote, "a few of the pledges were kept, but Willkie's tragic death damped and almost extinguished the reforms he stimulated" (S. Neal, *Dark Horse*, 276). The stereotyping thus continued. For more on White's efforts in Hollywood, see Janken, *Biography of Walter White*, 267–73.

113. For a monograph-length study of the Detroit riot, see Capeci and Wilkerson, *Layered Violence*. For contemporary comment, see *Crisis* 49 (July 1943): 199, 200. For a brief account of the riot, see Wynn, *The Afro-American and the Second World War*, 68–71.

114. *NYT*, 25 July 1943.

115. Ibid.; also cited in Barnard, *Wendell Willkie*, 408; and S. Neal, *Dark Horse*, 275.

116. *NYT*, 25 July 1943. For another sympathetic appraisal of the African American plight, see Arthur Krock, "The President and Mrs. Roosevelt Can Help," ibid., 3 August 1943. Krock was not always so understanding of the situation faced by African Americans. See also Turner Catledge, *New York Times Magazine*, 8 August 1943. For the NAACP's view of the riots, see the *Crisis* throughout 1943, in particular, "The Riots," editorial (July 1943): 199; Chester B. Himes, "Zoot Suit Riots Are Race Riots" (July 1943): 200–201, 222; Thurgood Marshall, "The Gestapo in Detroit" (August 1943): 232–33, 246; "Riot Report Blames Negroes" (September 1943): 280; and Louis E. Martin, "Detroit—Still Dynamite" (January 1944): 8–10.

117. Barnard, *Wendell Willkie*, 497.

118. This article was reprinted in the *New York Times*, 13 June 1944. This formed the basis of a draft platform that Willkie submitted to the Republican Platform Committee. Willkie's platform, which was ignored, was published in the *New York Times* in July 1944.

119. Barnard, *Wendell Willkie*, 497.

120. Draft of "Our Citizens of Negro Blood" article for *Collier's* 114 (7 October 1944), Willkie MSS, Speeches, 1944; also cited in Barnard, *Wendell Willkie*, 496.

121. Ibid.

122. Ibid.

123. *Newark Evening News*, 2 April 1943, Willkie MSS, NAACP file, 1943.

124. Walter White to George Gallup, 29 May 1944, cited in S. Neal, *Dark Horse*, 276.

125. *NYT*, 29 October 1943. Interestingly, respondents were not offered a choice of Democratic or Republican nominees; they were merely asked the question: "Do you favor Wendell Willkie as the Republican presidential candidate for 1944?" This poll, although not the question it asked, is also cited in Sitkoff, in Madison, *Hoosier Internationalist*, 83.

126. *CD*, 14 October 1944, and the *Pittsburgh Courier*, October 14, 1944, cited in Madison, *Hoosier Internationalist*, 86. The NAACP named its new headquarters building in New York in memory of Willkie. For further information, see *Willkie Memorial Building Fund* pamphlet, ER, reel 20, frames 0011–18.

127. Elmo Roper to Russell Davenport, 26 July 1943, cited in S. Neal, *Dark Horse*, 276

128. *One World* would go on to be one of the best-selling books during the war.

129. Viorst, *Fall from Grace*, 176. Conrad Joyner agrees: "the Republicans accepted Willkie because they did not know him and as they got to know him they dropped him" (*Republican Dilemma*, 68).

130. Willkie's biographers, including Joseph Barnes, Warren Moscow (both journal-

ists who knew Willkie well), Ellsworth Barnard, Donald Bruce Johnson, and Steve Neal, are, by and large, extremely positive about his impact on American politics. The most recent major work is Neal's *Dark Horse*, an exhaustive and, in many ways, praiseworthy study that does not analyze the impact of Willkie sufficiently. The main exception to this is Mary Earhart Dillon's *Wendell L. Willkie*. With the possible exception of Dillon, all agree that Willkie was a genuine advocate of civil rights. Some of the more general literature on the Republican Party is less kind. Conrad Joyner, for example, describes Willkie as "politically inept" (*Republican Dilemma*, 68), while Viorst sees Willkie as an unwelcome interloper within the GOP. George Mayer, while recognizing his talents and appeal, faults Willkie's inexperience and unwillingness to accept the advice of GOP regulars in 1940.

131. There were even rumors about Willkie becoming Roosevelt's vice president in 1944. This has been attributed to Roosevelt biographer James MacGregor Burns, who in 1955 recalled Roosevelt wanting to join forces with Willkie in a "really liberal party" (*New York Times Magazine*, 2 January 1955, 42, cited in Kirk and McLellan, *Political Principles of Robert A. Taft*, 51).

Chapter 4. The Totally Political Man

1. Darilek, *Loyal Opposition*, 18.

2. Taft to Richard Scandrett, 26 January, 1942, cited in Polenberg, *War and Society*, 185.

3. Polenberg, *War and Society*, 186.

4. Darilek, *Loyal Opposition*, 42.

5. Ibid., 44.

6. Ibid., 44–45.

7. Ibid., 52.

8. Ibid., 53.

9. Ibid.

10. Ibid.

11. White to Martin, 24 September 1942, and Martin to White, 30 September 1942, NAACP, pt. 18, ser. C, reel 29, frames 0110, 0107. White did, however, praise the party's commitment to victory without a negotiated peace.

12. White to Ira Lewis, editor of the *Pittsburgh Courier*, 30 October 1942, ibid., frame 0119.

13. Ibid. The other editors were: P. B. Young (*Norfolk Journal and Guide*), McNeal and Lechard (*Chicago Defender*), Carl Murphy (*Baltimore Afro-American*), and A. C. Powell (*New York People's Voice*). See letters from White to the above, ibid., frames 0126–30.

14. *Norfolk Journal and Guide*, 7 November 1942, ibid., frame 0136.

15. Darilek, *Loyal Opposition*, 55. For the Republican assessment of the election see PRP, Part II, Reports and Memoranda of the Research Division of the Headquarters of the Republican National Committee, 1938–1980, "The 1942 Election" (henceforth "The 1942 Election"), reel 1, frames 0269–0300. This dealt with regions rather than particular groups of voters; therefore, there is no mention of African Americans.

16. Darilek, *Loyal Opposition*, 53. The GOP's own analysis confirms that core Democratic voters, such as the young and the working class, stayed at home, while many migrant war workers were not registered, and soldiers did not use their absentee ballots, all leading to the low turnout (PRP, Research Division, "The 1942 Election," reel 1, frames 0269–0300).

17. PRP, Research Division, "The 1942 Election," reel 1, frames 0269–0300.

18. Undated, cited in Blum, *V was for Victory*, 232.

19. Earl Brown, "Negro Vote," *Harper's* 189 (July 1944): 152, cited in Butler, "The Political Significance of Negro Migration from the South, 1940–1962," in Vander, *The Political and Economic Progress of the American Negro, 1943–1963*, 9. Brown stated that a majority of African Americans in New Jersey, Ohio, Illinois, Indiana, Missouri, West Virginia, New York, and Kentucky had registered as Republicans. Timothy Thurber has also suggested that a majority of African Americans had voted for the GOP in 1942 ("Seeds of the Southern Strategy," 5).

20. Darilek, *Loyal Opposition*, 54. The Republicans concurred, arguing that if they could maintain their fortunes, they would win the presidency and both houses of Congress in 1944 (PRP, Research Division, "The 1942 Election," reel 1, frames 0269–0300). The Democrats felt that the results may have been different if the Allied invasion of North Africa had taken place the week before the election rather than the week after.

21. PRP, Research Division, "The 1942 Election," reel 1, frames 0269–0300.

22. Darilek, *Loyal Opposition*, 63.

23. Ibid., 91.

24. Ibid., 94.

25. For more detail on Vandenberg's role, see Meijer, "Hunting for the Middle Ground." For further comment, including criticism of the Mackinac Charter, see Stephen Tompkins, *Vandenberg*, 210–13. Tompkins sees Mackinac as helping to facilitate eventual Republican support for the United Nations (213). Vandenberg was widely praised by Republicans for his handling of the Mackinac meeting (Darilek, *Loyal Opposition*, 117).

26. Darilek, *Loyal Opposition*, 99–100.

27. Willkie's support suggests that Mackinac was acceptable to the internationalists within the party, but Mayer believes it was "primarily designed to outflank Willkie and to placate public opinion" (*Republican Party*, 462). Nevertheless, Willkie remained the major threat to party unity as the election of 1944 approached. A journalist attending the Mackinac meeting paid a bellboy to page Willkie, apparently causing Old Guard Republicans to "rush into huddles of fear" (Democratic report of Dewey's political plans, 7 September 1943, FDRP-PSF, pt. 4, reel 9, frame 0913).

28. Dalfiume, "Forgotten Years," 95.

29. The demand for labor in 1940 and 1941 had little impact upon African American unemployment; however, from 1941 to 1944 the number of African Americans employed by the federal government tripled (Blum, *V Was for Victory*, 183–84).

30. For more detail on the March on Washington Movement, see Wynn, *Second World War*, 43–48. Wynn suggests that the priority of the movement was to ensure

employment for African Americans in the war industries rather than desegregation of the military.

31. Blum, *V Was for Victory*, 208. Interestingly, Randolph viewed the *Courier* as the despicable "spokesman for the petty black bourgeoisie" (ibid.).

32. *Crisis* 49 (January 1942): 7; resolutions of the 1942 NAACP annual conference, 18 July 1942, NAACP, *Annual Report*, 1942, cited in Berg, *Ticket to Freedom*, 101.

33. Dalfiume, "Forgotten Years," 99–100. The Detroit, Michigan, branch, for instance, was aiming to have twenty thousand members by the end of 1943 (*Crisis* 50 [May 1943]: 140). Figures for NAACP membership in 1946 from NAACP press release, 15 November 1946, NAACP, pt. 18, ser. C, reel 29, frames 0201–02.

34. For more detail on the FEPC's effectiveness, or lack of it, see Wynn, *Second World War*, 48–55. One bright point was the integration of San Francisco's shipyards.

35. Polenberg, *War and Society*, 105. Dalfiume suggests that African American protest was actually circumscribed by the war ("Forgotten Years," 55). This view is supported by Sitkoff, "Coming of Age of Civil Rights"; and Finkle, "Black Protest." In "World War II in the Lives of Black Americans," Modell, Goulden, and Magnusson examine the impact of the war on individual African American veterans. J. Edgar Hoover launched an investigation of "foreign-inspired agitation among American Negroes," which, although undertaken because of African Americans' perceived "aggressiveness and militancy," found them to be "fundamentally loyal" in August 1943 (Berg, *Ticket to Freedom*, 103). For a brief discussion of African Americans during the war, see Lawson, *Running for Freedom*, 1–29.

36. "A Declaration by Negro Voters," *Crisis* 51 (January 1944): 16–17. (The Declaration can also be found in Broderick and Meier, *Negro Protest Thought*, 238–43.)

37. Ibid.

38. Ibid.

39. Spangler to White, 6 December 1943, NAACP, pt. 18, ser. C, reel 29, frame 0161.

40. White to Spangler, 11 December 1943, ibid., 0162–64.

41. Special meeting of the NAACP Board of Directors, 31 July 1944, NAACP, pt. 18, ser. C, reel 15, frame 0805.

42. "Declaration by Negro Republican Workers in Chicago," February 11–12, 1944, NAACP, pt. 18, ser. C, reel 15, frames 0736–38. See also *Plaindealer*, 18 February 1944.

43. Ibid.

44. Ibid.

45. Joseph V. Baker, *Philadelphia Inquirer*, 7 May 1944, Thomas E. Dewey Papers (henceforth TED), ser. 4, box 11, file 8.

46. Ibid. According to the 18 February 1944 *Plaindealer*, the Chicago convention was wracked by disputes and was often bad-tempered. Eastern African American Republicans later met in Philadelphia to urge the Republican National Convention in June to take action to end the discriminatory practices "which have developed under the New Deal." Seventy-five delegates from New York, New Jersey, Connecticut, Massachusetts, Pennsylvania, Maryland, Delaware, and the District of Columbia attended. This seems to have been an exercise in endorsing Republican policy and an excuse to condemn the

New Deal, rather than any attempt to address African American problems seriously (*Plaindealer*, 19 May 1944).

47. Ibid., 25 February 1944.

48. *Crisis* 51 (March 1944).

49. Ibid.

50. *Plaindealer*, 10 March 1944.

51. Although given the clashes between African Americans from the two parties and between White and various African American Republicans, genuine cooperation was a distant prospect. A good indication that African Americans from all shades of the political spectrum shared certain core goals is to be found in Logan's *What the Negro Wants* (1944), which featured contributions from many of the leading African American figures of the day, including Bethune, Du Bois, Randolph, Wilkins, Langston Hughes, and Gordon B. Hancock.

52. According to Wynn, only 2,208 African Americans refused induction into the military between 1941 and 1946 (*Second World War*, 103). The jazz musician Dizzy Gillespie told his draft board that, having never seen a German, he would not know who to shoot. Elijah Muhammad, the leader of the Nation of Islam and later Malcolm X's mentor, was imprisoned for three years during the war. See also Plummer, *Rising Wind*, 74–75. Bayard Rustin and Paul Robeson also refused to serve, with the former going to prison as a result.

53. Moos, *The Republicans*, 425; Sterling Morton to Alfred Landon, 3 January 1947, Reinhard, *Republican Right*, 40; James A. and Nancy F. Wechsler, "The Road Ahead for Civil Rights—The President's Report: One Year Later," *Commentary*, October 1948, 297–304, NAACP, pt. 18, ser. C, reel 26, frames 0303–10.

54. *PM*, 5 October 1944, NAACP, pt. 18, ser. C, reel 21, frame 0194.

55. Dewey to Landon, 6 June 1944, cited in Beyer, *Thomas E. Dewey*, 73; also cited in Polenberg, *War and Society*, 210.

56. "Statement made by Thomas Dewey for the *Pittsburgh Courier*," 12 February 1942, TED, ser. 12, box 2, file 42.

57. Republican manifesto for the 1942 New York gubernatorial election, 29 August 1942, cited in NAACP Papers, pt. 18, ser. B, reel 11, frame 0296.

58. Thomas Dewey, campaign speeches dated 19 October 1942 and 26 October 1942, cited in ibid., frame 0291–92.

59. Thomas Dewey, interview with Carl Lawrence, *Amsterdam Star-News*, 29 August 1942, ibid., frame 0296–97. This was not the most rigorous of interrogations.

60. "Interview with Mr. Dewey for *Amsterdam Star-News*," 26 October 1942, TED, ser. 9, box 10, file 11.

61. Ibid. This again echoed the statements of Willkie.

62. Ibid.

63. "Address by Thomas E. Dewey at Union Baptist Church, New York City, October 19, 1942," ibid., ser. 9, box 10, file 2.

64. Ibid.

65. Ibid. Omitted from the final draft was the following passage: "it wasn't long ago that we read in the newspapers of a factory producing army trucks in Detroit that was

closed down because hundreds of white employees refused to work with a handful of colored workers."

66. This speech was made several months after Willkie's "Imperialisms at Home" speech to the NAACP convention.

67. "Address by Thomas E. Dewey, Republican candidate for governor, at a rally in public school 136, Edgecomb Avenue and 135th Street, Monday evening, Oct. 26, 1942," TED, ser. 9, box 10, file 11. (This speech is also available in NAACP, pt. 18, ser. B, reel 11, frames 0516–19.)

68. For details on Democratic splits in New York, see Darilek, *Loyal Opposition*, 52.

69. Julia Baxter of the NAACP analyzed Dewey's speeches during his first few months as governor. Reporting to White, she concluded: "I have examined them but have found no specific promises on Dewey's part to appoint outstanding Negroes to responsible jobs in the State government set up" (memorandum for Julia Baxter to Walter White, 4 May 1943, NAACP, pt. 18, ser. B, reel 11, frame 0293). This turned out to be something of a Dewey trait; writing in *Harper's* in 1944, Richard H. Rovere said of Dewey: "his speeches . . . say nothing in crisp rhythmical prose." He dodged issues or hedged and relied on polls when determining policy (18, no. 1128 [May 1944]: ibid., frame 0558–59). For Rivers's appointment, see *NYT*, 14 September 1943.

70. *NYT*, 14 September 1943.

71. *Amsterdam Star-News*, 25 September 1943, TED, ser. 7, box 62, file 43. For biographical detail on Rivers and further comment on his appointment, see the *New York Age*, 25 September 1943, ibid., ser. 7, box 62, file 43. See also *NYT*, 14 September 1943.

72. *Amsterdam Star-News*, 25 September 1943, TED, ser. 7, box 62, file 43.

73. Tobias to Dewey, 4 November 1943, TED, ser. 4, box 185, file 18.

74. *NYT*, 19 March 1944. Beyer believes that the findings of the first committee were "conflicting and overly partisan" (*Dewey, 1937–1947*, 158).

75. *New York Post*, 26 March 1944, cited in NAACP, pt. 18, ser. B, reel 11, frame 0339. See also *Plaindealer*, 7 April 1944.

76. Sender Garlin, "Is Dewey the Man?" original source unknown, TED, ser. 2, box 15, file 4.

77. *NYT*, 13 April 1944.

78. "Interview with Mr. Dewey for *Amsterdam Star-News*," 26 October 1942, TED, ser. 9, box 10, file 11.

79. NAACP press release, 23 March 1944, NAACP, pt. 18, ser. B, reel 11, frame 0338; also quoted in *Plaindealer*, 31 March 1944. Dewey was also attacked by the National Negro Congress (*Plaindealer*, 7 April 1944). Wilkins, writing to Joseph Gavagan, who was now on the New York State Supreme Court, dismissed the new commission as a "meaningless gesture" (Wilkins to Gavagan, 21 March 1944, NAACP, pt. 18, ser. B, reel 11, frame 0333). Wilkins was acting secretary of the association at this time as Walter White was touring American military bases around the world.

80. Garlin, "Is Dewey the Man?" TED, ser. 2, box 5, file 4.

81. Telegram from Church to Dewey, 15 March 1944, NAACP, pt. 18, ser. B, reel 11, file 0329.

82. *NYT*, 18 March 1944; telegram from Church to Dewey, 15 March 1944, NAACP, pt. 18, ser. B, reel 11, frame 0329.

83. Copy of speech drafted by Rivers during the 1938 campaign; Rivers to Hickman, 22 September 1942, TED, ser. 9, box 10, file 11. For other comment on Dewey's attitude to the bill, see Paul Lockwood to Roy Wilkins, 17 April 1944, NAACP, pt. 18, ser. B, file 11, frames 0343–44. For Wilkins's reply, see Wilkins to Lockwood, 18 April 1944, ibid., frames 0341–42.

84. *Plaindealer*, 12 May 1944. Tobias originally made this allegation in *Congress View*, the monthly magazine of the National Negro Congress, which had also criticized Dewey.

85. *Plaindealer*, 12 May 1944. Other elements in the press shared this suspicion; see, for example, "Two Strikes on Dewey," *Crisis* 51 (April 1944): 104. The National Non-Partisan League, a pro-Roosevelt African American organization, later echoed Tobias's allegation, stating that on the day Dewey killed the New York State FEPC, his lieutenant was in North Carolina assuring party leaders in the state that the governor was not a "Negro lover" (*Plaindealer*, 27 October 1944). The *New York Post* also suggested that the blocking of the law was linked to North Carolina lily-whites who wanted to draft Dewey for president (*New York Post*, 31 March 1944, NAACP, pt. 18, ser. B, reel 11, frame 0530).

86. *Plaindealer*, 12 May 1944. See also *New York Post*, 26 March 1944, NAACP, pt. 18, ser. B, reel 11, frame 0339.

87. National Citizens Political Action Committee (PAC), press release, 21 August 1944, NAACP, pt. 18, ser. C, reel 21, frames 0207–09.

88. *New York Post*, 31 March 1944, ibid., pt. 18, ser. B, reel 11, frame 0530.

89. *Philadelphia Inquirer*, 7 May 1944, TED, ser. 4, box 11, file 8.

90. Walter White to Thomas Dewey, 8 June 1944, NAACP, pt. 18, ser. B, reel 11, frames 0371–72. For those appointed to the new committee, see *NYT*, 1 June 1944. See also NAACP press release, 6 August 1944, NAACP, pt. 18, ser. B, reel 11, frame 0539. Frank L. Weil of the United Services Organization (USO), for example, had helped to prevent the publication of a pamphlet entitled *The Races of Mankind*, which attacked myths of racial superiority (White to Dewey, 9 June 1944, NAACP, pt. 18, ser. B, reel 11, frame 0371).

91. *Crisis* 51 (April 1944): 104.

92. *Plaindealer*, 3 March 1944.

93. Ibid., 18 February 1944. See also Wilkins to Dewey, 10 February 1944, NAACP, pt. 18, ser. B, reel 11, file 0327; and the NAACP press release regarding the soldier vote bill, 10 February 1944, ibid., frame 0523. Eastland felt that the passage of his bill would prevent any further moves for an anti–poll tax bill (Sullivan, *Days of Hope*, 131).

94. Figures for the number of soldiers voting from PRP, Part II, Reports and Memoranda of the Research Division of the Headquarters of the Republican National Committee, 1938–1980, "The Presidential Election—1944," March 1945 reel 1, frames 0339–42; and ibid., April 1945, frames 0471–0500. Over half of these votes were cast in California, Pennsylvania, Illinois, New Jersey, New York, and Ohio (ibid.).

95. The poll tax states were Mississippi, Virginia, Georgia, Alabama, South Carolina, Texas, Arkansas, and Tennessee. Louisiana, North Carolina, and Florida had abolished the poll tax during the 1930s and, as a result, saw dramatic increases in voting (Sullivan, *Days of Hope*, 106–8). The *Crisis* reported that in the presidential election of 1940 just over 5 percent of the population of South Carolina voted; in Mississippi, the figure was 8 percent; and only around 10 percent voted in Georgia, Arkansas, and Alabama. Less than 20 percent voted in Virginia (12.9 percent), Louisiana (15.7 percent), Texas (16.2 percent), and Tennessee (17.9 percent), about a quarter voted in North Carolina (23.3 percent) and Florida (25.7 percent), and a third in Kentucky ("Democracy[?] at the Ballot Box," *Crisis* 48 [January 1941]: 7). The poll tax was, therefore, "the single most important reason" for low voter turnout in the South (Berg, *Ticket to Freedom*, 104).

96. Sullivan, *Days of Hope*, 114. According to Berg, the NAACP's leadership was wary of the NCAPT due to the presence of prominent leftists, including New York congressman Marcantonio (*Ticket to Freedom*, 108–9).

97. Sullivan, *Days of Hope*, 116.

98. For Bender's continued opposition to the poll tax, see *Congressional Record* 93 (1947): 80–81, appendix A4080–1; Extension of Remarks of Hon. George H. Bender, 26 July 1947. Bender noted that in 1946, 47 percent of people in non poll tax states voted, compared to 9.58 percent in those that maintained the tax.

99. Berg, *Ticket to Freedom*, 104.

100. Sullivan, *Days of Hope*, 119.

101. Ibid., 121.

102. George H. Bender to Dewey, 4 June 1943, TED, ser. 4, box 207, file 22.

103. Ibid.

104. Telegram from White to Dewey, 9 May 1944, ibid.

105. Telegram from Dewey to White, 11 May 1944, ibid.

106. Telegram from White to Dewey, 11 May 1944, ibid. Rivers urged Dewey to support cloture but leave the constitutional merits of the bill to the Senate (telegram from Francis Rivers to James C. Hagerty, a Dewey aide, 12 May 1944, ibid.).

107. "R. R. Church, Republican Head, Urges Walter White to Seek Roosevelt Aid in Poll Tax Fight," unattributed press release, 13 May 1944, ibid., ser. 4, box 32, file 29.

108. Ibid. Randolph, echoing Church, noted that White's "friend" Roosevelt had no problem passing legislation if he wanted to and concluded that the NAACP leader was "hunting for excuses to condemn" the GOP (*Plaindealer*, 21 July 1944).

109. *Washington Post* editorial, 13 May 1944, TED, ser. 4, box 207, file 22.

110. *Crisis* 51 (June 1944): 185.

111. White to Dewey, 1 August 1944, TED, ser. 4, box 207, file 22.

112. *Plaindealer*, 21 July 1944.

113. *NYT*, 1 August 1946. The *Times* does not say which state contributed two votes.

114. Ibid., 6 February 1948.

115. Ibid., 29 July 1948.

116. Ibid.

117. Ibid., 30 July 1948.

118. Alben Barkley to Walter White, 12 August 1948, NAACP, pt. 18, ser. B, reel 9, frame 0208.

119. *Crisis* 51 (January 1944): 21.

120. "Weekly Survey of the Negro Press," 3 April to 9 April 1944, 1, TED, ser. 4, box 127, file 6.

121. *Baltimore Afro-American*, 8 April 1944, cited ibid. Similar sentiments were expressed in the *Pittsburgh Courier*, 8 April 1944; the *Washington Tribune*, undated; and the *New York People's Voice*, 8 April 1944, TED, ser. 4, box 127, file 6.

122. *NYT*, 13 June 1944. Willkie's platform was published in the *New York Times* on 11 July 1944.

123. *Plaindealer*, 16 June 1944.

124. Ibid.

125. Ibid.

126. Ibid.

127. *NYT*, 13 June 1944; also cited in Sitkoff, in Madison, *Hoosier Internationalist*; and S. Neal, *Dark Horse*, 274.

128. Johnson and Porter, *National Party Platforms*, 412.

129. This was all the more surprising as Taft was in charge of the platform committee and had a role in writing the civil rights plank.

130. *Plaindealer*, 23 June 1944.

131. Ibid., 7 July 1944.

132. Ibid., 30 June 1944.

133. Johnson and Porter, *National Party Platforms*, 404; Moon, *Balance of Power*, 33; *Plaindealer*, 28 July 1944; *Crisis* 51 (August 1944): 251.

134. *Crisis* 51 (August 1944): 249.

135. *New Republic*, 28 August 1944, 241–43, cited in Thurber, "Seeds of Southern Strategy," 7.

136. *Crisis* 51 (August 1944): 251.

137. Ibid., 250.

138. For more detail on these statements, see ibid., 251; *Plaindealer*, 23 June 1944; and NAACP press release, NAACP, pt. 18, ser. B, reel 10, frame 0696. A similar appeal appeared in the *Pittsburgh Courier* (1 July 1944, cited in Plummer, *Rising Wind*, 102).

139. *Plaindealer*, 18 August 1944.

140. *Look*, 5 September 1944, TED, ser. 2, box 15, file 4. The states in question were Connecticut, Massachusetts, New Hampshire, Pennsylvania, Illinois, Minnesota, Missouri, New Jersey, New York, Ohio, Wisconsin, and Wyoming.

141. *Plaindealer*, 20 October 1944.

142. Ibid., 22 September 1944.

143. Ibid., 28 July 1944.

144. Ibid., 29 September 1944.

145. Ibid.

146. S. D. Redmond to Herbert Brownell, 5 October 1944, TED, ser. 4, box 151, file 7.

147. Mayer, *Republican Party*, 464.

148. Address by Roosevelt to the Teamsters Union, Washington, D.C., 23 September 1944, Rosenman, *Public Papers*, 289. This was Roosevelt's famous "Fala speech," in which he attacked the Republicans for making "libelous statements about my dog." Republicans had suggested that Roosevelt had sent a destroyer to the Aleutian Islands to collect his dog. During the 1944 election, Beyer comments that "sarcasm and ridicule were his [Dewey's] principal weapons—wit, humor and downright warmth he sorely lacked" (Beyer, *Dewey, 1937–1947*, 231).

149. *Crisis* 51 (November 1944): 344. Hillman was also referred to as a "foreign-born" labor leader by the GOP (*Plaindealer*, 22 September 1944).

150. Democratic campaign pamphlet, 1944, *Win with FDR*, TED, ser. 2, box 15, file 3. The pamphlet also declared, "if you're screwy, vote for Dewey."

151. *PM*, 2 November 1944, NAACP, pt. 18, ser. C, reel 21, frame 0298.

152. Thomas Dewey, campaign speech, Philadelphia, September 7, 1944, in Schlesinger et al., *Presidential Elections*, 8: 3074.

153. Thomas Dewey, campaign speech, New York, November 4, 1944, ibid., 8: 3088.

154. *Plaindealer*, 13 October 1944.

155. Franklin Roosevelt, campaign speech in Boston, 4 November 1944, Schlesinger et al., *Presidential Elections*, 8: 3089–93.

156. In spite of this, the Republicans claimed the support of some of the biggest African American newspapers, including the *Baltimore Afro-American*, the *Amsterdam Star-News*, the *Pittsburgh Courier*, and the *Kansas City Call*. Yet Roosevelt carried each of the cities and the states in which these papers were based (*Plaindealer*, 10 November 1944). Roosevelt's backers included the *Chicago Defender*, the *Michigan Chronicle*, the *St. Louis Argus*, the *Norfolk Journal and Guide*, and the *New York People's Voice*. See also "*Courier* Calls on Negroes to Support Dewey," *New York Herald Tribune*, 29 September 1944, NAACP, pt. 18, ser. B, reel 11, frame 0583.

157. Stimson was also quoted as saying: "leadership is not embedded in the Negro race yet, and to try to make commissioned officers to lead men into battle—colored men—is only to work disaster to both" (*Crisis* 51 [April 1944]: 115; also cited in Wynn, *Second World War*, 31; and Winkler, *Home Front U.S.A*, 66).

158. *Plaindealer*, 13 October 1944.

159. Gordon B. Hancock, ANP, "Wendell Willkie: Moral Giant," ibid., 20 October 1944. As well as writing a syndicated column for the ANP, Hancock was the dean of Virginia Union University (an African American institution) and a clergyman. For a detailed appraisal of Hancock's long and distinguished career, see Gavins, *Perils and Prospects*.

160. *Plaindealer*, 3 November 1944.

161. Ibid.

162. "The 1944 Vote for President in the Ten Largest Cities," TED, ser. 2, box 15, file 5.

163. Darilek, *Loyal Opposition*, 173.

164. These states were Illinois, Michigan, Missouri, New York, New Jersey, Pennsylvania, West Virginia, Delaware, Maryland, and Kentucky. Michigan, along with Cali-

fornia, had seen the largest increase in African American population during the war (Wynn, *Second World War*, 62).

165. These states were Connecticut, Delaware, Idaho, Illinois, Kentucky, Maryland, Massachusetts, Nevada, New Hampshire, Michigan, New Jersey, New Mexico, Oklahoma, Oregon, and Pennsylvania (Republican National Committee press release, 11 November 1944, TED, ser. 2, box 38, file 15). See also "Dewey Needed Shift of Only 303,414 Votes," *New York Herald Tribune*, 12 November 1944, NAACP, pt. 18, ser. B, reel 11, frame 0622. For the Republican assessment of the election, see PRP, Part II, Reports and Memoranda of the Research Division of the Headquarters of the Republican National Committee, 1938–1980, "The Presidential Election-1944," March 1945, reel 1, frames 0339–0342; and ibid., April 1945, frames 0471–0500. This analysis suggests that a switch of 395,000 votes in Illinois, Massachusetts, Michigan, Missouri, New York, New Jersey, and Pennsylvania would have given the election to Dewey. However, "it is granted that statistical analysis of this kind can be readily turned in the other direction and show that a shift of a few votes in certain Republican States would have placed them in the Roosevelt-Truman column" (PRP, 0339–42).

166. RNC press release, 11 November 1944, TED, ser. 2, box 38, file 15.

167. Chairman's Report, Indianapolis, 22 January 1945, TED, ser. 2, box 38, file 15.

168. *Plaindealer*, 10 November 1944.

169. *Crisis* 51 (December 1944): 376.

170. *Plaindealer*, 24 November 1944.

171. Mayer, *Republican Party*, 465.

Chapter 5. Jockeying, Buck-Passing and Double-Talk

1. For a brief overview of Truman's prepresidential record on civil rights, see Berman, *Politics of Civil Rights*, 8–23.

2. Roosevelt endorsed a permanent FEPC on the day of his death (ibid., 7).

3. McCoy and Ruetten, *Quest and Response*, 21.

4. *NYT*, 20 April 1945, and 29 June 1945.

5. McCoy and Ruetten, *Quest and Response*, 22.

6. *NYT*, 4 July 1945.

7. Ibid., 8 July 1945.

8. McCoy and Ruetten, *Quest and Response*, 23.

9. *NYT*, 13 July 1945.

10. Ibid., 14 July 1945.

11. Ibid., 8 August 1945.

12. Ibid., 7 September 1945.

13. Ibid., 27 September 1945. The *Pittsburgh Courier* questioned Truman's commitment to the FEPC in his twenty-one-point plan of 1945 as he refused to use his power to prevent southerners from stalling the measure (*Pittsburgh Courier*, 22 September 1945, cited in Berman, *Politics of Civil Rights*, 28). A. Philip Randolph agreed with the *Courier's* analysis (ibid.).

14. *NYT*, 22 December 1945.

15. *Crisis* 53 (January 1946): 8. Berman argues that Truman had to sacrifice the FEPC

to appease the South and, therefore, protect his domestic program (*Politics of Civil Rights*, 31). During the strike by Capital Transit workers in Washington, D.C., in late 1945, Truman seized the company but refused to allow the FEPC, which had investigated Capital Transit for three years, to intervene to end its discriminatory practices. The *Crisis* asserted that this failure to act all but killed the FEPC. For further details on the Capital Transit case, see Berman, *Politics of Civil Rights*, 29–31.

16. Berman, *Politics of Civil Rights*, 34.

17. *Crisis* 53 (February 1946): 40, 72. The bill was defeated three days before Lincoln's birthday commemorations. At various Lincoln Day speeches, no senior Republican mentioned the FEPC debate.

18. Ibid.

19. *NYT*, 16 February 1946.

20. *Crisis* 53 (March 1946): 73.

21. Church to Brownell, 19 March 1945, TED, ser. 4, box 32, file 29. Church had attended every Republican national convention from 1912 to 1940. Charles Michelson had been the Democrats' publicity director in 1940.

22. Ibid.

23. Ibid.

24. Letter from Robert R. Church, president of United Minorities, to African American Republican leaders, 1 August 1945, ibid., ser. 4, box 32, file 29.

25. Ibid.

26. Republican American Committee (henceforth RAC), "Declaration to the Republican Party," 24–25 August 1945, NAACP, pt. 18, ser. C, reel 29, frame 0170–72; capitals in original. The committee thanked Dewey and Senators Langer (North Dakota), Morse (Oregon), Ball (Minnesota), Burton (Ohio), Aiken (Vermont), Capper (Kansas), Ferguson (Michigan), Wherry (Nebraska), and Smith (New Jersey), as well as Representatives La Follette (Indiana), Baldwin (New York), Keefe (Wisconsin), and Bender (Ohio). This, of course, did not mean that any of these Republicans actually endorsed the demands of the committee. African American signatories included T. Gillis Nutter, George A. Parker, Bishop D. H. Sims, Eunice H. Carter, and, perhaps surprisingly, C. B. Powell.

27. *Baltimore Afro-American*, 6 December 1946, cited in McCoy and Ruetten, *Quest and Response*, 69.

28. *Pittsburgh Courier*, 4 January 1947, cited in Berman, *Politics of Civil Rights*, 59. Almost a year earlier, during the death throes of the FEPC bill, J. W. Ivy had alleged what Martin now confirmed. He stated that the "Republican proclamation of support of a permanent FEPC at Chicago [in 1944] was simply political expediency and a device for snaring Negro votes in pivotal northern and western states" (*Crisis* 53 [March 1946]: 72). For a sympathetic, if not entirely convincing, account of Martin's attitude toward civil rights, see Kenneally, "Black Republicans."

29. Berman does not intimate who attended this meeting or whether its content was meant for public consumption. It seems unlikely, however, that Martin, potentially writing off the African American vote, would have wanted this to be common knowledge (*Politics of Civil Rights*, 59).

30. RAC press release, 27 August 1948, NAACP, pt. 18, ser. C, reel 29, frames 0216–

17. African American Republicans from Cleveland made similar demands in June 1948 (Clayborne George, "Committee of Citizens in Cleveland Ohio," submission to the Republican Platform Committee, 9 June 1948, NAACP, pt. 18, ser. C, reel 29, frames 0268–69.

31. Herbert Brownell, "Chairman's Report, Republican National Committee Meeting, Chicago, December 7, 1945," TED, ser. 2, box 38, file 15. This report also dealt with appeals to female voters, veterans, and young Republicans.

32. RNC News Release, "Report of Herbert Brownell, Jr., Chairman to the Republican National Committee," 1 April 1946, ibid. The states Brownell mentioned were Pennsylvania, Illinois, New York, Kentucky, Maryland, Ohio, California, Michigan, New Jersey, Missouri, Tennessee, Indiana, and Virginia.

33. Ibid.

34. Ibid. One of Washington's first tasks was to carry out a survey among African American voters in seven marginal congressional districts.

35. Herbert Brownell, Republican Party chairman, undated memorandum, TED, ser. 2, box 38, file 15.

36. Ibid.

37. Ibid. Irving Ives, another trusted Dewey lieutenant, warned the governor in early 1948 that the issues of antilynching, anti–poll tax, antidiscrimination, and antisegregation "are almost as difficult for the Republicans as for the Democrats" ("Outline of Subjects for Inclusion in a Discussion of National Affairs: Part IV, Civil Rights." Ives to Dewey, 17 March 1948, ibid., ser. 10, box 22, file 5).

38. J. N. Wagner, "Wake up, Republicans," *Republican*, October 1947, NAACP, pt. 18, ser. C, reel 29, frame 0220.

39. Ibid.

40. Ibid.

41. *Republican*, October 1947, cited in *Congressional Record*, 93 (1947): 80–81, appendix A4393, "Negroes," Extension of Remarks of Hon. William Langer, 26 November, 1947.

42. NAACP press release, 30 March 1946, NAACP, pt. 18, ser. C, reel 29, file 0177.

43. White to Thurgood Marshall, draft of statement to the Republican National Committee by the Continuations Committee of Negro Organizations, 27 March 1948, NAACP, pt. 18, ser. C, reel 29, frames 0284–86. In common with the earlier "Declaration by Negro Voters," the NAACP and particularly White were the prime movers in this exercise. White wanted the committee to appear at the Republican convention (White to Carroll Reece, 20 May 1948, ibid., frame 0266).

44. *NYT*, 4 January 1945; also quoted in Smith, *Thomas E. Dewey*, 443. For a brief account of the progress of the antidiscrimination bill, see ibid., 443–48.

45. *NYT*, 29 January 1945.

46. Ibid. The Urban League, NAACP, CIO, National Lawyers Guild, NNC, and the National Conference of Christians and Jews were among the groups publicly backing the SCAD (*NYT*, 4 February 1945). For more on the SCAD's findings, see ibid., 29 January 1945. The New York Chamber of Commerce and the Association of the Bar of the City of New York were among those organizations opposing the SCAD. See *NYT*,

1 January 1945, and 22 February 1945. For Ives's defense of the bill, see ibid, 13 February 1945. For further reports on opposition, see ibid., 7 January 1945, and 1 February 1945.

47. Smith, *Thomas E. Dewey*, 446.

48. *NYT*, 17 February 1945.

49. Ibid., 21 February 1945.

50. Ibid., 1 March 1945. The bill was actually drafted by Charles Tuttle, the chairman of the temporary commission appointed by Dewey the previous year (ibid., 15 March 1945). For the terms of the bill, see ibid., 1 and 6 March 1945.

51. Ibid., 17 March 1945. In July, Dewey picked the five members of the SCAD. Henry C. Turner, a lawyer and former president of the New York City Board of Education, was chairman. He was joined by Elmer F. Carter, editor of *Opportunity* and an NAACP member; Edward J. Edwards, a labor leader; Julian J. Reiss, a director of the International Tailoring Company; and Mrs. Leopold K. Simon, an attorney and member of the State Workmen's Compensation Board. Carter declared: "in the field of human relations, this is the most important step since the Emancipation Proclamation." Roy Wilkins praised the composition of the commission (ibid., 7 July 1945). For Dewey's signing of the bill into law, see ibid., 13 March 1945.

52. *Crisis* 52 (April 1945), 109. The CIO also praised Dewey (*NYT*, 26 March 1945). For praise of Dewey from Adam Clayton Powell and the *Pittsburgh Courier*, see Smith, *Thomas E. Dewey*, 447. Neither reference is cited.

53. Dewey to James E. Allen (New York NAACP), 28 March 1945, TED, ser. 4, box 245, file 54.

54. *NYT*, 5 May 1945.

55. Ibid., 12 May 1945.

56. Smith, *Thomas E. Dewey*, 663. Journalist Warren Moscow recounted this conversation to Smith.

57. Dewey to Mark Starr, Negro Labor Committee, 11 February 1946, TED, ser. 4, box 127, file 6.

58. *NYT*, 6 April 1948, 15 September 1948. Religious institutions were exempted.

59. Smith, *Thomas E. Dewey*, 448.

60. In May 1945, Connecticut passed an antidiscrimination bill based on the Ives-Quinn law (*NYT*, 2 May 1945).

61. Moon, *Balance of Power*, 198. Henry Lee Moon also expounded his theory in the *New Republic*; see *Plaindealer*, 22 October 1948.

62. Walter White, "Will The Negro Elect Our Next President?" *Collier's*, 22 November, 1947, cited in Moon, *Balance of Power*, 214. See also *Plaindealer*, 21 November 1947. There were now seventeen states—New York, Illinois, Pennsylvania, California, Ohio, Indiana, Michigan, New Jersey, Missouri, West Virginia, Maryland, Connecticut, Delaware, Kansas, Kentucky, Oklahoma, and Massachusetts—where the African American vote could prove crucial.

63. Gosnell, *Truman's Crises*, 311.

64. New York entertainer Billy Rose suggested that W. C. Fields would make a better president, stating: "if we're going to have a comedian in the White House, let's have a good one" (McCullough, *Truman*, 521).

65. Ibid., 522.

66. The election also saw the Republican Party begin to make inroads into urban areas due to the shift in African American, labor, and veteran votes (PRP, Part 2, Reports and Memoranda of the Research Division of the Headquarters of the Republican National Committee, 1938–1980, reel 1, frame 0630). The return of African American voters to the Republican Party also helped to account for victories in Delaware, Maryland, Kentucky, Missouri, and Michigan. Gains were also reported in Harlem (ibid., frame 0642). See also the Report of the Colored Division, 5 December 1946, Republican Party Papers, Republican National Committee, pt. 1, ser. A, reel 8, frames 0062–63. Party chairman Carroll Reece singled out Val Washington for particular praise.

67. PRP, Part 2, Reports and Memoranda of the Research Division of the Headquarters of the RNC, 1938–1980, reel 1, frame 0652.

68. Sitkoff, "Coming of Age of Civil Rights," 599. In 1944, the Supreme Court ruled in *Smith v. Allwright* that the Democratic all-white primary election was unconstitutional. The NAACP campaigned against the Democratic primary in Texas as the state had prevented African Americans from participating in the election. For a brief account of the case, see Lawson, *Running for Freedom*, 13–15.

69. NAACP press release, 20 September 1946, NAACP, pt. 18, ser. C, reel 26, frame 0430. The committee represented forty-seven organizations. For more details on the lynchings in question, see Zangrando, *Crusade*, 173–77.

70. Berman, *Politics of Civil Rights*, 51–52. According to Walter White, on hearing of the situation in the South, Truman exclaimed: "My God! I had no idea it was as bad as that! We have to do something" (White, *A Man Called White*, 330–31). For further detail on mob violence and the formation of the PCCR, see Donaldson, *Truman Defeats Dewey*, 104–9.

71. Berman, *Politics of Civil Rights*, 77. As Berg notes, "Truman began building his own coalition, with the black vote of the urban north as its cornerstone" (*Ticket to Freedom*, 27). Truman was also sensitive to the Cold War context, particularly after an NAACP delegation including White, Du Bois, and Bethune presented African American grievances to the United Nations in October 1947, greatly embarrassing the American government.

72. For correspondence between the association and the PCCR, see NAACP, pt. 18, ser. B, reel 25, frames 0526–0727. For editorial comment on the PCCR and the response of leading Republicans to it, see ibid., frames 0826–52. Gary Donaldson argues that, "in many ways, the PCCR became an arm of the NAACP" (*Truman Defeats Dewey*, 107).

73. Zangrando, *Crusade*, 178. White believed that Truman had put his political career on the line by endorsing civil rights (McCullough, *Truman*, 570).

74. Wayne Morse and Eleanor Roosevelt also spoke at the convention. For the full text of the address, see *NYT*, 30 June 1947. Truman's advisers were keen to make the speech as uncontroversial as possible (memorandum, including a draft of the speech, from David K. Niles to Matthew J. Connelly, 16 June 1947, Papers of Harry S. Truman: Files of Clark M. Clifford, Merrill, *Documentary History of the Truman Presidency*, 320–22). Truman, according to Berman, ignored this advice (*Politics of Civil Rights*, 61).

For Walter White's speech at the convention see Merrill, *Documentary History of the Truman Presidency*, 331–33.

75. See *To Secure These Rights*, in McCoy and O'Connor, *Readings in Twentieth-Century American History*, 531–34. For White's praise of the PCCR's findings, see *Plaindealer*, 21 November 1947.

76. Sitkoff, "Coming of Age of Civil Rights," 600.

77. *Plaindealer*, 23 January 1948.

78. *NYT*, 3 February 1948. Ironically, considering the poll tax and the effective disenfranchisement of African Americans, there were some southerners who questioned the influence that the electoral system gave to African Americans and minorities. Representative Ed Gossett of Texas declared: "our archaic electoral system has placed control of the two major parties in the hands of minorities in New York and Chicago. Both parties get down on their bellies and crawl in the dirt and kiss the feet of the minorities" (*NYT*, 4 February 1948). Berman argues that Truman was more concerned about Wallace than any bolt by southerners (*Politics of Civil Rights*, 87; see also McCullough, *Truman*, 587).

79. *Washington Post*, 3 February 1948, cited in Donaldson, *Truman Defeats Dewey*, 109.

80. Donaldson, *Truman Defeats Dewey*, 110.

81. This was despite the committee's chairman, Robert Taft, voting with the southerners on the issue (Berman, *Politics of Civil Rights*, 88). Ives had been elected to the Senate in 1946.

82. *NYT*, 6 February 1948.

83. Ibid., 16 February 1948.

84. Ibid. *Commentary* attributed the good record of these states to the "comparative enlightenment" of their Republican administrations (James A. and Nancy F. Wechsler, *Commentary*, October 1948, 297–304, NAACP, pt. 18, ser. C, reel 26, frames 0303–10).

85. Berman notes that "southerners who were inclined to revolt, of course, failed to understand that Truman was engaged in symbolic action, that his rhetoric was a substitute for a genuine legislative commitment." Berman firmly believes that the threat of a southern revolt prevented any action on civil rights (*Politics of Civil Rights*, 95).

86. *NYT*, 10 April 1948.

87. Ibid., 21 April 1948.

Chapter 6. Dewey Defeats Truman

1. "The Politics of 1948" is often attributed to Clark W. Clifford, but it was actually written by James Rowe. The more famous Clifford version of this memorandum appeared in November 1947. Clifford took credit for the "Politics of 1948" because Rowe was a law partner of Thomas Corcoran, whom Truman disliked (McCullough, *Truman*, 590). The memo dealt with other voting groups aside from African Americans, with Alonzo Hamby suggesting that winning the West was the main focus of the memo (Hamby, *Beyond the New Deal*, 210).

2. Interestingly, Rowe argued that the only time African Americans had voted Republican since 1932 was in New York in 1946 (James Rowe Jr., confidential memorandum, "The Politics of 1948," 18 September 1947, Papers of Kenneth Hechler, Merrill, *Documentary History of the Truman Presidency*, 14: 29–51).

3. Ibid.

4. Ibid.

5. Kirkendall, "Election of 1948," in Schlesinger et al., *Presidential Elections*, 8: 3106–7. Rowe, as Gosnell notes, seriously underestimated the depth of feeling in the South over civil rights (*Truman's Crises*, 367).

6. Undated memorandum from Oscar Ewing to Clark Clifford, cited in Donaldson, *Truman Defeats Dewey*, 100. The *U.S. News* reported that Truman's "popularity with Negro voters in the North has risen in about the same proportion as it had dropped among white voters in the South. . . . A Truman victory in a big state like Pennsylvania, with thirty-five electoral votes, would almost offset the loss of Alabama, Arkansas, Mississippi and South Carolina" (21 May 1948, cited in ibid., 111).

7. Unsigned memorandum, "Should the President Call Congress Back?" 29 June 1948, Merrill, *Documentary History of the Truman Presidency*, 14, 249–50.

8. *Harper's*, September 1948, cited in Joyner, *Republican Dilemma*, 76.

9. Unsigned memorandum, "Should the President Call Congress Back?" 29 June 1948, Merrill, *Documentary History of the Truman Presidency*, 14, 249–50.

10. Clark Clifford et al., "Memorandum for the President," November 1948, Student Research File, "B File," Harry S. Truman Papers, cited in Karabell, *Last Campaign*, 36.

11. For the strengthened plank and Hubert Humphrey's speech on the subject, see Schlesinger et al., *Presidential Elections*, 8: 3182–83, 3184–86. Truman called Humphrey and the ADA "crackpots."

12. For more on the Democrats' debate on the civil rights plank, see *NYT*, 13 July 1948. For the Dixiecrat walkout and adoption of civil rights plank, see *NYT*, 15 July 1948. See also Gosnell, *Truman's Crises*, 376–81; McCoy and Ruetten, *Quest and Response*, 123–27; and Ross, *Loneliest Campaign*, 116–22. Truman later took credit for the civil rights plank in his memoirs, claiming "I was perfectly willing to risk defeat in 1948 by sticking to the civil rights plank" (Truman, *Years of Trial and Hope*, 182).

13. McCullough, *Truman*, 638–40.

14. Truman was also aided by the fact that voters viewed Wallace, not him, as the communist threat. "The result was," Donaldson argues, "big votes for Truman from the northern-urban-liberal-black coalition that his strategists had targeted" (*Truman Defeats Dewey*, 215). On 13 September 1948, however, the *New York Times* reported that the southern revolt was helping the Republicans.

15. The *Baltimore Sun* asserted that the orders were "politically inspired" (27 July 1948, cited in Berman, *Politics of Civil Rights*, 118). On 18 August, Randolph, convinced of Truman's sincerity, called off plans for resistance to the draft (ibid.).

16. Hugh M. Gloster, "The Southern Revolt," *Crisis* 55 (May 1948): 137–39, 155–56.

17. *Cleveland Call and Post*, undated, cited in Moon, *Balance of Power*, 208. "Taft," Patterson concludes, "like most white Americans . . . simply failed to appreciate the

plight of the black man in American society, for little in his own experience had exposed him to it" (*Mr. Republican*, 304–5).

18. Quoted from the *Congressional Record* 89 (14 October 1943), NAACP, pt. 18, ser. B, reel 9, frame 0404.

19. Joseph Ferguson, *Philadelphia Inquirer*, 2 December 1947, TED, ser. 5, box 11, file 14. For criticism of Taft by Walter White about the lack of civil rights legislation, see *Plaindealer*, 28 May 1948.

20. *NYT*, 5 and 6 June 1948. Dewey also went south before the convention, visiting Maryland, Virginia, and North Carolina (ibid., 9 June 1948). For more on Taft and African Americans, see *Crisis* 55 (January 1948): 9.

21. "Appointments of Colored People in State Employ Made by Governor Dewey," undated, TED, ser. 7, box 63, file 11.

22. Joseph Ferguson, *Philadelphia Inquirer*, 3 December 1947, TED, ser. 5, box 11, file 14.

23. The 25 June 1948 *Chicago Sun-Times* called Dewey's nomination "a triumph of the art of political synthetics" (cited in Hamby, *Beyond the New Deal*, 241). For reports that Stassen and Taft were joining forces to thwart Dewey, see *NYT*, 21 June 1948. The votes of two African American members of the Credentials Committee at the convention ensured the seating of a pro-Dewey delegation from Georgia. This was particularly ironic as the two committeemen were Taft delegates from other states. They voted against the pro-Taft Georgia delegation due to its perceived lily-whitism. Dewey's forces had apparently pointed out to African American delegates that Taft had not ensured the passage of any civil rights legislation in the Senate (*Plaindealer*, 2 July 1948). See also *NYT*, 22 June 1948; and W. J. "Bill" Shaw to White, 4 June 1948, NAACP, pt. 18, ser. C, reel 29, frame 0253.

24. *NYT*, 25 June 1948.

25. Joyner attests that Republicans "were not exultant about Dewey's candidacy" (*Republican Dilemma*, 75). For more detail on the Republican convention, see Donaldson, *Truman Defeats Dewey*, 150–56; and Karabell, *Last Campaign*, 148–49.

26. Dewey certainly felt that Taft was too conservative to be elected. Thompson, *Lessons from Defeated Presidential Candidates*, 104. In fact, Dewey "intensely disliked" Taft, according to McCullough (*Truman*, 672). Taft commented that "I had to struggle constantly against the idea that I could not be elected" (Patterson, *Mr. Republican*, 417). Nevertheless, he remained confident that Dewey would win and be president for eight years. For more information on the rivalry between the two men, see ibid., 423–27.

27. *NYT*, 27 June 1948.

28. Joyner, *Republican Dilemma*, 5.

29. Biographical details from: Katcher, *Earl Warren*; Warren, *Memoirs of Earl Warren*; Moon, *Balance of Power*; and Karabell, *Last Campaign*, 149. Warren was, according to Karabell, "affable, centrist and bland. . . . No one would have guessed that this was the man who would almost unilaterally transform American civil rights as chief justice of the Supreme Court" (149).

30. *NYT*, 26 June 1948, quotation from Karabell, *Last Campaign*, 149.

31. Phillips, *The 1940s*, 331.

32. Abels, *Jaws of Victory*, 68, 152. Warren and Dewey, according to Gould, "did not get along" (*Grand Old Party*, 316).

33. Johnson and Porter, *National Party Platforms*, 450.

34. Beyer, *Dewey, 1937–1947*, 189. According to Beyer, the platform was adopted in twenty seconds.

35. Later in the same edition, the *Plaindealer* described the Republican platform as a "forthright document, definite in its pledges" (2 July 1948).

36. Ibid.

37. Ibid., 9 July 1948.

38. NAACP press release, 17 June 1948, NAACP, pt. 18, ser. C, reel 29, frame 0300.

39. The Continuations Committee of Negro Organizations consisted of representatives from twenty-one African American organizations (NAACP press release, 18 June 1948, NAACP, pt. 18, ser. B, reel 10, frame 0844).

40. *Crisis* 55 (June 1948): 189.

41. *Baltimore Afro-American*, 3 July 1948; McCoy and Ruetten, *Quest and Response*, 123.

42. McCoy and Ruetten, *Quest and Response*, 123.

43. *NYT*, 23 June 1948.

44. Blinkoff was a Jewish Republican.

45. Rivers to Charles Breitel, Counsel to the Governor, 20 July 1948, TED, ser. 5, box 280, file 30.

46. Ibid. Randolph and fifty of his supporters had picketed the Republican convention demanding an end to Jim Crow in the military (*Plaindealer*, 2 July 1948). For more details on Randolph's campaign to desegregate the armed forces, see Berman, *Politics of Civil Rights*, 97–100.

47. Rivers to Breitel, 20 July 1948, TED, ser. 5, box 280, file 30.

48. Ibid.

49. Ibid.

50. Ibid.

51. Ibid.

52. Memorandum by Francis Rivers and Jack Blinkoff, 20 July 1948, TED, ser. 5, box 280, file 30.

53. For biographical details on Washington, see *Negro Statesman*, 15 March 1946, TED, ser. 2, box 46, file 1; and Cotter and Hennessy, *Politics without Power*, 161. The *Negro Statesman*, a monthly magazine for African American Republicans, hailed Washington's appointment as evidence of the Republican Party's commitment to African Americans (*Negro Statesman*, 15 March 1946, TED, ser. 2, box 46, file 1). Washington was not limited solely to African American concerns; in 1947, he toured the country at the request of Brownell, assessing Republican strength in various areas (Washington to Brownell, 8 June 1947, 16 June 1947, and 16 August 1947, ibid.).

54. Cotter and Hennessy, *Politics without Power*, 161–62. It would not be until 1960 that the GOP would permit Washington to approach African American churches as a way to gain African American support. Cotter and Hennessy assert that "he was prevented [previously] because of the fear that such an approach, directed almost exclu-

sively to Protestant churches, might be interpreted as evidence of bigotry" (ibid.). Hugh Bone argues that "less is known about the work of the minorities sections than about any other activities of the national office." This is partly because they were inactive for most of the year and only really had a properly defined purpose at election time (*Party Committees and National Politics*, 90).

55. *Plaindealer*, 13 August 1948.

56. Ibid., 10 September 1948.

57. Washington to White, 24 April 1946, NAACP, pt. 18, ser. C, reel 29, frame 0194. White, used to moving in grander circles, dismissed Washington as an "underling." For further details on the dispute between White and Washington, see Topping, "Supporting Our Friends and Defeating Our Enemies."

58. *Commonweal* 68, no. 17 (6 August 1948), NAACP, pt. 18, ser. C, reel 26, frames 0254–55. The *Commonweal* also reported the comments of Democratic senator Howard McGrath of Rhode Island, who declared: "If the Republicans are smart, they will enact this program."

59. James A. and Nancy F. Wechsler, "The Road Ahead for Civil Rights—The President's Report: One Year Later," *Commentary*, October 1948, 297–304, NAACP, pt. 18, ser. C, reel 26, frames 0303–10.

60. Ibid.

61. Ibid.

62. *NYT*, 3 October 1948.

63. Press release by Archibald M. Crossley of the Crossley Poll, 15 October 1948, TED, ser. 2, box 4, file 6.

64. Karabell, *Last Campaign*, 189. For more information on polls predicting a Dewey victory, see Donaldson, *Truman Defeats Dewey*, 209–10; and Gosnell, *Truman's Crises*, 407–9.

65. For more information on Dewey's failure to inspire audiences, see Karabell, *Last Campaign*, 202–3. Karabell describes Dewey's speeches as "numbingly anodyne."

66. McCoy and Ruetten, *Quest and Response*, 137.

67. Ibid.

68. *NYT*, 22 October 1948.

69. Patterson confirms that Taft was "forced" to go south in 1948 by Dewey's campaign team (*Mr. Republican*, 422).

70. *Plaindealer*, 29 October 1948, and 12 November 1948.

71. Ibid., 7.

72. For more information on the perceived threat of Wallace, see the ADA's analysis, "Henry A. Wallace: The First Three Months," Merrill, *Documentary History of the Truman Presidency*, 14, 172–74.

73. *NYT*, 26 June 1948.

74. Ibid., 23 June 1948. Actor and singer Paul Robeson and W.E.B. Du Bois were among those African Americans attending the Progressive convention on 20 July 1948 in Philadelphia (Berman, *Politics of Civil Rights*, 115). This was a far cry from 1944, when White, in his *Chicago Defender* column, was fulsome in his praise of the former vice president and went so far as to advocate a Willkie-Wallace ticket, claiming that both

men had "placed their political principles and personal integrity above holding a job" (*CD*, 5 August 1944).

75. *NYT*, 14 October 1948. Hastie "campaigned vigorously" for the Democrats, according to Hamby (*Beyond the New Deal*, 250).

76. *NYT*, 13 September 1948.

77. McCoy and Ruetten, *Quest and Response*, 139. Schuyler was a former Socialist and had been a member of the NAACP's public relations team. Berg asserts that the association's alliance with Truman was "realpolitik, pure and simple" (*Ticket to Freedom*, 129).

78. McCoy and Ruetten, *Quest and Response*, 141. Berman states that the decision to speak in Harlem was made at the last minute (*Politics of Civil Rights*, 126).

79. *NYT*, 21 July 1948, 1. The *Baltimore Afro-American* rejected Brownell's explanation (31 July 1948, cited in McCoy and Ruetten, *Quest and Response*, 132).

80. K. M. Landis II, *Chicago Sun-Times*, 4 August 1948, NAACP, pt. 18, ser. C, reel 26, frame 0258.

81. According to McCoy and Ruetten, *Quest and Response*, 132.

82. *NYT*, 15 September 1948. The Maine victory was at least in part due to AFL/CIO backing.

83. Ibid., 1 November 1948.

84. Thompson, *Lessons from Defeated Presidential Candidates*, 106–7.

85. Smith, *Thomas E. Dewey*, 524. By mid-October, Truman had reduced the gap to a statistical dead-heat (Karabell, *Last Campaign*, 257).

86. Karabell, *Last Campaign*, 203–4. Jaeckle was also concerned that Dewey was giving speeches that had been written weeks previously and had not been updated to take into account recent events. Warren expressed concern about the farm vote and Truman's attacks on Congress, but this went unheeded (ibid., 204).

87. Thompson, *Lessons from Defeated Presidential Candidates*, 108.

88. Ibid.

89. *Plaindealer*, 29 October 1948.

90. Phillips, *The 1940s*, 341.

91. Abels, *Jaws of Victory*, 275. In the aftermath of the election, the Republican Party's Research Division reported that Gallup overestimated the Republican vote by 4.4 percent, Crossley by 4.4 percent, and Elmo Roper by 7.1 percent. Ironically, Gallup and Crossley allowed for a 4 percent margin of error, which was less than the margin of victory in twenty-one states totaling 290 electoral votes ("The 1948 Election: A Statistical Analysis, May 1949," PRP, Part 2, Reports and Memoranda of the Research Division of the Headquarters of the RNC, 1938–1980, reel 1, frame 0774). For additional analysis of the press and pollsters' reaction to Truman's victory, see Ross, *Loneliest Campaign*, 232–37.

92. Abels, *Jaws of Victory*, 270.

93. Karabell, *Last Campaign*, 257.

94. *CD*, 13 November 1948, NAACP, pt. 18, ser. C, reel 18, frame 0358.

95. Abels, *Jaws of Victory*, 296. Indeed, it is very likely Dewey would have won Il-

linois had Wallace been on the ballot. Figures for African American voting are also available in McCoy and Ruetten, *Quest and Response*, 142.

96. Martin, *Stevenson of Illinois*, 345–46.

97. *Pittsburgh Courier*, 13 November 1948, NAACP, pt. 18, ser. C, reel 18, frames 0355–56.

98. "The 1948 Election: A Statistical Analysis, May 1949," PRP, Part 2, 1938–1980, reel 1, frame 0771. See also Abels, *Jaws of Victory*, 290. The Democratic chairman, J. Howard McGrath, agreed that the African American vote was an extremely important factor in carrying these three states (*Truman*, 713).

99. "The 1948 Election." PRP, Part 2, Reports and Memoranda of the Research Division of the Headquarters of the RNC, 1938–1980, reel 1, frame 0793. This analysis did not suggest what percentage of African Americans voted for the Democrats. It did, however, question the basis for Walter White's contention that 69 percent of African Americans had voted Democrat.

100. Berman, *Politics of Civil Rights*, 130–31.

101. Lubell, *Saturday Evening Post*, no date, quoted in McCullough, *Truman*, 714. Polls carried out by the Democratic Party itself invariably predicted a Truman victory (Gosnell, *Truman's Crises*, 407–9).

102. "The 1948 Election," PRP, Part 2, 1938–1980, reel 1, frame 0772. Moos also emphasizes the loss of the farm vote as the vital factor in Dewey's defeat and notes that 682,382 people voted for congressmen but not for president (*Republicans*, 444–45).

103. Thompson, *Lessons from Defeated Presidential Candidates*, 107.

104. Dewey to Henry Luce, 15 December 1948, cited in Donaldson, *Truman Defeats Dewey*, 212; and Smith, *Thomas E. Dewey*, 544. For further detail on the farm vote, see Karabell, *Last Campaign*, 207–8.

105. Abels, *Jaws of Victory*, 290. These states were Ohio, Illinois, Indiana, Michigan, Montana, Nebraska, Kansas, Missouri, Iowa, and Wisconsin. Abels argues that "the farm vote turned out to be the key to the election result" (171). Smith agrees, citing the loss of Wisconsin, Ohio, Illinois and Iowa as the key to Dewey's defeat (*Thomas E. Dewey*, 544). The Democrats were able to portray the Republicans as the enemies of the farmer, particularly after Stassen had accused the administration of keeping food prices high. Abels comments: "the Stassen charge was as disastrous to the Dewey cause as any single incident in the 1948 campaign" (*Jaws of Victory*, 173). Gould also attributes Truman's victory to the farm vote (*Grand Old Party*, 318).

106. Truman's majorities in Wisconsin, Iowa, and Wyoming were wafer-thin (Schlesinger et al., *Presidential Elections*, VIII, 2311).

107. Truman interview with R. Alton Lee, 3 August 1961, cited in Donaldson, *Truman Defeats Dewey*, 202.

108. For the impact of the labor vote, see Karabell, *Last Campaign*, 257–58.

109. Donaldson, *Truman Defeats Dewey*, 203. In some parts of the country it was the labor movement that supplied the strongest support for the Democrats, sometimes doing more than party organizers to get the vote out (Ross, *Loneliest Campaign*, 17).

110. Donaldson, *Truman Defeats Dewey*, 216–17.

111. *Pittsburgh Courier*, 13 November 1948, NAACP, pt. 18, ser. C, reel 18, frames 0355–56.

112. *CD*, 13 November 1948, ibid., frame 0358.

113. NAACP press release, 27 January 1949, ibid., frame 0374.

114. Smith, *Thomas E. Dewey*, 524.

115. Kirkendall, "Election of 1948," in Schlesinger et al., *Presidential Elections*, 8: 3139–40.

116. *Crisis* 55 (December 1948): 361. The desire not to "waste" votes was almost certainly a factor as well.

117. Thompson, *Lessons from Defeated Presidential Candidates*, 105.

118. Ibid., 106.

119. Abels, *Jaws of Victory*, 165.

120. McCoy and Ruetten, *Quest and Response*, 144. For the Democrats' propaganda efforts among African Americans, see ibid., 139–40.

121. Albert D. Butler estimates that 1.5 million people, almost all African American, left the South between 1940 and 1950 ("Negro Migration from the South," in Vander, *Progress of the American Negro*, 3).

122. Brownell and Burke, *Advising Ike*, 96. Brownell also maintained, in the face of overwhelming proof of the opposite, that Dewey's "strong pro–civil rights stance led to lasting support in his . . . presidential and gubernatorial campaigns" (ibid., 44).

123. "Dewey had a complex about the Negro vote," concludes Abels, "which he had always courted in New York but never got" (*Jaws of Victory*, 220).

124. Smith, *Thomas E. Dewey*, 524.

125. Beyer, *Dewey, 1937–1947*, 241.

126. Mayer, "The Republican Party, 1932–1952," in Schlesinger et al., *History of U.S. Political Parties*, 3: 2285.

127. Both Berman and Smith hint that Dewey was actively courting the South, but this is dismissed by Abels. See Berman, *Politics of Civil Rights*, 130–31; Smith, *Thomas E. Dewey*, 524; and Abels, *Jaws of Victory*, 194.

128. Abels, *Jaws of Victory*, 276.

129. Ibid., 277–78. It was reported that Taft was not especially disappointed by Dewey's defeat, but he did not make these sentiments public (ibid., 278–79).

130. *NYT*, 16 November 1948. Gould describes Kelland as "an influential conservative" (*Grand Old Party*, 321). For other comments by Kelland, see Donaldson, *Truman Defeats Dewey*, 211–13.

131. Smith, *Thomas E. Dewey*, 525.

Permission Note: Parts of this chapter have appeared previously in "'Never Argue with the Gallup Poll': Thomas Dewey, Civil Rights and the Election of 1948," *Journal of American Studies* 38, no. 2 (August 2004): 179–99.

Chapter 7. The Elephant and the Skunk

1. *CD*, 1 January 1949, 6. Truman's sincerity was again questioned when a letter he allegedly wrote to Congressman Frank W. Boykin was made public, stating: "Frank, I

don't believe in this civil rights program any more than you do, but we've got to have it win." The comments were apparently made before the election, but Truman only denied them privately (McCoy and Ruetten, *Quest and Response*, 149).

2. Henry Lee Moon, "What Chance Civil Rights?" *Crisis* 56 (February 1949): 42–44.

3. *CD*, 8 January 1949.

4. Berman, *Politics of Civil Rights*, 135.

5. Donovan, *Tumultuous Years*, 23.

6. *NYT*, 6 January 1949. The 5 February 1949 *Chicago Defender* described Truman's inaugural as "one of the greatest and most important declarations of an American president." For further comment, see McCoy and Ruetten, *Quest and Response*, 154–55.

7. *NYT*, 16 January 1949. Krock restated this view the following month (see *NYT*, 13 February 1949). Krock, interviewing Truman in 1950, perhaps revealed his feelings about African Americans when he said "you know intimately the conditions of the Negro race and the limitations of its capacity to fill certain kinds of employment" (*Crisis* 57 [March 1950]: 170).

8. *NYT*, 21 January 1949. White pointed out that Elmo Roper put the cost of discrimination to the American economy at billions of dollars and the propaganda benefits to Communists of continued discrimination (telegram from White to Eisenhower, 19 June 1952, NAACP, pt. 18, ser. B, reel 14, frames 44–45). White forwarded this telegram to Ives, Rivers, Morse, Dewey, Case, Driscoll, Hoffman, Cabot Lodge, and James Duff. For more on the Cold War aspect of the civil rights struggle, see Berg, *Ticket to Freedom*, 116–40; and McCoy and Ruetten, *Quest and Response*, 180.

9. *CD*, 29 January 1949. An association survey revealed that Truman had won 69 percent of the African American urban vote, while outside of New York and Los Angeles, votes for Wallace were negligible. In Virginia, African Americans voted for Republican congressional candidates by a margin of six to one, but they also backed Truman four to one; African Americans backed Truman in Los Angeles by a margin of seven to one (*NYT*, 26 January 1949; see also *Crisis* 56 [February 1949]: 42–44). For Moon's full analysis of the election, see Henry Lee Moon, "What Chance Civil Rights?" *Crisis* 56 [February 1949]: 42–44.

10. *Crisis* 56 (February 1949): 42–44.

11. The *Chicago Defender* regarded Morse, Ives, Cabot Lodge, and Ferguson as African Americans' main Republican friends (2 April 1949).

12. *Crisis* 56 (February 1949): 41; *NYT*, 26 January 1949. Ives also remained concerned that supporters of civil rights legislation were not sincere (*CD*, 5 February 1949).

13. Myers had helped to draft the original civil rights plank in 1948 (Berman, *Politics of Civil Rights*, 138).

14. *Crisis* 56 (February 1949): 41.

15. *NYT*, 1 February 1949.

16. Telegram, Walter White to Arthur Vandenberg, 25 February 1949, NAACP, pt. 18, ser. B, reel 9, frame 264.

17. McCoy and Ruetten, *Quest and Response*, 171. When Vandenberg made his ruling in 1948, he was sustaining a point made by Richard Russell of Georgia.

18. *CD*, 12 March 1949. Taft had denied allegations of a deal with the Dixiecrats to a delegation of labor, church, and minority leaders.

19. Ibid.

20. Berman, *Politics of Civil Rights*, 147.

21. Ibid., 141.

22. Ibid., 142 and 147.

23. *NYT*, 3 March 1949.

24. Berman, *Politics of Civil Rights*, 149. For reaction to Truman's 4 March statement on cloture, see *NYT*, 5 March 1949. For criticism of Truman, see *NYT*, 7 March 1949.

25. Berman, *Politics of Civil Rights*, 148. See also McCoy and Ruetten, *Quest and Response*, 173. Many of the Republican votes against changing the cloture rule were from states such as Maine, Nebraska, Minnesota, and Wisconsin where there were very few African American voters (Aronson and Spiegler, "Does the Republican Party Want the Negro Vote?" *Crisis* 56 [December 1949]: 368).

26. Berman, *Politics of Civil Rights*, 149.

27. Ibid., 150.

28. "Roll Call on Barkley Ruling, 11 March 1949," NAACP, pt. 18, ser. B, reel 9, frame 270. White wrote to Vandenberg "to ask and plead" with him to use his "great prestige" to sustain the Barkley ruling (White to Vandenberg, 11 March 1949, NAACP, pt. 18, ser. B, reel 9, frame 272). Twenty-three Republicans voted to overrule, including Bricker, Jenner, Mundt, Vandenberg, and Wherry. Ferguson, Ives, Knowland, Cabot Lodge, McCarthy, Morse, Saltonstall, and Taft were among those voting to sustain the Barkley ruling.

29. Wilkins to Archibald Carey, 10 November 1952, cited in Berman, *Politics of Civil Rights*, 150. For more details on the recriminations, see McCoy and Ruetten, *Quest and Response*, 175.

30. *Baltimore Afro-American*, 19 March 1949, cited in McCoy and Ruetten, *Quest and Response*, 176.

31. Berman, *Politics of Civil Rights*, 152. Lucas was essentially a conservative on civil rights and had been against the 1948 plank. This made him an acceptable choice as majority leader to Russell; indeed, although Hamby describes Lucas as "an easygoing moderate," he argues that Lucas was "hand-picked by the southern conservatives" (*Beyond the New Deal*, 313). Donovan believes that Lucas had a "liberal veneer over conservative instincts" (*Tumultuous Years*, 119). For more on Lucas's role, see Hamby, *Beyond the New Deal*, 317–18.

32. *Crisis* 56 (April 1949): 105.

33. *NYT*, 18 March 1949.

34. "Roll Call Vote on Amendment to Senate Rule XXII, 17 March 1949," NAACP, pt. 18, ser. B, reel 9, frame 271. See also press release, 14 April 1949, ibid., pt. 18, ser. B, reel 9, frame 279.

35. *NYT*, 16 and 17 March 1949.

36. Ibid., 18 March 1949. See also ibid., 16 March 1949. The *Crisis* noted that it had never been possible to secure a two-thirds vote in the Senate for cloture (56 [April 1949]: 105).

37. *NYT*, 18 March 1949.

38. Ibid., 16 March 1949

39. Ibid., 17 March 1949. Lucas failed to mention that twelve nonsouthern Democrats also voted for the measure.

40. Ibid., 18 March 1949. Figure for the Dixiecrat vote from ibid.

41. Ibid., 17 and 24 March 1949, 22. Five members of the Republicans' nine-strong policy committee, as well as fifteen GOP senators who had demanded that Lucas take up the measure, voted with southern Democrats on the issue of cloture (*Crisis*, 56 [December 1949]: 368).

42. *CD*, 26 March 1949. See also ibid., 2 April 1949. Ironically, Wherry would soon write to Wilkins to express "my sincere support for legislation to expand equality of opportunity for all our people" (Wherry to Wilkins, 14 April 1949, NAACP, pt. 18, ser. B, reel 9, frames 374–78).

43. *Crisis* 56 (April 1949): 105.

44. Ibid.

45. Ibid.

46. *NYT*, 8 April 1949.

47. *CD*, 26 March 1949.

48. *Crisis* 56 (December 1949): 412.

49. Ibid., 368.

50. *NYT*, 29 April 1949. For details of the omnibus civil rights, anti–poll tax, and FEPC bills, see Berman, *Politics of Civil Rights*, 158–59; and McCoy and Ruetten, *Quest and Response*, 178–79.

51. *NYT*, 8 May 1949.

52. Ibid., 11 May 1949.

53. Ibid., 27 May 1949.

54. Ibid., 12 May 1949. Eight states had FEPC laws by August 1949: New York, New Jersey, Connecticut, Massachusetts, New Mexico, Oregon, Rhode Island, and Washington. For Humphrey's comments, see ibid., 12 May 1949. The four states that had laws relying primarily upon persuasion settled 1,200 cases between August 1947 and August 1948 without having to resort to their powers of enforcement (ibid., 27 May 1949).

55. Ibid., 3 June 1949. See also *CD*, 4 June 1949.

56. *NYT*, 7 June 1949. See also *CD*, 11 June 1949. Ferguson later wrote to the *New York Times* to point out that his antilynching bill differed from that proposed by the PCCR because of the effort he had taken to ensure the constitutionality of his bill (*NYT*, 12 June 1949). Support for an antilynching bill also came from Attorney General Tom Clark (*NYT*, 17 June 1949). While the debate continued there was a lynching in Georgia. Two whites were quickly arrested but were freed within ten days by an all-white jury (*NYT*, 5 and 15 June 1949).

57. Berman, *Politics of Civil Rights*, 159. Statement from an NAACP press release, 26 May 1949.

58. *NYT*, 13 July 1949. Wilkins's message was sent to Lucas, McGrath, Taft, and Martin.

59. Ibid., 27 July 1949. Voting for the bill were 151 Democrats and 121 Republicans; 25 Republicans voted against.

60. Berman, *Politics of Civil Rights*, 161.

61. Ibid., 161–62. See also *NYT*, 16 September 1949. Eastland's appointment also ended the already dim prospect of a purge of 1948 Dixiecrats, and amply demonstrated Truman's reluctance to exacerbate Democratic splits. Truman had discussed the prospect of attempting to purge the party of Dixiecrats with Sam Rayburn, but the Speaker, a good friend of the president, felt that this would cost the Democrats control of Congress (Donovan, *Tumultuous Years*, 17). According to Donovan, although an opponent of civil rights legislation, which he felt would fail, Rayburn was "no racist." For the friendship between Rayburn and Truman, see ibid., 19–20.

62. *NYT*, 22 September 1949.

63. Ibid., 4 October 1949.

64. Ibid., 20.

65. *Crisis* 56 (December 1949): 365.

66. Ibid., 413.

67. Ibid., 414.

68. Ibid., 415.

69. Ibid., 416.

70. Ibid.

71. "Statement of Hon. Kenneth S. Wherry, Republican United States Senator from Nebraska on Civil Rights Legislation, 7 January 1950," NAACP, pt. 18, ser. B, reel 9, frames 374–78.

72. *NYT*, 5 January 1950. See also Berman, *Politics of Civil Rights*, 167.

73. *NYT*, 8 January 1950.

74. Ibid. Supporters of the Mobilization Committee included Lucas, Ives, Humphrey, Morse, A. C. Powell, and Javits, as well as Val Washington of the RNC and William Dawson of the DNC (*Crisis* 57 [February 1950]: 107).

75. *NYT*, 8 January 1950. Russell had sought compromise with Truman on the basis of the "Arkansas Plan" but had been rebuffed (Berman, *Politics of Civil Rights*, 160).

76. *NYT*, 14 January 1950.

77. Berman, *Politics of Civil Rights*, 168.

78. *NYT*, 21 January 1950. For further background on the House Rules Committee, see ibid., 22 January 1950.

79. Ibid., 21 January 1950.

80. Donovan, *Tumultuous Years*, 118.

81. *NYT*, 21 January 1950.

82. Ibid., 17 February, 1950.

83. Ibid., 24 January 1950. This was because, ironically, the Republicans would be celebrating Lincoln's birthday on 12 February.

84. Ibid., 21 February 1950. The sponsor of the substitute measure was Samuel K. McConnell of Pennsylvania, the ranking Republican member of the Education and Labor Committee.

85. Ibid., 22 February, 1950.

86. Ibid.

87. Ibid., 23 February, 1950. The NAACP immediately telegrammed congressmen to tell them that the substitute bill was unsatisfactory (ibid.). Large crowds gathered in the public galleries to watch the debate.

88. *Crisis* 57 (March 1950): 170. The 221 congressmen who supported the McConnell bill consisted of 117 mostly southern Democrats and 104 Republicans.

89. *NYT*, 24 February 1950.

90. Ibid.

91. Ibid. Throughout the controversy, Krock argued that the FEPC was being used as a campaign issue for 1950. He questioned Truman's sincerity on the issue as it was not mentioned at a recent White House conference between Truman and Democratic congressional leaders. He concluded that "most of the principals in the parliamentary farce now going on want to keep the FEPC issue alive for campaign purposes" (ibid., 26 January 1950).

92. Ibid., 14 April 1950; Berman, *Politics of Civil Rights*, 173.

93. A closed meeting of the Republican Policy Committee, chaired by Taft, was believed to be discussing the FEPC bill (*NYT*, 13 April 1950).

94. Ibid..

95. Ibid, 13 May 1950.

96. Ibid., 16 May 1950.

97. Ibid., 20 May 1950.

98. Ibid., 8.

99. Ibid., 14.

100. *Crisis* 57 (June 1950): 374–75. Among the Republicans in favor were: McCarthy, Vandenberg, Brewster, Knowland, Saltonstall, Taft, Bricker, Ferguson, Ives, Wherry, and Jenner. Six of the thirty-two votes against were from Republicans, including Mundt.

101. *NYT*, 17 May 1950.

102. Ibid.

103. Ibid., 21 May 1950.

104. Memorandum from Stephen Spingarn, 5 July 1950, Spingarn, MSS, Harry S. Truman Library, cited in Hamby, *Beyond the New Deal*, 346; italics in original. Hamby argues that Spingarn's strategy had much wider, more positive, significance for civil rights.

105. *NYT*, 11 and 13 July 1950.

106. Ibid., 13 July 1950. For the most part, southern senators stayed out of the debate.

107. Ibid., 25 January 1949.

108. Ibid., 26 January 1949.

109. Smith, *Thomas E. Dewey*, 546–47. See also *NYT*, 26 January 1949; R. B Creager (Texas) was also highly critical of Scott (*NYT*, 28 January 1949).

110. *NYT*, 28 January 1949.

111. Ibid.

112. Ibid. Morse had expressed concern that those senators selected to attend the meeting were not representative of the party in the Senate (ibid., 25 January 1949). Those

selected were Wherry and Hugh A. Butler of Nebraska, Owen Brewster of Maine, and Homer Capehart of Indiana.

113. Ibid., 30 January 1949. By contrast, liberals such as Lodge and Ives blamed the Eightieth Congress for Dewey's defeat (Patterson, *Mr. Republican*, 427).

114. *NYT*, 28 January 1949. Senator Owen Brewster of Maine and former senator John Townsend of Delaware would be the cochairmen of the new committee. The other members of the committee were: Homer Ferguson (Michigan), Henry Cabot Lodge Jr. (Massachusetts), H. Alexander Smith (New Jersey), Hugh Butler, (Nebraska), Zales N. Ecton (Montana), Edward J. Thye (Minnesota), and John J. Williams (Delaware).

115. For further details, see Patterson, *Mr. Republican*, 427–29.

116. *NYT*, 30 January 1949.

117. Ibid., 9 February 1949.

118. Ibid.

119. Ibid.; also cited in Smith, *Thomas E. Dewey*, 547.

120. *NYT*, 9 February 1949.

121. Ibid., 13 February 1949.

122. Ibid., 18 February 1949.

123. Ibid.

124. Ibid., 15 July 1949.

125. Ibid., 20 July 1949.

126. Ibid., 29 July 1949.

127. Ibid., 5 August 1949.

128. Ibid., 7 August 1949.

129. Ibid., 5 August 1949. Friends of Gabrielson described him as "an Iowa farm boy made good," although he was now a successful lawyer and businessman (ibid.).

130. Ibid., 29 July 1949. The New Deal and Fair Deal were compared to Soviet policy, including a claim that *Toward Soviet America*, a book published in 1932 by Communist leader William Z. Foster, had many similarities with Truman's recent message to Congress (*NYT*, 29 July 1949).

131. Ibid., 30 July 1949.

132. Ibid., 15 October 1949. Colorado, Illinois, Iowa, Kansas, Michigan, Minnesota, North Dakota, South Dakota, Montana, Nebraska, New Mexico, Utah, Wisconsin, and Wyoming were all represented.

133. Ibid., 16 October 1949.

134. Ibid., 20 December 1949.

135. Ibid., 2 February, 1950. The governors were: Duff of Pennsylvania, Fred G. Aandahl (North Dakota), Sherman Adams (New Hampshire), William S. Beardsley (Iowa), Val Peterson, (Nebraska), and C. A. Robins (Idaho). For the full text of the of the Republican Party's statement of principles and objectives, see ibid., 7 February 1950.

136. Ibid., 2 February, 1950.

137. Ibid., 7 February, 1950.

138. Ibid.

139. Ibid., 5 March, 1950.

140. Javits's speech at the National Republican Club in January 1950, cited in Javits and Steinberg, *Javits*, 153.

141. *NYT*, 7 February 1950.

142. Ibid., 5 March 1950.

143. Ibid., 9 February 1950.

144. Ibid., 12 February 1950.

145. Ibid., 5 March 1950.

146. Ibid., 13 February 1950.

147. Wilkins to Ives, 9 February 1950, NAACP, pt. 18, ser. B, reel 9, frame 382. See also NAACP press release, 9 February 1950, ibid., 397. See also "Report of the Acting Secretary for the March 1950 Meeting of the Board," ibid., pt. 18, ser. C, reel 29, frame 335.

148. *Crisis* 57 (April 1950): 238–39.

149. *NYT*, 22 April, 1950.

150. Javits and Steinberg, *Javits*, 153; and *NYT*, 2 July 1950. The committee originally was going to be known as the "Republican Committee for American Action."

151. *NYT*, 13 February, 1950. For more on regional divisions within the GOP, see *NYT*, 15 January 1950. Of Republican division, Mayer argues that "to call it a sectional position would be an oversimplification" (*Republican Party*, 482–83).

152. *NYT*, 16 September 1950.

153. Ibid., 2 October 1950. Dewey even claimed some credit for Jackie Robinson signing for the Brooklyn Dodgers.

154. *CD*, 4 November 1950. White was also extremely frustrated by the failure of so many African Americans to exercise their right to vote. See "Memorandum from White to all Branch Officers," 14 March 1952, ibid., 530–31; and also "NAACP Primer for Political Action," NAACP, pt. 18, ser. C, reel 23, frames 522–25.

155. *CD*, 4 November 1950.

156. Ibid.

157. Patterson, *Mr. Republican*, 458. Patterson comments: "it was Taft's good fortune that he never had to face a truly formidable foe in Ohio" (ibid.).

158. *CD*, 18 November 1950.

159. *Crisis* 57 (December 1950): 714.

160. *NYT*, 28 November, 1950.

161. *CD*, 18 November 1950.

162. *NYT*, 9 December, 1950.

163. Ibid.

164. Memorandum from Clarence Mitchell to Walter White, 9 November 1950, NAACP, pt. 18, ser. B, reel 9, frame 450. For the association's perspective on the election, see memorandum from Edna B. Kerin to Gloster Current, 20 November 1950, NAACP, pt. 18, ser. C, reel 22, frame 3.

165. *Akron Beacon Journal*, 20 November 1952, ibid., pt. 18, ser. C, reel 18, frame 385.

166. *NYT*, 7 February 1951.

167. *Baltimore Afro-American*, 24 March 1951, NAACP, pt. 18, ser. C, reel 20, frame 451.

168. Ibid.

169. Press release from the *New Orleans Times-Picayune*, 27 April 1951, ibid., pt. 18, ser. C, reel 29, frames 386.

170. "Should the GOP Merge with the Dixiecrats?" *Collier's*, 28 July 1951, NAACP, pt. 18, ser. C, reel 29, frames 360–67. Case spoke at the NAACP convention in 1952 and announced the posthumous award of the annual Spingarn Medal to murdered Florida civil rights activist Harry T. Moore (speech by Clifford P. Case, to the 43rd Annual Convention of the NAACP, 27 June 1952, ibid., pt. 18, ser. B, reel 9, frames 653–56). The association later praised Case's appointment to the Ford Foundation's Fund for the Republic in 1953 (NAACP press release, 28 May 1953, ibid., 597).

171. *Collier's*, 28 July 1951, NAACP, pt. 18, ser. C, reel 29, frames 360–67.

172. *NYT*, 18 September 1951. The states represented included: Texas, Alabama, New York, New Jersey, Virginia, Nebraska, Minnesota, Maine, Pennsylvania, Oklahoma, Georgia, Tennessee, South Carolina, North Carolina, South Dakota, Wisconsin, and Florida (ibid.). The Committee to Explore Political Realignment soon appointed two cochairman, one Republican and one Democrat (ibid., 24 September 1951).

173. Ibid., 23 September 1951.

174. Ibid., 26 September 1951.

175. Ibid., 2 October 1951.

176. Ibid., 5 October 1951.

177. Ibid., 8 October 1951. Nixon's own propriety would, of course, be questioned during the 1952 campaign.

178. Ibid., 14 October 1951. For editorial comment on the Boyle-Gabrielson controversies, see ibid., 15 October 1951, and 28 October 1951.

179. Ibid., 21 October 1951.

180. Ibid., 8 November 1951.

181. Gabrielson, who had been linked at various times to Eisenhower, Taft, and Stassen, had declared his neutrality on the nomination.

182. *NYT*, 20 November 1951. At the University of Mississippi, most of the questions posed related to civil rights (although none were recorded by the *Times*).

183. Ibid., 10 December 1951.

184. The NAACP was testing the "separate but equal" mandate in the South on the basis of the discrepancy in funding for white and black schools and the knowledge that fulfilling its Constitutional responsibilities under *Plessy v. Ferguson* could bankrupt the region.

185. *NYT*, 10 November 1951.

186. For information on the NAACP's attempts to resist communist infiltration and avoid being labeled a Communist front organization, see Berg, *Ticket to Freedom*, 116–40; Jonas, *Republican Party*, 135–51; and Janken, *Biography of Walter White*, 319–23. Berg rightly praises the association for avoiding a witch hunt against members suspected of Communist sympathies while constantly reinforcing its anti-Communist credentials publicly. Throughout this period, the *Crisis* relentlessly reaffirmed the associa-

tion's opposition to communism. See, for example, editorial, *Crisis* 56 (March 1949): 72; Walter White, "The Negro and the Communists," ibid., 57 (August–September 1950): 502–6, 537–38; "Wilkins Denounced of Communists at the 1950 Convention, ibid., 57 (August–September 1950): 513; and Herbert Hill, "The Communist Party—Enemy of Negro Equality, ibid., 58 (June 1951): 365–67. In 1951, an amendment was adopted "restricting membership to those who support the principles and program of the NAACP," and "these principles include opposition to communist infiltration and control" (ibid., 58 [August–September 1951]: 476). This was reaffirmed in 1952, ibid., 59 (August–September 1952): 446.

Chapter 8. The Unfinished Business of America

1. *Crisis* 57 (December 1950): 685. For a diatribe against Taft, see *His Record Is Against Him: A Speaker's Handbook on Robert Alphonso Taft*, issued by the United Labor League of Ohio in 1950. This booklet attacks Taft's positions on most issues, including the FEPC, lynching, and the poll tax.

2. *Crisis* 57 (December 1950): 685. White complained to Perry Howard that Taft supporters from Ohio were using as campaign literature a *Crisis* editorial condemning the Democrats' failure on civil rights (White to Perry Howard, 19 October 1950, NAACP, pt. 18, ser. C, reel 29, frames 374–75). The letter was made public in a press release of the same date (NAACP, pt. 18, ser. C, reel 29, frame 376). Taft's reluctance to seek the nomination stemmed partially from his wife's poor health.

3. Smith, *Thomas E. Dewey*, 578.

4. Russell and McClellan, *Robert A. Taft*, 74. For further detail on Taft's standpoint, see Robert A. Taft, "What I Believe," *Collier's* 129, no. 15 (12 April 1952): 83, cited ibid.

5. *CD*, 9 February 1952.

6. *Crisis* 59 (March 1952): 171.

7. *CD*, 5 January 1952.

8. *NYT*, 28 June 1952.

9. Ibid., 28 January 1952. For further criticism, see Albert Barnett in *CD*, 26 April 1952.

10. *Crisis* 57 (December 1950): 685.

11. Ibid., 686. Moon was paying particular attention to Taft's comments in the campaign, especially in relation to segregated schools, states' rights against federal legislation, and the FEPC. By 1952, he wanted a "Taft folder" with all the senator's comments, and perhaps a press release with a selection of his pronouncements (memorandum, Moon to White, 3 March 1952, NAACP, pt. 18, ser. C, reel 23, frame 683).

12. *Crisis* 57 (December 1950): 686–87.

13. Ibid., 687. A good example of this came when he suggested "eating less and eating less extravagantly" when food prices soared (ibid., 690).

14. NAACP press release, 17 May 1952, NAACP, pt. 18, ser. C, reel 24, frame 529.

15. *Crisis* 57 (December 1950): 691.

16. *CD*, 5 April 1952.

17. *NYT*, 13 June 1952. For further detail on Taft's standpoint, see Taft, *Collier's*, April 1952, 83, cited in Russell and McClellan, *Robert A. Taft*, 74.

18. *CD*, 31 May 1952.

19. Smith, *Thomas E. Dewey*, 553; Halberstam, *The Fifties*, 4.

20. Smith gleans this information from Eisenhower's personal account of the meeting (*Thomas E. Dewey*, 554–55).

21. Ibid., 555.

22. Gould, *Grand Old Party*, 327; Smith, *Thomas E. Dewey*, 582.

23. *NYT*, 28 June 1952. For moves to draft Eisenhower, see Smith, *Thomas E. Dewey*, 577–84.

24. Brendon, *Ike*, 278.

25. Richardson, *Presidency of Eisenhower*, 105.

26. Michael S. Mayer, "Regardless of Station, Race or Calling: Eisenhower and Race," in Krieg, *Soldier, President, Statesman*, 34.

27. Brendon, *Ike*, 278.

28. Richardson, *Presidency of Eisenhower*, 106.

29. NAACP press release, 1 April 1948, NAACP, pt. 18, ser. B, reel 13, frame 865. Like many Americans, White admired Eisenhower's wartime contribution; in 1946, for example, he wrote to the general requesting an autographed picture (White to Eisenhower, 8 April 1946, NAACP, pt. 18, ser. B, reel 13, frame 807). Herbert Brownell visited Eisenhower when he was NATO commander and was surprised to hear that he was in favor of integration "in any area where the government properly belonged" and his view that military integration had worked well (Columbia University Oral History Project, interview with Herbert Brownell, 33, cited in Mayer, "Regardless of Station, Race or Calling," in Krieg, *Soldier, President, Statesman*, 36).

30. Excerpts from the Testimony of General Dwight D. Eisenhower, before the Committee on Armed Services, United States Senate, Friday April 2, 1948, vol., 2, Universal Military Training, 2591 to 96, NAACP, pt. 18, ser. B, reel 13, frames 868–70. See also Mayer, "Regardless of Station, Race or Calling," in Krieg, *Soldier, President, Statesman*, 34–35.

31. Memorandum, White to Moon and Wilkins, 8 April 1948, NAACP, pt. 18, ser. B, reel 13, frame 897. For Moon's reply, see memorandum, Moon to White, 6 April 1948, ibid., frame 898. The *New York Herald Tribune* column appeared before Eisenhower's testimony.

32. NAACP press release, 8 April 1948, ibid., frames 902–3.

33. Robert F. Burk, "Dwight D. Eisenhower and Civil Rights Conservatism," in Krieg, *Soldier, President, Statesman*, 52.

34. Morrow, *Four Years a Guinea Pig*, cited in M. Mayer, ibid., 35.

35. Robert F. Burk, "Dwight D. Eisenhower and Civil Rights Conservatism," in Krieg, *Soldier, President, Statesman*, 52. Morrow felt that Eisenhower "instinctively did the right thing" (Mayer, "Regardless of Station, Race or Calling," in Krieg, *Soldier, President, Statesman*, 36).

36. *NYT*, 26 September 1949. For more on Eisenhower's concerns, see Mayer, "Regardless of Station, Race or Calling," in Krieg, *Soldier, President, Statesman*, 36. Eisenhower was later questioned about the possibility of appointing Bunche to his cabinet

(*NYT,* 6 June 1952). Bunche would, however, endorse Stevenson later in the campaign (ibid., 6 September 1952).

37. *NYT,* 26 September 1949.

38. "Statement by Eisenhower on FEPC," undated, NAACP, pt. 18, ser. B, reel 14, frame 25.

39. Telegram, White to Eisenhower, 5 June 1952, ibid., frame 26. See also telegram from White to Eisenhower, 19 June 1952, ibid., frames 44–45. White forwarded the latter telegram to Ives, Rivers, Morse, Dewey, Case, Driscoll, Cabot Lodge, and James Duff. Driscoll replied, vowing to fight for a compulsory law to be included in the party's platform (Driscoll to White, 26 June 1952, ibid., 51–53).

40. Wilkins to White, 6 June 1952, ibid., 30.

41. *NYT,* 6 June 1952.

42. Ibid., 7 June 1952.

43. Ibid., 8 June 1952.

44. Ibid., 10 June 1952.

45. Ibid., 15 June 1952.

46. *CD,* 14 June 1952.

47. Ibid.

48. Ibid.

49. Ibid.

50. *NYT,* 30 June 1952.

51. *CD,* 5 July 1952.

52. Ibid., 19 and 26 April 1952.

53. Ibid., 3 May 1952. Oscar De Priest, another Republican African American stalwart, had died the previous year.

54. Ibid., 19 April 1952.

55. *Crisis* 59 (June–July 1952): 345.

56. *CD,* 7 June 1952.

57. "What the Negro Wants in 1952," NAACP, pt. 18, ser. C, reel 24, frames 284–88. See also NAACP press releases, 5 and 19 June 1952, ibid., frames 536, 540–41.

58. Ibid.

59. NAACP press release, 22 June 1952, ibid., 389–90.

60. "Elmo Roper, Speaking on the National Broadcasting Company, 22 June 1952," ibid., pt. 18, ser. C, reel 18, frames 395–98.

61. The NAACP's aim was to double the 1 million registered African American voters in the South by the time of the 1952 election ("NAACP Primer for Political Action," ibid., frames 522–25).

62. "Elmo Roper, Speaking on the National Broadcasting Company, 22 June 1952," ibid., 395–98.

63. Ibid.

64. Ibid.

65. *NYT,* 13 July 1952. For more background on the convention, see Krock, "In the Nation," *NYT,* 17 July 1952; and Gould, *Grand Old Party,* 329–30.

66. For the machinations surrounding the credentials of the Texas delegation, see Smith, *Thomas E. Dewey*, 586–87; and Patterson, *Mr. Republican*, 538–45.

67. *NYT*, 4 July 1952.

68. *CD*, 12 July 1952.

69. *NYT*, 30 June 1952.

70. Ibid., 13 July 1952.

71. White had asked Gabrielson for a full day for the NAACP and fifty-one other national organizations, representing 35 million Americans, in front of the Republican Platform Committee, but they were allowed only three hours (telegram from White to Gabrielson, 6 May 1952, NAACP, pt. 18, ser. C, reel 29, frame 398). The *New York Times* viewed the hearings before the subcommittee on civil rights as "one of the more important" of the convention (2 July 1952). The association had set up a civil rights headquarters at Roosevelt College for the duration of the Republican and Democratic conventions (NAACP press release, 2 July 1952, NAACP, pt. 18, ser. C, reel 29, frame 412).

72. *NYT*, 12 June 1952.

73. Ibid., 4 July 1952. There were thirty-nine African American delegates from seventeen states, including ten border and southern states, the Virgin Islands, and Washington, D.C., at the Republican convention, and most were backing Taft (*CD*, 21 June 1952).

74. Richard Norton Smith, interview with Cabot Lodge, 1980, cited in Smith, *Thomas E. Dewey*, 589. Smith refers to the two rebellious Harlem delegates without naming them, one—presumably Burton as he remained at the convention—had, as noted, his livelihood threatened, while the other, presumably Hill, had to return home due to the death of his daughter. Dewey exerted this kind of extreme pressure, threatening the removal of patronage jobs, on other members of the New York delegation (ibid., 590).

75. *NYT*, 9 July 1952.

76. Ibid..

77. Ibid., 1 and 10 July 1952.

78. Ibid., 10 July 1952.

79. Ibid., 19 July 1952. For the text of the Republican civil rights plank, see *CD*, 12 July 1952; and *Crisis* 59 (October 1952): 480–81.

80. *NYT*, 11 July 1952. See also *CD*, 12 July 1952. For a brief account of Driscoll's efforts in securing civil rights legislation in New Jersey, see *NYT*, 6 April 1949.

81. *CD*, 12 July 1952.

82. *NYT*, 11 and 13 July 1952.

83. Ibid., 29 July 1952.

84. Ibid.. Perry Howard, attending his twenty-eighth convention since 1912, had earlier made the headlines by making a "stump speech" lying down. He was resting in his hotel room to conserve energy for the convention. Supporting Taft, he declared that the Ohioan "has a colossal mentality with the suavity of a modest maiden" (ibid., 4 July 1952).

85. *CD*, 2 August 1952. Burton had earlier written to Brownell asking that Reynolds be appointed to head the GOP's Colored Voters Division.

86. Ibid.

87. Ibid., 19 July 1952.

88. Ibid., 12 July 1952.

89. *CD*, 19 July 1952.

90. Ibid.

91. McCoy and Ruetten, *Quest and Response*, 320.

92. *Crisis* 59 (August–September 1952): 412.

93. NAACP press release, 10 July 1952, NAACP, pt. 18, ser. C, reel 29, frames 417–18.

94. *CD*, 2 August 1952.

95. Roderick Stevens to Vandenberg, 29 July 1952, NAACP, pt. 18, ser. B, reel 14, frames 63–64. He enclosed a column by Krock on the issue.

96. *NYT*, 12 and 13 July 1952. For a biography of Summerfield, see ibid., 26 November 1952.

97. Ibid., 13 July 1952.

98. Ibid.

99. According to Patterson, Taft was apparently willing to consider the vice-presidential slot on the ticket, but Eisenhower's preference was for Knowland, Driscoll, or Nixon (*Mr. Republican*, 564–65). Dewey's choice was Nixon (Smith, *Thomas E. Dewey*, 582).

100. McCoy and Ruetten, *Quest and Response*, 314.

101. *NYT*, 31 March 1952.

102. According to Stuart Brown, Truman actually offered Stevenson the nomination and his endorsement in January 1952 (*Adlai Stevenson*, 75).

103. McCoy and Ruetten, *Quest and Response*, 316.

104. *CD*, 15 March 1952.

105. Ibid., 24 May 1952.

106. Ibid., 12 April 1952.

107. Ibid., 24 May 1952.

108. Ibid.

109. McCoy and Ruetten, *Quest and Response*, 322. For the text of Truman's Howard University speech, see *NYT*, 14 June 1952; and *CD*, 21 June 1952. The *New York Times* suggested that Truman "was not in a fighting mood" during the speech (14 June 1952).

110. *CD*, 19 July 1952. For the NAACP's efforts to influence the convention, see *NYT*, 20 July 1952; and NAACP press release, 17 July 1952, NAACP, pt. 18, ser. C, reel 24, frame 550.

111. McCoy and Ruetten, *Quest and Response*, 323.

112. "Statement by Walter White, Leadership Conference on Civil Rights and Executive Secretary of the NAACP, 24 July 1952," NAACP, pt. 18, ser. C, reel 18, frame 413.

113. Ibid. For other reaction to the plank, see "Democratic Plank Hailed as Civil Rights Victory" NAACP press release, 24 July 1952, NAACP, pt. 18, ser. C, reel 24, frame 552. For the text of the plank, see *NYT*, 24 July 1952. White expressed similar sentiments of William Dawson but privately voiced serious concern about the nomination

of Sparkman (White to William Dawson, 31 July 1952, NAACP, pt. 18, ser. C, reel 23, frame 795).

114. McCoy and Ruetten, *Quest and Response*, 325.

115. *NYT*, 25 July 1952.

116. Statement by White, 26 July 1952, NAACP, pt. 18, ser. C, reel 18, frame 415; also reported in *NYT*, 27 July 1952.

117. *NYT*, 3 August 1952.

118. *CD*, 2 August 1952.

119. Ibid., 9 August 1952 Sparkman asked Clarence Mitchell and the NAACP for some leeway on civil rights, which he claimed to support (Mitchell to White, 1 August 1952, cited in Berg, *Ticket to Freedom*, 192).

120. *Crisis* 59 (August–September 1952): 412. For a meeting between White and Stevenson, where the Democratic candidate was again notably vague, see NAACP press release, 14 August 1952, NAACP, pt. 18, ser. C, reel 24, frames 557–58.

121. *NYT*, 10 August 1952. The eight states were New York, Pennsylvania, New Jersey, Michigan, Indiana, Connecticut, Delaware, and Maryland. The other three of these eleven marginal states were Ohio, California, and Illinois, the states in which the African American vote had delivered victory to Truman in 1948.

122. Ibid.

123. Ibid.

124. Ibid.

125. Ibid., 4 August 1952. Members of the group included: Ives, Driscoll, Saltonstall, Case, Javits, Hugh D. Scott (Pennsylvania), and Burton and Hill from Harlem. See also McCoy and Ruetten, *Quest and Response*, 325.

126. *NYT*, 6 August 1952.

127. Ibid., 17 August 1952.

128. Ibid., 5 August 1952. See also NAACP, pt. 18, ser. B, reel 14, frame 148.

129. *CD*, 23 August 1952, 21.

130. Ibid.

131. Ibid., 6 September 1952.

132. McCoy and Ruetten, *Quest and Response*, 326.

133. *Look*, 23 September 1952, NAACP, pt. 18, ser. B, reel 17, frames 616–23.

134. *NYT*, 20 August 1952.

135. *Crisis*, 59 (October 1952): 539.

136. *NYT*, 3 October 1952. This speech was broadcast on radio as well. Ives also attacked Sparkman (ibid.).

137. Ibid., 9 October 1952. Dewey restated his "white supremacy" claims on 11 October (ibid., 12 October 1952).

138. Ibid., 4 October 1952.

139. Ibid., 8 October 1952.

140. Research Division, RNC, "The Civil Rights Voting Record of Republicans and Democrats in the Senate and House of Representatives, 1933–1952," NAACP, pt. 18, ser. C, reel 29, frame 59.

141. *NYT*, 27 August 1952. Ives also went out of his way to praise Taft for "his sports-

manship and party loyalty" (ibid.). As far as the *Chicago Defender* was concerned, Ives had confirmed that he had failed to persuade Eisenhower about the need for an FEPC law (6 September 1952).

142. *NYT*, 9 October 1952.

143. Ibid., 25 October 1952.

144. Ibid., 6 September 1952, citing *U.S. News and World Report*.

145. Sherman Adams telegraphed Wilkins on behalf of Eisenhower, to arrange a meeting with the NAACP at the end of August. For details of the arrangements for the meeting, see telegram, Wilkins to Eisenhower, 6 August 1952, NAACP, pt. 18, ser. B, reel 14, frame 69; telegram Sherman Adams to Roy Wilkins, 10 August 1952, ibid., frame 73; and William L. Pfeiffer to Wilkins, 22 August 1952, ibid., frame 74. Spaulding was a Philadelphia attorney

146. NAACP press release, 28 August 1952, ibid., pt. 18, ser. C, reel 24, frame 561–63.

147. Wilkins and Mathews, *Standing Fast*, 212. "Eisenhower was a fine general and a good and decent man," Wilkins continued, "but if he had fought World War Two the way he fought for civil rights, we would all be speaking German today" (ibid., 222). For further information about the meeting, including the claim that the meeting lasted forty-five minutes, see NAACP press release, 28 August 1952, NAACP, pt. 18, ser. C, reel 24, frames 561–63.

148. Quotations from *Crisis* 59 (August–September 1952): 412; and Parmet, *Eisenhower*, 438, respectively. See also O'Reilly, "Racial Integration," 110.

149. McCoy and Ruetten, *Quest and Response*, 326.

150. *NYT*, 30 August 1952.

151. Ibid., 4 September 1952. Eisenhower spoke to around one hundred thousand people on this tour. An ulterior motive of the trip was to force the Democrats to campaign in the region more than they had wanted to and thus divert their resources from key northern states (ibid.).

152. Ibid., 19 September 1952.

153. *NYT*, 1 October 1952. The *New York Times* reported the crowd's silence. Clarence Mitchell soon demanded to know whether Eisenhower had made a "secret deal" with Byrnes on civil rights (13 October 1952). For the full text of the speech, see ibid., 1 October 1952, or "Text of the Address by Dwight D. Eisenhower, Republican Nominee for President, Delivered at Columbia, South Carolina, Tuesday Afternoon, September 30, 1952," NAACP, pt. 18, ser. B, reel 14, frames 105–10.

154. McCoy and Ruetten, *Quest and Response*, 327.

155. Quotations from the *Greenville Piedmont*, 1 October 1952; and *Greenville News*, 21 October 1952, NAACP, pt. 18, ser. B, reel 14, frames 88. Leaflets dropped from planes in North Carolina warned of "Negro bosses" if Stevenson were elected, while stressing that Eisenhower was against the FEPC (*CD*, 22 November 1952).

156. Telegram from White to Eisenhower, 6 October 1952, NAACP, pt. 18, ser. B, reel 14, frame 91.

157. Sherman Adams to White, 7 October 1952, ibid., frame 92.

158. NAACP press release, 9 October 1952, ibid., frame 93.

159. Telegram from White to Adams, 14 October 1952, ibid., 97.

160. "Memorandum to the Board of Directors from Roy Wilkins, 8 September 1952. Re: Interviews with Republican and Democratic Nominees for President," ibid., 81.

161. Parmet, *Eisenhower*, 438.

162. "Draft Resolution for Consideration of Board of Directors at Its Meeting, September 8 1952," NAACP, pt. 18, ser. C, reel 22, frame 40.

163. *Crisis* 59 (October 1952): 518; also reported in *NYT*, 10 September 1952. White moved swiftly to reassure the New York NAACP that this was not an endorsement of Stevenson (telegram from White to the New York NAACP, 11 September 1952, NAACP, pt. 18, ser. C, reel 22, frames 45–46). White also wanted the Associated Press to correct the implication that the association was endorsing the GOP (telegram from White to the Associated Press, 12 September 1952, ibid., frame 44).

164. *NYT*, 14 September 1952. Nixon also urged an end to the poll tax while speaking in Virginia (ibid., 3 October 1952).

165. David E. Langley to Wilkins, 11 September 1952, NAACP pt. 18, ser. C, reel 22, frames 57–58.

166. Wilkins to David E. Langley, 15 September 1952, ibid., frames 54–55.

167. Wilkins to Clarence Mitchell, 24 September 1952, ibid., frame 61. For the association's policy and attempts to maintain its nonpartisanship, see "Memorandum from White to all Branch Officers," 14 March 1952, NAACP, pt. 18, ser. C, reel 23, frames 530–31.

168. "Excerpts from Comments by Walter White, Executive Secretary, National Association for the Advancement of Colored People, Annual Ohio State Conference of Branches, Columbus, Ohio, 21 September 1952," ibid., frames 615–18.

169. Ibid.

170. *CD*, 27 September 1952. The eight key states were: Illinois, New York, Pennsylvania, Ohio, Massachusetts, California, Michigan and Texas; the black vote was also considered an extremely important factor in New Jersey, Connecticut, Indiana, Missouri, Delaware, Maryland, Kentucky, West Virginia, and Kansas.

171. *Look*, 23 September 1952, NAACP, pt. 18, ser. B, reel 17, frames 616–23.

172. Ibid. For a reminder of White's earlier praise of the Democratic platform, see "Statement by Walter White, Leadership Conference on Civil Rights and Executive Secretary of the NAACP, 24 July 1952," ibid., pt. 18, ser. C, reel 18, frame 413 (see also page 343 and note 112).

173. *Look*, 23 September 1952, ibid., pt. 18, ser. B, reel 17, frames 616–23.

174. Ibid. For other comment on African Americans and the election, see the special edition of the *Nation*, 27 September 1952. This included an editorial entitled "The Southern Negro: 1952"; "The Negro Vote in the South: 1952," by Henry Lee Moon; "The Negro's Growing Political Power," by R. H. Brisbane; "Democrats Versus Dixiecrats," by Clarence Mitchell; and "Ah, Gettysburg, Where Is Thy Sting?" by Tarleton Collier (*Nation*, 27 September 1952, 243–73, NAACP, pt. 18, ser. B, reel 17, frames 632–59).

175. Daisy Lampkin to White, 10 September 1952, NAACP, pt. 18, ser. C, reel 22, frames 49–50. For the full article, see "NAACP Backs Stevenson," *Pittsburgh Post Gazette*, 10 September 1952, ibid., frame 51.

176. Daisy Lampkin, on behalf of the Republican National Committee, 23 October 1952, ibid., pt. 18, ser. C, reel 29, frames 426–27. See also undated clipping from the *Pittsburgh Courier*, ibid., pt. 18, ser. C, reel 23, frame 858. Lampkin, like many other Republicans, noted Alabama's "white supremacy" ballot when referring to Sparkman.

177. James P. Spencer to White, 27 October 1952, ibid., frame 918.

178. Undated telegram, White to Lampkin, ibid., frame, 919. Lampkin to White, 29 October 1952, ibid., frames 920–21.

179. Telegram, White to Lampkin, 30 October 1952, ibid., frame 924; White to Lampkin, 30 October 1952, ibid., frame 925. Lampkin was field secretary from 1930 to 1948.

180. Telegram, White to Arthur Summerfield, 31 October 1952, ibid., pt. 18, ser. C, reel 29, frame 432; see also NAACP press release, 31 October 1952, ibid., pt. 18, ser. C, reel 24, frame 605. White also recognized that there was crossover between the mailing lists of the association and the *Courier*.

181. Pearson Broadcast, 12 October 1952, ibid., pt. 18, ser. C, reel 29, frame 420. See also *CD*, 1 November 1952.

182. McCoy and Ruetten, *Quest and Response*, 327–28. A small but significant change took place when, on 29 October in Chicago, Truman started talking about "integration" rather than "desegregation" (ibid.). For additional detail on the whistle stop tour, see Hamby, *Beyond the New Deal*, 501.

183. *NYT*, 12 October 1952.

184. Ibid., 12 October 1952. For the full text of Truman's Harlem speech, see ibid. Truman moderated his tone slightly in Brooklyn, seeing civil rights as an issue that could bring the GOP back to its "great—but almost forgotten—tradition of freedom and human rights." Instead, however, Eisenhower preferred "crass equivocations" and the "contributions of Dixiecrat millionaires" (ibid., 19 October 1952).

185. *NYT*, 12 October 1952.

186. Ibid., 15 October 1952.

187. Ibid., 12 October 1952.

188. Hamby, *Beyond the New Deal*, 498.

189. Martin, *Stevenson of Illinois*, 720–21.

190. *NYT*, 10 and 17 October 1952.

191. Ibid., 18 October 1952. In remarks that were not broadcast, Nixon stated that the fight against discrimination had to be intensified because "we can still lose the struggle with worldwide Communism for men's minds, hearts and souls" (ibid., 20 October 1952).

192. Ibid., 24 October 1952.

193. Kansas City *Call*, 10 October 1951, cited in McCoy and Ruetten, *Quest and Response*, 327. For the full text of Eisenhower's speech, see *NYT*, 26 October 1952.

194. Ibid., 25 and 26 October 1952.

195. Ibid., 26 October 1952. Dewey spoke briefly.

196. Ibid. The *Chicago Defender* claimed that Eisenhower "drew a chilly response" from the mere five thousand who showed up (1 November 1952).

197. *NYT*, 28 October 1952. A mention of Sparkman elicited some boos from the crowd.

198. Ibid., 31 October 1952.

199. *Look*, 23 September 1952, NAACP, pt. 18, ser. B, reel 17, frames 616–23.

200. *NYT*, 19 September 1952. Morse also condemned the "Jekyll and Hyde" Republican platform.

201. Patterson, *Mr. Republican*, 578. Taft claimed to have written most of the statement that he and Eisenhower issued (ibid, 577). Stevenson noted sardonically that Taft had "lost the nomination, but won the candidate" (*NYT*, 28 October 1952). Indeed, Patterson notes that Taft "carried on as if he were the nominee" and continued to insist that he could have won (*Mr. Republican*, 580). Taft also insisted that there be no cabinet post for Dewey, something Eisenhower was not keen on anyway (Smith, *Thomas E. Dewey*, 599, 605).

202. *NYT*, 19 September 1952.

203. Ibid., 25 October 1952.

204. "The 1952 Elections, A Statistical Analysis: A Statistical Analysis of the 1952 Presidential, Senatorial, Congressional and Gubernatorial Elections with Supporting Tables," Prepared by the Research Staff, Republican National Committee, 1626 Eye St., N.W., Washington 6, D.C., October 1953, Homer H. Gruenther Records, 1953–60, box 7, "The 1952 Elections—A Statistical Analysis (Booklet)" (henceforth "The 1952 Elections, A Statistical Analysis," RNC, October 1953), 1.

205. Elmo Roper to White, 12 November 1952, NAACP, pt. 18, ser. C, reel 23, frames 996–97.

206. Ibid.

207. *Crisis* 59 (December 1952): 616.

208. "Supplement to Survey of the Negro Vote in the 1952 Presidential Election," NAACP, pt. 18, ser. B, reel 17, frames 652–56. For a comprehensive account of African American voting trends, see ibid.; and also Henry Lee Moon, "The Southern Negro Vote, 1943–1953," paper presented at Tenth Annual Institute of Race Relations, Fisk University, Nashville, Tenn., 10 July 1953, 14, NAACP, pt. 18, ser. B, reel 17, frame 686. Moon reported in December 1952 that Stevenson had carried 99 percent of the vote in Darlington, South Carolina (*Crisis* 59 [December 1952]: 616).

209. NAACP press release, 6 November 1952, NAACP, pt. 18, ser. C, reel 24, frame 631. The cities surveyed were: New York, Chicago, Philadelphia, Los Angeles, Detroit, Houston, Miami, Newark, Memphis, Pittsburgh, Richmond, Durham, and Montclair, New Jersey. No African American incumbent was defeated in the election (*CD*, 15 November 1952). For further analysis, see ibid., 8 November 1952.

210. *Crisis* 59 (December 1952): 616.

211. "The 1952 Elections, A Statistical Analysis," RNC, October 1953, 30.

212. Ibid., 1. Southern governors believed that Eisenhower's victory would not lead to a two-party South (*NYT*, 17 November 1952).

213. "The 1952 Elections, A Statistical Analysis," RNC, October 1953, 2.

214. Archibald J. Carey to Wilkins, 6 November 1952, NAACP pt. 18, ser. C, reel 29, frames 434–35. Carey ended the letter with, "I still love you and tell Walt and everybody 'howdy.'"

215. Wilkins to Carey, 10 November 1952, NAACP, pt. 18, ser. C, reel 29, frames 436–38. Wilkins wrote that "the most tragic thing that could happen to this country would be to have Richard M. Nixon as president."

216. "The 1952 Elections, A Statistical Analysis," RNC, October 1953, 2.

217. Ibid., 2–3.

218. Ibid., 3.

219. *Crisis* 59 (December 1952): 617.

220. Ibid., 646.

221. Ibid.

222. NAACP press release, 13 November 1952, NAACP, pt. 18, ser. C, reel 24, frames 632–33. See also *Crisis* 59 (December 1952): 654, and "Suggested Draft of Statement on the Election," undated, NAACP, pt. 18, ser. B, reel 14, frame 122.

223. Ibid.

224. *CD*, 22 November 1952, 11. Du Bois had, of course, famously urged African Americans to "close ranks" during the Great War and forget their "special grievances" until the conflict's conclusion.

225. NAACP press release, 28 November 1952, NAACP, pt. 18, ser. C, reel 24, frame 503.

226. *CD*, 13 December 1952. Bunche, for whom Eisenhower had "expressed admiration," was invited to but unable to attend the meeting.

227. Ibid.

228. NAACP press release, 22 January 1953, NAACP, pt. 18, ser. B, reel 14, frame 154.

229. "Report of the Secretary for the Month of November 1952," ibid., pt. 18, ser. C, reel 24, frame 609.

230. *NYT*, 23 December 1952. Eisenhower told Edgar Brown that he was keen to appoint a suitably qualified African American to his cabinet (*CD*, 15 November 1952).

231. *CD*, 6 December 1952.

232. Wilkins to Arthur M. Carter, 16 December 1952, NAACP, pt. 18, ser. B, reel 14, frame 137. See also Carter to Wilkins, 5 December 1952, ibid., frame 139.

Sources

Primary Sources

PAPERS AND COLLECTIONS

Akerson, George B. Papers. Herbert Hoover Library, West Branch, Iowa.

Congressional Record, 1945–48.

Dewey, Thomas E. Papers. Rush Rhees Library, University of Rochester, New York.

Hoover, Herbert. Papers. Herbert Hoover Library, West Branch, Iowa.

Landon, Alfred M. Papers. Kansas State Historical Society, Topeka.

NAACP Papers. Cambridge University.

Republican Party Papers. Part I: Meetings of the Republican National Committee, 1911–1980.

Republican Party Papers. Part II: Reports and Memoranda of the Research Division of the Headquarters of the Republican National Committee, 1938–1980. Edited by William Leuchtenberg (general editor) and Paul L. Kesaris (editor). Maryland: University Publications of America, 1986.

Roosevelt, Eleanor. Papers. Roosevelt Study Center, Middelburg, the Netherlands.

Roosevelt, Franklin. Papers. Roosevelt Study Center, Middelburg, the Netherlands.

Strauss, Lewis L. Papers. Herbert Hoover Library, West Branch, Iowa.

Willkie, Wendell L. Papers. Lilly Library, University of Indiana, Bloomington.

JOURNALS AND NEWSPAPERS

Chicago Defender, 1948–52

Crisis, journal of the NAACP, 1928–52

Fortune, 1936 and 1940

New Republic, 1936 and 1940

New York Times, 1936–52

Opportunity, journal of the National Urban League, 1932–48

Topeka and Kansas City Plaindealer, 1932–48

Secondary Sources

Abels, Jules. 1959. *Out of the Jaws of Victory*. New York: Holt, Rinehart and Winston.

Ambrose, Stephen. 1984. *Eisenhower, 1890–1952*. London, Boston, and Sydney: George Allen and Unwin.

Badger, Anthony J. 1989. *The New Deal: The Depression Years, 1933–1940*. London: Macmillan.

Bain, Richard C. 1960. *Convention Decisions and Voting Records*. Washington, D.C.: Brookings Institution.

Barnard, Ellsworth. 1966. *Wendell Willkie: Fighter for Freedom.* Marquette: Northern Michigan University Press.

Barnes, Joseph. 1952. *Willkie.* New York: Simon and Schuster.

Benson, Edward G., and Paul Perry. "Analysis of Democratic-Republican Strength by Population Groups." *Public Opinion Quarterly* (September 1940): 465–473.

Berg, Manfred. 2005. *"The Ticket to Freedom:" The NAACP and the Struggle for Black Political Integration.* Gainesville: University Press of Florida.

Berman, William C. 1970. *The Politics of Civil Rights in the Truman Administration.* Columbus: Ohio State University Press.

Bernstein, Barton J. 1970. *Politics and Policies of the Truman Administration.* Chicago: Quadrangle Books.

Beyer, Barry K. 1979. *Thomas E. Dewey, 1937–1947: A Study in Political Leadership.* New York and London: Garland.

Billington, Monroe. 1973. "Civil Rights, President Truman and the South." *Journal of Negro History* 58, no. 2 (April): 127–39.

Blaustein, A. P., and R. L. Zangrando. 1968; repr., 1991. *Civil Rights and African-Americans: A Documentary History.* Evanston, Ill.: Northwestern University Press.

Blum, John Morton. 1976. *V Was for Victory: Politics and American Culture During World War II.* New York and London: Harcourt Brace Jovanovich.

Bone, Hugh A. 1949. *American Politics and the Party System.* New York, Toronto, and London: McGraw-Hill.

———. 1958; repr., 1968. *Party Committees and National Politics.* Seattle and London: University of Washington Press.

Brendon, Piers. 1987. *Ike: The Life and Times of Dwight D. Eisenhower.* London: Secker and Warburg.

Brewer, W. M. 1953. "Robert R. Church." *Journal of Negro History* 38, no. 2 (April): 249–51.

Broderick, Francis L., and August Meier, eds. 1965. *Negro Protest Thought in the Twentieth Century.* Indianapolis, New York, and Kansas City: Bobbs-Merrill.

Brogan, D. W. 1937. "The Future of the Republican Party." *Political Quarterly,* 8, issue 2, (April–June): 180–93.

Brown, Stuart Gerry. 1960. "Civil Rights and National Leadership: Eisenhower and Stevenson in the 1950s." *Ethics* 70, no. 2 (January): 118–34.

———. 1965. *Adlai Stevenson, A Short Biography: The Conscience of the Country.* Woodbury, N.Y.: Barron's Woodbury Press.

Brownell, Herbert, with John Burke. 1983. *Advising Ike: The Memoirs of Herbert Brownell.* Lawrence: University Press of Kansas.

Bruce, Harold R. 1952. "Racial Religious and Sectional Interests in the 1952 Election." *Annals of the American Academy of Political and Social Science* 283 (September): 141–47

Buchanan, A. Russell. 1977. *Black Americans in World War II.* Santa Barbara, Calif., and Oxford, England: Clio Books.

Bunche, Ralph J. 1973. *The Political Status of Negroes in the Age of FDR.* Chicago and London: University of Chicago Press.

Buni, Andrew. 1974. *Robert L. Vann of the Pittsburgh Courier: Politics and Black Journalism.* Pittsburgh: University of Pittsburgh Press.

Burdette, Franklin. 1972. *The Republican Party: A Short History.* Princeton, N.J.: D. Van Nostrand.

Burk, Robert F. 1984. *The Eisenhower Administration and Black Civil Rights.* Knoxville: University of Tennessee Press.

———. 1986. *Dwight D. Eisenhower: Hero and Politician.* Boston: Twayne.

Capeci, Dominic J., Jr., and Martha Wilkerson. 1991. *Layered Violence: The Detroit Rioters of 1943.* Jackson and London: University of Mississippi Press.

Carmines, Edward G., and James A. Stimson. 1989. *Issue Evolution: Race and the Transformation of American Politics.* Princeton, N.J.: Princeton University Press.

Casey, Ralph D. 1937. "Republican Propaganda in the 1936 Campaign." *Public Opinion Quarterly* 1, no. 2, (April): 27–44.

Cashman, Sean Dennis. 1989. *America in the Twenties and Thirties: The Olympian Age of Franklin Delano Roosevelt.* New York and London: New York University Press.

———. 1991. *African Americans and the Quest for Civil Rights.* New York and London: New York University Press.

Chafe, William H., Raymond Gavins, and Robert Korstad, eds. 2001. *Remembering Jim Crow: African Americans Tell about Life in the Segregated South.* New York: New Press.

Cochran, Bert. 1967. *Adlai Stevenson: Patrician among Politicians.* New York: Funk and Wagnalls.

Cook, Robert R. 1998. *Sweet Land of Liberty? The African-American Struggle for Civil Rights in the Twentieth Century.* London and New York: Longman.

Cotter, Cornelius, and Bernard Hennessy. 1964. *Politics without Power: The National Party Committees.* New York: Atherton Press.

Cox, Oliver C. 1951. "The Programs of Negro Civil Rights Organizations." *Journal of Negro Education* 20, no. 3 (Summer): 354–66.

Dalfiume, Richard. 1968. "The Forgotten Years of the Negro Revolution." *Journal of American History* 55, no. 1 (June): 90–106.

———. 1969. "Military Desegregation and the 1940 Presidential Election." *Phylon* 30, no. 1 (1st quarter, 1969): 42–55.

Daniel, Pete. 1986. *Standing at the Crossroads: Southern Life Since 1900.* New York: Hill and Wang.

———. 2000. *Lost Revolutions: The South in the 1950s.* Washington, D.C. Chapel Hill and London: University of North Carolina Press for the Smithsonian National Museum of American History.

Darilek, Richard E. 1972. *A Loyal Opposition in Time of War: The Republican Party and the Politics of Foreign Policy from Pearl Harbor to Yalta.* Contributions in American History, Number 49. Westport, Ct., and London: Greenwood Press.

David, Paul T., Ralph M. Goldman, and Richard C. Bain. 1960. *The Politics of National Party Conventions.* Washington, D.C.: Brookings Institution.

Day, David S. 1980. "Herbert Hoover and Racial Politics: The De Priest Incident." *Journal of Negro History* 65, no.1 (Winter): 6–17.

Dillon, Mary E. 1952. *Wendell L. Willkie*. Philadelphia and New York: Lippincott.

Divine, Robert A. 1971. *Second Chance: The Triumph of Internationalism in America During World War II*. New York: Atheneum.

Donaldson, Gary A. 1999. *Truman Defeats Dewey*. Lexington: University Press of Kentucky.

Donovan, Robert J. 1982. *Tumultuous Years: The Presidency of Harry S. Truman, 1949–1953*. Columbia and London: University of Missouri Press.

Downes, Randolph C. 1966. "Negro Rights and the White Backlash in the Campaign of 1920," *Ohio History* 75 (Summer): 85–107.

———. 1970. *The Rise of Warren Gameliel Harding, 1865–1920*. Columbus: Ohio State University Press.

Dray, Philip. 2003. *At the Hands of Persons Unknown: The Lynching of Black America*. New York: Modern Library.

Evjen, Henry O. 1952. "The Willkie Campaign: An Unfortunate Chapter in Republican Leadership." *Journal of Politics* 14, no. 2 (May): 241–56.

Fausold, Martin L. 1985. *The Presidency of Herbert C. Hoover*. Lawrence: University Press of Kansas.

Finkle, Lee. 1973. "The Conservative Aims of Militant Rhetoric: Black Protest during World War II." *Journal of American History* 60, no.3 (December): 692–713.

Fuess, Claude M. 1939; repr. 1965. *Calvin Coolidge: The Man from Vermont*. Westport, Ct.: Greenwood Press.

Garcia, George F. 1972. "Herbert Hoover's Southern Strategy and the Black Reaction." Master's thesis, University of Iowa.

———. 1979. "Herbert Hoover and the Issue of Race." *Annals of Iowa*, 44, no.7 (Winter): 507–15.

Gavins, Raymond. 1977. *The Perils and Prospects of Southern Black Leadership: Gordon Blaine Hancock, 1884–1970*. Durham, N.C.: Duke University Press.

Goings, Kenneth W. 1990. *"The NAACP Comes of Age" The Defeat of Judge John J. Parker*. Bloomington and Indianapolis: Indiana University Press.

Goodwin, E. Marvin. 1990. *Black Migration in America from 1915 to 1960: An Uneasy Exodus*. Studies in Twentieth-Century American History, vol. 3. Lewiston, Queenston, and Lampeter: Edwin Mellen Press.

Gosnell, Harold Foote. 1935; repr. 1967. *Negro Politicians: The Rise of Negro Politics in Chicago*. Chicago and London: University of Chicago Press.

———. 1980. *Truman's Crises: A Political Biography of Harry S. Truman*. Westport, Ct., and London: Greenwood Press.

Gould, Lewis L. 2003. *Grand Old Party: A History of the Republicans*. New York: Random House.

Halberstam, David. 1993. *The Fifties*. New York: Villard Books.

Hamby, Alonzo L. 1973. *Beyond the New Deal: Harry S. Truman and American Liberalism*. New York and London: Columbia University Press.

———. 1992. *Liberalism and Its Challengers: From FDR to Bush*. 2nd ed. New York and Oxford: Oxford University Press.

Handlin, Oscar. 1958. *Al Smith and His America*. Boston and Toronto: Little, Brown.

Harnsberger, Caroline. 1952. *A Man of Courage: Robert A. Taft*. Chicago, Toronto, and New York: Wilcox and Follett.

Harrell, James A. 1968. "Negro Leadership in the Election Year 1936." *Journal of Southern History* 34, no.4 (August): 546–64.

Hart, George L. 1936. *Official Report of the Proceedings of the Twenty-first Republican National Convention*. New York: Tenny Press.

———. 1940. *Official Report of the Proceedings of the Twenty-second Republican National Convention*. Washington D.C.: Judd and Detweiler.

Hicks, John D. 1960. *Republican Ascendancy 1921–1933*. London: Hamish Hamilton.

Hodgson, Godfrey. 1990. *The Colonel: The Life and Wars of Henry Stimson, 1867–1950*. New York: Knopf.

Hoover, Herbert. 1952. *The Memoirs of Herbert Hoover: The Cabinet and the Presidency, 1920–1933*. London: Hollis and Carter.

Hughes, Langston. 1962. *Fight For Freedom: The Story of the NAACP*. New York. Norton.

Jack, Robert L. 1943. *History of the National Association for the Advancement of Colored People*. Boston: Meador.

Janken, Kenneth Robert. 2003. *White: The Biography of Walter White, Mr. NAACP*. New York: New Press.

Javits, Jacob K. 1964. *Order of Battle: A Republican's Call to Reason*. New York: Atheneum.

———, with Rafael Steinberg. 1981. *Javits: The Autobiography of a Public Man*. Boston: Houghton, Mifflin.

Johnson, Donald Bruce. 1960. *The Republican Party and Wendell Willkie*. Urbana: University of Illinois Press.

Johnson, Donald Bruce, and Kirk H. Porter. 1973. *National Party Platforms*. 5th ed. Urbana: University of Illinois Press.

Jonas, Gilbert. 2005. *Freedom's Sword: The NAACP and the Struggle against Racism in America, 1909–1969*. New York and London: Routledge.

Jones, Charles O. 1965. *The Republican Party in American Politics*. New York: Macmillan; London: Macmillan/Collier.

Josephson, Matthew, and Hannah Josephson. 1969. *Al Smith: Hero of the Cities*. London: Thames and Hudson.

Joyner, Conrad. 1963. *The Republican Dilemma*. Tucson: University of Arizona Press.

Karabell, Zachary. 2000. *The Last Campaign: How Harry Truman Won the 1948 Election*. New York: Knopf.

Katcher, Leo. 1967. *Earl Warren: A Political Biography*. New York and London: McGraw-Hill.

Kellogg, Charles Flint. 1967. *NAACP: A History of the National Association for the Advancement of Colored People*. Vol. 1, *1909–1920*. Baltimore: Johns Hopkins University Press.

Kenneally, James J. 1993. "Black Republicans during the New Deal: The Role of Joseph W. Martin, Jr." *Review of Politics*, 55, no. 1 (Winter): 117–39.

Kirby, John B. 1974. "Ralph J. Bunche and Black Radical Thought in the 1930s." *Phylon* 35, no. 2 (2nd quarter): 129–41.

Kessner, Thomas. 1989. *Fiorella La Guardia and the Making of Modern New York*. New York: McGraw-Hill.

Key, V.O. 1949. *Southern Politics in State and Nation*. New York: Vintage Books.

———. 1952. *Politics, Parties and Pressure Groups*. 3rd. ed. New York: Thomas Y. Crowell.

Kinder, Donald R., and Lynn M. Sanders. 1996. *Divided By Color: Racial Politics and Democratic Ideals*. Chicago and London: University of Chicago Press.

Kirby, John B. 1980. *Black Americans in the Roosevelt Era: Liberalism and Race*. Knoxville: University of Tennessee Press.

Kirk, Russell, and James McClellan. 1967. *The Political Principles of Robert A. Taft*. New York: Fleet Press.

Klarman, Michael J. 2004. *From Jim Crow to Civil Rights: The Supreme Court and the Struggle for Racial Equality*. Oxford and New York: Oxford University Press

Kleppner, Paul. 1982. *Who Voted? The Dynamics of Electoral Turnout, 1870–1980*. New York: Praeger.

Krieg, Joann P., ed. 1987. *Dwight D. Eisenhower: Soldier, President, Statesman*. Westport, Ct.: London and New York: Greenwood Press.

Lacey, Michael J., ed. 1989. *The Truman Presidency*. Cambridge: Woodrow Wilson International Center for Scholars and Cambridge University Press.

Ladd, Everett Carll. 1966. *Negro Political Leadership in the South*. Ithaca, N.Y.: Cornell University Press.

Landon, Alfred M. 1936; reissued 1971. *America at the Crossroads*. Port Washington, N.Y., and London: Kennikat Press.

Lash, Joseph P. 1972. *Eleanor and Franklin*. London: Book Club Associates.

Lawson, Stephen F. 1997. *Running for Freedom: Civil Rights and Black Politics in America since 1941*. New York and London: McGraw-Hill.

Levy, Eugene. 1973. *James Weldon Johnson: Black Leader, Black Voice*. Chicago and London: University of Chicago Press.

Lewinson, Edwin R. 1974. *Black Politics in New York City*. New York: Twayne.

Lewinson, Paul. 1963. *Race, Class and Party: A History of Negro Suffrage and White Politics in the South*. New York: Russell and Russell.

Lichtmann, Allen J. 1979. *Prejudice and the Old Politics: The Presidential Election of 1928*. Chapel Hill: University of North Carolina Press.

Lisio, Donald J. 1985. *Hoover, Blacks and Lily-Whites*. Chapel Hill and London: University of North Carolina Press.

Logan, Rayford. 1944. *What the Negro Wants*. Chapel Hill: University of North Carolina Press.

Lowi, Theodore J. 1995. *The End of the Republican Era*. Norman and London: University of Oklahoma Press.

Lubell, Samuel. 1951. *The Future of American Politics*. New York: Harper and Brothers.

Madison, James H., ed. 1992. *Wendell Willkie: Hoosier Internationalist*. Bloomington and Indianapolis: Indiana University Press.

Martin, John Bartlow. 1976. *Adlai Stevenson of Illinois: The Life of Adlai E. Stevenson*: Garden City, N.Y.: Doubleday.

Mayer, George H. 1965. "Alf M. Landon, as Leader of the Republican Opposition, 1937–1940." *Kansas Historical Quarterly* 32, no.3 (Autumn): 325–333.

———. 1967. *The Republican Party 1854–1966*. 2nd. ed. New York: Oxford University Press.

McCoy, Donald R. 1966. *Landon of Kansas*. Lincoln: University of Nebraska Press.

———. 1967. *Calvin Coolidge: The Quiet President*. New York: Macmillan.

———. 1973. *Coming of Age: The United States in the 1920s and 1930s*. Baltimore: Penguin Books.

———. 1984. *The Presidency of Harry S. Truman*. Lawrence: University Press of Kansas.

McCoy, Donald R., and Raymond G. O'Connor. 1963. *Readings in Twentieth-Century American History*. New York: Macmillan; London: Collier/Macmillan.

McCoy, Donald R., and Richard T. Ruetten. 1973. *Quest and Response: Minority Rights in the Truman Administration*. Lawrence: University Press of Kansas.

McCullough, David. 1992. *Truman*. New York and London: Simon and Schuster.

McElvaine, Robert S. 1993. *The Great Depression: America, 1929–1941*. New York: Three Rivers Press.

McGinnis, Patrick E. 1967. "Republican Party Resurgence in Congress, 1936–1946." Ph.D. diss., Tulane University.

McKenna, Marian C. 1961. *Borah*. Ann Arbor: University of Michigan Press.

McMillen, Neil, R. 1982. "Perry W. Howard: Boss of Black-and-Tan Republicanism in Mississippi, 1924–1960." *Journal of Southern History* 48, no. 2 (May 1982): 205–24.

Meier, August, and John H. Bracey Jr. 1993. "The NAACP as a Reform Movement, 1909–1965: 'To Reach the Conscience of America.'" *Journal of Southern History* 59, no. 1 (February): 3–30.

Meijer, Hank. 1993. "Hunting for the Middle Ground: Arthur Vandenberg and the Mackinac Charter, 1943." *Michigan Historical Review* 19, no. 2 (Fall) 1–21.

Merrill, Dennis, general editor. 1996. *Documentary History of the Truman Presidency*. Vols. 11, 12, and 14. Bethesda, Maryland: University Publications of America.

Merrill, Taylor. 1938. "Lynching the Anti-Lynching Bill." *Christian Century*, 23 February. 238–40

Milkis, Sidney M., and Jerome M. Mileur, eds. 2002. *The New Deal and the Triumph of Liberalism*. Amherst and Boston: University of Massachusetts Press.

Modell, John, Marc Goulden, and Sigurdur Magnusson. 1989. "World War II in the Lives of Black Americans: Some Findings and an Interpretation." *Journal of American History* 76, no. 3 (December): 838–48.

Moley, Raymond. 1962. *The Republican Opportunity*. New York: Duell, Sloan and Pearce.

Moon, Henry Lee. 1948. *Balance of Power: How the Negro Voted*. Westport, Ct.: Greenwood Press.

Moos, Malcolm. 1956. *The Republicans: A History of Their Party*. New York: Random House.

Moscow, Warren. 1968. *Roosevelt and Willkie*. Englewood Cliffs, N.J.: Prentice Hall.

Muller, Herbert J. 1968. *Adlai Stevenson: A Study in Values*. London: Hamish Hamilton.

Murray, Robert K. 1969. *The Harding Era: Warren G. Harding and His Administration*. Minneapolis: University of Minnesota Press.

———. 1973. *The Politics of Normalcy: Governmental Theory and Practice in the Harding-Coolidge Era*. New York: Norton.

Neal, Donn C. 1983. *The World beyond the Hudson: Alfred E. Smith and National Politics, 1918–1928*. New York and London: Garland.

Neal, Steve. 1984. *Dark Horse: A Biography of Wendell Willkie*. New York: Doubleday.

Norrell, Robert J. 1985. *Reaping the Whirlwind: The Civil Rights Movement in Tuskegee*. New York: Knopf.

———. 2005. *The House That I Live In: Race in the American Century*. New York and London: Oxford University Press.

Nowlin, William F. 1931; reissued 1970. *The Negro in American Politics*. New York: Russell and Russell.

O'Dell, Samuel. 1987. "Blacks, the Democratic Party and the Presidential Election of 1928: A Mild Rejoinder," *Phylon* 48, no.1 (Spring): 1–11.

O'Reilly, Kenneth. 1997. "Racial Integration: The Battle General Eisenhower Chose Not To Fight." *Journal of Blacks in Higher Education*, no. 18 (Winter): 110–19.

Osofsky, Gilbert. 1963; repr. 1971. *Harlem: The Making of a Ghetto, Negro New York, 1890–1930*. New York: Harper Torchbooks.

Parmet, Herbert S. 1972. *Eisenhower and the American Crusade*. New York: Macmillan; London: Collier Macmillan.

Parris, Guichard, and Lester Brooks. 1971. *Blacks in the City: A History of the National Urban League*. Boston and Toronto: Little, Brown.

Patterson, James T. 1967. *Congressional Conservatism and the New Deal: The Growth of the Conservative Coalition in Congress, 1933–1939*. Lexington: University of Kentucky Press.

———. 1972. *Mr. Republican*. Boston: Houghton, Mifflin.

———. 1996. *Grand Expectations: The United States, 1945–1974*. New York and Oxford: Oxford University Press.

Payne, Charles M., and Adam Green, eds. 2003. *Time Longer Than Rope: A Century of African American Activism, 1850–1950*. New York and London: New York University Press.

Perry, Elizabeth Israels. 1987. *Belle Moskowitz*. New York: Oxford University Press.

Pfeffer, Paula F. 1990. *A. Philip Randolph: Pioneer of the Civil Rights Movement*. Baton Rouge and London: Louisiana State University Press.

Phillips, Cabell. 1975. *The 1940s: Decade of Triumph and Trouble*. New York: New York Times Chronicle of American Life; London: Collier/Macmillan.

Plesur, Milton. 1962. "The Republican Congressional Comeback of 1938." *Review of Politics* 24, no. 4 (October): 525–562.

Plummer, Brenda Gayle. 1996. *Rising Wind: Black Americans and U.S. Foreign Affairs, 1935–1960*. Chapel Hill and London: University of North Carolina Press.

Pohlmann, Marcus D. 1990. *Black Politics in Conservative America*. New York and London: Longman.

Pohlmann, Marcus D., ed. 2003. *African American Political Thought*. Vol. 5, *Integration vs. Separatism: The Colonial Period to 1945*. London and New York: Routledge.

———. 2003. *African American Political Thought*. Vol. 6, *Integration vs. Separatism: 1945 to the Present*. London and New York: Routledge.

Polenberg, Richard. 1972. *War and Society: The United States, 1941–1945*. Westport, Ct.: Greenwood Press.

Redding, Louis L. 1936. "Borah—What *Does* He Stand For?" *Crisis* 44 (March): 70–2 and 82.

Reed, Christopher Robert. 1997. *The Chicago NAACP and the Rise of Black Professional Leadership: 1910–1966*. Bloomington and Indianapolis: Indiana University Press.

Rees, Matthew, 1991. *From the Deck to the Sea: Blacks and the Republican Party*. Wakefield, N.H.: Longwood Academic.

Reinhard, David W. 1983. *The Republican Right Since 1945*. Lexington: University Press of Kentucky.

Research Division of the Republican National Committee. 1940. *Campaign Textbook of the Republican Party, 1940*. Washington, D.C.: Republican National Committee.

Richardson, Elmo. 1979. *The Presidency of Dwight D. Eisenhower*. Lawrence: Regents Press of Kansas.

Rivlin, Benjamin, ed. 1990. *Ralph Bunche: The Man and His Times*. New York and London: Holmes and Meier.

Robinson, Edgar E., and Vaughn Davis Bornet. 1975. *Herbert Hoover: President of the United States*. Stanford, Calif.: Hoover Institution Press, Stanford University.

Rosenman, Samuel I. 1950. *The Public Papers and Addresses of Franklin D. Roosevelt, 1944–45*. Vol 13, *Victory and the Threshold of Peace*. New York: Harper and Brothers.

Ross, Barbara Joyce. 1972. *J. E. Spingarn and the Rise of the NAACP, 1911–1939*. New York: Atheneum.

Ross, Irwin. 1968. *The Loneliest Campaign: The Truman Victory of 1948*. New York: New American Library.

Rowell, Chester H. 1938. "The Resources of the Republican Party." *Yale Review* 27, no. 3 (March): 433–49.

Russell, Francis. 1968. *President Harding: His Life and Times*. London: Eyre and Spottiswoode.

Rutland, Robert Allen. 1996. *The Republicans from Lincoln to Bush*. Columbia and London: University of Missouri Press.

Schlesinger, Arthur et al., eds. 1985. *History of American Presidential Elections*. New York: Chelsea House.

———, eds. 1973. *History of U.S. Political Parties*. Vol. 3, *1910–1945: From Square Deal to New Deal*. New York: Chelsea House, in association with Bowker.

Schneider, Mark Robert. 2002. *"We Return Fighting": The Civil Rights Movement in the Jazz Age*. Boston: Northeastern University Press.

Shannon, Jasper B. 1951. "Political Obstacles to Civil Rights Legislation." *Annals of the American Academy of Political and Social Science* 275 (May): 53–60.

Sherman, Richard B. 1964. "The Harding Administration and the Negro: An Opportunity Lost." *Journal of Negro History* 49 (July).

———. 1966. "Republicans and Negroes: The Lessons of Normalcy." *Phylon* 27.

———. 1973. *The Republican Party and Black America from McKinley to Hoover, 1896–1933*. Charlottesville: University Press of Virginia.

Sievers, Rodney M. 1983. *The Last Puritan? Adlai Stevenson in American Politics*. Port Washington, N.Y.: National University Publications, Associated Faculty Press.

Sitkoff, Harvard. 1971. "Harry Truman and the Election of 1948: The Coming of Age of Civil Rights in American Politics." *Journal of Southern History* 37, no. 4 (November): 597–616.

———. 1978. *A New Deal for Blacks: The Emergence of Civil Rights as a National Issue*. New York: Oxford University Press.

Smith, Richard Norton. 1982. *Thomas E. Dewey and His Times*. New York: Simon and Schuster.

Sternsher, Bernard, ed. 1969. *The Negro in Depression and War: Prelude to Revolution, 1930–1945*. Chicago: Quadrangle Books.

Stimson, Henry L., and McGeorge Bundy. 1948. *On Active Service in Peace and War*. London and New York: Hutchinson.

St. James, Warren D. 1958. *The National Association for the Advancement of Colored People: A Case Study in Pressure Groups*. New York: Exposition Press.

Stolberg, Mary M. 1995. *Fighting Organized Crime: Politics, Justice and the Legacy of Thomas E. Dewey*. Boston: Northeastern University Press.

Sullivan, Patricia. 1996. *Days of Hope: Race and Democracy in the New Deal Era*. Chapel Hill and London: University of North Carolina Press.

Tatum, Elbert Lee. 1951; repr. 1974. *The Changed Political Thought of the Negro*. Westport, Ct.: Greenwood Press.

Thompson, Kenneth W., ed. 1994. *Lessons from Defeated Presidential Candidates*. Lanham, N.Y., and London: University Press of America.

Thomson, C.A.H. 1939. "Research and the Republican Party." *Public Opinion Quarterly* 3, no.2 (April): 306–313.

Thurber, Timothy. 2001. "Seeds of the Southern Strategy: The Republican Party and African Americans, 1940–1952." Paper presented at British Association for American Studies conference, April.

Tompkins, C. David. 1970. *Senator Arthur H. Vandenberg: The Evolution of a Modern Republican, 1884–1945*. Lansing: Michigan State University Press.

Topping, Simon. 1999. "'In No Election since 1860 Have Politicians Been So Negro-Minded as in 1936:' Courting the African American Vote in the Election of 1936." *OVERhere* 18, no. 3 (Autumn): 72–82.

———. 2000. "'Turning Their Pictures of Abraham Lincoln to the Wall': The Republican Party and African Americans in the Election of 1936." *Irish Journal of American Studies* 8 (May): 35–59.

———. 2004. "'Never Argue with the Gallup Poll': Thomas Dewey, Civil Rights and the Election of 1948." *Journal of American Studies* 38, no. 2 (August): 179–99.

———. 2004. "'Supporting Our Friends and Defeating Our Enemies': Militancy and Non-partisanship in the NAACP, 1936–1948." *Journal of African American History* 89, no.1 (Winter): 25–27.

Trani, Eugene P., and David L. Wilson. 1977. *The Presidency of Warren G. Harding*. Lawrence: Regents Press of Kansas.

Trotter, Joe William, Jr., ed. 1991. *The Great Migration in Historical Perspective: New Dimensions of Race, Class and Gender*. Bloomington and Indianapolis: Indiana University Press.

Truman, Harry S. 1956. *Memoirs*. Vol. 2, *Years of Trial and Hope*. Garden City, N.Y.: Doubleday.

United Labor League of Ohio. 1950. *His Record Is Against Him: A Speaker's Handbook on Robert Alphonso Taft*. Published by the United Labor League of Ohio.

Vandenberg, Arthur H., Jr., ed. 1953. *The Private Papers of Senator Vandenberg*. London: Victor Gollancz.

Vander, Harry J., III. 1968. *The Political and Economic Progress of the American Negro, 1943–1963*. Dubuque, Iowa: William C. Brown Book Co.

Viorst, Milton. 1968. *Fall from Grace: The Republican Party and the Puritan Ethic*. New York: New American Library.

Walker, Stanley. 1944. *Dewey: An American of this Century*. New York and London: Whittlesey House, McGraw-Hill.

Walton, Hanes, Jr. 1969. *The Negro in Third-Party Politics*. Philadelphia: Dorrance.

———. 1972. *Black Political Parties: An Historical and Political Analysis*. New York: Free Press; London: Collier/Macmillan.

———. 1972. *Black Politics: A Theoretical and Structural Analysis*. Philadelphia, New York, and Toronto: Lippincott.

———. 1975. *Black Republicans: The Politics of the Black and Tans*. Metucken, N.J.: Scarecrow Press.

———. 1985. *Invisible Politics: A Multidimensional Analysis of Black Political Behavior*. Albany: State University of New York Press.

Walton, Hanes, Jr., and Robert C. Smith. 2000. *American Politics and the African American Quest for Universal Freedom*. New York: Longman.

Ward, Paul W., "Wooing The Negro Vote," 1936. *Nation* 143 (1 August).

Warren, Earl. 1977. *The Memoirs of Earl Warren*. Garden City, N.Y.: Doubleday.

Watson, Richard L., Jr. 1963. "The Defeat of Judge Parker." *Mississippi Valley Historical Review* 50, no.2 (September): 213–34.

Weed, Clyde P. 1994. *The Nemesis of Reform: The Republican Party during the New Deal*. New York: Columbia University Press.

Weiss, Nancy J. 1974. *The National Urban League, 1910–1940*. New York: Oxford University Press.

———. 1983. *Farewell to The Party Of Lincoln: Black Politics in the Age of FDR*. Princeton, N.J.: Princeton University Press.

White, Walter, 1948. *A Man Called White: The Autobiography of Walter White.* Athens: University of Georgia; London: Brown Thrasher Books.

———. 1955. *How Far the Promised Land?* New York: Viking Press.

White, William Allen. 1938. *A Puritan in Babylon.* New York: Macmillan.

White, William Smith. 1954. *The Taft Story.* New York: Harper and Brothers.

Wilkins, Roy, with Tom Mathews. 1982. *Standing Fast: The Autobiography of Roy Wilkins.* New York: Viking.

Willkie, Wendell L. 1943. *One World.* New York: Simon and Schuster.

Wilson, Joan Hoff. 1975. *Herbert Hoover: Forgotten Progressive.* Boston and Toronto: Little, Brown.

Winkler, Allan M. 2000. *Home Front U.S.A.: America during World War II.* 2nd ed. Wheeling, Ill.: Harlan Davidson.

Wolf, Thomas P., William D. Pedersen, and Byron W. Daynes, eds. 2001. *Franklin Roosevelt and Congress.* Vol. 2, *The New Deal and Its Aftermath.* Armonk, N.Y., and London: M. E. Sharpe.

Wolters, Raymond. 1970. *Negroes and the Great Depression: The Problem of Economic Relief.* Westport, Ct.: Greenwood Press.

Wunderlin, Clarence E., Jr., ed. 1997. *The Papers of Robert A. Taft.* Vol. 1, *1889–1939.* Kent, Ohio, and London: Kent State University Press.

———, ed. 2003. *The Papers of Robert A. Taft.* Vol. 3, *1945–1948.* Kent, Ohio, and London: Kent State University Press.

Wynn, Neil A. 1976. *The African-American and the Second World War.* London: Paul Elek.

Young, Roland. 1956. *Congressional Politics in the Second World War.* New York: Columbia University Press.

Zangrando, Robert L. 1965. "The NACCP and a Federal Anti-Lynching Bill, 1934–1940." *Journal of Negro History* 50, no.2 (April): 106–107.

———. 1980. *The NAACP Crusade against Lynching, 1909–1950.* Philadelphia: Temple University Press.

Index

Simon Topping is a lecturer in American Studies at the University of Plymouth, England. He has written several scholarly articles on topics of twentieth-century African American history.